REAPING A GREATER HARVEST

Number Fourteen:
Sam Rayburn Series on Rural Life

Sponsored by Texas A&M University–Commerce
M. Hunter Hayes, General Editor

REAPING A GREATER HARVEST

AFRICAN AMERICANS, THE EXTENSION SERVICE, AND RURAL REFORM IN JIM CROW TEXAS

DEBRA A. REID

TEXAS A&M UNIVERSITY PRESS

College Station

Library of Congress Cataloging-in-Publication Data

Reid, Debra Ann, 1960–
    Reaping a greater harvest : African Americans, the extension service, and rural reform
in Jim Crow Texas / Debra A. Reid. — 1st ed.
        p.   cm. — (Sam Rayburn series on rural life ; no. 14)
    Includes bibliographical references and index.
    ISBN-13: 978-1-58544-571-4 (cloth : alk. paper)
    ISBN-10: 1-58544-571-1 (cloth : alk. paper)
    1. Texas Agricultural Extension Service.   2. African American agriculturists—
Texas.   3. Agriculture and state—Texas.   4. African Americans—Texas—History.
5. Rural extension—Texas.   6. Rural development—Texas.   I. Title.   II. Series.
S544.3.T4R45   2007
    630.71′5—dc22   2006021742

In memoriam,

ROBERT A. CALVERT

CONTENTS

List of Illustrations   IX

Series Editor's Foreword   XI

Acknowledgments   XIII

Introduction   XIX

1   African Americans and Rural Reform in Texas, 1891–1914   1

2   Forming Separate Bureaucracies: The Negro Division of the
      Texas Agricultural Extension Service, 1915–20   22

3   Segregated Modernization: Taking the Message into African
      American Fields and Farm Homes   48

4   Public Reform in Black and White: The Maturation of a
      Segregated Division   86

5   Building Segregated Social Welfare: Texas' Negro Division
      and Roosevelt's New Deal   114

6   Beyond the Farm: Cultivating New Audiences and Support
      Systems at Home and Abroad   145

7   Separation Despite Civil Rights   177

    Conclusion: Measuring Greater Harvests   191

Notes   195

Bibliographic Essay   257

Manuscript and Archival Sources   263

Index   269

ILLUSTRATIONS

FIGURES

1. Robert L. Smith, ca. 1928 4
2. John McQuinney and Walter C. Porter, ca. 1928 8
3. Robert L. Smith with unidentified group 27
4. Robert L. Smith with farmers at McKinney, Texas, 1923 28
5. Seth T. Toney, Seguin, Texas, inoculating pigs, January 1937 51
6. Unidentified couple feeding their chickens 55
7. Home of W. T. Lewis and family, Antioch Community,
   Texas, April 1933 57
8. Willie Mae Lewis's bedroom, Antioch Community, Texas,
   April 1933 58
9. Ira Bearden, Gay Hill, and his prize-winning corn crop, 1923 60
10. Armelia Marsh, Elysian Fields, after 1924 Dallas Fair 61
11. Meeting to discuss canning, ca. 1933 66
12. Mrs. Callie Byrd and Mrs. Fannie Hollaway sealing tin cans, 1924 . . . 71
13. Buildings suitable for community canning plants 72
14. Community canning house, Pyrtle Community, Texas, April 1933 . . . 73
15. Brick furnace in Pyrtle Community, Texas, canning house,
    April 1933 74
16. Beulah Community canning house, Palestine, Texas, April 1933 75
17. Office of J. V. Smith and Miss Ruby O. Phelps, McLennan County,
    Texas, April 1933 93
18. Duroc Jersey sow with her litter, owned by Hathaway Goodlow,
    near Waco, Texas, April 1933 104
19. Club boys butchering hogs, Kendleton Community, Texas, 1937 106
20. Miss Bankhead, Sunny Side, Texas, 1931 107
21. Soil conservation demonstration at Ernest Stein's farm, Mount
    Enterprise Community, Texas, April 1933 127

22. Checking terrace elevations, R. P. Pervey's farm, Browndale
Community, Texas, April 1933 128

23. Evans Spring club women, Neches, Texas, refinishing a bedstead,
April 1933 139

24. Ruby O. Phelps conducting slipper chair–making demonstration,
Harrison Community, Texas, April 1933 140

25. Nathan and Ellitie Harvey family, Burleigh Community,
Texas, 1940 143

26. Leigh 4-H Club girls' display, 1946 Central East Texas Fair 148

27. Lula Foreman, Limestone County, Texas, showing new
refrigerator, 1949 152

28. Mrs. R. H. Franc, Smith County, Texas, inspecting modern electric
sewing machine, June 1955 153

29. Jim Foreman and sons with hogs they planned to show, July 1949 154

30. Annie L. Barrett presenting chicks to African American youth,
April 1946 155

31. Southern District Sears, Roebuck Cow-Sow & Hen Program,
Gilt & Boar Show 156

32. Third Annual Meat Show, Tyler, Texas, March 1942 158

33. Judging entries at a Negro hog show, 1940 165

34. Jim Foreman and sons with ribbons from State Fair, 1948 166

35. Charles E. Trout and Henry S. Estelle watch farmers unload
cucumbers, September 1947 174

36. Mrs. Lea Etta Lusk, Washington County, Texas, 1954 178

37. Political cartoon published in *Washington Afro-American,*
March 1965 186

MAPS

1. Percentage of black-owned farms, 1910, and location of Negro
Division activities, 1915 26

2. Percentage of improved land in cotton, 1910, and location of
Negro Division activities, 1915 30

3. Counties featured in the narrative, representing Texas' demographic
and geographic diversity 49

4. Map of Harrison County, Texas, drawn by Annie L. Barrett, 1946 ... 54

5. Percentage of black-owned farms, 1930, and counties with
Negro Division agents, 1925–34 116

6. Percentage of improved land in cotton, 1930, and counties with
Negro Division agents, 1925–34 121

SERIES EDITOR'S FOREWORD

More than half a century after the Supreme Court's landmark 1954 decision in *Brown v. Board of Education,* we continue to confront the lingering ramifications of segregation and the "Jim Crow" laws that buttressed racial and social inequality throughout the South following the Reconstruction era. In *Reaping a Greater Harvest: African Americans, the Extension Service, and Rural Reform in Jim Crow Texas,* Debra Reid's diligent research and lucid writing reveal the social and political processes that deeply affected rural Texas during this tumultuous period.

As tempting as it might be for writers to lose focus when facing a barrage of legal and historical data, Reid's perspective remains trained firmly on the people most directly affected by social and political race-based obstacles. She reminds readers that African American agrarians faced not only these artificial impediments but also natural obstacles—"uncontrollable threats" ranging from weather conditions to invasive pests—that they shared with white landowners. These struggles did not disappear with the Civil Rights Act of 1964 but continue even now in apparent and subtle modes. By examining this history and explaining the ways in which black Texans were denied the social and economic rights and privileges that were available to whites, Reid reminds her readers that the past, present, and future remain inextricably linked; as she writes in her conclusion, "advocates of rural southern minority rights still struggle to effect change." Reid successfully wrenches the derogatory "Jim Crow" image—a persona dating back to minstrel pantomimes—away from the yoke of cliché to reveal the men, women, and children occluded beneath the image. Rather than a simple synecdoche of racial injustice, the Jim Crow figure becomes in Reid's hands the embodiment of a complex social and political system.

In *Texas, Cotton, and the New Deal,* the seventh volume in the Sam Rayburn Series on Rural Life, Keith J. Volanto examines the effects on the Texas cotton industry of Roosevelt's policies and institutions such as the Agricultural Adjustment Administration. Although *Reaping a Greater Harvest* likewise presents a cogent study of cotton farming in Texas, Reid hones in on the social and political processes that thwarted African American landowners and farmers. These are complementary texts, revealing much about the varied history of Texas, this major crop, and the men and women who labored in and around the cotton fields of east Texas. More importantly, Debra Reid and *Reaping a Greater Harvest* stand on their own merits. It is a pleasure to have Reid and her book in the Rayburn Series.

This year marks the tenth anniversary of the Sam Rayburn Series on Rural Life. Sponsored by Texas A&M University-Commerce, since 1997 the Rayburn Series has operated under the auspices of Texas A&M University Press at College Station, publishing notable volumes on a diverse range of topics that provide a fresh and keen understanding of life in the East Texas region. As Debra Reid's evocative title suggests, this region is fruitful and productive, yielding a multitude of harvests.

—M. Hunter Hayes

ACKNOWLEDGMENTS

Reaping a Greater Harvest emerged out of the last dissertation that Texas historian Robert "Bob" Calvert supervised. He urged me to study female employees of the Negro Division of the Texas Agricultural Extension Service (TAEX), but I wanted to include male as well as female employees and their relationships with white as well as black Texans. Archives offered rich evidence of African Americans pursuing rural reform during the late nineteenth century and the ways their private efforts helped launch a publicly funded program delivered by African Americans to African Americans during the early twentieth century. My dissertation, "Reaping a Greater Harvest," won the first Gilbert C. Fite Dissertation Award in 2001, but instead of seeking a publisher then, I expanded the study temporally and conceptually. Many helped me pursue my goals, but it took more than eight years of research and revision.

The Negro Division operated out of Prairie View, Texas, between the 1910s and the 1960s. Historical files are housed in the University Archives, John C. Coleman Library, Prairie View A&M University. Mrs. Jimmizine B. Taylor, archivist, and her work-study assistant, Angela Johnson, pulled box after box for me during 1998 and 1999. Mrs. Taylor and Ms. Phyllis Earles provided photographic reproductions for this book during final editing in 2005 and 2006. Their help proved invaluable. Original issues of the *Prairie View Standard,* also in the Prairie View A&M archive, recount services that agents provided. Cliff Jones spent a hectic day in the archives collecting relevant data from this resource as I prepared to relocate to Eastern Illinois University (EIU) during summer 1999. Staff at the Cooperative Extension Service, Prairie View A&M, expressed interest in the study and offered their assistance, helping me locate informants who corroborated the written record and provided information beyond that documented in the archives.

David Chapman, archivist, Texas A&M University, suggested I research black extension agents when I visited Cushing Memorial Library and Archives, on the College Station campus, during fall 1997. Records created by black agricultural agents and home demonstration agents intrigued me. Between 1997 and 2000, Angus Martin and Melanie Hill satisfied my repeated requests to consult TAEX historical files. Late in 2005, Valeria Coleman and Melissa Zajicek helped me acquire photographic reproductions. Jennie Kitching, retired associate director for human sciences, TAEX, shared her efforts to organize historical materials not yet transferred to Texas A&M's archives. She helped me access files temporarily housed at the Texas A&M Riverside campus during 1999. Thanks go to Dr. Kitching and Edna Eisfeldt, AV librarian, TAEX, who kept the doors open so I could read the partially catalogued collection. Fred Mitchell, payroll manager, TAEX, expressed interest in my research and allowed me access to the microfilm copies of payroll records and of annual reports that agents submitted to their supervisors. I spent too little time reading these records between 1997 and 2000.

National repositories contain information critical to understanding the Negro Division. Joe Schwarz and Tab Lewis at the National Archives and Records Administration II (NARA), College Park, Maryland, helped me navigate the U.S. Department of Agriculture records. Archivists at the regional National Archives and Records Administration repository in Fort Worth offered Farm Security Administration (FSA) files relevant to local projects. Holly Reed, Still Pictures Reference, NARA, deserves special thanks for hours spent researching my requests. She confirmed negative numbers and assured me access to Federal Extension Service (FES) images.

I wanted to relate the Negro Division to other African American reform efforts that preceded it. Special thanks to Kent Keeth, director of the Texas Collection, Baylor University, and Ellen Kuniyuki Brown, archivist, for encouraging me to study two relevant collections—the papers of the Farmers' Improvement Society (FIS) of Texas and the George S. and Jeffie O. A. Conner Papers. Mike Stein, archivist at the Nesbitt Memorial Library in Columbus, Texas, provided background information on Robert L. Smith and his in-laws, the Isaacs family. Sandra M. Burrell, Sam Houston Regional Library and Research Center, a branch of the Texas State Library and Archives Commission in Liberty, Texas, shared photographic reproductions of black farm families in Liberty County. Joshua Mason, EIU graduate assistant, pored over the *Chicago Defender* looking for information on black farmers. Gail Biel, Marshall, Texas, gave me Negro county agent narrative reports from Harrison County that had been discarded.

Cartographers Ron Finger and Chris Blakely translated statistical analysis into maps that I had conceptualized. Finally, in the latter stages of manuscript preparation, as I sought more context for the Texas-based study, librarians at Eastern Illinois University, including Sue Abel and Christine Young, processed interlibrary loan requests indefatigably, and staff at the University of Illinois–Champaign (UIUC) extended faculty loan privileges to me so I could take obscure published primary sources home instead of camping out in the cavernous library. I pursued several funding options to reduce my dependency on Texas A&M University as I researched and wrote about a service that the university housed and administered for decades. In addition to funds provided by the Department of History, the Office of Graduate Studies, the Women's Studies Program, and the Center for Interdisciplinary Studies, all at Texas A&M, I received a Council on Faculty Research grant from Eastern Illinois University. Additional funding came from the East Texas Historical Association (Ottis Lock Endowment Award) and the Center for American History (Miss Ima Hogg Student Research Travel Award), the University of Texas at Austin. Anonymous reviewers' comments on applications submitted to the National Endowment for the Humanities in 2001 and 2003 helped me hone my thesis.

Panel presentations over the course of the project generated useful comments and offshoot publications. At the 1998 Social Science History Association conference, Joseph Barton compared the experiences of black agents to E. P. Thompson's English working class and prompted me to think about the long-term significance of co-option. At the 1999 Agricultural History Society symposium, Roy V. Scott and John E. Lee Jr. sharpened my focus by simply renaming my paper "Rural African Americans and Progressive Reform." A version of that paper appeared in *Agricultural History* (Spring 2000). I expanded it, with the permission of *Agricultural History,* for inclusion in *The Countryside in the Age of the Modern State: Political Histories of Rural America,* edited by Catherine McNicol Stock and Robert D. Johnston (2001). My involvement in the symposium "Who Owns America? III: Minority Land and Community Security," sponsored by the Land Tenure Center at the University of Wisconsin–Madison in 2001, and subsequent discussions with Jess Gilbert resulted in the refinement of my ideas about African American farmers in Texas in the southern context and the publication of another article in *Agricultural History* (Spring 2003). Other presentations tested ideas that appear herein, and I thank program chairs for affording me opportunities to share them.

Thought pieces have appeared in occasional publications. These include an article on canning in *Localités/Localities,* a special issue of EIU's *Research and Review Series* (Spring 2000) and a paper on Negro home demonstration agents presented at an international conference on rural studies in 1999 and published in *Rustica Nova: The New Countryside and Transformations in Operating Environment,* edited by Kalle Pihlaimen and Erik Tirkkonen (Turku, Finland: University of Turku, 2002). A paper on the Negro Division and pig breeding appeared in *Biological Progress in Agriculture, Proceedings of CIMA XII: The International Congress of Agricultural Museums, Poznan, Poland, 12–16 October 1998* (Szreniawa, Poland, 2001). Most recently, the Association for Living History, Farm and Agricultural Museums, (ALHFAM) published a paper (*ALHFAM Bulletin* [Spring 2003]) that I presented at the 2003 joint conference of the Rural Women's Studies Association and ALHFAM's Western and Mountain-Plains regions. It focuses on the importance of establishing historical sites that document rural black life. These presentations and subsequent revision for publication helped me refine my thoughts.

Many colleagues have taken time from their busy schedules to discuss this research. Informal conversations with Martin Hardeman, Lynnea Magnuson, and Michelle LeMaster, and sustained discussions with Jacqueline Wehrle, who gave generously of her limited time and exceptional editing skills have, collectively, helped me clarify my argument. Martin gave me the needed kick in the pants to finish the manuscript, and I am forever indebted to him for that. He never tired of asking how much longer it would take. Orville Vernon Burton and attendees at his Southern History Reading Group in Urbana, Illinois, provided valuable feedback on early versions of the two *Agricultural History* submissions. Thom Moore invited me to present highlights from my research at a brown bag lunch held for graduate students in community psychology at UIUC and has eagerly shared his thoughts on my work. A chance encounter with Joel Williamson on a return flight from the 2001 Organization of American Historians conference led to a discussion of book titles. He preferred "Reaping a Greater Harvest" more than another option I considered. I followed his advice.

Finally, to members of my committee, who read the entire dissertation more than once and remained supportive—a special thanks. Rebecca Sharpless inspired me with her work on women on the Blackland Prairie. Her ability to link private lives to regional and national history established a benchmark. David Vaught provided the theoretical approach that I needed to steer me away from a straight descriptive narrative and a good model for me to consider as I sought a more complete understanding of the complexity of modernizing agriculture. Albert Broussard supported me and encouraged me to broaden my pool of primary sources. His insightful comments shared in courses and casual conversation helped me turn exciting research into a viable dissertation topic. And finally, my mentor, Bob Calvert—his concise instructions suited my frenetic nature and helped keep me focused. His own doctoral dissertation on the southern Grange helped me organize my thoughts and think about political and economic relationships and differences between public and private reform. His philosophy of life, expressed eloquently as he battled cancer, inspired me to face the future. We co-taught Texas history at Texas A&M University during the summer of 2000, his last offering and my first as a newly minted PhD. He died in November 2000.

He wanted me to look for a teaching position in Texas, but I found employment in my home state of Illinois. He wanted me to publish this study at his press of choice, Texas A&M University Press, and I followed his advice. He wanted me to do less and think more . . . So I conclude as I began, by recognizing Bob's contributions, regretting that I could not act on all of them, and reaffirming the belief that this topic warrants the effort. I believe the study reflects his inspiration and would certainly have been better had it received more of his direct influence.

INTRODUCTION

Science changed agriculture and rural life in unprecedented ways during the twentieth century, and land-grant colleges became official conduits to channel new ideas into the countryside. Increased knowledge of plant and animal genetics and diseases revolutionized crop and stock farming. Technological innovations ranging from tractors to synthetic chemicals contributed to the revolution, making hand labor increasingly obsolete and financial investment requisite to success in agriculture. Increased knowledge of nutrition and health care, an abundance of household conveniences, and greater access to markets changed the home as well as the farm. Land-grant colleges cooperated with the U.S. Department of Agriculture (USDA) to operate experiment stations and agricultural extension services. A select clientele benefited, specifically, farm families that sought change and could afford to invest to improve their quality of life. A symbiotic relationship developed between recognized experts employed by state and national government and families seeking their advice.[1]

Agricultural modernization did not occur evenly across the rural South. Various factors accounted for this, including widespread poverty as well as farmers' resistance to outside influence, but, most important, prejudice affected decision making. White southerners refused to share findings broadly across race and class lines. *Reaping a Greater Harvest* focuses on the process by which race-based decision making limited rural reform in Texas. The contest was quintessentially political. Rather than allow blacks full participation in the production and distribution of information, white Texans limited black involvement and influence. Ultimately, whites legally separated the races to accomplish their ends. The Negro Division, established by the Texas Agricultural Extension Service in 1915, became a model of progressive rural, black-led reform, but it began, in part, to keep black Texans isolated from positions of influence. Ample evidence on the Negro Division's forma-tion, maturation, and decline helps us understand the history of legalized segregation. Earlier successful all-black organizations, namely, the Farmers' Improvement Society of Texas, provided a model that Negro Division staff used to lend their program credibility. Black advocates of farming and rural life turned to it for information, advocacy, and professional status, just as whites depended on it to perpetuate race and class biases. Over fifty years, between 1915 and 1965, the Negro Division grew into a powerful professional organization that influenced white decisions but never broke free of white authority.[2]

Data collected by census enumerators in 1900 and 1910 made it clear that African Americans had to be involved in the exchange if southerners hoped to harness technological innovations to their advantage. Until 1900, no com-prehensive data quantified African American contributions to agriculture, the largest sector of the southern economy. When racial information was added to census statistics in that year, black involvement became obvious. The Bureau of the Census commissioned W. E. B. Du Bois, a Harvard PhD and professor of economics and history at Atlanta University, to interpret the findings. His analysis revealed that African Americans operated just over one-quarter of all southern farms but they grew two-fifths of all cotton pro-duced in the South, making them, as a group, more dependent on cotton as their principal source of income than were white farmers. Black farm-ers accounted for one-half of all farmers reporting cotton as their principal source of income. Such evidence led Du Bois to assert that "agricultural in-dustry is dependent to a very large degree upon the cooperation of the negro farmer." Yet, southern whites did not recognize black authority in agriculture or credit blacks with any influence in the system. They were effectively ex-cluded from politics by the early twentieth century and thus powerless to stabilize their standard of living. White landlords and merchants squeezed blacks economically, and legislators ensnared them legally, codifying race-based discrimination in a strategy to ensure black dependency.[3]

Du Bois confirmed black farmers' economic marginalization. While blacks operated more than one-quarter all farms in the South, they culti-vated only one-sixth of all the improved land, produced only one-sixth of the South's gross product, and controlled only one-ninth of southern farm prop-erty values. Nonetheless, Du Bois portrayed economic mobility as well. He documented black landowners who steadily accumulated property despite discrimination. Those who purchased land chose to settle where "economic conditions [were] favorable" and where they could "enjoy a fair degree of agricultural prosperity." Owning land gave them opportunities to improve their lives materially. They invested their labor, capital, and skill into "restoring the soil and making permanent improvements in buildings, fences, etc." They put floors and glass windows in their houses, and some even bought new furniture. Du Bois recognized potential in their efforts and labeled them "coproducers of the wealth of the land." The census statistics indicated that, despite racism and legalized discrimination, African Americans still subscribed to deep-seated values that linked landownership to economic and personal independence.[4]

Du Bois did not trace such aspirations to any particular person or political approach. Rather, he claimed that "thrifty" black farmers had to ally with "well-disposed [white] landowners and honest merchants" to realize their goals. Education often provided them the foundation to make intelligent and responsible decisions that helped them manage marginal soils and build a rural support system. Rural settlements and kinship groups across the South provided safety nets for black landowners, which helped them build, as historian Steven Hahn has indicated, a "new political nation . . . embedded in persons, places, and land, in the relations and aspirations of rural family and community life."[5]

In their efforts to improve their lives, progressive black landowners faced many challenges. Some they shared with their white counterparts, in particular, uncontrollable threats such as weather, creditors, a volatile cotton market, and even pests that could ruin them financially. With only the trappings of economic security, however, black landowners also faced debilitating threats to their humanity, namely, the refusal of individuals and bureaucracies at the local, state, and national levels to grant them full citizenship. While hard work, social networks, and well-meaning reformers could aid the material advancement of blacks, equality remained elusive for much of the century. As early as 1903, Du Bois was worrying that material progress provided a false sense of equality, as well as a false sense of security. African Americans had to affect the legislative process to secure full protection of their civil rights and their hard-earned material gains.[6]

White Democrats and Republicans alike recognized that blacks were steadily accumulating property and wielding some influence in the countryside and devised ways to preserve white legal superiority at the expense of this acquisitive farming class. The struggle highlighted the contradiction at the heart of the American political ideal: a nation founded on principles of equality and justice refused to grant full citizenship and civil rights to minority farmers, who obviously bought into the American ideal of economic independence and personal autonomy.

Comparison of 1900 and 1910 census data indicates that the number of black farmers in the South increased by more than 20 percent during the decade, despite the systematic challenges to their position. The number of white farmers increased as well, but only by 17.4 percent. Analysts concluded that, during this decade, "agriculture became, relatively to other fields of employment, more important among Negroes . . . and less important . . . among Whites." Many expressed their preference for farming over other occupations by investing hard-earned income in land. The value of land operated by blacks more than doubled between 1900 and 1910. Furthermore, black farmers invested in land before machinery, stock, or farm buildings. The statistics indicated that black farmers had increasingly vested interest in agriculture and reasons to pursue scientific advances and rural reform.[7]

Gaining access to information, however, proved difficult. As the rural reform movement progressed, white southerners responded to black farmers in contradictory ways. While individuals and institutions sometimes furthered black landowners' goals and provided access to information to help improve farming practices, across the South whites refused to engage blacks as equals in the reform process. Texas provides an excellent case study of this dynamic because it offered blacks seeking land both unparalleled opportunities to acquire it and inconceivable threats to holding it. At the turn of the twentieth century, 30.7 percent of black farmers in Texas owned land, the highest ratio of owners to operators in the Cotton Belt. Du Bois attributed this to "the chances of the free West," to "cheap and plentiful land," and to the absence of a large plantation system, opportunities that other states did not afford blacks. Furthermore, the presence of Mexican laborers created additional racial tensions in the Texas countryside that did not exist in the rest of the South, and this caused whites to favor African American landownership more than Mexican because of white and black Texans' cultural similarities. But in general, black-white relations in Texas were culturally akin to those in the rest of the South because most residents had migrated from other southern states.[8]

While offering relative opportunity, life in Texas posed significant challenges as well. The boll weevil, a pest that migrated north out of Mexico during the early 1890s, threatened cotton crops. Texas farmers depended on cotton as a cash crop more than did farmers in other southern states, and black farmers in Texas depended on it to an even greater degree. In 1900,

87.1 percent of black Texans raised cotton compared to only 67.3 percent of white Texans. Furthermore, 85.6 percent of all black Texas farmers grew cotton as their principal source of income. Both races could have benefited from pest-eradication research, but the significant proportion of black landowners in Texas wielded little influence in the post-Populist era. White landowners often controlled local government and exerted most influence at the state and national levels. They assured access for themselves by establishing experiment stations in places convenient to them and by appointing their peers to positions of authority at the state land-grant college and, ultimately, the Agricultural Extension Service. This helped white farmers control not just the production of information but its dissemination. Serving black farmers was not high on their priority list. Texans helped set the standard by expecting blacks to ask for the service from white experts and by excluding black experts from employment in publicly funded agricultural reform efforts.[9]

Contemporaneous with research into pest eradication, but separate from it, the USDA looked for ways to change farming methods. In 1902, officials appointed a special agent for the promotion of agriculture in the South, Dr. Seaman A. Knapp. He traveled to Texas during early 1903 to test a strategy he had devised that required communities to indemnify a local farmer willing to demonstrate new methods. Residents of Terrell agreed to support Walter C. Porter, a large landowner farming on the Blackland Prairie, a fertile swath that ran between heavily wooded East Texas and the more arid western portion of the state. Porter's tenant applied Knapp's ideas to help launch Farmers' Cooperative Demonstration Work, a program administered by the USDA and from which the Federal Extension Service emerged. Farmers who wanted to participate had to volunteer their time, land, and labor to implement the experts' suggestions, no small request for cash-strapped farmers. Those who demonstrated new practices saw their yields increase, though skepticism proved difficult to overcome.[10]

Though Knapp's influence among southern farmers remains debatable, white farmers considered Farmers' Cooperative Demonstration Work another aspect of rural reform that they should control, but black farmers wanted access. They volunteered their land, time, and labor, as white farmers did, yet, they could not secure appointments as experts though white farmers could. Cooperative demonstration work developed as a fulcrum on which black and white reformers jockeyed for position over more than ten years, between 1904 and 1915.[11]

To further demonstration work, Knapp negotiated with officials at Agricultural and Mechanical College of Texas (hereafter Texas A&M) to cooperate in the service. Texas A&M developed as the white land-grant institution, founded during Reconstruction in compliance with the 1862 Morrill Land-Grant Act to support higher-level public education. In 1912, Texas A&M signed a memo of agreement with the USDA to house the newly formed Texas Agricultural Extension Service. This agreement undermined efforts by the University of Texas and the Texas Department of Agriculture to offer similar programs to farmers and their families to improve rural conditions and increase farm and household efficiency and health. African Americans remained marginalized in the new service, prohibited from delivering advice and therefore relegated to the role of consumer.[12]

After more than a decade of testing Farmers' Cooperative Demonstration Work, the U.S. Congress passed the Smith-Lever Agricultural Extension Act in 1914. This act created the Federal Extension Service (FES) as a branch of the U.S. Department of Agriculture responsible for disbursing federal funds to white land-grant colleges in each state. The act vested authority in Texas A&M and allowed its white administrators to distribute federal funds. Empowered by *Plessy v. Ferguson,* an 1896 U.S. Supreme Court decision that established the precedent of separate but equal, Texas created the Negro Division within its extension service and hired three African Americans in 1915 to disseminate information to black farmers and their families. The creation of the separate division resulted from the resolve of white Texans to restrict black participation and to protect white power structures. By 1922, all eleven of the former Confederate states, including Texas and the border states of Maryland, West Virginia, Kentucky, Oklahoma, and Missouri, employed black agents, often cordoned off in separate divisions, to serve black farm families.[13]

Whites created the Negro Divisions in response to black demands for inclusion, and the Negro Division developed as an exercise in contradictions. Classic Hegelian dialectics played out in the Texas countryside. The Negro Division in Texas reflected black agency as well as black subjugation. It grew because of black talent as well as white racism. For fifty years, from the summer of 1915 through the summer of 1965, it thrived, relatively speaking. Black Texans routinely secured more funding and employed more agents through the Negro Division than did staff in any other division in the South. Yet, employees earned less than their white counterparts and worked longer hours with fewer benefits. Regardless, black employees became as vested in the success of the division as were white supremacists.

Initially, middle-class African Americans claimed the Negro Division as their platform for advocating for rural modernization. As demographics shifted and black owners began leaving the land at an accelerated pace after World War II, Negro Division employees used the division to promote their profession. Black agents continued to conduct successful programs and increased employment standards, but neither effort undermined the race-biased foundation on which the Negro Division rested. Segregation, however, proved less defensible as civil rights displaced economic rights as the rallying cry for rural black reformers. After 1964, when legal segregation became illegal, whites again assaulted black influence by obliterating the professional division that blacks had built. On June 30, 1965, those black staff members who did not retire were subsumed into subordinate positions within an integrated TAEX.

The Negro Division provided opportunities for rural blacks within the limitations imposed by social, economic, and civil inequity. In this book I shall explore the factors that affected the formation and maturation of the Negro Division in Texas and evaluate the efforts and results of workers in the field and the obstacles they faced. Themes of race, gender, and class run throughout the narrative.

The first chapter considers how black farmers and reformers negotiated with white politicians to protect their positions in the rural South. After the demise of the Populist challenge to two-party politics, both Democrats and Republicans turned their backs on black farmers and began competing with each other over the best way to address the needs of white Texas farmers. As whites jockeyed for position, they refused to involve blacks in any publicly funded program as more than consumers of services. Blacks addressed their own needs through private all-black efforts such as the Farmers' Improvement Society of Texas. Black reformers in other states realized modest inclusion after they convinced USDA officials to allocate funds provided by northern philanthropists to hire black agents. Texans did not follow suit but instead waited until the state had complete authority over Farmers' Cooperative Demonstration Work. Then they hired black agents and cordoned them off in the Negro Division.

Chapter 2 analyzes the critical five-year period between 1915 and the end of the Great War. The first three African American employees of the Texas Agricultural Extension Service laid the foundation for a viable division but also set a precedent for doing more with less. They met the unrealistic expectations that TAEX officials set because they worked with landowning farm families already active in private reform efforts such as the FIS. These farmers took suggestions offered by the agents to heart and delivered the first cotton bale to the gin, canned copious amounts of vegetables and meat, and even earned premiums for the best pigs exhibited at local agricultural fairs. Yet, the visible evidence of their success exacerbated racial tension. Whites expected rural blacks to farm but not to outperform white farmers, and they expected the extension agents to maintain the racial status quo. Black employees, on the other hand, had to justify their position with measurable accomplishments within the constraints imposed by white bureaucrats. Doublespeak became pro forma.[14]

Chapter 3 analyzes the ways agents employed in the Negro Division worked with African Americans individually, in groups, and through communities to build networks of support and influence during the 1920s. Farm families gained advocates, communities gained boosters, and churches and schools found new causes through cooperation with agents. Agents did not just help individuals raise better corn or cotton and rehabilitate clothing; they facilitated leadership training through club activities, they focused community action through health campaigns, and they advocated economic entrepreneurship through community canning centers. They strengthened rural communities but, at the same time, they strengthened the separate bureaucracy. Nonetheless, the color-sensitive bureaucracy trapped the black employees, supervisors and field agents alike, by undervaluing their contributions, co-opting their ideas, manipulating their appointments, and systematically discriminating against them.

The success of black agents in the field related directly to their ability to negotiate interracially. Chapter 4 explores the relationships that developed at all levels because of the legal segregation of Negro Division staff from white residents, representatives of local government, and state and national officials, and the constant interaction that nonetheless occurred. Whites defined the modern South as rational, efficient, and white, and they denied blacks equal standing in the system, no matter how essential progressive blacks made their reform agenda. As long as the minority agents emphasized goals that white southerners could support, specifically, goals that strengthened the Texas economy by creating sustainable black farms, the Negro Division received financial support from many sources, white as well as black. Thus, agents retained their appointments and farmers retained their advocates. Gender relations proved as fluid as race relations. White as well as black female professionals faced limitation. Regardless, racial stereotypes that white men projected onto black women made it possible for black women to secure education and enter public service more readily than their white counterparts, and also to exert more authority than black men were allowed to wield. Black women bore responsibility for much public contact and fund-raising, while black men found themselves emasculated, earning half the salary paid their white male counterparts, but an amount equal to that paid their female co-workers.[15]

Chapter 5 covers the complicated decade of the 1930s and the limited benefits that New Deal legislation provided for Texas' black farmers. Few blacks received New Deal services, but those who did participated because of their relationship to individuals affiliated with the Negro Division. The division did not pursue class equity in the countryside. It had focused on services for landowners and prosperous tenants from its inception, and these farmers garnered social welfare benefits during the New Deal. Sharecroppers largely did not. Black agents motivated their constituents to sign up for the cotton buyout program administered through the Agricultural Adjustment Administration, to build canning houses, to stuff mattresses, and to manage their limited finances as efficiently as possible, given new credit opportunities. Despite economic hard times, several African Americans gained relatively stable employment because of their continued work for black farmers who remained committed to the land.

The growth in the Negro Division during the depression years continued into the 1940s, largely because of agent involvement in World War II and cold war initiatives. Chapter 6 explores the ways that agents expanded their programs into towns and cities and used media such as photographs, exhibits, and radio to convey reform ideas to nonfarm audiences, black and white alike. Agents reached more Texans indirectly through public festivals even as the number of farm owners declined steeply. Adult and 4-H club membership decreased as well during the 1940s and the 1950s. The loss of constituents prompted supervisors to defend their position within the separate bureaucracy that they had helped construct. They developed higher standards of employment and created professional organizations to stabilize their support networks, but agents and other black professionals also became increasingly vocal about inequity in pay, benefits, and access. Agents had to balance their efforts to preserve their position with an increased need to save black farmers.

Another distraction arose, however, in the form of opportunities abroad for a select few agents. During the cold war, U.S. foreign relations goals resulted in the formation of the Office of Foreign Agricultural Relations within the USDA, and Point Four, administered by the Department of State. These offered Negro Division employees opportunities for foreign service. The United Nations Food and Agriculture Organization provided attractive assignments for black agents to serve abroad as well. Most Negro Division staff who enlisted in foreign projects, particularly in Africa, realized greater personal freedom. Their participation seemed ironic to international detractors, who criticized the United States for not living up to the ideals stated in both the U.S. Constitution and the United Nations' Declaration of Human Rights.

Chapter 7 focuses on the civil rights movement, the role of Negro agents in the movement, and the movement's effect on the Negro Division. The separate bureaucracy within TAEX survived until the U.S. Congress passed the Civil Rights Act in 1964. Integrating TAEX, however, did not proceed in the spirit of equality and justice for all. African American professionals found themselves demoted and even more beholden to white administrators. Some staff, Dempsey Seastrunk, for example, became key members of the TAEX headquarters staff in College Station, Texas, but others lamented the demise of the fifty-year-old bureaucracy.

Advocates of separate services for minority farmers renewed their quest during the 1970s. In response, the U.S. Congress passed legislation creating a new Extension Service across the South designed to serve racially diverse and economically disadvantaged rural Americans by advocating alternative, sustainable approaches to agriculture. The previously all-black land-grant institutions, founded as a result of the 1890 Morrill Land-Grant Act, assumed responsibility for the program, including Prairie View A&M University in Texas. It received funding directly from the U.S. government and authority over the new public reform program, a realization of separatist goals. The 1890 Cooperative Extension Program that developed, however, remained marginal to the large-scale production goals that drove agricultural reform at TAEX headquarters.

While trying to improve farming techniques and general material prosperity, Negro Division staff members and the farmers they served engaged in a collective struggle against poverty, hardship, ignorance, inequality, and subordination. They did not, however, always agree on the best solution. Some believed that economic efficiency would earn them equal treatment. Others believed that they should secure rights because they were part of the body politic. A small percentage of African American farmers and reformers in Texas prospered economically, and on this basis the Negro Division grew. Ironically, however, the material evidence of their success as farmers and reformers both sustained government funding and generated opposition to their quest for more equal inclusion. The rhetoric used by minority employees of TAEX and their constituents reflects the essence of politics, a struggle between unequals to make the government more responsive to minority needs. The structure of the Negro Division and the function of its staff indicate the ways that a bureaucracy grew out of color consciousness and then shifted to appease whites as well as blacks over a fifty-year period.[16]

African American reformers fell short of their ultimate goals to serve black farmers and strengthen their own profession. Economies of scale forced most black farmers out of business. Their low-capital operations made it difficult for them to compete against white agribusiness, and agents did not make subsistence agriculture a viable alternative. Neither farmers nor reformers secured justice. Race-biased decisions kept blacks marginalized from government programs, even though the Negro Division gave them a legitimate voice. Integration, in many ways, silenced that voice, as black agents lost their jobs and black farmers who persevered lost their advocate in policy decisions in Texas.[17]

REAPING A GREATER HARVEST

I

African Americans and Rural Reform in Texas, 1891–1914

African Americans strove to improve conditions in rural Texas after emancipation, but the most organized and sustained effort developed during the Populist era of the late 1880s and the early 1890s. Politics affected white decisions to support black-led reform efforts, specifically, the Farmers' Improvement Society of Texas, because whites believed such alliances weakened Populist challenges to the two-party system. After the demise of Populism, Texas Democrats and Republicans abandoned rural blacks and began competing with each other over the best way to address the needs of whites. Blacks remained influential but marginalized from growing opportunities in government-funded reform aimed nearly completely at white audiences. The Texas Department of Agriculture, the Agricultural and Mechanical College of Texas, and experiment stations authorized by the U.S. Department of Agriculture and supported by Texas A&M provided information to select groups. White Texans kept a firm grasp on knowledge by prohibiting black involvement in research and refusing to employ blacks as purveyors of information. African Americans had to ask for services and depend on white Texans to deliver. Ultimately, sustained requests for information combined with an evident commitment to agriculture and rural life on the part of black farm families forced Texas officials to hire African Americans. They believed that separating them into the Negro Division of the Texas Agricultural Extension Service would reduce their influence.

Robert Lloyd Smith first organized blacks in Oakland, Texas, in 1889 to circumvent exploitation by whites, "a class," according to Smith, "that calculated, almost to the pound, his productive capacity, and then gave him credit up to this estimate and occasionally beyond it." By 1891, he had shifted his goals from home and yard improvement because he realized that farmers could not afford even modest repairs. Instead, he advocated more politicized agendas, specifically, abolishment of the credit system. He believed black farmers could circumvent the Texas lien law, which trapped them in poverty, by raising foodstuffs at home and using cash to purchase cooperatively. Raising crops and stock for home consumption required changing the crop culture, so he encouraged members of his newly constituted Farmers' Improvement Society of Texas to discuss topics of interest to farmers and thereby "create, encourage, and foster an intelligent and lively interest in improved methods of farming." The FIS used prize money to reward farmers for improving their fields, garden crops, and livestock. Smith expected the farmers to take their hard-earned funds and contribute some to the FIS mutual-benefit fund to insure member families against loss, but he also expected them to invest in real and personal property, specifically, land and a home.[1]

Smith's reform agenda appealed to a growing group of middle-class African Americans which included his in-laws, William H. and Catherine Isaacs. Isaacs, the community blacksmith, had purchased a town lot in the unincorporated community of Oakland in April 1866, soon after emancipation, adding an acre at the edge of town to his holdings the next year. Only three other African Americans owned land in the county before him. The Isaacses' status as landowners added leverage to their pursuit of education for their several children. By the mid-1880s, Smith had arrived in Freedmantown, the name white Oakland residents conferred on the black settlement at the edge of town, to teach. He helped build better schools and professionalize black teachers. He allied with Isaacs fully by marrying one of his daughters, Francis Isabella "Belle" Isaacs, in 1890.[2]

Smith's alliance with the Isaacses proved fortuitous, and the FIS became a family affair. Smith administered the organization and, with the help of his brother-in-law, William Isaacs Jr., developed the FIS cooperative purchasing system. His wife, Belle Isaacs Smith, coordinated the Women's Barnyard Auxiliary, the FIS branch that helped women turn eggs, poultry, and butter into valuable additions to farm income. As a team they engaged in a form of economic warfare, encouraging black farm families to practice improved methods of farming, invest their income in their own homes and land, and thus distance themselves from white control. Farmers could improve their status from sharecropper to tenant to farm owner and gain personal security as a result. New landowners also gained influence in local decision-making. Members of secure farm communities could hire educators, ministers, tradesmen, doctors, and even lawyers to work in their interests. Property ownership, particularly landownership, assured them some influence, even during an era of increased disfranchisement and de facto discrimination. At the same time, though, landowners paid more taxes, including poll taxes, and they committed their limited resources to education. Reformers allied with landowners to improve conditions in Texas, bringing to rural blacks the gleanings from their own education. Thus, land became a tool that blacks used to reap a greater harvest, economically and constitutionally.[3]

Smith's efforts coincided with the rise of the most significant third-party challenge in the history of the United States. The Colored Farmers National Alliance and Cooperative Union had originated in nearby Houston County, Texas, in 1886. It offered blacks excluded from the Farmers Alliance because of their race and disgusted with existing party politics a voice in local, state, and national politics. Smith founded the Village Improvement Society three years later as an alternative to the alliance and the Populist challenge. His shift in goals in 1891, signified by his renaming the society the Farmers' Improvement Society and adding cooperative buying, indicates the ways he positioned his organization in direct competition with the Colored Farmers National Alliance goals. In this way he hoped to cultivate support for white Texas Republicans.[4]

White Republicans needed rural black votes to defeat the growing third party, and the countryside proved a fertile place to recruit them. In October 1896, on the eve of the presidential election, Smith revised the FIS constitution to facilitate institutional expansion into three neighboring counties. As white votes split between Democratic and Republican candidates, Smith secured black votes for the Republicans. As a result, white Republicans became beholden to him and his noncontroversial goals of economic security through private property ownership, self-improvement, and local autonomy.[5]

Colorado County Republicans thanked Smith by electing him twice as their representative to the state legislature, in 1895 and 1897. During the 1896 campaign, he even ousted influential black Texan Norris Wright Cuney as the Republican leader, so much had Smith become the indispensable black Republican. Concomitantly, the FIS became the indispensable reform organization for property-holding black farmers.[6]

Smith and the FIS illustrate the ways that rural African Americans used grassroots politics to sustain reform on a large scale. They often accomplished their goals through self-segregated efforts, and this caused some to refrain from challenging segregation outright when they were in positions of influence. For example, Smith did not question segregation of public schools when he sat in the Texas legislature, because African Americans exercised some control over their schools. Eliminating black schools would have diminished the little authority that blacks had in the color-sensitive South, making them

Figure 1. Robert L. Smith, ca. 1928. (Smith-Cobb
Family Papers, Texas Collection, Baylor University)

more dependent, not less, on white southerners. He supported construction
of a land-grant school for African American youth and another bill that gave
black trustees responsibility for black public school administration and authority over their children's education. Smith challenged other aspects of segregation, however, as the 1896 U.S. Supreme Court decision, *Plessy v. Ferguson,*
legalized separation of races in places of public accommodation. He opposed
separate waiting rooms in depots. He pursued the cause of civil liberty by
supporting antilynching legislation. This issue interested all blacks, including economically successful farmers, who faced intimidation and violence as
inflated cotton prices fueled race-based violence. He sought an amendment
to the 1874 Landlord and Tenant Act to prevent landlords from exacting more
from tenants than the harvest warranted. Ultimately, he favored free access
to the vote, even as Democrats and Republicans systematically denied blacks
the franchise (Fig. 1).[7]

Yet, white Republicans and Democrats quickly abandoned Smith and his
rural constituency. In 1900, he chaired the Republican State Convention,

whose platform urged Republicans to censure Democrats' efforts to "disfranchise colored voters who exercised, for years, the 'sacred right of suffrage.'" Nothing came of the request, and Democrats enacted legislation over the next seven years that virtually excluded blacks and poor whites from the political process. This legislation included a poll-tax amendment in 1902; the Terrell Election Law of 1903, instituting the white primary in Texas; and refinements of that law in 1905, 1907, 1913, and 1918 that severely restricted black and poor white voters. The namesake of these bills, Judge A. W. Terrell, led Democrats who refused to share authority with black Texans or count poor whites as their constituents. In 1905, an exasperated Smith wrote Booker T. Washington decrying the state of southern politics: "Lynch laws, peonage, whitecapping, and all kindred evil have their root in the rape of the ballot." [8]

As white Texans stripped political power from black Texans, they also strengthened their authority over new scientific information related to agriculture. The process began during Reconstruction, when whites appropriated public lands set aside by the Morrill Land-Grant Act of 1862 to support training in agriculture and mechanical arts. The land-grant college that emerged in Texas further consolidated information in the hands of white Texans. Subsequent national legislation, including the Hatch Act of 1887, expected such colleges to form agricultural experiment stations. Texas Agricultural Experiment Station, organized in 1888 and connected with Texas A&M University, pursued three agendas: investigating threats to Texas agriculture; teaching students to investigate and mitigate these threats; and conveying the information learned to people who were not college students. The public program claimed to "solve problems which the private individual cannot afford, and is not prepared, to solve for himself." Whites realized most benefits. [9]

Some Texans did not rely on national authority to further agricultural reform but took matters into their own hands. In 1887, they created the State Bureau of Agriculture and incorporated it into an existing department, renamed the Department of Agriculture, Insurance, Statistics, and History. Officials of the bureau had the responsibility for accumulating data on agriculture and, after 1889, stock raising. In 1904, USDA officials employed special agents to work with farmers in Texas. This prompted another reorganization of the Texas department in 1905, and states' rights Democrats appointed a commissioner and made him responsible for protecting trees, plants, and shrubs from infectious diseases. In this way, Texas Democrats exerted some control over agricultural reform in their state by indirectly resisting USDA incursions into Texas. White supremacy also motivated them. [10]

Texans who led the movement to consolidate agricultural reform included Edward Reeves Kone, a white farmer, lawyer, county judge, and leading Democrat. He became the first elected commissioner of agriculture for the reconstituted Texas Department of Agriculture (TDA) in 1908. A native Texan whose father fought for the Confederacy, Kone celebrated when Democrats recaptured the state legislature from Republican influence in 1873. He understood that rural blacks sought reform, and he conveyed this through his advocacy of the 1896 Democratic State Convention pledge to protect "all classes and races . . . in the enjoyment of life, liberty, and the pursuit of happiness." He also understood black efforts to control their own schools and to enlarge Prairie View Normal School and convert it to a university for black Texans. Yet, his apparent support of such black agendas reflected his opposition to Populism more than real support. While such strategizing may have drawn some African American support away from the Colored Farmers National Alliance and Smith's Republicans, the Democrats, including Kone, left little doubt about which race should control Texas. By 1904, Kone had endorsed the Terrell Election Law as "wise and efficient" reform. His persistence helped him secure leadership of the TDA, a position he held for three terms, to 1915.[11]

As white Democrats sought authority over agricultural information, the boll weevil moved north out of Mexico and threatened Texas' primary cash crop, cotton. Planters and cotton brokers became concerned as cotton bolls failed to mature and yields declined. In 1894, two years after the infestation began, C. H. DeRyee of Corpus Christi notified the USDA. The national government encouraged Texas legislators to intervene by prohibiting farmers from planting cotton in the infested area, but officials in Texas failed to act, perhaps in resistance to national suggestions. By the early twentieth century, the pest had spread into Central Texas. The 1902 crop suffered, but the 1903 crop proved a disaster, with yields cut in half. In October 1902, as gins turned out cotton bales, entomologists with the USDA issued a memo advocating a three-part approach, including planting of early-maturing seed, fertilizing and cultivating to hasten maturity, and destroying stalks as early as possible in the fall. Information did not reach farmers effectively, however, and existing cultivation methods facilitated infestation. The problem required immediate action to change farming practices.[12]

Not all Texans resented national influence. Railroad businessmen, intent on expanding agricultural production, sought information from the USDA's new special agent for the promotion of agriculture in the South, Dr. Seaman A. Knapp, appointed in 1902. In early 1903, Knapp arrived in Terrell,

Texas, at the invitation of the president of the Texas Midland Railway Company, E. H. R. Green, and his agents. Knapp, the consummate educator, was eager to test a new method of peer instruction. He asked Terrell residents to pick a farm and a farmer willing to try new crops and methods of cultivation and to share what he learned with his neighbors. Eight businessmen and farmers picked Walter C. Porter as the demonstrator and indemnified him against loss. Of his eight hundred–acre farm in the heart of the Blackland Prairie near Terrell, Porter volunteered an unfertilized seventy-acre plot that had been planted in corn and cotton for nearly thirty years. His black tenant farmer, John McQuinney, implemented Knapp's instructions, planting cotton, corn, peas, sorghum, sweet potatoes, kafir corn, and milo maize. At the end of the 1903 harvest, Porter proclaimed success, earning seven hundred dollars more on the tract than he would have earned using old methods (Fig. 2).[13]

Cooperative demonstration work seemed the most democratic of all agricultural reform methods. In theory, literate black or white owners or tenants could secure the information and guidance of the government through published reports or personal contact and could implement the suggestions. McQuinney gained access to USDA recommendations because he implemented them. Other black and white Texans could read about them in local newspapers that carried information about demonstration work and advertisements for early-maturing cotton seed, which developed bolls before weevil eggs hatched. Newspapers also featured testimonials from landowners offering incentives to their tenants to purchase the seed. The *Terrell Times-Star* reported that Houston Haynie, of Kemp, offered to pay one-fourth of the cost of the early-maturing (North Carolina) seed for spring planting. One of Haynie's tenants remarked that, if all the landlords encouraged their tenants in such a way, "it would hasten the adoption of new methods and result in much good to this section." Blacks could access the *Terrell Times-Star* and could read about such offerings and the recommendations of the USDA. This gave them access to information about scientific farming techniques, but on white terms. Other African Americans appealed to USDA special agents.[14]

The first five USDA agents received their appointments in late January and February 1904. One of them, J. A. Evans, a white farmer selected because of his practical nature and ability to encourage farmer participation, enrolled two black Texas farmers on his first day at work. Agents remembered spending about one-quarter of their time during the early years of cooperative demonstration work serving black farmers. African Americans accounted for approximately 20 percent of all Texas farmers in 1905, and most of them

Figure 2. John McQuinney (left) and Walter C. Porter (right). The prototype demonstration that evolved into Farmers' Cooperative Demonstration Work was created on Porter's farm, near Terrell, Kaufman County, Tex., in 1903. McQuinney worked the seventy-acre tract. This photo was taken ca. 1928 to commemorate the twenty-fifth anniversary of the founding of Farmers' Cooperative Demonstration Work. Photograph published in *Silver Anniversary,* 40; Martin, *The Demonstration Work,* 33; and *Acco Press* 31, no. 2 (Feb. 1953.): 8. (Neg. 33-S-17943, Ed C. Hunton, copy negative, 1952, FES, USDA, NA)

depended on cotton as their principal cash crop. Yet, they cultivated only about 14 percent of all land devoted to cotton in Texas. Such statistics make it difficult to assess whether special agents spent an equitable amount of time with black farmers. Given the degree to which black farmers depended on cotton, they warranted at least the attention agents claimed they received, if not more.[15]

White landowners concerned about the dire economic circumstances that prompted black tenants and laborers to leave farming sometimes asked agents to talk with them. As many as five hundred tenants in Harrison County in one year decided to move to the city or to work in nearby mines or lumber camps. White landowners asked Knapp to help them keep blacks on the land. Knapp authorized J.L. Quicksall, the special agent in the area, to call a meeting of black farmers in the county and offer them information on scientific farming. The county agent in Kaufman County, home of the first demonstration and of the McQuinney family, was working with forty black tenant families by 1907.[16]

Knapp encouraged the special agents to work with black farmers because they grew considerable cotton in the Blackland Prairie, predominantly on white owners' lands. By 1904, with the release of Du Bois's analysis of 1900 census data in "The Negro Farmer," Knapp and his agents knew the responsibility that black farmers bore for the crop and understood the need to involve them as demonstrators. Yet, racist attitudes affected Knapp's judgment about the level of information they could ingest. He believed that "the colored race [must] start at the bottom. In attempting to raise the condition of the colored man we frequently start too high up, and in talking of the higher progress talk right over his head. When I talk to a negro citizen I never talk about the better civilization, but about a better chicken, a better pig, a whitewashed house."[17]

Knapp did not want to hire black agents because he believed whites would serve both races while blacks would concentrate only on programs for members of their race. That comment reflected more white farmers' refusal to accept instruction from blacks than blacks' refusal to share. Knapp advised white agents to work with black farmers, but only if they requested the service. Extension officials believed black farmers who wanted information would ask for it, and white agents should not spend their time recruiting black demonstrators.[18]

Knapp shared racist attitudes with the white Democrats who ran Texas' institutions. He depended on men such as David F. Houston, president of Texas A&M, to help promote Farmers Cooperative Demonstration Work.

Knapp and Houston may have agreed on limiting services to black Texans, but they disagreed about other things. Knapp, who did not respect academics, though he had been one, left a meeting with Houston late in 1903 unimpressed with his "small potato ideas." Houston may have given Knapp a cool welcome because he resented the northerner's intrusion into Texas' affairs and feared that Knapp's demonstration work would compete with the land-grant institution's mission to educate Texans about agriculture. In contrast to Knapp, James Wilson, U.S. secretary of agriculture, believed that Texas A&M was "more nearly fulfilling its mission than any other similar institution in the United States," and that Houston had much to do with its success. Houston and Knapp eventually agreed to share staff. A professor from Texas A&M would work as one of Knapp's agents to help recruit students to Texas A&M, and three of Knapp's agents would reside at Texas A&M for a period to learn about the attitudes within the land-grant college. This agreement focused agents' efforts on prosperous white farmers, not the masses of farmers dependent on cotton.[19]

Knapp did not limit his promotional efforts to Texas A&M. He opened an office in Houston, Texas, in January 1904 and appealed to agricultural agents employed by Texas railroads to distribute information. During 1905, as federal appropriations remained inadequate and the boll weevil continued to spread, he visited David Houston and Texas A&M again. While there, he met Dr. Wallace Buttrick, secretary of the General Education Board (GEB), a fund John D. Rockefeller had endowed in late 1902. Buttrick was looking for ways to educate rural residents with GEB funds. While Houston may have set aside his states' rights and antimonopoly leanings to listen to Buttrick's ideas, the meeting did not result in GEB money for agents in Texas. Instead, Knapp and Buttrick laid the groundwork for sustained funding of demonstration work in noninfested areas, with local matches of GEB funds.[20]

General Education Board funds supported the employment of the first black agents, but not in Texas. The GEB and the USDA agreed in April 1906 that the GEB would pay all direct and indirect costs to carry cooperative demonstration work to areas of the South not covered by government appropriations, that is, not part of the regions infested by the boll weevil. The USDA maintained authority over all agents hired with GEB funds. Until November 1906, those agents were all white. On November 12, 1906, Booker T. Washington negotiated with a USDA official to hire the first Negro agent in the South, Thomas M. Campbell, and allow him to operate out of Tuskegee Institute in Alabama. Within days, the GEB provided additional funds to hire J. B. Pierce to work out of Hampton Institute in Virginia, and within a year, GEB funds had enabled Mississippi blacks to call on the services of J. A. Booker, stationed at Mound Bayou. Black agents were hired in Georgia and in the Carolinas in 1908. The national government did not legislate the hiring of black agents, thus respecting each state's right to respond to the majority of its citizens rather than protect minority citizens' rights.[21]

Texas did not qualify for GEB funds because the 1906 agreement between the U.S. secretary of agriculture and the secretary of the GEB limited funding to noninfested areas. Consequently, the GEB did not support efforts in Texas to the same degree that the endowment supported other areas of the South. Critics abounded. Educators who convened at the University of Texas at Austin in 1907 noted: "The general education board, to which Mr. Rockefeller has recently given $32,000,000, and the Southern Educational Board have done much to promote education in other States, but these boards have refused aid to Texas on the ground that Texas is able to help herself and needs no charity." Another reason GEB funding lacked popular support in Texas related to the antitrust sentiment in the state, particularly toward railroads. This made state officials less than receptive to Rockefeller's philanthropy.[22]

Without GEB funding, blacks did not gain positions as purveyors of scientific information in Texas. As a result, black farmers continued to rely on white agents for guidance. USDA agents reported that black farmers in Walker County were "becoming greatly interested in the work" in 1909 due to the potential to double yields. The local agent, J. B. Cauthen, claimed that "fully sixty percent" of the county's population was black, but records do not document how many of his 550 demonstrators were black. At least he recognized that black farmers sought advice to improve their cultivation practices and increase their income.[23]

USDA agents also praised black farmers who excelled in implementing advice. In 1909, J. W. Williams won twenty-three dollars at the Mineola Corn & Cotton Show for raising three thousand pounds of seed cotton per acre. The county agent, C. E. Allen, commented that Williams had five more acres just as fine as the award-winning acre. By publicizing the event, Allen believed that he would appeal to more African American farmers in counties such as Wood with small black populations. He had staged the corn and cotton show as a public relations event to generate interest in demonstration work, and it was just as important to appeal to black as to white farmers to ensure the broadest coverage in the county. Obviously, agents responded to local circumstances, and despite USDA directions not to recruit black farmers, agents' decisions indicate that appealing to black farmers helped them fulfill their larger reform agendas.[24]

Successful reform depended on youth involvement. White as well as black reformers called for programs for their youth, and many youth clubs already existed. The Texas Farmers' Congress, a Texas A&M offering that began in 1898, supported the Farmer Boys' and Girls' League in 1903 and had enrolled 1,200 white youth by 1904. When funds were cut in 1905, demonstrators supported it and helped it continue. This set a precedent for cooperation between federal and state government nine years before the relationship was codified in the Smith-Lever Act of 1914. African Americans involved youth in rural reform as well. The all-black Farmers' Improvement Society began its Juvenile Branch in 1907 and quickly enrolled black youngsters.[25]

USDA agents likewise believed that training youth could further the agricultural reform agenda efficiently. J. L. Quicksall, state agent in Texas, recounted how Capt. F. S. White, the horticultural commissioner of the Rock Island and Frisco Railroad lines, visited Jacksboro, Texas, in 1907, and suggested the establishment of corn clubs. Tom Marks, the agent in Jack County in West Texas, had enrolled 111 white boys by spring 1908. He involved the county superintendent, teachers, and parents in organizing viable corn-contest clubs. R. P. Elrod, the agent in Lee County in South Central Texas, realized even greater success with youth enrollment the next year, reporting 230 white boys involved in corn clubs by December 1909. Businesses and interested citizens contributed to a fund to purchase improved seed corn and to offer premiums at the fall corn club show. African American boys wanted to compete but could do so only if separate classes for Negroes existed, or if separate fairs were held. Forty-two African American boys formed one of Elrod's corn clubs, and the agent reported that he had "equally good results shown with them as with the white boys," possibly because they enjoyed the incentive of exhibiting at the FIS annual fair in Lee County in 1910.[26]

Smith and members of the FIS realized that black youth could benefit from the scientific information that government agents had to offer and praised USDA officials to ensure that support continued. Trustees of the Giddings (Lee County) FIS branch wrote a letter in 1910 that thanked R. P. Elrod for his "tireless" efforts "to show that farming is a paying proposition." His "stirring speeches" and the printed matter he distributed increased interest in farming among the black population and caused "a greater harvest to be reaped on the same acreage." The letter landed on Seaman Knapp's desk.[27]

Nearly one-third of the Lee County population was black, so the ratio of black to white youth in Elrod's clubs reflected county demographics. Yet, racism cooled white Texans' enthusiasm for including black youth. Howard H. Williamson, the agent in charge of boys' and girls' club work in Texas, expressed a lukewarm attitude when he reported that the boys involved in Negro clubs were "almost as prompt as the white boys in reporting on their work." Regardless, agents and supervisors had to admit that some black farmers made good farmers.[28]

The letter from the FIS trustees represented one of the few strategies rural blacks could use to counter such racist thinking. By the fall of 1909, black agents had been at work in Alabama, Virginia, and Mississippi between two and three years. Robert L. Smith, FIS president, certainly knew of this work, given his personal relationship with Booker T. Washington, who had facilitated Smith's hiring. Smith had interacted with many of the agents through farmers' institutes that met at Tuskegee Institute beginning in 1897. Yet, white administrators provided services only grudgingly. Williamson stressed that demonstration work in Texas "never made any direct attempt to do any extensive work with negro boys [but was confined] to a few counties where the negro boys requested that they be enrolled as members" of corn clubs. The boys also had to ask for bulletins, circulars, and other materials that demonstration agents distributed. The government satisfied individual demands, but it avoided making services more generally available, even as the number of black farmers increased and they remained disproportionately responsible for cotton cultivation.[29]

Blacks in other states turned to state departments of agriculture to gain information when the USDA proved unresponsive. They argued that neither black farm owners nor tenants could produce bountiful yields even on prime farmland if white southerners withheld information. Black educators believed that states should bear the burden for delivery. If departments provided services for white farmers, they should provide equal services for blacks. Texas' commissioner of agriculture, Edward R. Kone, disagreed. He initiated farmers' institutes, sponsored by the TDA, in April or May 1909 with the understanding that USDA special agents would participate. This placed the TDA in direct competition with Texas A&M for the agents' limited time. But Kone had little intention of inviting black farmers or reformers to institutes. Some may have attended, but no effort to involve blacks as peers occurred initially.[30]

Though black Texans could not secure demonstration agents of their own race, Texas' black land-grant institution tried to fill the void. Edward L. Blackshear, principal of Prairie View Normal & Industrial Institute (hereafter Prairie View A&M), supported farmers' congresses because they provided an opportunity to publicize the all-black land-grant school and to distribute needed information to rural African Americans. Blackshear believed that the farm on campus offered opportunities to conduct educational programs and make them widely available. He inaugurated short courses at Prairie View A&M in 1909, and these often utilized the farm for instruction. The short courses followed the model piloted at Tuskegee in 1905. In 1909, Tuskegee's two-week short course had drawn 960 men, women, and children. Blackshear believed that Alabama's black farmers realized their farmwork had greater significance beyond the daily routine, and he hoped to generate the same sentiment in Texas. In addition to agricultural instruction, the Prairie View A&M courses instructed farmers and rural men, women, and children in trades such as leatherworking and in home economics. In keeping with progressive reform goals, instructors also discussed morality. In 1915, the school's white board of directors authorized Calvin H. Waller, professor of agriculture, to "deliver agricultural lectures at different gatherings" and to be reimbursed for associated expenses.[31]

Accounts of informal education conducted at Prairie View A&M appeared in white newspapers, and reporters stressed the nonpolitical content. Editors of the San Antonio Daily Express assured their readers that "the discussion . . . will take a wide range, but it embraces only those economic questions which are of practical interest and which make for material progress and advancement." Farmers heard presentations on truck farming, dairying, hog and poultry raising, home gardening, organizing school farms, and improving rural schools. The programs gave farmers a sense of purpose and a forum for self-governance as they organized a board of officers and planned to share the information with neighbors.[32]

Attendees credited Blackshear with providing inspiration and leadership for expanding farmer education. A reporter for the Prairie View Standard quoted Blackshear's praise of reform-minded African Americans: "The negro farmer is rapidly becoming a diversifier, a farmer of the modern and most progressive type."[33]

Not all black farmers believed what they read in the newspapers. Farmers often resisted reform efforts, and agents had almost as much trouble convincing them to listen to their advice as to get white officials to support the work. Agents became frustrated as they strove to spread the message of self-determination to a people seeking release from oppression. The farmers lost faith in agents who implied that they, the farmer, and not the economic system in which they functioned, were responsible for the South's social and economic shortcomings.[34]

Black farmers also understood that improvements could have repercussions. Better homes led to increased rents, thus allowing the white landlord to reap additional rewards from the tenant's labor. Class conflict within the black community also challenged agents. They appeared to be representatives of the landlord class, the ones sapping the strength from the poor rural blacks, and tenant farmers and sharecroppers resented their advice. Some tenants showed their lack of support for the program by choosing migration.[35]

Despite the general lack of support from white Texans, and the lack of unity among black farmers, black reformers in Texas kept working to further rural reform. Three events occurred in 1911 that increased African Americans' awareness of if not their access to demonstration work in the state. Booker T. Washington toured the Texas countryside during late September and early October. In Houston he praised Smith for the work undertaken to help black Texans "get homes, become farmers, save their money and lead useful lives." The biggest, most boisterous crowd greeted the party in Waco, Smith's home at the time. Certainly, Smith gained wider name recognition as a result of the trip. He accompanied Washington for a portion of it, as did Edward L. Blackshear. Texans became more acquainted with Washington's philosophy, and the enthusiasm to put his ideas into practice influenced rural and small town reform. It did not, however, prompt Texas officials to appropriate funds for black agents.[36]

During 1911, Texas legislators authorized county commissioners to fund white demonstration agents. This increased the number of agents working, because federal funds went further when supplemented with local matches. White agents worked with black farmers in poor counties with large black populations because, if their property values increased, they paid more taxes. These taxes became part of county general funds, the source of agents' salaries. At least one county agent reported the importance of this tax base to furthering demonstration work. Counties with strong FIS branches often had significant percentages of black landowners as members, and these landowners influenced newly funded white agents as well.[37]

Some agents called open meetings in county courthouses to distribute information to black farmers, even though agents often had to attain permission from the commissioners' court to hold the meetings. They occurred in the spring, when blacks could still implement the information. TAEX administrators claimed that responding to black property owners' requests helped increase the number of blacks who benefited from the services.[38]

Also during 1911, Texas A&M's Educational Trains provided another opportunity for black farmers to acquire information. The trains made fifty-five stops in the first half of December, covering 2,217 miles and reaching 31,455 people. Blacks gained access to the information conveyed by these lecture trains, because they gathered with whites at depots to hear the lecturers and view the exhibits carried in the cars. The trains ran on several main railways, including the Midland and East Texas, the Texas Central, and the Missouri, Kansas & Texas, all of which cut through counties with a large black population. The cooperative demonstration agents relied on the trains to convey information again in 1914. The Katy–A&M College Agriculture Train ran in March and the Katy–A&M College Good Roads Special ran in August. Farmers who missed the train stop but subscribed to the local paper could still read about the information imparted. The Dallas and Galveston newspapers reported the service.[39]

Even the Texas Agricultural Experiment Station responded to black farmers' needs by providing scientific information related to an important cash crop that many grew. In 1914, its division of plant pathology and physiology, directed by F. H. Blodgett, secured private funding to conduct research in watermelon blossom-end blight. Blodgett, with the support of C. H. Waller, professor of agriculture, located the field studies on the farm at Prairie View A&M. Dr. J. J. Taubenhaus, a plant pathologist, supervised research, and E. T. Williams, who had studied with Waller, assisted. Farmers in the region could then hear about the important research through lectures Waller gave.[40]

In August 1912, responsibility for agricultural reform became consolidated at Texas A&M. The board of directors announced that the college "should be of great service in many ways to the citizens residing throughout the State . . . co-operating in agricultural and engineering lines with the people, the tax-payers of their state." A committee clarified the role and function of the new Texas Agricultural Extension Service that fall, and the USDA and Texas A&M signed a memorandum of understanding on October 1, 1912, which gave Texas A&M authority over farm demonstration and boys' and girls' club work in the state, conducted under the auspices of TAEX.[41]

Opinions about the agreement varied. Women involved in extension education in 1912 wondered if the partnership would threaten their limited participation, because Texas A&M did not admit women, and advocates of rural reform worried that the land-grant institution would not support women's work. Edna W. Trigg became the first white female appointed to do USDA-related work in Texas and began organizing canning clubs in January 1912. Trigg worked with sixteen canning agents who received $75 per month, paid by the GEB, for two months' work with girls. The agents organized the girls into clubs and taught them how to grow and can tomatoes. The University of Texas sponsored similar programs, maintained a traveling library service, and held "better baby" clinics to improve rural life. The Texas Department of Agriculture also offered programs to women and girls, implemented by women. These all received inadequate resources to operate when compared to the allocations that men received, and men and women criticized the state as a result. The U.S. secretary of agriculture at the time, David Houston, was president of Texas A&M when demonstration work began. He fielded these complaints adroitly and distributed fifty-five thousand copies of a letter in October 1913 to the wives of USDA crop correspondents, asking for their comments and an itemization of their needs. Women sought more official responsibility and worried that gender bias would limit their influence as employees and recipients of reform.[42]

Women questioned the decision that authorized Texas A&M, a public all-male university, to administer funds designated for canning clubs, and they asked TAEX's first director, Clarence Ousley, and Houston to provide equal funding to male and female agents. The General Federation of Women's Clubs led the challenge but ultimately acquiesced, settling for a 25 percent allotment of funds for women agents. Black women, even those in the Texas Association of Colored Women's Clubs, organized in 1905, wielded less leverage and did not gain positions as a result of the 1912 agreement. And white women in Texas, generally, suffered from fewer services as a result of the exclusive contract between Texas A&M and the federal government. The University of Texas at Austin redirected its education initiatives toward urban adults and away from rural audiences, which the new extension service at Texas A&M would serve henceforth.[43]

African Americans found no reason to celebrate the memo of understanding between Texas A&M and the USDA either. By 1912, the USDA, with funds from the GEB, had placed thirty-two black agents in nine southern states, excluding Texas. On June 30, 1915, eleven states reported a total of sixty-six black agents. These agents, in theory, had to serve approximately four million men, women, and children living on black-operated farms. Texas ranked fifth in the nation in the number of black farmers, but no provision mandated their inclusion in programs provided by TAEX.[44]

African Americans lobbied the USDA for more positions for African Americans equal to those held by white agents. In 1913, the National Association for the Advancement of Colored People (NAACP) argued that segregating civil service employees would create inequity on the job, punish capable employees who had done nothing wrong, violate the idea of "fair play and equal treatment," reduce the efficiency of both white and black agents in the service, and set a precedent that would have far-reaching consequences.

USDA officials denied that the agency had a segregation policy and claimed that no employees had complained of discrimination. Yet, race affected decision making. Bradford Knapp and O. B. Martin, USDA policy makers, concurred in 1913 that boys' and girls' clubs for African American youth should incorporate "Negro" in the name to distinguish them from similar programs for white children. Martin, fearful that similarity would "cause trouble and conflict with the Canning Club work among the white girls," sought even more distinct titles. He suggested that black agents work with girls and their mothers and emphasize home improvement rather than home canning, which white girls and their mothers pursued. He suggested "Home Making Clubs" as a more accurate and less controversial name for black groups. Both Knapp and Martin agreed that black children would earn "separate badges, of different design . . . they can not wear the same badges the white boys wear."[45]

Race-based decisions, such as *Plessy v. Ferguson,* prompted Texans, and other southerners, to go one step further and create separate agencies as homes for the black staff, and headquarters for their separate programs and awards. The pernicious segregation created a conundrum for blacks seeking appointments and services: Negro Divisions marginalized blacks but also ensured access; the segregated divisions gave African American reformers more visibility and a modicum of legal protection. In other words, segregation gave black reformers legitimacy. Some embraced the opportunities that the Negro Divisions allowed while others believed that separation perpetuated inequality.

Southern legislative support for the Smith-Lever Act, passed in May 1914, eliminated the use of private funding and northern influence in southern agriculture. The Smith-Lever Act also gave states the authority to distribute public funds as they saw fit, without national intervention. Only then did officials in Texas create a separate extension service, the Negro Division, in August 1915, to serve black farmers. TAEX staffed it with qualified adults knowledgeable in modern scientific practice. The structure of the bureaucracy, with whites overseeing blacks at all levels, reinforced Jim Crow race relations. Furthermore, white supervisors appropriated inadequate funds and expected African American staff members to supplement their salaries with local support, produce measurable results from their black constituents, and work with little to no office support. These factors made the black agents dependent on patronage to retain positions. Thus, the new federal reform program, enabled by a partnership between the national and state governments, reinforced grave inequities on the southern landscape, in particular, the marginal and subordinate status of black and poor white Americans.[46]

Pres. Woodrow Wilson considered the Smith-Lever Act "one of the most significant and far-reaching measures for the education of adults ever adopted by the government . . . to ensure the retention in rural districts of an efficient and contented population." His optimism, however, did not mirror the sentiments of African Americans. A concerned northern senator asked during the debate how the bill involved black land-grant colleges in the administration of the appropriated funds. Sen. Hoke Smith of Georgia, the floor leader for the bill, replied: "We will put it in our white agricultural college. We would not appropriate a dollar in Georgia to undertake to do extension work for the negro agricultural and mechanical school. It would be a waste of money." The bill included the provision that the legislature in each southern state have the authority to designate which land-grant college, authorized in either 1862 or 1890, received the funds. This gave state bureaucracies tacit permission to administer the whole fund through the white colleges. Northern senators, representatives of the NAACP, and other concerned citizens realized that this removed African Americans from the process.[47]

Even though Texas had a relatively large and concentrated black population and clearly lay within the jurisdiction of the southern extension office, Texans waited more than a year after passage of the Smith-Lever Act to expand offerings to rural blacks. Clarence Ousley conferred with Howard H. Williamson early in 1915 about involving more African American boys in corn clubs. Williamson responded that work with blacks was "an unexplored field" and should be entered cautiously to avoid "spending a large sum of money unwisely." Williamson recommended a one-year trial period to survey the situation and plan for the future. He suggested that the new segregated program could be conducted as part of existing club work, but it would be administered out of Prairie View A&M. A state leader for the segregated division could coordinate activities from Prairie View A&M and report weekly to the director at extension headquarters at Texas A&M. Williamson proposed limiting the agent's range to "a rather small territory" around Prairie View A&M and limiting the materials distributed to only those previously involved in Farmers' Cooperative Demonstration Work. He even advocated simpler materials, because, "due to their illiteracy," black youth could not take full advantage of TAEX publications.[48]

Williamson went even further in his attempts to limit black agents. He outlined their schedule, with the months of October, November, December, and January devoted to visiting communities and organizing clubs, and February and March devoted to instructing in seed testing, spacing, fertilizing, and planting. He envisioned the agent discussing late-summer cultivation and seed selection from standing crops in June and July. The end of the crop season marked the end of the agent's program. The agent would arrange for exhibits and collect reports in August and September. Throughout the year, the agent would visit all clubs every sixty days and hold lectures in school-houses and other locations in the field to reach more junior and adult African Americans. Williamson stressed the importance of competition as a motivating factor, and he recommended that the agent receive authority to organize exhibits devoted to the work of black club members at county fairs and to secure special fair premiums for them. These special prizes regularly amounted to only one-half to one-third the fair premiums awarded to white boys for the same effort.[49]

Williamson's recommendations left little room for modification by African American agents. Yet, his assertion that rural blacks would require simplified bulletins and circulars proved incorrect. Booker T. Washington routinely received letters from farmers asking for information. He used these as evidence to convince Knapp and other officials to increase the number of black agents. Members of the FIS reported that USDA bulletins helped members of corn clubs make "splendid exhibits" of corn and cotton at the FIS fair. Prairie View A&M faculty shared published information with participants at farmers' institutes and congresses. Ousley even advertised a bulletin on seed corn selection produced by the Department of Experimental Agronomy and a USDA bulletin entitled "School Lessons in Cotton" in the *Prairie View Standard* in 1915. Later that year, he brought two more pamphlets to the attention of readers; one discussed the proper storage of sweet potatoes, and the other, cotton value. Though illiteracy limited some rural blacks, the literate profited greatly from the printed word. This exacerbated the divide between a rising black middle class and the impoverished majority.[50]

White Extension Service personnel did not acknowledge black middle-class activism. A paternalistic mind-set shaped the attitudes of TAEX officials, including Ousley and Williamson, and this led them toward segregation. Ousley, TAEX director and a southerner active on Democratic state committees, explained that "racial and social distinctions" set African Americans apart from white club members. Furthermore, he believed that blacks needed special service provided by "their own people," and white southerners needed to manage it. This sentiment reflected the views held by many whites, who believed that African Americans accepted their second-class status. C. Vann Woodward describes this attitude as wrongheaded. He argues that southerners might have imagined that "the Negro had by now 'discarded the foggy notions of the Reconstruction,'" but evidence indicates otherwise. Some whites actually feared the potential blacks exhibited, and this led them to take coercive and even violent measures to maintain racial superiority. The TAEX's bureaucratic structure made black appointees answer to white authority, yet black farmers, disfranchised and lacking authority, still affected TAEX decisions. The segregated Negro Division evolved partially in response to their goals.[51]

The changing nature of agricultural reform in Texas indicates the ways that black reformers influenced white decision-making. Blacks navigated the quagmire of southern race relations by working with high-ranking officials, white experts, and black farmers as well as working around many white farmers and legislators opposed to expanding public services. Black reformers across the South, from FIS trustees in Lee County, Texas, to Booker T. Washington at Tuskegee Institute, influenced the decisions of white policymakers, but black reformers found themselves limited by racialized policies. Each reformer made decisions based on larger goals of rural reform as well as personal and career goals, but structures such as the segregated division proved difficult to surmount. Those involved in public programming realized many benefits but found themselves constrained by segregation despite a modicum of influence.[52]

2

Forming Separate Bureaucracies

The Negro Division of the
Texas Agricultural Extension Service, 1915–20

Texas became the twelfth state to segregate extension services when TAEX administrators created the Negro Division during 1915. The division quickly became the largest in the nation, securing more federal funding, more staff, and more participants than any other. It developed as a model of progressive reform, with college-educated African Americans instructing black youth and adults about farm and home management and efficiency and serving as agents of modernization. They had to devise strategies that appealed to poor farmers inclined toward self-improvement but cash poor and racially disadvantaged. They also had to face the backlash of white, middle-class progressivism and its racist tendencies and accomplish their goals despite this.

TAEX officials picked the first agents carefully, believing that they would convey only information that did not threaten white authority. The TAEX director, Clarence Ousley, asked Prairie View A&M principal, Edward L. Blackshear, to recommend a woman and two men to undertake the work. Ousley interviewed Mrs. Mary Evelyn V. Hunter, an Alabama native and recent graduate of Prairie View A&M, in late July 1915 and appointed her first. He then selected Robert L. Smith, a college-educated South Carolinian and the FIS president, and Jacob H. "Jake" Ford, a Texan, teacher, farmer, and veteran of Farmers' Cooperative Demonstration Work. Texas A&M president, William B. Bizzell, approved the appointments. The three traveled to TAEX headquarters on the Texas A&M campus for a conference with Ousley shortly after their appointment, and he impressed on them the importance of their work. Smith recounted that "we were told by our chief, Colonel Ousley, to get results from our work or the Negro Division would be abolished." Hunter remembered Ousley saying that "if we succeeded others would be added to the force and if we failed that there would be no other Negro agents employed in the near future." According to Hunter, the three "accepted this challenge with the determination to win and establish for ever in the minds of those in authority that some Negroes will plan and develop large organizations if permitted to do so."[1]

Hunter, Smith, and Ford represented a group of progressive-minded rural blacks, credentialed and committed to improving rural life, but their treatment indicates that their white colleagues did not consider them equals. White male administrators resisted appointing white women for demonstration work, yet, they appointed Hunter before appointing any black men, an indication of systemic devaluing of black masculinity by the same paternalists. White administrators apparently did not resent the black staff members; rather, descriptions indicate that they were considered useful. TAEX home demonstration agent Bernice Carter described Hunter as "a very efficient woman and [one who] will doubtless do a good work among the negroes of this state." Other officials described Smith as "an exceptionally strong negro [who had] already done a great work among the colored farmers of this state." The white county agent who had worked with Ford praised him for "his earnest desire to be helpful to the negro race." TAEX administrators appointed Smith as the first director of the Negro Division (see Table 1), Ford served as agronomist, and Hunter as home demonstration agent. With their appointments, white staff could take comfort that black farmers were being served, and black staff could celebrate, according to Hunter, the "large and worthwhile contributions to American citizenry" they made.[2]

TAEX administrators publicly announced the formation of the Negro Division in September 1915. White promoters believed that newly hired agents could "awaken" among the black farmers "a full realization of their opportunities in agriculture." Reporters covering the announcement indicated that "work with the negroes of Texas will begin for the first time." Both perspectives fail to convey the efforts made over the previous thirteen years through demonstration work with black farmers or the FIS-led reform that had served black farmers in several counties for nearly twenty-five years. Yet, administrators based their hiring decisions on previous experience, and Hunter remembered Ousley directing them to work with "those communities where the interest was great enough to justify . . . entering." This restriction basically directed staff to serve acquisitive black farm families already familiar with the FIS or earlier demonstration work. While this apparently reduced the burden staff members bore for creating an effective service in a short time, Hunter, Smith, and Ford targeted landowning families throughout the eastern half of the large state. This proved no small feat, as 21,000 black landowners farmed in Texas.[3]

TABLE 1. Texas Agricultural Extension Service Negro Division State Leaders

Name	Title	Tenure
Robert Lloyd Smith	State leader	Aug. 1, 1915–June 30, 1919[*]
Edward Lavoisier Blackshear	Special agent	Oct. 1, 1916–June 30, 1918
	Assistant state leader	July 1, 1918–June 30, 1919
	State leader	July 1–Dec. 12, 1919[†]
Calvin Hoffman Waller	Professor (Prairie View)	Sep. 1907–Dec. 31, 1919
	State leader	Jan. 1, 1920–Apr. 15, 1941[†]
Edward Bertram Evans	Veterinarian & professor (Prairie View)	1918–41
	Acting state leader	May 1–31, 1941
	State leader	June 1, 1941–Apr. 15, 1945
	State leader	July 1–Aug. 31, 1946[††]
William Cullen David	County agent (Madison)	Mar. 21, 1934–Mar. 15, 1943
	District agricultural agent	Mar. 16, 1943–July 4, 1944
	Acting state leader	Apr. 16–June 30, 1945
	Assistant state leader	July 1–Aug. 31, 1946
	State leader	Sep. 1, 1946–Mar. 31, 1959[§]
Marshall V. Brown	County agent (Brazoria)	May 1, 1937–Apr. 15, 1941
	Administrative assistant	Sep. 15, 1941–Mar. 31, 1959
	Acting state leader	Apr. 1–30, 1959
	State leader	May 1, 1959–Jan. 22, 1964[†]
Alton E. Adams	County agent (Fort Bend)	Apr. 16, 1933–Apr. 5, 1944
	Emergency war food assistant	Apr. 6–Oct. 15, 1944
	County agent (Fort Bend)	Oct. 16, 1944–Nov. 30, 1954
	Farm & home development specialist	Dec. 1, 1954–May 31, 1959
	Assistant state leader	June 1, 1959–Mar. 31, 1964
	Acting associate state leader	Apr. 1, 1964–June 30, 1965
	Staff assistant	July 1, 1965–June 30, 1970[§]

Source: D. H. Seastrunk, "Fifty Years of Negro Extension Work in Texas, 1915–1965," working draft, PV; E. B. Evans, "Down Memory Lane."
[*]Resigned
[†]Died in office
[††]Promoted to principal of Prairie View A&M
[§]Retired

Underfunding defined the division's financial condition throughout its existence. During its formative years, 1915 to 1921, it received only 4.1 percent of the total TAEX budget, though it employed between 6.5 and 9.8 percent of the office staff. In 1915, the TAEX provided one allotment of $4,900 to fund the three staff positions, travel and administrative costs, and supplies for one year's worth of home and agricultural demonstrations. Agents relied on their clientele as well as local agencies and county governments to supplement the meager appropriations. The TAEX even debated who should pay for franking privileges so the agents could mail information rather than travel incessantly. Ousley reported in 1915: "I am pleased to say that the negro workers have proved themselves to be very efficient, that the negro leaders of the State have given me very great assistance, and that their people are responding very satisfactorily to the instruction we are offering." White administrators doubled the allotment in fiscal year 1916–17. Another "lecturer in agronomy and a woman on home economics" joined the Negro Division staff in 1916. They were handpicked, as well. The lecturer was likely Edward L. Blackshear, former Prairie View A&M principal and recommender of the first appointees; and the woman was Pinkie Rambo, likely related to Smith.[4]

Despite different perceptions of blacks' duties, whites and blacks shared goals that they believed the Negro Division could fulfill. The black agents adopted the white extension education model, enrolling black farm families as volunteer demonstrators and cooperators. The men, women, and children who participated committed their farms, fields, homes, and labor to projects that served as models for their neighbors. Other residents pledged to cooperate in the demonstration by providing moral support, labor, and sometimes financial aid. Participation required a financial outlay as well, through dues to clubs and purchases of supplies. Hunter, Smith, and Ford realized the commitment necessary and worked as efficiently as possible to reach as many as possible in the shortest period of time. They traveled together initially, meeting with whole communities at traditional gathering spots such as churches or schools and at FIS convocations and county fairs to generate support. Hunter later recalled that their "untiring energy" as public servants along with the support offered by communities generated "a firm basis" for the division.[5]

The first three agents could waste no time as they worked to improve rural life. Smith, the most experienced organizer, had pursued reform since the mid-1880s, and he continued doing so as Negro state leader. He concentrated on "getting the people out and organizing them" while "the actual

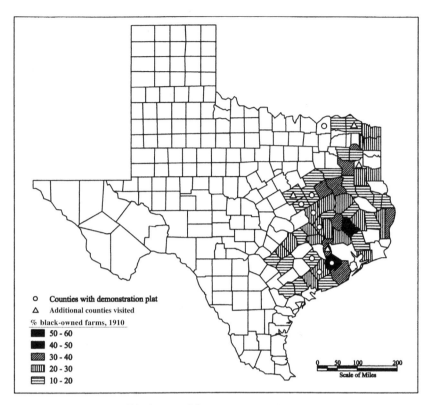

Map 1. Percentage of black-owned farms, 1910, and location of Negro Division activities, 1915. (U.S. Bureau of the Census, *Thirteenth Census of the United States, 1910,* vol. 7, *Agriculture,* 632–54, 678–700; county personnel, TAEX Historical Files). Drawn by Chris Blakely and Ron Finger; revised by Richard Riccio.

work was entirely Mr. Ford's and Mrs. Hunter's." They concentrated initially on basic needs, "raising feed crops for stock and food for man," but worked only in "localities settled by negro farmers who were in a position to govern their own farms." They launched a public relations campaign to convince potential club members that the government program had their best interests at heart. The *Prairie View Standard* editor noted that "when the colored people shall have been thoroughly and completely organized . . . the results will show vast improvements in all phases of rural and civic activity on the part of the negro citizenship." Such efforts helped them convince families to "make their farms object lessons for the community." Their efforts laid the groundwork for the employment of black agents throughout East Texas.[6]

Smith, Hunter, and Ford began by identifying eight counties where they believed they could generate support for the public reform. They traveled

Figure 3. Robert L. Smith (center) with an unidentified group. (Smith-Cobb Family Papers, Texas Collection, Baylor University)

across East Texas, from Red River and Fannin counties in the north to Wharton and Fort Bend counties in the south, to select one acre in each of eight counties to serve as a demonstration plat, but they also organized co-operative clubs in all twelve counties they visited. The eight counties selected as sites for demonstration plats represent the variables under which black farmers operated (see Map 1). Seven of the counties, those in South Texas and in the Brazos River bottoms, had many black residents, descended from slaves brought by some of the first Euro-Americans in Texas. A plantation culture developed in Wharton, Fort Bend, and Colorado, all counties in the Gulf Coastal Plain that depended on stock raising, cotton, and sugar production. In four Central Texas counties—Brazos, Robertson, Falls, and Limestone—the fertile Brazos River bottom soil lured southerners prior to the Civil War, and planters brought their slaves to expansive cotton fields. The first black extension agents also developed a plat in Fannin, a county in far North Texas with only 12 percent black population. Yet, the private school established by the FIS in 1906 and opened in 1908 to educate black youth about agriculture was located there (Fig. 3). Other counties visited by agents included Red River, a neighbor of Fannin; Gregg, another plantation county in the forests of Northeast Texas with a history of FIS involvement; Waller, a plantation county in South Texas and home of Prairie View A&M; and McLennan, the only targeted county in the Blackland Prairie and the home of Smith and the FIS.[7]

Figure 4. Robert L. Smith (back left) with farmers at McKinney, Tex., July 1, 1923. (Smith-Cobb Family Papers, Texas Collection, Baylor University)

Those involved in the early meetings recognized the critical role communities played in establishing extension work in Texas, regardless of demographics. The first agents used trains, wagons, buggies, and sometimes automobiles to cover the miles between farmers' residences and community gathering spots. Smith remembered that "roads were bad and autos few," but the effort paid off as they reached large numbers of rural people (Fig. 4). African American administrators documented the positive aspects and the large turnouts at demonstration sites and club meetings as a way to convince TAEX administrators to continue funding the service. The strategy worked, as the annual report for 1917 indicates: "From the results obtained it is apparent that the money expended on negro extension work in the State of Texas is bringing satisfactory results." Others remembered gatherings as less glamorous: "Attendance of these early meetings was scarce because of the long distance that had to be walked over the muddy roads and of the uncleared forest."[8]

TAEX program goals for the black and white divisions were amazingly similar, initially. During 1915, TAEX administrators stressed diversification. They wanted farmers to realize "the unwisdom of a system of farming dependent chiefly upon cotton as the only or main source of income." This led agents to emphasize the ways diversification helped farmers secure "agricultural abundance and independence." Other TAEX goals for 1915 depicted diversified farmers as the "safest basis of credit and the best insurance of continuing prosperity in an agricultural State." Ousley reported at the end of 1917 that extension programs caused Texans to think about "breaking the all-cotton habit of fifty years."[9]

Diversification proved more difficult for black agents to implement than for white agents, however, because black farmers depended more on cotton. Farmers in five of the twelve counties visited by the first TAEX Negro agents planted cotton in 50 to 60 percent of their improved acres, and farmers in four more devoted between 30 and 50 percent to cotton. Farmers in only two of the counties visited devoted 20 percent or less of their improved land to cotton in 1910. This reflected the tendency throughout the state to concentrate resources on "white gold" (Map 2).

Ford, the agronomist, speaking to farmers who devoted most of their resources to raising cotton, had to tailor his message carefully. He urged farmers to grow more corn and cereals to feed their families and their stock and delivered his message via the cooperative demonstration model. Farmers had to volunteer their acre as "an object lesson in good methods of farming." Few black farmers, however, had the resources to devote such energy to demonstrations. One agent recalled that the service was "confined to one or two communities . . . with no particular direction of action or purpose." Regardless, Smith believed that those who met with Ford gained "practical instruction in the preparation of the soil, proper cultivation, and seed testing," with an emphasis on raising corn. Participants had to be patient because it took at least a season to realize returns, and this caused many to remain skeptical of the advice.[10]

Ford presented his lectures to a variety of audiences. He regularly appeared at fairs sponsored by local FIS branches and at county unions and

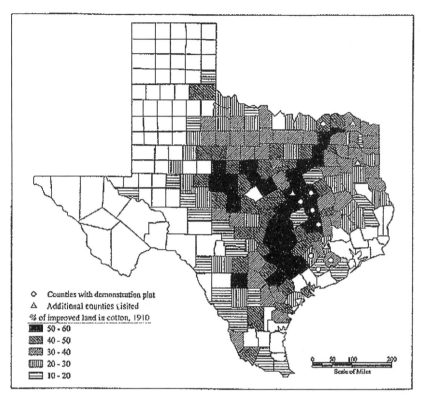

Map 2. Percentage of improved land in cotton, 1910, and location of Negro Division activities, 1915. (U.S. Bureau of the Census, *Thirteenth Census of the United States, 1910,* vol. 7, *Agriculture,* 632–54, 678–700; county personnel, TAEX Historical Files). Drawn by Chris Blakely and Ron Finger; revised by Richard Riccio.

state convocations. He also lectured at Prairie View A&M's short course. Correspondents to the FIS newspaper and the *Prairie View Standard* enthusiastically recounted information he imparted, all of which touted the "A&M way." Ford recommended that farmers prepare their seedbeds in the fall and deep plow in October to turn under any green vegetation so the soil would hold moisture through the winter. He instructed farmers to open their land in the spring with "four good mules" hitched to a "middle buster," a plow with a double moldboard that moved dirt to either side of a central furrow. Farmers could then plant in the deep furrow with a walking planter, covering the corn with not more than three inches of dirt. He also recommended that they cultivate with a buzzard-wing sweep, vernacular for a plow sweep with a wide span, set shallow. All methods guaranteed the conservation of moisture, part of the repertoire of white as well as black agents for improving cultivation techniques. A flyer advertising the "Great Food and Feed Campaigns" of World War I declares that "the Ford System of raising a corn crop, when followed it has never been known to fail."[11]

Ford's recommendations indicate his target audience: progressive farmers with the freedom to determine their own schedules and the equipment they needed. Plowing in October worked for land not dedicated to cotton. Furthermore, farmers picked cotton past the first frost, often into November and December, despite advice to harvest earlier and destroy stalks, which served as vectors for weevils. Few black farmers had four mules at their disposal to break the land in the spring, or the specialized equipment to cultivate. Such recommendations seemed inappropriate for impoverished farmers, even for landowners who operated on the edge of overextension, and beyond their ability to implement. Farmers who wanted the information devised more practical solutions within their means.

The farm agents worked to make farms paying propositions, with "sufficient income for the comfort of the family and to educate the children." But farmers did not passively accept the recommendations. They challenged agents and created competitions that pitted the A&M way against tradition. Agents recounted that the A&M plot grew better than the farmers' and that this persuaded at least competing farmers to adopt the extension suggestions. Hunter described such an encounter between Jacob Ford and a Mr. Wilson, an old farmer set in his ways. Ford planted one acre of corn on the Wilson farm and Wilson's son cultivated it following Ford's recommendations. Wilson planted a second acre of corn and cultivated it following his traditional methods. When the corn was ready to harvest, officials as well as farmers from around the county came to observe and measure. Wilson's patch yielded 12.5 bushels while Ford's yielded 50 bushels and 12 bushels of peas. Hunter remembered that the publicity convinced many to adopt their agents' advice, but converts were hard won.[12]

While men worked in the fields, Hunter met with women and girls to stabilize the household economy and improve farm family health. Her approach focused on gardening, food preservation, and poultry raising, all of which theoretically reduced dependency on landlords and merchants. Whites considered the effort worthy because second-year funding provided Hunter with an assistant, Pinkie Rambo, who began in October 1916 (see Table 2).[13]

Families that owned land could implement recommendations more easily than could sharecroppers and tenants, who did not control their own labor. Regardless, agents had to convince cash-poor farmers of the wisdom

TABLE 2.   Supervisors of Negro Home Demonstration Work, Texas

Name	Title	Tenure
Mrs. Mary E. V. Hunter	Home economics demonstrator	Aug. 1, 1915–Sep. 30, 1930
	Acting district agent	July 1–Sep. 15, 1931*
Mrs. Minnie O. Graves	County agent (Grimes)	Nov. 11, 1925–Sep. 30, 1930
	Acting district agent	Oct. 1–Dec. 22, 1930†
Mrs. Iola W. Rowan	County agent (Nacogdoches)	Nov. 16, 1927–Sep. 15, 1930
	Acting district agent	Jan. 1–June 30, 1931
	District agent	Sep. 16, 1931–Oct. 8, 1942
	Supervisor—district agent	Feb. 1, 1943–Sep. 28, 1946
Mrs. Pauline R. Brown	County agent (Gregg)	June 1, 1933–Sep. 30, 1942
	Acting district agent	Oct. 1, 1942–Jan. 31, 1943
	Assistant district agent	Feb. 1–June 30, 1943
	District agent	July 1, 1943–Sep. 30, 1946
	Supervisor	Oct. 1, 1946–June 30, 1965††
	Staff assistant to director	July 1, 1965–May 31, 1967§

Source: Seastrunk, "Fifty Years of Negro Extension Work in Texas, 1915-1965"; Hutchison, "The Texas Agricultural Extension Service," 135 .
* Resigned
† Died in office
†† Position discontinued July 1, 1965
§ Retired; day and month unknown

of building privies, draining farmyards, and investing in other home and farm improvements to stabilize the health of the family and the productivity of the farm. Hunter devised annual campaigns that emphasized "better homes one year, more home gardens the next, and more canned goods the next year." Under her leadership, farm families with adequate resources undertook home construction, renovation, and budgeting.[14]

Hunter's records laud the accomplishments, but others indicate resistance to early home demonstration work. Irene Sanders, the widow of the first Negro farm agent in Anderson County recounted that "limited knowledge" and inadequate education hindered black farmers' ability to "plan their needs" or "execute their plan." She blamed the farm operators for their plight and exhibited middle-class values toward the lower-class tenants, who "cared nothing about the upkeep and sanitation of the places in which they lived." She also criticized landowners and described some farmers as "land poor"; that is, they had followed the advice of "persons who placed emphasis on 'Getting

Land' in quantities" and thus overextended themselves and ignored the need to build "comfortable homes."[15]

Paternalism affected black home demonstration work, as it affected white women's work. Hunter documented gender discrimination, though she did not label it as such, and she did not complain about the apparent inequity. She worked just as much as the male agents, but she made less. Yet, her salary was much closer to that of her black male colleagues than were white women agent's salaries to that of their white male colleagues. Hunter's cohort also had fewer opportunities in the service because fewer permanent positions were available for women than for men. This meant that the household economy, so important to sustaining marginal family farms, did not receive as much support as agriculture traditionally associated with the male's domain received. Of the first eight counties served by the Negro Division, all but Limestone employed male agents in permanent positions during the first five years of the program, but none employed women permanently. Women worked only temporarily as emergency funds allowed.[16]

Progressives often imposed order on agricultural reform by creating bureaucracies. Texans accomplished this through the chain of command that linked the Negro Division to the white TAEX from its inception. Starting with the establishment of the Negro Division in 1915, Texas A&M presidents met regularly with Prairie View A&M principals. Regular contact between the white and black land-grant college administrators, as well as between white extension officials and black supervisors, ensured continuity of service and attitude, particularly as administrators changed during the formative years (see Table 3).

Negro Division staff members knew that their white supervisors, both land-grant presidents and extension office directors, held paternalistic if not racist views. William B. Bizzell, Texas A&M president between 1914 and 1925, had a relatively open mind about race relations. He took his responsibility for Prairie View A&M as a branch of Texas A&M seriously and visited the campus regularly. On one occasion, he spoke at a Prairie View A&M convocation and discussed the migration of African Americans to the North. He contended that "people should go wherever and whenever they wished to go—and unmolested." This contrasted with the philosophy of the first TAEX director, Clarence Ousley, which helped institutionalize segregation.[17]

Changes in white administrators shifted individuals but not the commitment to racial segregation. After Ousley left to work as U.S. assistant secretary of agriculture, his replacement, Thomas O. Walton, brought experience to the position, having worked in Farmers' Cooperative Demonstration Work

TABLE 3. Texas Agricultural Extension Service Organizational Chart, 1926–27

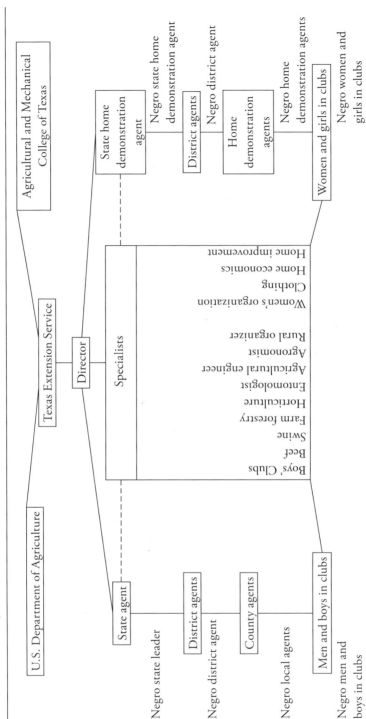

Source: Adapted from O. B. Martin and I. W. Hill, "Inspection Report of Cooperative Extension Work, Texas, 1926–1927," July 28–August 3, 1927, n.p., Annual Inspection Reports of Cooperative Extension Work in the Field, ES, RG 33, NA.

Note: The boxed terms identify white administrators and white agencies; the terms below the boxed items identify Negro Division employees. Contemporary titles used in Martin and Hill's chart are preserved.

and then as a TAEX county agent. Contemporaries described Walton as "homespun, down-to-earth, . . . and a self-made educator from East Texas." Walton, however, "had reservations about Negroes and would often say that 'Negroes are not self-starters; they have to be cranked up every day.'" His influence, first as director, and then as president of Texas A&M, affected extension activities for more than twenty-five years.[18]

Bizzell's and Walton's affirmation of Smith and then Blackshear as directors of the Negro Division satisfied selected groups of white as well as black Texans. Thousands of farmers in Texas knew these men as the leading black agrarians and educators in the state. Strong defenders of Blackshear considered him an outstanding educator, and J. Sheb Williams, a member of the Prairie View A&M board of directors in 1915, ranked him above Booker T. Washington for his "efficiency" as an educator and the "high moral example" that he set for his race. Smith's and then Blackshear's approaches appealed to African Americans who remained committed to rural southern life.[19]

White politicians' preference for these men during the formative years indicates that African Americans who had associated with Booker T. Washington obviated most white criticism of black involvement in public rural reform. Their appointments also indicate white support for self-help, self-segregation, and materialism after Washington's death in 1915, even as black Americans refocused reform goals. When younger agents introduced different ideas, older supervisors cautioned them to avoid trouble by respecting the parameters of race relations in Texas, but older supervisors, at the same time, used forced segregation to build influential and relatively autonomous reform programs.[20]

Smith and Blackshear both worked to build black authority in the countryside. Smith operated as Ousley's peer, leading the Negro Division during its initial growth phase from August 1, 1915, to his resignation on June 30, 1919. He combined his duties as president of the FIS with his responsibilities as Negro state leader and maintained extension headquarters in Waco, probably working out of the FIS offices. The TAEX funded a stenographer with extension appropriations to assist him. Smith accepted the responsibility because it increased the potential to help black farmers and their families diversify production and thus avoid the crop lien. He also recognized that the Negro Division depended on community networks he had established with the FIS, and he wanted to protect the integrity of his private organization. Ironically, his support of public reform eventually led to the co-option of FIS strategies and the economic collapse of the nongovernmental organization. The Negro Division sapped FIS members' limited resources.[21]

Smith had returned to his duties as FIS grand president full time by mid-1919, and the Negro Division's headquarters moved to Prairie View A&M, thus consolidating publicly funded rural reform at the black land-grant institution as whites had done at Texas A&M. This laid the foundation for the bureaucracy that, though underfunded and understaffed, still served half of the Texas counties with measurable black populations.

The division's relative success motivated race-conscious Texans to create thorough trails of race-specific paperwork. This supported further race-based decisions at all bureaucratic levels.[22]

Such documentation highlighted services even as black farmers became victims. Black staff members had to protect their appointments and clientele by negotiating race protocol. This proved complicated because even economic goals furthered by diversifying production, changing cultivation practices, improving breeds, preserving excess, and creating more sanitary and comfortable homes could anger whites. The *Chicago Defender* carried a photograph of a lynching of four Texans on its front page in October 1915. The headline read "Father and Three Sons Assassinated for Raising the First Cotton, News Never Reached World from Texas." The *Defender,* a leading African American newspaper, urged readers to study the reproduced image: "See these men hanging from a limb of a tree simply because they raised better cotton than their white neighbors." Chicago included many former farmers who had left the rural South in favor of a growing metropolis. These farmers and their families knew the risk involved in raising cotton that matured earlier or yielded more per acre than that planted by their white peers. Certainly, the image of farmers lynched for raising cotton got the former farmers' attention. It came as no surprise to them that farmers did not have to rape a white woman or assault a white man to face a lynch mob. Simply competing with middle-class whites for markets could get them into trouble.[23]

Depressed cotton markets might have exacerbated passions that led to race crimes. Earlier in 1915, the *Chicago Defender* had reported that the war in Europe left southerners with a surplus of cotton. As foreign markets closed to imports, the price for cotton fell. Furthermore, farmers had increased acreage to compensate for potential boll weevil infestations, and surpluses hastened the price decline. White farmers felt the pinch at harvest and reacted violently to any black family that sold cotton at the beginning of the ginning season at a higher price.[24]

Growing less cotton, or abandoning it altogether, could release farmers from cash-crop dependency, but this was a change in mind-set hard to accomplish. Scientific agriculturalists urged farmers to diversify, to grow products that consumers demanded—grains and stock, specifically. The *Defender* implied that by doing so, poor farmers of both races could stop fighting with each other over the volatile cotton market and start earning a livelihood. Diversification took on political significance as the *Defender* told its African American readership that "owning or operating as we do about 15 percent of the farm land, the change means much to us from every point of view. That we are equal to the new regime there is no question. We have been tried and found not wanting." The paper praised the African American extension agents who worked with farmers across the South, injecting "new methods, new spirit and new life" into southern agriculture. It proved difficult, however, for southern agents to negotiate changing race relations, convey scientific information, and help progressive farmers avoid becoming victims.[25]

Correspondence between Blackshear and his colleagues in 1919 addressed the delicate issue of race relations. Blackshear reminded them to not mix "other problems with the extension work that have no official connection with it," and to "avoid mooted religious, political or racial problems because these problems involve questions as to which the public entertains various opinions." He provided an example of what agents should not discuss, sharing his sectarian beliefs about the Baptist faith, and advised his colleagues to avoid such discussions. On the "race problem," however, he remained vague, and his language conveys the ambiguity of Washingtonian rhetoric: "Our opinions are doubtless identical on this problem, but there is a large body of citizens who do not think on this problem as we do, hence when we refer to the race problem it should be done judiciously and in a way to make peace between the races and not discord." He urged his colleagues to let other intelligent men and women express the "negro view on the race question" and to concentrate on the extension work that they were employed to undertake.[26]

Blackshear's missive eventually crossed Bradford Knapp's desk. Knapp, chief of the southern state extension office and the son of Seaman Knapp, forwarded the letter to Secretary of Agriculture David Houston, a colleague of Blackshear's from the years when they had both served as principals of the Texas land-grant institutions. Blackshear concluded the letter with laudatory remarks about the white extension workers and their service to Negro farmers, sentiments expressed for the benefit of white administrators. Knapp assured Houston that Blackshear and two other African American agents retained by the Federal Extension Service to quell the racial agitation "running all through the South" were "doing fine work."[27]

But Blackshear's advice highlighted the unequal position of black agents and white administrators. He urged agents not to engage in discussions "that would awaken antagonism among the white people toward black people," because the "other side is even more capable of awaking antagonism against us and backing it up than we are." He encouraged building relationships based on "confidence and friendship" rather than "suspicion and distrust." He implied that any extension worker who pursued the "race problem" broke the "bounds of authority, reason, and common sense" expected of appointees, justifying white beliefs that "black people" could not hold responsible positions in government. Blackshear's stance represented increasingly old-fashioned ideas, even in 1919.[28]

Not all blacks, however, believed that the agents did good work. In fact, some believed they hurt the race. In 1921, Charles E. Hall, African American section chief in the Division of Agriculture, Bureau of the Census, expressed frustration with inadequacies in agricultural extension work in the South, claiming that it left much to be desired because of a "lack of intelligent effort, due I have been informed, to the selection of demonstration agents whose qualifications as 'Good Negroes' overshadow their ability to disseminate vital agricultural knowledge." He shared serious and cutting criticisms alleged by extension employees' peers with USDA officials. Hall quoted Ralph W. White, West Virginia Department of Agriculture, who believed that "the agents spend most of their time in building up the State political machine." Hall recounted that William A. Bailey from Oklahoma said that "the work of the States Relation Service in Oklahoma is a joke . . . It is simply a political machine and does not function agriculturally for the benefit of this racial group." Mr. Cardwell of North Carolina called farm demonstration agents in his state "racially disloyal" because they had "joined Editor Poe in his propaganda advocating the segregation of Negro farm owners in our State, thereby alienating the confidence of the people among whom they were SUPPOSED to work." John H. Polk called them "just spokes in the political machinery of the State," a scathing commentary that implied that black agents conspired with white Democrats and exacerbated black subordination.[29]

White perceptions of black extension accomplishments differed as well, usually based on different perceptions of political loyalties. White extension officials rejected criticisms of black political pandering because, "of all of the agents in the field, the negro agents are freer from politics than any other class." They dismissed the criticisms as coming from persons "not well informed, or [who] have not seen the best phases of extension work carried on among the negroes." White administrators, almost exclusively white Democrats, expected agents to do their job and stay out of politics. Black agents, however, recognized the political nature of their job as they advocated for farmers aspiring to middle-class status, inclusion in progressive reform, and influence in the modernizing South. They sometimes went beyond the parameters TAEX officials set for them to work in areas with established programs, and they ventured beyond prescribed territory. This led federal inspectors to criticize Negro Division administrators as ineffective.[30]

The Great War affected the development of the Negro Division in profound ways, providing a needed boost in funding and staffing. By 1917, mobilization preceding U.S. involvement pressured Smith, Ford, and Hunter, with the help of two nine-month workers in the field, to reach "practically a population of 700,000 people," but federal appropriations helped make the expectation a bit more reasonable. In August 1917, Congress passed the Food Production and Food Control acts to secure the support of the Federal Extension Service for the war effort. These acts provided $6.1 million for personnel to work in counties that previously had not benefited from extension personnel. The TAEX received $148,000 in emergency appropriations to facilitate the home army. This supported the appointment of female and male agents of both races. Appropriations from the federal Emergency Fund paid the salaries of nearly half of the twenty-three Negro Division employees in 1918, five male and six female agents.[31]

The Extension Service proved critical to mobilization, because Pres. Woodrow Wilson considered it the primary vehicle for reaching people, "the only organization in the country, nation-wide in its scope, through which government policies can be transmitted to the remotest rural communities within a few hours." The war effort infused new life into extension offerings, as well. Clarence Ousley described the war as "that great calamity" and credited it with emphasizing "the unwisdom of a system of farming dependent chiefly upon cotton as the only or main source of income." The European market for cotton closed when the war began, and extension efforts thus focused on diversification as a result. Agents shared ways to make farmers wiser producers, and Ousley believed that "a system of farming which makes food and feed its first requirement is the surest method of . . . independence."[32]

As mobilization intensified, African American agents expanded their programs. They participated to a limited degree in Saturday Service Leagues, a farm organization that emerged from a meeting of Alabama extension workers at Tuskegee Institute in 1918. Thomas M. Campbell coordinated the leagues in an effort to increase production. They provided incentives for tenants to work six days per week and for landlords to increase their wages. Agents encouraged farm families to invest this income in Liberty bonds and War savings stamps. Agents also raised money for the Red Cross, as did the white agents. Edward L. Blackshear reported that the extension agents directly and indirectly influenced one-third of all black Texans to sign up for war securities.[33]

African Americans lobbied the USDA to recognize the work blacks were doing across the South. The USDA responded by creating another level of bureaucracy, adding three black special agent positions in 1918. Robert R. Moton, principal of Tuskegee Institute, wrote Bradford Knapp, chief, FES, suggesting the appointment of an African American to the Department of War as "a measure to stimulate colored farmers in the South." Knapp outlined a plan to Dr. Alfred True, claiming that he had discussed the idea with "a number of our negro workers," who shared it with others, including Moton. Knapp believed that "the common, every-day negro in the South" did not want another political appointment to the Department of Labor, or the War Department, or the Food Administration, or other agencies involved in administration. Furthermore, Knapp argued, "to bring a negro in here [the FES] . . . would be like the fifth wheel to a wagon, a useless part of the organization."[34]

Instead, Knapp proposed a solution to involve African Americans officially in the wartime agricultural programs without "disorganizing the extension machinery." He believed that this would satisfy black reformers who wanted the USDA to publicly recognize the "negro farmer and the negro farmer problem." He also believed that the three new agents could create a "more effective and earnest extension work for the negroes in each of the States where there is a large negro farming population." Agents would distribute information on "problems of production and farm labor" and help "get the best service from them during the war." Finally Knapp believed that appointees had an intimate knowledge of the "morale of the negro farming people of the South and a consistent effort to maintain that morale on a proper basis."[35]

By appointing the special agents, the federal government acknowledged the increased responsibilities prompted by war mobilization. After all, the number of employees in Negro Divisions across the South had increased from 70 in April 1917 to 320 in September 1918. Regardless, existing black agents could not satisfy demand, and white agents had to serve black farmers as a result. The sustained lobbying for more services to black farmers prompted the USDA to appoint three men, including Edward L. Blackshear, as special field agents. Blackshear served the trans-Mississippi region and apparently continued to do so until his death in December 1919, even as he led Texas' Negro Division. His involvement with the Extension Service at the national level increased TAEX's and Prairie View's prestige even though his service was brief. This overextension vested Negro Division staff in Texas with even more responsibility.[36]

War mobilization encouraged white administrators to cooperate for the first time in a decade, and sometimes opportunities for a select number of blacks resulted. The efforts to increase food and fiber supplies for World War I resulted in a temporary reconciliation between Texas A&M and the University of Texas. These competing schools had each administered extension programs prior to the Smith-Lever Act in 1914. Interest in the "extension" of college offerings to adults via informal delivery was high, and many institutions of higher education expanded their curriculum to serve their audiences better. The University of Texas, located in the state capital of Austin, focused on courses that would interest urban dwellers, while the land-grant institution lived up to its agricultural and mechanical purpose by focusing on extension courses that appealed to a rural constituency. During the war years, the institutions combined limited emergency appropriations to further the conservation of food in urban areas. An advisory board of representatives from twelve women's organizations met in Dallas in October 1917 and planned a program to prevent duplication and foster collegiality. In 1918, two black agents received appointments to undertake demonstrations in the use of substitutes, canning, drying, and planning home orchards. Black agents embraced canning demonstrations. They held ninety-eight meetings, conducted demonstrations in six towns, and awarded three certificates to women who then supervised the construction of community canning centers through which they reached 1,518 individuals.[37]

Not all Texas Democrats welcomed the increased opportunities for blacks provided by federal funding, even if Democrats at TAEX headquarters administered the funds. In fact, increased federal funding led to increased competition between the Texas Extension Service and the Department of Agriculture. Federal inspectors described relations between the competing purveyors of scientific farming information—the TAEX and the TDA—as "not good" in 1917. "There is not understanding between them," and this led to "duplication, confusion, and more or less friction." Inspectors wished that the TDA would agree to focus on "regulatory matters, statistics, and similar lines" and allow the TAEX to concentrate on "all the educational work along agricultural and home economic lines in the State." The TDA did not listen. In 1921, inspectors again reported "friction" between the two and that the trouble was "long standing" and impossible to solve. Blacks became pawns in the power struggle. In 1917, the TDA had apparently followed the TAEX model, involving blacks in programs when they asked for service.[38]

Joseph Elward Clayton became TDA's first official black volunteer to co-ordinate "colored" institutes in 1917. Clayton, a teacher and reformer, knew firsthand the importance of grassroots reform and black community involvement. His wife, Brittie, was the daughter of a successful farmer in Littig, a freedman's community near Manor, Texas. Clayton shared Smith's and Blackshear's ideas that public funding and involvement in public programs could further rural black reform, and this led to his exploitation by the TDA. He acquiesced to additional restraints on his personal liberty in exchange for status as the first African American appointed to conduct TDA business. He volunteered rather than demanding pay and pledged to pursue only economic objectives. He told white attendees at the 1917 state institute that "you white friends must help us train the negro how to intelligently and successfully till the soil, because we are getting them to more and more love the occupation of farming." He went even further in 1921, assuring his white audience that black farmers would remain as loyal as antebellum slaves.[39]

He secured rail passes, as did other Texas State Farmers' Institute employees, to facilitate meetings with blacks throughout East Texas, though this did not make up for no pay. The mobility helped him reach twelve counties in just thirty days in 1917. He justified his appointments for the next four years with numbers. Over a twelve-month period in 1918 and 1919, he organized 289 colored institutes to convey information to rural blacks, and he spoke to 67,832 persons in mixed audiences. He visited 568 farms, organized 163 canning clubs, and demonstrated the technique to 5,418 men, women, and children. C. W. Rice, later a labor activist and newspaper editor in Houston, also organized institutes without expense to the state other than transportation. By August 1919, TDA was allotting $1,000 to each of the "colored field workers," and they justified the expenditure by reaching 67,000 through institutes and canning clubs. This represented 12.9 percent of the rural black population.[40]

The Negro Division played the numbers game, too. By 1920, 26 county agents had served more than 37,000 adults and juniors, just over 6 percent of the rural black population. In 1920 alone, they preserved 290,350 cans of fruit and vegetables, valued at $100,349. The accuracy of both reports remains debatable, given the pressures that administrators placed on black agents to show measurable progress.[41]

State legislators authorized commissioners' courts, the democratic governing bodies at the county level, to appropriate funds for canning work in 1917.

Thus, county dollars could build canning centers no matter which organization undertook the work—the FIS, the TAEX Negro Division, or TDA's colored farmers' institutes. Competition obviously existed between the divisions to secure what little local support there was.[42]

Clayton distinguished black TDA programs from TAEX Negro Division offerings because he indicated that he was responding to black tenant concerns. In 1919, he reported that the shift from tenancy to day labor placed a hardship on tenant farmers, and that the Texas State Farmers' Institute should use its influence to rent land to black tenants on the third and fourth shares. Yet, he furthered capitalist goals by helping black investors purchase large amounts of land to employ the tenants. The committee on organizing black farmers' institutes, under Clayton's leadership, also recommended that landlords require their tenants to plant cover crops to protect the soil from erosion and leaching over the winter months, and to remunerate the tenant for the work. Clayton and other TDA affiliates considered tenancy a vital component of capitalist agriculture. Tenants could expand production more readily and, with sound credit management, they had more opportunities than owners of small farms who avoided buying things on credit. Despite his efforts to distinguish his service with TDA from the Negro Division, Clayton did not retain TDA support after 1921.[43]

Other African Americans built on the support shown for the war to challenge the southern system. The NAACP began to organize branches in Texas in 1918, starting in San Antonio, in response to increasing racial violence. Although recruitment began in urban areas, African Americans from throughout Texas joined. Members included farm owners, tenants, and laborers who believed that "the time has come [for] the white man and the black man to stand upon terms of social equality." Rural blacks expressed this sentiment fleetingly before violence silenced them. Most secured charters and registered members of the NAACP in 1919 only. Steven Reich believes that thereafter the "activists lost their vehicle of organization, of connecting to broader national and global struggles." He continues: "The coercive resources of both state and federal governments . . . defeated these soldiers of democracy and, for the moment, made Texas safe for white supremacy."[44]

Texas government also defeated private self-help organizations such as the FIS. After Smith resigned as Negro state leader, he remained active in the FIS. Rather than encouraging FIS members to seek retribution after suffering violence, he asked them to pray. He suggested that branches discuss potentially controversial topics such as "Will the Negro Be as Free as Other Races after the War?" But instead of encouraging the members to ask for equality, he advised them to practice prudence and patience in the post–World War I period, because "the white people did not seem to be as cordial." He assured the members that "after a period of unrest and adjustment . . . things would come out all right." In other words, prewar conditions would return, and black farmers would resume their chores without fear of retribution. Blackshear urged similar restraint in 1919, but he never indicated that things would work out; rather, he suggested actions that would encourage white people to become confident in the abilities of African Americans and friendly toward them. Neither man could have anticipated how a combination of racist policy decisions, economic downturns, class bias, and personal choice would make farming a dirty word for many African Americans and undermine the quest for economic security that farm owners and agents pursued.[45]

After the Great War, Texas tried to retain black agents partially because the rural black population had grown. The number of black farm operators in the state had increased 11.2 percent between 1910 and 1920. This rate exceeded that across the South (3.9 percent). The TAEX positioned itself to be the primary conduit of information on scientific agriculture and home management to the growing black population. Black agents stood poised to assume additional responsibilities and professional recognition following their successful war mobilization efforts, and whites tended to support their economic and therefore nonthreatening agendas. The co-option of FIS community-based programming, the intimidation that had silenced NAACP branches, the withdrawal of TDA sponsorship of black farmers' institutes, and the redirection of programs offered by the University of Texas toward urban constituents sealed the Negro Division's monopoly on publicly funded rural reform.[46]

Its dominance, however, did not translate into adequate appropriations. The federal emergency fund was discontinued by mid-1919, after emergency appointees involved in home demonstration and urban demonstration work completed the canning season. In 1919, the state agent for home demonstration reported seventeen black female employees, including one district agent, three regular workers, and thirteen emergency agents employed for brief periods during the garden harvest season. When the fiscal year ended on June 30, 1919, only four black females and eleven black males remained employed. The staff increased to twenty-six agents in 1920, but much of this increase resulted from the employment of women as seasonal appointees, not an expansion of permanent positions. White administrators expected African American agents to accept their status, but a period "of unrest and transition" began as agents tried to realize some equity.[47]

Since 1911, state law had required counties to partially match the appropriation for county agents, providing at least $1,000.00 to fund each white agent. No law governed the minimum required to place a black agent, but the TAEX refused to place agents if commissioners did not contribute at least $300.00 for their salaries. After the war, a reduction in federal funds for agent salaries exacerbated the already limited financial support afforded the Negro Division. The TAEX offered low salaries initially, and black agents accepted at all levels of the bureaucracy. In 1915, Hunter earned $732.50 and Smith earned $1,000.00; black male agents in the field received between $390.00 and $500.00, and black female agents received between $58.00 and $385.00, depending on the duration of their appointment. In general, black agents earned salaries comparable to those of black schoolteachers. By 1918, the salaries had increased to $1,260.00 for Smith, $1,012.50 for Blackshear, $1,020.00 for Ford, and $1,020.00 for Hunter, but their salaries changed little thereafter.[48]

Some county commissioners appropriated $300 in matching funds to qualify for agents because they realized that tax-paying African Americans contributed to the county largesse. One white district agent noted that the taxes assessed on the increased production undertaken by black and white farmers in Brazoria County paid for the appropriation authorized by the county commissioners for the white county agent in 1918. Local appropriations to support the appointment of demonstration agents came out of the general tax fund, and blacks contributed their share to this resource. Thus, commissioners paid some attention to the needs expressed by black residents, but they also argued that financial resources were insufficient to support extension work. For example, Brazoria County, a large county with a relatively high percentage of black farm owners, provided funding for a white county agent and for a black home demonstration agent in June 1918. It did not fund a black county agent position until 1937. Convincing commissioners to fund African American positions proved to be a formidable challenge.[49]

During the early years, the ideology expressed by sage reformers such as Smith and Blackshear influenced the development of the Extension Service. They, along with Hunter, Ford, and Clayton, expressed middle-class beliefs that held the poor responsible for their misfortunes. This caused these reformers to aim their efforts at farmers who could put their recommendations into practice. They believed that by cooperating with the government they could spread progressive values. Their ambitions generated public support for rural improvement, and they became members of an elite group of black

TABLE 4. African American Participation in the Texas Agricultural Extension Service, 1915–40

Year	No. of Workers	No. of Families Reached	No. of Individuals Enrolled in Clubs	No. Rural African Americans in Texas	% Rural African Americans Involved in Extension	No. Counties w/ Male Agents	No. Counties w/ Female Agents
1915	3	1,000	3,919	*	*	0	0
1920	25	2,500	30,844	518,444	(5.9)	12	21
1925	49	6,780	78,956	*	*	24	22
1930	55	3,470	*	524,948	(8.0)	25	27
1935	74	10,047	66,127	*	*	38	31
1940	87	27,374	38,633	504,718	(7.7)	46	36

Source: "Growth in the Number of Families Reached by Extension Service in Five-Year Periods, 1915–1940," Calvin H. Waller Papers, 1915–40, Negro Extension Work, folio 3, PV; Biennial Report of the Director of Extension Service Agricultural and Mechanical College of Texas, 1915–1917, 9, 11; TAEX Annual Report 1920, 54–55; TAEX Annual Report 1925, 69; TAEX Annual Report 1930, 31; Extension Work in Texas, 1935, 28; Texas Extension Work in 1940, 41, 44. For statistics on the rural black population, see Negro Population 1790–1915, 43–44, 51, 91–92; Negroes in the United States, 1920–1932, 813; Sixteenth Census of the United States, 1940, vol. 2, Population, pt. 6, 763, 765.
*Not available

government employees. Yet, government officials realized that, by favoring them with appointments, they could provide new social programs to the underserved without committing adequate resources to the effort. Ultimately, these reformers' willingness to serve compromised their own objectives.

Women benefited from their involvement in private and public reform. They gained visibility and used their positions to do race work by fighting the economic causes of social problems that affected black families. This helped pave the way for a new profession using new methods and standards of home economics instruction as a model. Most who became involved in the TAEX gained their education at Prairie View A&M, and the Negro Division provided opportunities for these college-educated black women to express themselves, organize communities, and validate the importance of domestic production. They also gained entrance into an elite group. Only 2.5 percent of African American women in 1920 held professional positions, and they joined the growing middle class. But they did so on white terms and remained marginalized despite their activism.[50]

By 1924, the TAEX's Negro Division was receiving more federal money than those in other southern states, and it employed as many or more black agents as the other states with significant black extension programs, a total of thirty-six employees (see Table 4). The TAEX's Negro Division continued as the largest in the nation through the New Deal era, with the most staff, the largest territory, and durable funding from federal, state, and local resources. The bureaucracy created during the first ten years proved incredibly robust even if its success depended on complicity with white supremacy. Negro Division staff members' willingness to accept inadequate wages, offices, and resources perpetuated the separate but equal ideal, but their involvement with rural families provided a mechanism for some to gain access to previously white-only benefits.[51]

3

Segregated Modernization

*Taking the Message into African American
Fields and Farm Homes*

Negro agents disseminated scientific information about farm and home management to families throughout East Texas. During the 1920s, they worked with African Americans individually, in groups, and through communities to build networks of support and influence. The communal aspect of instruction was evident in all phases of program delivery. Although individuals volunteered to demonstrate new methods, they functioned as members of extended kinship and community groups. All participants gained leadership experience through club activities. They learned organizational skills by cooperating with preachers and teachers and businessmen interested in reform. They engaged economic entrepreneurship through formation of community canning centers and market-oriented but diversified agriculture. Freed from white oversight, black farm families tailored information to suit their needs. They negotiated poverty and racism to conduct demonstrations on their own terms, with their own resources, and with their own agendas. They stabilized their position, as a result, and helped strengthen rural communities. At the same time, they solidified the influence of the Negro Division. Nonetheless, the color-sensitive bureaucracy undervalued their contributions and systematically discriminated against them. Despite their relative autonomy, black agents and their constituents could accomplish only so much in white Texas.

Growth in the black Texas population prompted white administrators to sustain staffing levels after the Great War. Between 1920 and 1930, the number of black farm operators increased by 9.3 percent. This growth made Texas somewhat distinctive from the Old South, which experienced a drop of 4.9 percent in black farm operators. The number of black farm operators increased only in the trans-Mississippi states, including Mississippi, Louisiana, Arkansas, and Oklahoma, in addition to Texas. Even though Texas

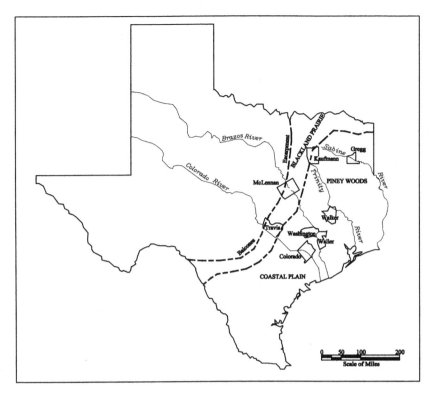

Map 3. Counties featured in the narrative. These counties represent the demographic and geographic diversity of East Texas. Drawn by Chris Blakely and Ron Finger; revised by Richard Riccio.

experienced the smallest percentage of growth among the five states, TAEX officials supported the Negro Division to a greater degree than segregated divisions were supported in other southern states (see Map 3).[1]

Agents knew that if club members communicated and cooperated they could accomplish major things and enjoy a more modern life. That ideal, however, seemed a long way off for many during the 1920s. Rural blacks remained caught in the Jim Crow South, where racism defined public and private encounters. Furthermore, sagging commodity prices, drought, floods, and the boll weevil added to the burden that black farmers bore. Families that heeded an agent's advice often found that they accomplished nothing—"the excessive rains and the large presence of the boll weevil swept away practically the whole cotton crop." County agents regularly prayed to God for relief, but they doggedly tried to change the system through organized club work.[2]

Diversification proved a difficult lesson to teach black farmers in Texas, who depended so much on one cash crop, cotton. Yet, agents indicated how crops and stocks, in addition to cotton, could increase income and help free families from dependency on crop liens. Agents urged farmers to relegate cotton to supplemental cash crop rather than primary crop. If farmers raised more corn than cotton they could keep hogs and could sell excess corn and pork; they could convert cotton fields to pasture, keep dairy cattle, and market cream; they could plant orchards and sell fruit. Income from numerous sources, not a concentration on cotton, could help farmers become solvent. Farm women could do this as well as men. Mrs. Smoot in Washington County became a landowner because she reduced expenses by canning, increased income by raising poultry, and put the money she made from her cotton into land and a home.[3]

Farm agents, however, faced their greatest challenge in attempts to convert their farmers to diversification. From the time the black agronomist Jacob Ford learned about cotton reduction at Texas A&M in 1916, agents committed to reducing cotton dependency. Extension agents advocated diversification to stabilize the market, but "white gold" exerted a greater influence on farmers' decisions than did agents' advice. In 1919, Robert Hines, agent in McLennan County, discouraged farmers from growing cotton but, to satisfy their demands for information about the cash crop, he introduced a better class of cotton that increased yields. Several agents wrestled with the paradox of trying to reduce cotton acreage but supporting use of prolific varieties. Agents and farmers both knew what a good crop could help them accomplish. They could purchase their first land or add to existing holdings, cover mortgages, make up for lost earnings, and pay the inflated prices for necessities. Jeffie O. A. Conner, the home demonstration agent in McLennan County in 1924, reported that "our people have bought more land in the past year than in many years. This was brought about by the influence of our work, plus a good cotton crop, last fall was the first time for some years that the farmers had very much money." When prices were good, women cultivated patches of cotton as a form of investment and bought things they wanted for the home with their income, just as men improved the farm with the proceeds.[4]

Farm agents encouraged diversification by introducing improved methods of cultivation for feed crops such as corn and alternative cash crops such as wheat. These demonstrations appealed only to those farmers with acreage that they could devote to corn or wheat. Tenants who were forced by lease agreements to put their resources into cotton realized little benefit from these

Figure 5. Seth T. Toney, agent, Seguin, Guadalupe County, Tex., inoculating pigs with his Pig Club boys, Jan. 1937. (J. B. Coleman Library, Special Collections/Archives Dept., Prairie View A&M University)

programs. Bulletins explained the merits of growing other crops, and agents provided these to any farmer who asked. But farmers needed incentive and, in many cases, permission.[5]

Robert Hines, the agent in McLennan County, tried to "get a pig in every home," and his technique proved successful and popular. Pigs required little investment, reproduced rapidly, and thus contributed to farm income quickly. A farmer who raised pigs had more expendable income and could boast "that he has food enough for himself and team for the next year" (Fig. 5).[6]

During the 1920s, many tenants owned pigs to help them break out of the crop lien cycle, but cows brought increased status. Cows cost more and thus represented a greater risk, but they also could return high profits if dairies and creameries existed to process the milk. Dairy products also improved family nutrition. For these reasons, both male and female agents encouraged their clients to purchase cows. In 1926, Mary E. V. Hunter reported that 95 percent of "our club members" owned a cow and consumed fresh milk during eight months of the year. The quality of cow mattered, too. Hunter did not appreciate poor scrub cattle, as those failed to make a return on the investment.[7]

Not all tenants could participate, but agents identified those tenants who did in their annual reports. John Lusk converted tenant farmer John Sharpe of Brenham into an extension supporter between 1926 and 1933. When Lusk first approached Sharpe in 1926, Sharpe lived in a tenant house "of the very worst sort, . . . rearing a large family, working them hard as an all-cotton farmer, with no comforts nor conveniences." At first, "Sharpe did not care very much as to the services of an agent," but Lusk called on reinforcements. With the assistance of district agent Henry Estelle, Lusk helped Sharpe plan his crops, diversify, and market other products such as vegetables and poultry. But Sharpe remained unconvinced and "many times . . . would not even ask [the agents] in doors." Not until Sharpe "banked almost all of his cotton money" did he become a convert. By 1933, he owned, free and clear, a six-room house on fifty-six acres on a public road.[8]

Marketing opportunities helped convince Sharpe and farmers in other parts of Texas to invest more money in livestock, especially dairy animals. Waco, situated in the center of McLennan County, provided a market for fresh milk, and Hines knew that black farmers on the edges of the city could profit from the sale of surplus production. He urged them to "fight the mortgage and credit system" by participating in the "Get a Cow" movement. He believed this movement awakened interest "in the real value of the cow on the farm."[9]

Many farmers in the county had the resources to participate, so they responded by purchasing fifteen "good graded cows." Community cooperation proved especially important when farmers began their dairy herds. Two Texas communities agreed to exchange their purebred bulls after two years for their mutual benefit.[10]

Communities with little disposable income had to wait for credit from outside sources. John Lusk secured credit in 1924 for the first purchase of Jersey cows by black farmers in his county. By 1930, he described a twelve-month financing plan extended by the Washington County State Bank and two Jersey breeders, Otto E. Weiman and G. G. Sayles. This arrangement led to the placement of eighteen cows in the county. Before the credit arrangements, "our people had no dairy cows [but] each year we take a few farmers who we feel will pay off the note, promptly, making it easy for our project the next year, and recommend these for pure bred jersey cows." All but two repaid in full in 1930, and the two farmers who did not received an extension. The efforts paid off with increased farm income due to milk, cream, and butter production and with improved family health.[11]

The need to improve existing stock to increase yields led some agents to introduce pure-bred pigs, poultry, and cattle into communities. John V. Smith, agent in McLennan County, relied on peer pressure to help him improve the turkey flocks raised for market in the county. One of the demonstrators, L. A. Smith, bought purebred bronze breeding turkeys at a high price and provided birds from his flock to his neighbors at market price. John Smith encouraged several club members to buy these birds, but the members resisted. Instead, they bought lighter grade birds for a cheaper price. When L. A. Smith took his six-month-old, twenty-pound birds to market, they sold for twenty to twenty-three cents per pound. The other farmers had to sell two and a half birds to earn what Smith earned from one of his turkeys. Agents and agrarians believed that this evidence proved the value of improving stock, but farmers without adequate resources found the project prohibitively expensive.[12]

Agents became involved in stock care so they could help farmers protect their investment. They provided instruction in preventive care and simple treatment for horses, pigs, and cattle. In addition to lectures and demonstrations on vaccinating pigs for cholera, William Isaacs Jr., the agent in Colorado County, advocated the elimination of disease, particularly tick fever. As a result, he assisted in a county election that led to the construction of five new dipping tanks in the county, a controversial treatment that the USDA and state experiment stations used to combat tick fever.[13]

Large-scale producers interested in marketing their beef nationally and in improving their stock looked for a cure for the disease. Resulting state and county legislation enforced fencing and the use of dip tanks to kill the vector, the cow tick. Small farmers opposed the solutions because they sold their cattle locally not nationally, did not control enough land to fence, and resented government control of their personal lives. They resorted to violence, cutting fences and bombing dip tanks. Contemporaries considered these actions evidence of poor farmers' ignorance, but they really reflected "the frustration and political expression of the marginalized." Other farmers took less radical steps in their opposition, either ignoring the recommendations or expressing ambivalence about the role of the federal government in local and state affairs. Black extension employees, acting as agents of the state, supported scientific improvement.[14]

Agents faced more than resistance and ignorance in their efforts to improve rural life. Inadequate monetary and physical resources made it difficult for them to hold regular meetings and instill a sense of cooperation among their constituents. In 1922, Calvin Waller, Negro state leader, borrowed an organizational structure used by community councils of agriculture, an elective body that made decisions about white extension programming at the county level. Thereafter, he expected agents to organize twelve geographically distributed community clubs, hold elections to constitute a county council, and elect a county president. This provided members an opportunity

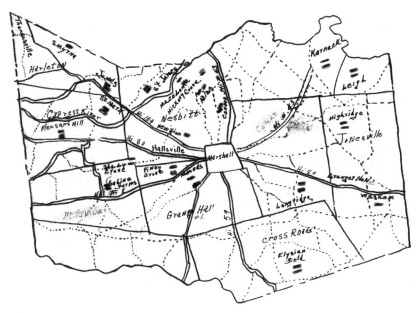

Map 4. Map of Harrison County, Tex., drawn by Annie L. Barrett, home
demonstration agent, and appended to her 1946 annual narrative report. To ensure
geographic coverage, she located twelve adult and child councils at crossroads communities. With such grassroots involvement, Barrett could reach rural blacks on
secondary and tertiary roads and distant from major population centers, specifically, the county seat, Marshall. (Annie L. Barrett, "Annual Narrative Report,"
Harrison County, Tex., Dec. 1, 1945–Nov. 30, 1946; original in author's possession)

to participate in a governing body, a right effectively denied most blacks
(see Map 4).[15]

The creation of community organizations depended on local support, and
this took time to generate. Mary Hunter believed the undertaking might
"require a number of months or a period of years to mature." It took time for
recent appointees to make the contacts necessary to organize twelve clubs.
If the appointee was a stranger, it took longer; if communities already had
an aptitude for reform, it was quicker. Rufus G. Johnson, agent in Gregg
County, involved any resident interested in extension work. Numerous freedmen colonies existed in the small county, and numerous market opportunities motivated them to organize. He quickly established twelve community
councils, and the members influenced program and project selection and implementation. Representatives from each of the community councils formed
a county council, and Johnson met with its members four times each year.
Members of the county council recommended programs to Johnson and also

Figure 6. Unidentified couple feeding their chickens. (Courtesy of the Lucille Burton Douglas Family Photograph Collection, Sam Houston Regional Library and Research Center, Texas State Library and Archives Commission)

helped secure local aid. Local councils such as these, according to Darlene Clark Hine, offered "safe havens [that] sustained relationships and wove networks across communities served."[16]

The organization that agents imposed on counties helped members learn proper management, and agents believed that such instruction met "one of the greatest needs" among rural African Americans. Through programs such as "Live at Home" and "Own Your Home," members learned budgeting, planning production needs, and managing credit. Mary Hunter even devised programs such as "The Balanced Woman," through which girls and women learned "something about everything pertaining to the farm." With management training, black youth and adults could then implement practical information they gained about poultry raising, gardening, cooking, sewing, health and sanitation practices, and home improvements (Fig. 6).[17]

Regular interaction with farm families helped agents share the latest scientific information, but families participated only if the programs reflected their needs. Agents quickly learned that they had to let the farm families plan

TABLE 5.   Modern Conveniences in Rural African American Homes, 1930

	All Farms	No. of Farms with Telephone	No. of Farms with Electric Lights	No. of Farms with Water Piped into Dwelling	No. of Farms with Water Piped into Bedrooms
Alabama	93,829	145	206	152	68
Arkansas	79,579	398	121	75	43
Louisiana	73,700	164	133	212	98
Mississippi	182,888	383	189	328	127
Oklahoma	22,937	1,129	389	394	311
Texas	86,063	793	196	412	164

Source: Adapted from *Negroes in the United States, 1920–1932,* table 41, 591.

their programs. One agent in Colorado County believed that, before county councils made programming decisions, "farm people [felt] that they were doing you a favor to carry out the program suggested, but due to County Councils and people given a chance to help in making the plans they are to work on, they are beginning to feel responsible for the success of the demonstration." Irene Sanders, working in Anderson County by the late 1920s, concurred. Over time, she realized that the women and girls had to take responsibility for the work to make the programs successful. She met with club members and discussed conditions in their areas, analyzed problems, and prioritized needs. Then women worked to realize their goals. They produced extra crops or canned goods for sale so they could purchase a can of paint to rehabilitate old bedroom furniture. Girls involved in home improvement made furniture from milk crates and rehabilitated clothing instead of buying new. Women and girls used expert advice to meet real needs. Sanders believed that, ultimately, "instead of programs being based to a great extent on production and preservation of products as in former years, they are taking a more farm and home management view on the farm business of the community." This approach helped the Extension Service "influence the rural people to solve some of their important problems." It increased their knowledge,

Figure 7. Home of W. T. Lewis and family, Antioch Community, Tatum, Rusk County, Tex., Apr. 1933. The Lewis family built their nine-room house, which included four bedrooms, in 1927. Mr. Lewis owned 495 acres, with 115 acres in a variety of crops. (Neg. S-16816-C, George W. Ackerman, photographer, FES, USDA, NA)

increased their production and perhaps their income, and inspired them to have "better homes with convenient surroundings."[18]

If participants could tie the program to their own goals, they became interested. For example, comprehensive farm rehabilitation proved overwhelming, but girls accomplished amazing things when given the freedom to manage their own situations. In one case, three sisters improved their rooms following the directions of their club leader. Then they decided that they wanted to plant a patch of cotton to increase their expendable income, and their father gave them permission to do so. They planted a big enough patch to pick six bales of cotton, and they used the proceeds to rehabilitate more furniture for their rooms. The remainder they put in the bank. The father then decided that their rooms made the rest of the house look shabby, so he built a new house. No doubt, he outfitted the family's stylish new home with modern conveniences (Table 5). Stories such as this became extension folklore as agents used them to emphasize the merits of planning and investment (Figs. 7 and 8).[19]

The girls who prompted their father to build them a new house worked outside of traditional white gender divisions of labor, but this reflected the

Figure 8. Willie Mae Lewis's bedroom, Antioch Community, Tatum, Rusk County, Tex., Apr. 1933. Willie Mae, one of five children of a landowning family, conducted the bedroom demonstration with the assistance of Mrs. Ethel W. Thomas, home demonstration agent. Willie Mae spent $2.80 on fabric and much labor to appliqué the quilt, pillowcases, chair cushion, and curtain panels to make the room "comfortable and livable." (Neg. S-16814-C, George W. Ackerman, photographer, FES, USDA, NA)

flexibility of Negro Division work with boys' and girls' clubs and adult clubs. Generally, Negro home demonstration agents worked with women and girls to increase their contributions to farm income and family health while Negro county agents concentrated their services on helping men and boys diversify and improve agricultural marketing. Several factors, however, prevented the gender-based divisions from being rigidly enforced. While boys usually became involved in corn clubs and girls in canning clubs, boys and girls could help diversify income sources by raising pigs and poultry. They could improve the attitude of the family by undertaking projects that improved farm appearance and reduced expenses. Finally, they could become healthier children and adults by adopting better health and sanitation practices. Girls learned how to prepare more nutritious meals; boys dug new outhouse holes. Both screened windows. Such actions improved the health of the family and its earning potential and reflected practices within black farm families.

Several men worked alone in counties, with no home demonstration agent. These men organized clubs that included men, women, boys, and girls. In this way, they addressed the needs of all their constituents, though they relied on women to help them create successful programs. William Isaacs Jr. adopted this strategy as the lone extension agent in Colorado County. He received support from the Colorado County Union of the FIS, and all fourteen of the clubs that he formed included men, women, and children. He provided separate instruction to the men who joined and to the boys' club members, but mothers instructed the girls in poultry and canning clubs.[20]

Ideally, counties employed men and women as agents. Sometimes, husbands and wives worked as agents in the same county, and this facilitated program development along gender lines that helped black farmers survive. Lea Etta Lusk, home demonstration agent in Washington County, emphasized work with farm youth, as did her husband, county agent John M. Lusk. In 1923, she devoted three-fourths of her time to girls' clubs, supervising twelve in the county. The girls raised a variety of animals, including hares and chickens. Annie B. Sharp managed to save $127 after raising Belgian hares for two years. Lillian Spencer, an award-winning seamstress, earned a tidy sum by sewing and investing her earnings in livestock. She bought a purebred Poland China pig for $15, twelve Rhode Island Red pullets and one cockerel for $14, and deposited her remaining $23 in the bank. Lusk influenced nine girls to attend college in 1923. These girls contributed to their families' income and managed to save enough for their college education.[21]

John M. Lusk reached out to children of owners and tenants alike in a county dominated by cotton production. Ira Bearden, son of renters in Gay Hill, planted Ferguson's Yellow Dent seed corn to great effect, raising the best corn in his part of Washington County two years in a row (Fig. 9). Bearden's success prompted eight other parents to involve their boys in club work. Some boys grew better corn than adults grew. Joe Franklin Jr., a club member in Chappell Hill, exhibited the best corn in the county three years in a row, and he won first prize at the county fair in 1923. The public recognition helped Franklin profit even more. He sold fifty bushels of seed corn for one dollar per bushel and invested the proceeds into a purebred Duroc-Jersey sow. One of Lusk's club boys joined exhibitors from other counties who won prizes for their corn and maize exhibited at the Dallas State Fair (Fig. 10). Other boys used their proceeds to offset education expenses. Tommie Bolton, also of Chappell Hill, won a scholarship to Prairie View A&M because of his entry in the county's corn-growing contest. Four other boys also entered college in 1923 due to Lusk's influence.[22]

Figure 9. Ira Bearden, son of renters from Gay Hill, Washington County, Tex., and his prize-winning corn crop, 1923. (J. B. Coleman Library, Special Collections/ Archives Dept., Prairie View A&M University)

Figure 10. Armelia Marsh, Elysian Fields, won first prize for prolific corn at the 1924 Dallas State Fair. (James M. Benton, Harrison County–Negro Agent, 1924, Material Submitted with Annual Narrative and Statistical Reports, 1914–44, Other Regular Reports Concerning Field Extension Work, ES, RG 33, NA)

Agents emphasized education, and examples of success motivated youth throughout the 1920s to take advantage of the possibilities that club work provided. In 1930, Robert Burks financed his first year at Brenham High School with money he raised from his Poland China sow and litter demonstration and his two acres of Yellow Dent corn. Eddie Lawrence undertook demonstrations with a Poland China gilt and an acre of Sure Cropper corn with the same intention of saving money for school.[23]

Families that applied scientific management to agriculture and home life became role models within the community and beyond. John Lusk featured the accomplishments of W. M. Spencer, his wife, and their ten children in his 1923 annual narrative report. The father became a demonstrator and four of the sons joined the boys' club in 1920. Lusk encouraged them to participate in the "Own Your Home" campaign. Over the course of three years, they planned their strategy, planted crops for feed, raised more chickens, and sold more eggs. Spencer paid off all his debts and ultimately bought a farm with an eight-room house and 160 acres of land. Lusk believed the effort proved even more noteworthy because Spencer had spent more than forty years in the same run-down shack that he, and his parents before him, had rented. The coordinated efforts of ten children and their parents made the difference in acquiring land.[24]

Agents provided opportunities for club members to analyze crops and stock. Judging contests trained farm youth in agribusiness. Boys' club members routinely observed judges at fairs and then practiced their skills in judging contests. This helped them learn to recognize quality stock and crops. County agent John Hogg encouraged boys to enter cattle- and hog-judging contests at the first "fair for negro[e]s" in Houston County in 1923. He advised them to get a score card and inspect the stock exhibited. Boys privileged enough to attend the annual short course at Prairie View A&M often participated in the judging contests there as well. John Lusk's club boys won first prize in cow and hog judging at the 1930 short course. All agents undertook this work and frequently mentioned the judging contests in their reports.[25]

Concerted efforts to engage girls and boys ensured participation. The number involved in extension work grew steadily throughout the 1920s and into the 1930s. Girls learned management and leadership skills, saved money, attended school, and became better-informed citizens. Boys participated in the same organizational, production, and marketing activities that girls did. The extension agents thus prepared the next generation of black extension agents, rural educators, and reformers, but, ironically, professional involvement forced the youth to leave the farm.[26]

Extension agents did not take the loss of farm youth to other pursuits lightly. Edward B. Evans, Negro state leader and later Prairie View A&M president, commented on the value of vocational agriculture instruction in training leaders, but he also expressed concern over the small number of Prairie View A&M graduates who took advantage of opportunities to manage farms or ranches in Texas. He dismissed lack of capital as the cause, because many of the graduates came from farm-owning families. Instead, he believed teachers needed to be more committed to farming as a profession. Extension agents also could foster an appreciation for farm life that could help retain the brightest and most promising young people and thus reverse the trend of out-migration.[27]

Extension agents devised other strategies that depended on group involvement to solve individual needs. In 1900, the average African American lived to forty years of age while the average white lived to fifty-one. By 1940, the average black male in the rural South lived fifty-six years while black females lived fifty-eight years. White males lived, on average, sixty-four years, and white females lived, on average, sixty-seven years. Malnutrition and inadequate sanitation negatively affected rural health, generally, but the impoverished conditions that affected many African Americans increased the health risks. Unscreened windows admitted mosquitoes and flies during the summer, and the lack of outhouses increased the threat of contamination to water supplies. The Extension Service addressed these problems directly, encouraging families to improve their diets and the sanitary conditions around the farm and to eliminate infectious disease as a way to increase life expectancy.[28]

Agents engaged entire communities in health reform. African American women began sanitation campaigns in the early twentieth century, and in 1915, Negro Health Week began to focus national attention on the deficiencies in public health care for African Americans. Extension agents in Texas coordinated local cleanup efforts as part of the national campaign. African Americans in Harrison County in April 1923 got a boost from members of the black Medical and Dental Society who volunteered their services to lecture and examine children. Doctors provided basic information about the uses of lime to dissuade flies from breeding in outhouses, the proper location of wells to reduce the risk of contamination, and reducing the transmission of disease, including venereal disease and tuberculosis. Extension agent James Morgan Benton concentrated his efforts on home and yard sanitation and community cleanup. As a result of the public programs, rural blacks cleared their yards, lots, and stables and promised to screen their houses and cement their wells in an effort to reduce outbreaks of typhoid fever. Benton estimated that programs in eight communities, including the county seat, involved two thousand residents. Lea Etta Lusk organized health and cleanup campaigns as part of Negro Health Week as well. She and Benton and other agents throughout the state engaged in a "war on rats, flies, and mosquitoes" by screening windows and doors, but they also took the campaign into the streets, cleaning up all cans and rubbish in and around schools, churches, and other public places frequented by African Americans.[29]

Health reform also targeted infants. Home demonstration agents taught farm wives and girls to prepare balanced meals and pay special attention to the feeding of infants. Lea Etta Lusk targeted families with undernourished, underweight children. She presented demonstrations on preparing milk and milk dishes and eggs that the children could easily digest. She persuaded women to change their children's diets because children in families that increased milk consumption showed increased weight and better health.[30]

Churches, schools, and beneficent lodges, fulcrums around which communities grew, provided points of contact. The deep religious convictions held by many rural African Americans contributed to the growth of the TAEX. Supervisors and agents met with rural pastors and members of fraternal organizations and communicated with an estimated 125,000 black Texans in the process. They believed that they reached those in even the most backward communities in this way and cultivated important connections with black professionals. In 1921, Waller reported that ten fraternal societies had allowed agents to speak to an estimated 175,000 members, and three of the largest created departments for demonstrations and lectures.[31]

Agents recognized the role of the church as a hub of rural community life and appreciated the influence ministers exerted on their parishioners. Black agents often shared with ministers a deep sense of religious conviction and belief in the redeeming power of the church. The extension staff routinely opened monthly meetings with a prayer. Therefore, close connections with ministers proved invaluable in spreading the word about extension work. Waller welcomed the opportunity to speak with one hundred Methodist Episcopal ministers who attended the Rural Pastor's School at Wiley College in Marshall, Texas, in 1921. He credited them with making it possible for extension agents "to work with all church groups in Texas." James Benton, agent in Harrison County, relied on the Rev. J. E. Campbell,

St. John Church, to launch his Negro Health Week observance. Benton, and Drs. Sheppard and Hunter, members of the Medical and Dental Society, addressed the congregation following Sunday school and church.[32]

Ministers helped agents appeal to families that they needed to reach. Because rural pastors shared many objectives with agents, the relationship proved mutually beneficial. At the Rural Pastor's School, first conducted at Wiley College in 1918, pastors discussed the plight of small black communities and worked to introduce stable credit systems that would help farmers escape tenancy. The Federal Council of the Churches of Christ in America published a bulletin in 1925 titled "Social Aspects of Farmers' Co-Operative Marketing." By the 1930s, the council was distributing literature that supported landownership. A series of three bulletins discussed landownership by black farmers: the first provided information on organizing to buy land; the second discussed qualifications of land buyers and advocated the formation of landownership committees; the third proposed an extension-type solution, encouraging farmers to "live at home" by growing gardens. Churches in and around Harrison Switch in McLennan County had access to these bulletins because Jeffie O. A. Conner, a resident of the community and a home demonstration agent with considerable experience, informed parishioners of their existence (Fig. 11). In exchange for the support pastors provided to extension programs, agents advocated for church repair, and community clubs did the work.[33]

The Extension Service identified rural teachers as potential cooperators. Teachers helped convey information and reach rural African Americans who otherwise would not hear of ways to improve health, sanitation, and welfare. County superintendents in many counties authorized teachers to work with the agents. This gave agents a captive audience of children to organize into boys' and girls' clubs with the hope of ultimately reaching their parents. County superintendents also allowed agents to attend parents' meetings. Prairie View A&M associates served as presidents and officers of the Colored Teachers State Association of Texas from its founding, and this gave them legitimate reasons to interact with teachers.[34]

Agents recognized the deplorable conditions in rural black schools. One home demonstration agent commented that "inconvenient, uncomfortable school buildings . . . lessened the desire of the child to attend school, thereby making him an unfit subject for a good citizen." Agents involved clubs in complete community overhauls, which included the construction of new schoolhouses if necessary. Funding from the Anna T. Jeanes Foundation, a fund administered by the General Education Board, provided opportunities

Figure 11. Meeting in a church with an unidentified woman, possibly Mrs. Jeffie O. A. Conner, discussing canning, ca. 1933. The agent illustrated her demonstration with photographs of operating community canning houses. (J. B. Coleman Library, Special Collections/Archives Dept., Prairie View A&M University)

for collaboration. Jeanes appropriations allowed county superintendents to hire industrial supervising teachers to work in rural black schools. Jeanes teachers came late to Texas compared to other southern states, working in six counties by 1919.[35]

Jeanes teachers conveyed information similar to that of home demonstration agents. They organized clubs to improve the school and community, provided lessons in sanitation and cleanliness, and introduced simple home-based industries into rural school instruction. In some states, their visibility vastly exceeded that of the extension agents. White progressives supported Jeanes teachers. Oscar B. Martin, an agent of the USDA in 1913, encouraged their involvement, providing funds to help them establish Homemaker's Clubs in North Carolina. When Martin began as TAEX director in December 1927, Jeanes teachers were working in twenty-two counties in Texas, home demonstration agents in nineteen, and both extension agents and Jeanes teachers in five counties during academic year 1927–28. Most local officials did not support duplication of effort for the black schools, and counties rarely retained both a Jeanes teacher and a Negro extension agent for long.[36]

Agents relied on schools for access to constituents. Efforts to improve health and hygiene often began in the schools. County superintendents encouraged teachers to work with agents, and this allowed classrooms to function as platforms from which male and female agents could deliver instructions on cultivation and preservation. School classes sometimes formed their own clubs, and schools devoted land to gardens and other crops to improve nutrition. The agents encouraged families to provide a tin can for each child so students did not share a cup and transmit disease. This inexpensive solution proved popular, and in 1921, the Red Cross in Marshall requested information from the black agents to make enough cups to supply every schoolchild in the county.[37]

In 1923, John Hogg, the sole agent in Houston County, organized twenty sewing clubs in the public schools. He distributed the TAEX bulletin for "first year sewing," and twenty-five girls sewed 150 caps, aprons, bags, towels, and potholders. Mary Hunter distributed the certificates that the girls earned at the county fair that Hogg helped organized that year. Hogg also involved teachers more tangibly in supporting the Extension Service. He asked the teachers' institute to contribute $200 toward the salary for a county home demonstration agent. Annie G. H. Hall received an appointment in July 1924 as a result.[38]

Rufus G. Johnson, agent in Gregg County for more than twenty years, worked with Ned Williams, a schoolteacher in Elderville, a freedmen's settlement, to build a school. Williams had attended Bishop College, a Baptist school in nearby Marshall, and Tuskegee Institute. He eventually returned to his roots on the Martin plantation, believing that "we are an agricultural people . . . and we belong to the soil, not in the cities." Dissatisfied Exodusters likewise returned to Texas from Kansas, lured back by the offer of affordable farmland marketed by black farmers in and around the settlement that came to be called Elderville. The remainder lived on plantation land that their families had farmed for generations. They joined Johnson and Williams in establishing the school to train their children in methods suited to a life in the country.[39]

Through the school, Johnson coordinated clubs for women and girls and instructed them in gardening, screening windows, and canning. His clubs even built community canning centers. He took pride in the accomplishments of the Elderville residents and knew that they set a standard that other communities attempted to emulate. More than half of the Elderville residents owned land. Farm youth, women, and men all contributed to the household economies of families in Elderville. As a result, they joined tens of thousands of others in Texas in the 1920s as they attempted to improve their conditions, but like others following the advice of Negro Division agents, they differed from most blacks in Texas because they managed to accumulate property instead of debt as they struggled to live with white racism.[40]

Johnson worked in the county where the segregated service had held its first demonstration in September 1915. Members who attended that meeting remained active in the community and in the extension clubs throughout the 1920s. They persevered through the Great Depression and adopted better farming practices to remain viable agriculturists. They encouraged their children and grandchildren to participate in 4-H Clubs and taught them "the value of Extension Work and its far-reaching service."[41]

Yet, schools did not provide a panacea. Farm youth often could not participate in extension work, even through schools cooperated with agents. Teachers in McLennan County asked emergency agent Robert H. Hines to establish boys' clubs in 1919. The boys could not accomplish anything, however, "because the father[s] would not give [them] a chance." Ultimately, Hines chided adults: "[I] had to watch my community clubs close to keep them going and could not give the time required to make the boys' work a real success." The schoolteachers had no authority even if they supported the program.[42]

McLennan County agents did not give up on involving schools, however, despite the frustrations. By 1924, extension agent John V. Smith had fostered a relationship between businessmen and rural schools, with the businessmen assuming some responsibility for helping rural schools acquire musical instruments to aid in instruction. This helped schools expand their curriculum and shows extension's broader influence, but teachers still could provide only support for programs; they could not override parental authority.[43]

One of the most successful community-based reform efforts—the development of community canning centers—involved numerous special interests. The first meeting black agents conducted, in September 1915, involved families gathered at Ted Williams's place in Blackjack, a small community just a half mile east of the International & Great Northern Railroad line in Northeast Texas. Robert L. Smith and Mary Hunter explained the general plan of the Extension Service and relied on an exhibit of canned goods to emphasize the benefits for the family of increasing food production. Hunter then demonstrated the concept of canning the surplus. The Texas Home Canners Association existed by 1908, and commercial canning was gaining support by that time as well. White Texans began systematically conveying scientific information on canning to white audiences in 1914. Community canning plants provided an opportunity to pool resources and preserve for home use as well as for sale. Blackjack's residents had access to railway lines to ensure that their products reached urban markets in Texas and beyond.[44]

The community-based approach to educating rural blacks about canning helped more people realize its benefits in a shorter amount of time. By involving girls as well as women in the program, youthful enthusiasm and physical stamina combined with experience to help even the poorest communities can surplus for their own use and for sale. The most impoverished used cauldrons or lard cans or washtubs and laundry boilers over open fires to preserve meat, tomatoes, corn, and other vegetables and fruit. Agents advocated this "open-kettle method" when limited resources precluded any other approach. As club canning spread, the price of manufactured steam pressure canners declined and poorer communities could afford them, but even then black agents advocated homemade alternatives.[45]

The economic benefits of home and commercial canning appealed to landowning farmers, and they sought advice. A group with "large farms and fair houses" in Stump Toe, near Fredonia in Gregg County, stood to profit from commercial canning due to their proximity to the growing towns of Tyler and Longview and several railroad lines. They contacted Hunter to speak with them soon after the demonstration at Blackjack. She showed them how to preserve culled sweet potatoes. The economics of her argument swayed them, and by October 21, 1915, residents had purchased a hot water canner for community use. They invested in their center through World War I, and by 1922, they were using steam canning equipment, cooperatively owned, to can tomatoes and sweet potatoes for market.[46]

Canneries operated by African Americans increased from one in 1915 to 250 in 1918. Part of the growth resulted from domestic mobilization supported by state law. In 1917, the Texas legislature authorized commissioners' courts to appropriate money for canning. Lea Etta Lusk, a home demonstration agent in Washington County employed to increase domestic production during the Great War, recalled that she spent all of May, June, and July in 1919 helping demonstrators can surplus vegetables. In this way, she reached "all communities where our people were free to plant gardens." The farm families in Washington County had known nothing about the process because they lived in cotton country, where all their energies were focused on the one cash crop. High food prices during the war forced families to can for home use, and women and girls "showed a deep interest" as a result. They realized that canning freed them from dependency on commodities purchased at inflated prices. Robert Hines, the agent in McLennan County, reported that nearly every black farm family planted a home garden and preserved the majority of the harvest. This differed from the situation in 1917, when "practically no vegetables were saved and a very little fruit." Such efforts helped many avoid debt and increase income.[47]

Agents knew that canning helped improve the nutritional value and variety of foodstuffs families consumed, and this improved the health of their constituency. And a healthier black population had the potential to earn more and participate in society to a greater degree than those debilitated by pellagra and other diseases associated with the rural poor. The TAEX published booklets to educate members about the health benefits of properly canned foods, but white as well as black extension agents believed that inadequate education made it difficult for many rural blacks to absorb the information.

Mary Hunter faced this impediment directly. She simplified the instructions through her "Steps in Canning" program, which she introduced immediately in 1915. She explained to the women and girls that they could enjoy fresh vegetables from their gardens only four months of the year, leaving 240 days without vegetables. She encouraged each family to put up 240 cans of vegetables, so that they would have at least one can for each day of the year not supplied by the garden. Those who followed her advice had to create storage space for the canned goods, a luxury few residents of one- and two-room box-frame houses enjoyed. By 1919, thirteen agents were helping Hunter implement "Steps in Canning." At least 14,366 women and girls processed 298,445 jars of fruits and vegetables with a value of $98,058.80 in 1919. By 1921, Hunter believed that the sustained emphasis on the benefits of canning for home use and for sale had convinced individuals and clubs in "nearly every community in Texas" to make or purchase a canner. Canning proved so popular that communities in counties without a black home demonstration agent still purchased canners (Fig. 12).[48]

Farmers used canning centers as a means of defense. Some chose to can their beeves instead of selling cattle at low prices in times of drought or when counties passed stock laws that required farmers to fence their cattle in compliance with legislation passed to reduce Texas fever. Many black farmers, owners and tenants alike, had no land to fence. The stock sales that resulted forced the price of cattle down, and farmers could not sell their beef. The new home demonstration agent in Houston County, Annie G. H. Hall, set to work in the fall of 1924 to mitigate the loss to farmers. In a few months, she organized the farmers to construct six community canners. By working cooperatively, families could can their beef and still harvest their cotton

Figure 12. Mrs. Callie Byrd and Mrs. Fannie Hollaway sealing tin cans under the direction of Jeffie O. A. Conner (not pictured), McLennan County, Tex., 1924. (George S. and Jeffie O. A. Conner Papers, Texas Collection, Baylor University)

crops. Thus, they made their crop and realized some gain from their cattle, which "would have otherwise been a total loss to them."[49]

The drought of 1925 also forced farmers in Washington County to can their beeves. Lea Etta Lusk traveled throughout the county and, with her husband's help, reintroduced canning to communities that had forgotten about its usefulness since World War I. They convinced discouraged farm families to "can their beeves in order to have something to help tide their families through the winter." Some dried-up milk cows became chili during that harsh year, but canning softened the blow for those farmers who faced the loss of a significant capital investment in their stock.[50]

Agents took their message to related organizations in an attempt to further food preservation. Maggie Lee, the agent in Polk County, offered a steam canner as a prize at the FIS encampment and fair in Polk County in October 1919. The Gold Standard branch of the FIS, located in Goodrich, Texas, earned the award for having the best exhibit at the fair. The agents in Waller County, Mary A. Dixon and Jesse Wilson, organized canning exhibits there for the local FIS encampment in 1919. Mary Hunter spoke about the merits of canning at FIS encampments and fairs and with FIS school students. Two girls, Beatrice and Cleo Parish, canned fruits, berries, and vegetables from the FIS school garden and received state and national attention for their efforts. In these ways, the extension service expanded its influence.[51]

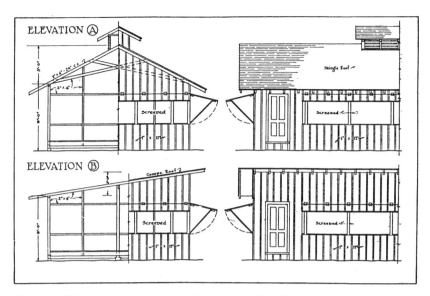

Figure 13. "End and side elevations of two types of buildings suitable for Community Canning Plants." (Walton Peteet, Chauncey Merwin, and Cornelia Simpson, *Community Canning Plants*, Agricultural and Mechanical College of Texas, Bulletin no. B-48 [College Station, 1919], 16)

The canneries became visible signs of the public and private partnership in rural development. Extension agents depended on voluntary labor and resources provided by club members. The men provided brick or stone and volunteered their services to build a furnace and small structures to protect it from the elements. The buildings varied, depending on the resources of the community. A TAEX bulletin, *Community Canning Plants,* provided elevations for a simple board-and-batten building with a shed roof measuring twenty by forty-eight feet. It resembled a typical farm shed of box construction and posed no challenge for a local carpenter. Some followed the recommendations and the effort paid off. By 1925, members in twenty-three counties, almost all of the counties with black agents, had built and rehabilitated 267 canning plants (Fig. 13).[52]

African Americans constructed canning centers from available materials because many had no resources to purchase materials. The experiences of residents in Flynn community provide an example. Iola Rowan, the Negro district state home demonstration agent, and William C. David, the county agent in Madison County, met with individuals in the Leon County community in 1933. The agents gave a canning demonstration on the creek bank, "because water was available at the creek but not at the home." They

Figure 14. Community canning house built for Pyrtle Community, Kilgore, Rusk County, Tex., Apr. 1933. Carpenters used plans furnished by the Negro Division, Prairie View, new lumber, corrugated roofing, and concrete, and spent $317.50. Albert Coss, Pyrtle School principal, and H. L. Brown, agent, assisted. (Neg. S-16822-S, George W. Ackerman, photographer, FES, USDA, NA)

constructed a furnace by digging a hole three feet long and three feet deep in the bank and laid a piece of galvanized iron sheeting over the hole to hold the retort and cookers. This made "an excellent furnace," and they processed three hundred cans of beef.[53]

Other communities seeking to operate on a commercial scale needed to meet government regulations for canned beef and vegetables (Fig. 14). They built buildings with brick furnaces and purchased steam canner outfits that consisting of a commercial-sized retort that cost $27, a sealer for tin cans that cost $16, and tin cans that cost as much as five cents each. Cooperation made it possible for four Gregg County clubs with a total of 180 members to save $200 on their equipment purchases in 1923. The multiple tasks necessary to build and outfit these centers provided practical instruction in at least six areas: economy, cooperation, sanitation, drainage, conveniences for the home, and landscaping. Residents then applied this knowledge to their

Figure 15. Brick furnace in Pyrtle community canning house, Kilgore, Rusk County, Tex., Apr. 1933. A furnace with two retorts, or steam pressure canners, might process five hundred to fourteen hundred cans per day, equivalent to thirty half-acre family gardens. (Peteet, Merwin, and Simpson, *Community Canning Plants,* 8, 11; neg. S-16820-C, George W. Ackerman, photographer, FES, USDA, NA)

Figure 16. Beulah Community canning house, Palestine, Anderson County, Tex., April 1933. Club women are cleaning green beans (right) and packing and sealing canned produce (left). Women in the background are loading the retort in preparation for pressure canning. Beulah residents built the structure in 1931. They used $75 in prize money won at the Anderson County Fruit Palace to purchase an old church building and salvage lumber for the new canning house. F. J. Robinson, agent, assisted. (Neg. S-16833-C, George W. Ackerman, photographer, FES, USDA, NA)

homes, churches, and schools, thus spreading the benefits of the knowledge gained in the canning centers (Fig. 15).[54]

Black families in Texas canned more than one million containers of food in 1929, an average of 115 cans or jars per family. This kept at least 368 community steam pressure canners busy during the canning season. Agents estimated the value of their work in gardening, canning, poultry, and dairying at $371,518.70 in 1929. Community residents had to cooperate to sustain this production. They had to agree on schedules for use of the facility, and they paid for the privilege with cans of food. Many adopted this toll method, paying a fixed fee set by the committee that managed the plant. If residents furnished the tin cans, the toll usually amounted to one-half of the finished product. The toll contributed to the operating costs of the plant. Yet, those who participated had to have the capital to invest in the tin cans or glass jars to start, and they had to control their own labor so they could plant the gardens and raise the beef that they canned (Fig. 16).[55]

Men, women, and children used the centers to process commodities for home use as well. Women and girls performed the bulk of the work associated with vegetable and fruit canning, but men processed syrup from the cane they grew and worked with the women when they processed beef. During the 1920s, Calvin Waller, Negro state leader, challenged agents to expand their services beyond the privileged communities that they had been serving. The agents relied on canning centers to accomplish the task, because the centers were both desperately needed by poor rural families and generally supported. Even the poorest communities could muster the voluntary labor needed to build the canneries, but only owners and some tenants could control their labor. With this measure of support promised, agents tailored the program to suit the resources of each club.[56]

Canning centers helped agents accomplish their goal of improving rural life because they stabilized rural communities. First, the cannery provided a means of generating common interest in the development of community life and a forum for introducing racial solidarity. Hunter recognized this in 1915 when she introduced the centers to rural African Americans. She believed that feuding and bickering created disunity that clergy and masters of competing churches and lodges often instigated. Operating a cannery required residents to cooperate to purchase seeds and negotiate a schedule for planting, harvesting, and preservation. Hunter believed that this created "a new community relation that had not been thought of before," and in 1925 she reported that the canning plants did more "to increase community interest than any one thing undertaken." The kitchens constructed in many plants also provided a new gathering place for functions, such as picnics and festivals, further strengthening local identity.[57]

Second, canning helped blacks nurture a sense of race solidarity through community cooperation. They had to cooperate to build structures, purchase canning supplies, and market the commodities. They elected governing councils to administer the operations, and they realized that they could take responsibility for their own actions and reduce their reliance on white landlords and other authority figures. The money they saved and earned gave farmers an opportunity to accumulate personal property, including land and homes. This created physical evidence of a minority culture eager to claim its economic and social equality.

Third, canning offered black Texans a way to stabilize their precarious existence. Money saved by using home-produced canned goods instead of store-bought goods protected many from indebtedness to some extent. Families that sold their canned goods gained income to invest in a pig, a dairy cow, or land. The accumulation of property, particularly the ownership of real estate, became one of the most blatant forms of black opposition to plantation agriculture and had political consequences. Black property holders paid taxes and had some say in local government expenditures as a result.[58]

Fourth, canning provided evidence of the challenge to the inequality of southern society. For example, canning contributed to the success of the E. D. Roberts family of Brenham. The Roberts family canned the extra food they grew while the patriarch "fertilized the soil, ploughed and planted as per the Agent's directions, . . . raised more chickens, sold eggs, fed cows a balanced ration, and sold more butter." With the proceeds, Roberts bought more tools, a better team of mules, paid off the debt on his first fifty acres, purchased fifty more, and even bought the family "a Ford car for their comfort, and as a means of hauling his produce to town." Agents presented Roberts as the model black farmer, and canning helped him realize economic solvency.[59]

Canning plants did not further economic development in all places. Roads and the markets that they served proved critical to the success of such undertakings. The need to gain access to constituents as well as markets motivated agents and their club members to support the good-roads movement. Most farmers lived on gravel or dirt roads prior to World War II. Such roads wreaked havoc on tires, and reformers encouraged public funding to maintain roads and increase the number of paved miles. Residents, however, balked at paying extra taxes to improve services. Proponents of good roads made an effort to educate rural Texans about the value they would gain from the modest increase in taxes to fund construction. The Texas Good Roads Association lobbied for road improvements as a means of increasing intrastate commerce. The association worked county by county, starting in the 1910s, to generate support to pave roads.[60]

Local boosters helped promote the movement through credit incentives. Chambers of commerce, creameries, local banks, and breeders provided loans to farmers to establish dairy herds. They targeted those who lived on main roads and had access to the market. Negro agents encouraged their constituents to participate. Creameries and dairy-processing plants purchased milk from any farmer, white or black, and in Harrison County a creamery purchased one-quarter of its supply from black farmers. Negro agents encouraged farmers to take advantage of the loans businesses provided and improve roads in anticipation of new markets. Farmers in McLennan, Houston, Harris, and Nacogdoches counties complied.[61]

Better roads helped agents as well. Automobiles made it easier for agents to meet with their club members and to participate in reform efforts beyond the farm and home. But the conditions of roads often limited the ability of agents to do their job. Those with cars incurred expenses that they had to cover with their limited salaries. John Hogg complained that he spent "nearly all of [his] time" traveling over rough roads on extension business in Houston County in 1923. His repair bill for his car, and gas for December, amounted to $80; for January, $50; and for February, $60. In April, he incurred an additional $20 repair bill when he tore up the rear of his car on a trip to the school grounds in Fodice. The program met with success, however. He reported that "the people cleared off and broke up four acres on School ground and had a rousing meeting." But he did not believe he received adequate compensation for the effort. He bought a horse to help him negotiate the roads when they became too muddy for his car.[62]

Hogg undertook road improvement as a way to make his work more efficient. He wrote: "We are trying hard to bring road results in this county. We are so far behind in this County in Road construction. The Commissioners are outlining and suggesting some special roads and offering some special teams to aid our cooperative efforts."[63]

Hogg proceeded to organize eight communities to improve local roads. He secured a $50 appropriation from the Houston County commissioners to aid the work, and he used part of the money to hire road plows and teams. His club members graveled four miles of public road and built and improved the roadbed on another ten miles. The efforts on the part of individual agents helped improve a small amount of mileage in Texas. Still, by 1930 only 3.8 percent of all black farm operators lived on concrete or paved roads while 77.8 percent lived on dirt roads (Table 6).[64]

Roads even provided new opportunities for defiance. Farmers who owned automobiles found cheaper prices elsewhere, and planters lost their labor as well as income from store sales. Planters had to provide cash as a way of keeping their laborers. Many Texas farmers found that the car gave them easier access to market as well. By 1930, at least 22,339 black farmers in Texas, 26 percent of farm operators, owned automobiles, while 1,317 owned trucks, and 242 owned tractors.[65]

Agents recognized the benefits of living along paved roads and owning automobiles, but also the risks. Some feared the automobile because those who invested unwisely would suffer the consequences. Robert L. Smith declared that "one great danger threatens our farming people, who are prosperous and that is the automobile craze. A man who hasn't an acre of land nor a house to live in has no moral right to buy an automobile and he ought to have sense enough to see it. Thirty-five cent cotton and a big crop do not come together every day or every year." Regardless, Smith interacted with automobile

TABLE 6. African American Farm Operators and Road Surfaces, Texas, 1930

State	Total Farms	No. on Concrete Rd.	No. on Asphalt/ Macadam or Brick Rd.	No. on Gravel Rd.	No. on Sand/Clay Rd.	No. on Improved Dirt Rd.	No. on Un-improved Dirt Rd.	No. on Other Rd. Type
Alabama	93,829	535	410	14,515	6,556	22,718	43,492	5,603
Arkansas	79,579	1,238	2,255	11,886	771	15,666	41,651	6,112
Louisiana	73,770	848	660	23,092	250	15,499	29,970	3,451
Mississippi	182,888	2,268	215	61,854	2,389	44,409	64,274	7,479
Oklahoma	22,937	239	88	1,366	275	8,604	10,200	2,165
Texas	86,063	1,012	2,237	7,957	2,529	26,278	40,712	5,338

Source: Adapted from *Negroes in the United States, 1920–1932*, table 40, 591.

owners regularly, and agents realized the importance of the automobile to helping rural black farmers removed from railway lines reach markets and attain economic viability.[66]

Many believed that increased access to markets offset the investment, but mobility brought increased temptation to leave the farm. Many rural African Americans living near the plantations where their parents and grandparents had labored as slaves feared the lure of the cities. They valued the life experiences they shared with neighbors, and they foresaw the demise of their fragile communities if the younger generation left. Extension services provided a means to keep children on the farm, some believed, but others feared that the service would lure them away. The girls' and boys' clubs certainly provided opportunities for youth to become leaders and productive citizens. Ironically, learning these skills often induced rural children to leave the farm for college, and college-educated youth rarely returned.

Managing extensive services over a large geographic area required regular meetings and strict adherence to policies. The Negro Division director and district agents held monthly meetings at the headquarters at Prairie View A&M to discuss issues affecting county agents. They assessed the status of each agent in the field, planned programs and itineraries, and outlined responsibilities associated with upcoming tasks. District agents reported on existing funding and plans under way to qualify counties for extension agents. They then carried this information and other material released by extension headquarters at College Station back to the field agents. Calvin Waller believed that "this method . . . keeps the Negro workers in constant contact with all phases of the work and each county working along the same program. We feel that in Turns, we know something about all phases of Extension work being projected in the United States."[67]

Waller advocated cooperation between Negro Division staff and Prairie View A&M to improve rural conditions. He helped make Prairie View A&M an integral part of black rural reform in Texas. The partnership, however, did not always run smoothly. Agents coordinated short courses, district meetings, summer encampments, and annual conferences and regularly presented at them. They depended on Prairie View A&M resources to make the programs successful. Administrative staff regularly secured the cooperation of professors by communicating initially with the principal. Yet, the college lacked the resources to offer additional financial support, and this became a bone of contention. In 1935, agents reported the largest attendance at a short course to date but also noted that the college contributed only limited financial assistance. Regardless, the underfunded black land-grant school and the underfunded Negro Division combined their limited resources to provide educational opportunities for farm families and agents.[68]

Such cooperation helped the Texas Negro Division grow during the 1920s and the early 1930s to reach thousands of rural blacks in more than fifty counties. As the number of staff members and the bureaucratic structure increased, district agents extended their public appearances to counties that did not have year-round agents. Hunter grouped between six and fourteen counties together, identified a central point to meet, and presented information on various subjects to the regional gathering. Interested individuals then returned to their counties and organized community clubs to further the work. This gave women opportunities to tailor the advice to their local situation and the responsibility of organizing and conducting the work. Organizing counties into districts and assigning agents to work with the agents and county councils facilitated training and increased communication and information sharing. It also increased the bureaucracy. District agents and state leaders used the monthly staff conference meetings to share information, discuss plans for major events both inside and outside the Extension Service, and strategize ways to expand their work. These meetings occurred without influence by white peers or supervisors or even black agents in the field. Agents organized state meetings during the 1920s as well, another development that facilitated communication between agents about the challenges they and their constituents faced and brainstorming about solutions. Farm families did not participate in these professional gatherings. Thus, as the Negro Division created bureaucratic structure to ensure some degree of consistency in its programs, it sometimes distanced itself from the constituents it served (Tables 7 and 8).[69]

The independence that rural blacks exercised through club work existed partially because of forced segregation. TAEX officials cordoned black agents off into the separate Negro Division, which removed them physically from TAEX headquarters in College Station. But black agents turned their marginalization into a platform that facilitated community development as well as self-development. Extension work helped rural men, women, and children learn how they could outmaneuver limitations imposed by economics. Diversified farming, often called "safe" farming, helped some families gain authority over their economic conditions.

Through community councils, black agents engaged their constituents in politicized activity as well. Children and adults found opportunities to elect officers, run meetings, and lobby for special projects, activities in which they

TABLE 7. Texas Negro District Agricultural Agents

Agent	Headquarters	Tenure
Jacob H. Ford	Wharton	Aug. 15, 1915–June 12, 1922*
A. J. Wood	Rusk	Oct. 1, 1916–July 30, 1920
Henry S. Estelle	Brenham	Aug. 1, 1920–June 30, 1924
	Waco	July 1, 1924–Aug. 31, 1935
	Prairie View	Sep. 1, 1935–Dec. 31, 1954†
Robert H. Hines	Waco	Oct. 1, 1921–June 30, 1924
[*McLennan County agent, 1919–21*]	Fort Worth	July 1, 1924–June 30, 1935
John H. Williams	Cameron (assistant)	July 1, 1934–Aug. 31, 1935
[*Milam County agent, 1925–32*]§	Prairie View (confirmed as district agent)	Sep. 1, 1935–Aug. 19, 1937
[*Austin County agent, 1937–43*]**	Prairie View	Aug. 20, 1937–Mar. 15, 1943
[*Travis County agent, 1944–45*]		
William Cullen David	Prairie View	Mar. 16, 1943–Dec. 31, 1944
[*Madison County agent, 1934–43*]		
[*Acting, assistant, and state leader, 1945–59*]		
W. H. Phillips	Prairie View	July 1, 1943–Aug. 31, 1947
[*Marion County agent, ??–1925*]		
[*Navarro County agent, 1925–31*]		
[*Milam County agent, 1932–39*]		
[*Navarro County agent, 1941–43*]		
Thomas A. Mayes	Prairie View (acting)	July 16, 1944–Feb. 28, 1945
[*Travis County agent, 1945–70*]		
John E. Mayo	Prairie View (acting)	Mar. 1, 1945–Dec. 31, 1952†
[*Lavaca County agent, 1924–28*]	(confirmed as district agent)	May 1, 1947–Dec. 31, 1952†
[*Guadalupe County agent, 1928–32*]		

(*continued*)

TABLE 7. *(continued)*

Agent	Headquarters	Tenure
[*Lavaca County agent, 1932–45*]		
John Vinson Smith	Prairie View (acting)	Sep. 1, 1947–June 30, 1948
[*McLennan County agent, 1921–44*]	(confirmed as district agent)	July 1, 1948–Aug. 31, 1955 †
[*Emergency food, labor assistant [1944–??*]		
William Benjamin Clark Jr.	Prairie View	Jan. 20, 1955–Feb. 28, 1973 † ††
[*Freestone County agent, 1936–40*]		
[*Falls County agent, 1940–47*]		
[*Wharton County agent, 1947–55*]		
Ruben A. Sanders	Prairie View	Sep. 16, 1955–Aug. 31, 19?? ††
[*Brazos County agent, 1938–42*]		
[*Guadalupe County agent, 1942–55*]		

Source: Seastrunk, "Fifty Years of Negro Extension Work in Texas, 1915–1965," TAEX Historical Files.
*Died in office
†Retired
††Title changed to area program specialist on July 1, 1965, as a result of the elimination of the dual extension organization as mandated by the Civil Rights Act of 1964. Clark remained at Prairie View. Sanders was assigned an office at Overton.
§Discrepancies exist between dates of transfer recorded in TAEX personnel records and dates on tables compiled by Seastrunk.
**This conflicts with service as "confirmed" district agent as noted by Seastrunk. It appears that Williams was confirmed as district agent but continued to serve as Austin County agent.

generally could not engage. When Mary Hunter created a state organization for county girls' clubs in 1925, she created opportunities for girls that had previously not existed. The president traveled to the State Teachers' Association conference in Dallas and presented a paper on club work to fifteen hundred teachers. By 1927, officers of county women's and girls' clubs had united in a state organization. The federation provided club members more experience in organizing, influence over extension programs beyond the local context,

TABLE 8. Texas Negro District Home Demonstration Agents

Agent	Location	Tenure
Pinkie Rambo	Prairie View	Oct. 12, 1916–[??], 1918
Mrs. Iola W. Rowan	Prairie View (acting)	Jan. 1–June 30, 1931
[*Nacogdoches County home demonstration agent (1927–30)*]	(Confirmed as district agent)	Sep. 16, 1931–Oct. 8, 1942
	(Supervisor/district agent)	Feb. 1, 1943–Sep. 28, 1946
Mrs. Jeffie Obrea	Waco	Oct. 1, 1932–Aug. 31, 1935
Allen Conner	Prairie View	Sept. 1, 1935–Oct. 31, 1949
[*McLennan County home demonstration agent, 1922–32*]		
Mrs. Pauline Rosalind Mason Brown	Prairie View	Feb. 1, 1943–Oct. 1, 1946
[*Gregg County home demonstration agent, 1933–42*]		
Myrtle Elwyn Garrett	Prairie View	Dec. 1, 1946–June 30, 1965
[*Falls County home demonstration agent, 1943–46*]		
Mrs. Ezelle M. Gregory	Prairie View	Dec. 1, 1949–Dec. 31, 1952

Source: Seastrunk, "Fifty Years of Negro Extension Work in Texas, 1915–1965," TAEX Historical Files.

and access to other government services. Yet, such efforts did not change the racist system that trapped African Americans in second-class citizenship.[70]

African American extension agents likewise worked diligently to improve their position relative to that of other black professionals. They worked in a service that required training in specialized areas related to agricultural science or home economics. They considered themselves part of an elite corps of several hundred individuals employed full time in salaried positions with titles. Their affiliation with the land-grant institutions elevated their status as informal educators. Rural Americans knew what people meant when they talked about the county agricultural agent or the home demonstration agent. Competition existed for the positions, and training did not guarantee placement. Once agents gained appointments, they had to participate in seminars regularly to remain competent in their field. As in any profession, the abilities of each individual varied, but the extension employees considered themselves experts, and they cooperated with Prairie View A&M to professionalize.[71]

Despite the successes negro agents and supervisors reported, they found themselves ultimately beholden to white power structures and frustrated at the limitations that legalized discrimination sanctioned. Ironically, segregation fostered interaction between white and black agents and supervisors, so each group could maintain its reform agenda. Negro Division staff depended on the strong community programs they built to maintain their strategic position within the biracial bureaucracy, but they had to regularly engage in interracial strategizing to preserve the Negro Division programs.

4

Public Reform in Black and White

The Maturation of a Segregated Division

As field workers, black agents were responsible for imparting scientific information to rural farm families and instructing their constituents in ways to improve their health, living conditions, farming practices, economic situations, and educational opportunities. As government employees, they were required to identify and solicit constituents, document progress, raise funds and maintain supporters, publicize events, and keep themselves informed and up to date through their own professional development. They also had to help plan future programs. They had to do all of this while negotiating the segregated South. Their responsibilities as government employees and state bureaucrats made them particularly conscious of the power structure that imposed segregation. Through their work they realized the significance of segregation because, while it allowed them authority within rural communities—authority denied them before the TAEX segregated its services—it also reinforced their separate and unequal status as citizens. Whites denied blacks equal standing but expected them to help Texas become part of the modern South. The agents received less pay but had to perform at the same level expected of white employees. They received less financial support and had to answer to white supervisors at all levels. Yet, they exerted some influence on white decisions, and this influence helped the segregated division become a stable feature of state government.

White bureaucrats at the national level carefully documented the development and significance of Negro extension programs. Three times between 1921 and 1926 the FES published circulars that indicated how rapidly the segregated division grew and how popular the programs were in most parts of the South, thus justifying segregationist decisions. The preface to the first treatise, *Extension Work among Negroes, 1920,* identifies four characteristics of employees that fit the accommodationist trope to which whites clung: "These Negro agents for the most part are well trained, have the right viewpoint, are earnest and conscientious workers, and are rendering valuable service." Valuable service entailed spreading "proper ideals" and improving rural conditions.[1]

A series of meetings in 1920, one of which occurred in Prairie View, Texas, and the others at Hampton Institute, Virginia, and Tuskegee Institute, Alabama, outlined a six-part platform for Negro extension agents to pursue. The six points mirrored goals Robert L. Smith had articulated thirty years before for his all-black FIS. The Negro Division goals, filtered through white authors, focused on (1) doing away with the mortgage system, (2) raising all food and feed, (3) owning and improving homes and farm equipment, (4) facilitating communication between farmers through meetings, fairs, and the like, (5) generating a more productive work ethic, and (6) focusing energies on building schools and churches and employing professionals to operate them. Blacks engaged in such reform would secure "comfort and independence, clean living, and useful citizenship." Whites looked for the "right kind of Negro leaders" to undertake the work, specifically, those with "judgment and discretion."[2]

In 1925, recognizing the twentieth anniversary of Thomas Campbell's employment as the first Negro extension agent in Alabama, the USDA published another circular, *Extension Work among Negroes, Conducted by Negro Agents, 1923*. The introductory remarks conclude: "The work of negro extension agents is of special significance and promises to be a possible means for the solution of some of the economic and other problems arising through the presences of negroes in such large numbers on southern farms." The author of the third circular, which appeared in 1926, recounted that agents' efforts to reach negro farmers and their families and to influence them to adopt better farm practices, to help them to increase their earning capacity, and to improve their living conditions; and also to interest negro boys and girls in farm activities, and to train them in the use of improved methods in farming and home making.[3]

While each author distinguished goals that differed subtly, black agents obviously focused on financial security. The third circular carries the subtitle *Land Ownership and Home Improvement Are Vital in Developing Negro Farm Life in the South*. It emphasizes economic lessons: "Energetic negroes soon learn thrift and have the ability to become good demonstrators." But the objective summations of black goals give way to racist sentiments tempered with respect for black accomplishments: "It is not surprising that it has taken a backward race a long time to acquire property and develop farms. It takes white agricultural college graduates quite a while to do that." The author, Oscar Baker Martin, directed the TAEX between 1928 and 1935 and believed that recognition from "leading white citizens" mattered to black demonstrators. Certainly white recognition mattered, but not because blacks craved it, as Martin implies. Rather, by 1926, segregation had demarcated race relations within the TAEX. Staff members understood the respective responsibilities for program delivery, fund-raising, and official reporting. White recognition of black agents mattered because whites held ultimate decision-making authority; but blacks exercised considerable autonomy in the service and affected white opinion in numerous ways.[4]

The TAEX let its authority over black agents be known during the hiring process. Agents could not work in counties until the counties "qualified" to host a black agent. Residents either had to express interest or Negro Division staff had to request a placement. A carefully scripted sequence of events ensured race protocol but supported black initiative nonetheless. After blacks in a given county expressed interest in extension programs, a Negro district agent and the Negro state leader visited the county to determine whether an agent was warranted and what level of support a county could provide. Calvin Waller, appointed director of the Negro Division in 1920, was familiar with the budget and funds available for his dispersal at the beginning of each fiscal year, and he and his staff prioritized counties needing agents and made their recommendations to the TAEX director. TAEX administrators assessed current expenditures and either accepted or rejected the county's request. Counties had to allocate only $300 toward black agents' salaries; not until 1937 did black administrators ask for at least $400. Even this small amount often created contention, and placements were delayed until funds became available. Black and white staff regularly communicated about needs and interest to make the process go as smoothly as possible. The interaction affected funding and resource allocations, but decisions always rested with TAEX administrators.[5]

In 1920, Waller publicly thanked white funding sources for their support, even though amounts provided black agents did not match amounts provided whites. He noted that commissioners' courts were the "main stay in establishing the work in various counties and in most cases they have given what their budget allowed in the furtherance of Negro work." In 1921, he reported that county commissioners, "though handicapped by the most critical conditions seen for some time," were "liberal in helping to keep the Negro work alive in many counties in Texas." Several courts approved the allocations without having to be approached, and others offered promises of support. He emphasized that "in no instance have Negro agents been told that the service was not needed or wanted in the county."[6]

Waller, however, publicly criticized the shortsightedness of some courts when the opportunity arose. He believed that the "peculiar misunderstanding that most Commissioners' Court[s] have, especially in counties where no negro agent has worked before" made fund-raising a challenge that demanded "courage, tact, and earnestness." He projected financial and social gains to convince counties not interested in participating. He believed the reward warranted the effort and expense because of the "inspiration that would be carried to this group of citizens actually on the land farming for a living."[7]

Placing and retaining agents posed a constant challenge. Limited funds often forced counties to choose between hiring a male or a female agent. Agents who worked in counties that employed only one did double duty. Counties justified hiring only a farm or home demonstration agent in various ways. Sometimes, not enough African American farmers lived in a county to warrant employment of two. In these counties, white agents continued working with black farmers, but they tended to serve only those who requested programs. This left black farmers underserved, but Negro Division staff lobbied on their behalf if the interest warranted it.

Once black agents received funding, counties expected them to show a steady increase in the number of residents served. Chambers of commerce throughout East Texas helped African American agents identify areas in need. Chamber members introduced the agent, often a stranger to the community, and helped establish the work by talking directly with interested residents. Such support came with the expectation that the Negro Division staff would improve conditions.[8]

Inadequate funding further challenged Negro Division staff. Matching funds provided by local partners indicated the race and gender biases that pervaded the service and the degree of discrimination that existed. During the early 1920s, the white male agent in McLennan County earned $3,200 while the black male agent earned $1,500 annually. The white home demonstration agent in McLennan County earned $2,190 annually while the black female agent earned $1,200. White agents regularly received other benefits such as expense accounts of $300 or more each year that defrayed costs they incurred in conducting their work. Some even received salary increases regularly. Black agents did not receive comparable benefits. By 1930, the county salary for the white male agent increased to $4,200 annually while the black male's decreased to $1,434; the white female's salary increased to

$3,000, and the black female's remained stagnant at $1,200. Length of service affected averages only negligibly. Thus, black women earned 40 percent of what white women earned, and black men earned 34.1 percent of what white men earned. Furthermore, black women earned 83.6 percent of the amount black men earned. These percentages varied slightly from county to county, but black agents rarely earned even half of what the white agents earned, and black women earned almost as much as black men. This reflected the ongoing attempts by white men to emasculate black men by paying them an amount nearly equal to that of black women, and it indicates that race more than gender determined salary.[9]

In the TAEX, women earned less and had fewer permanent positions open to them, but the structure that the Negro Division staff devised to support their profession provided women with opportunities for influence. African American home demonstration agents realized that they received inadequate pay, but most accepted it because they believed in the service. Vera Dial, the first home demonstration agent in Austin County, contended that agents had "the opportunity to serve humanity in a very educational and inspirational way [and the ability] to meet personally the men and women whose ideas and suggestions have made the Agricultural field an occupation that all men are proud of." Some valued the visibility associated with the appointment: "It gives an individual prestige and influence that no other profession can give."[10]

TAEX director Thomas Walton told federal inspectors in 1922 that "the return from funds invested in Negro Women workers is perhaps as great or greater than any of the other Extension projects." In 1924, Mary Hunter, the state leader for Negro home demonstration agents, indicated why TAEX officials believed her and her agents' service had proved so valuable to the state: "Not one of our club members have moved from our State during the ten years we have had the benefit of Extension Service. Home improvement has played an important part in satisfying our farmers." She continued: "As a whole our people are better satisfied with rural conditions than ever before." During the early to mid-1920s, white Texans needed labor to grow cotton. They advocated keeping African Americans on the land. Mrs. Hunter, in turn, worked with landowning black farmers predominantly, and with those in established rural communities who shared the goal of staying on the land. The outcome pleased whites and blacks alike.[11]

Shared goals motivated whites to advocate employment of black agents. Several citizens in Waco subscribed the sum of $275 to help pay the salary of the "colored assistant county agricultural agent," and the county commissioners appropriated $225 more in 1918. The agent began in February 1919. The Chamber of Commerce provided $300 in 1919, and the Commissioners' Court matched this to continue "work among the colored people." This amount was divided between the agricultural and the home demonstration agent working in the county. The new agricultural agent, Robert H. Hines, reported that the Waco Chamber of Agriculture, a select group of farmers, bankers, and businessmen, also supported his work. When commissioners in Colorado County appropriated $300 out of funds secured by public subscription to pay part of the black home demonstration agent's salary, newspapers declared that the county took "her place in the list of progressive and forward-looking counties." Ben H. Davis spent more than a year convincing "his white friends" in Colorado County to subscribe about $100. He supplemented this with help from the Weimar Chamber of Commerce and Garwood businessmen, collecting a total of $240. The Commissioners' Court provided the remaining $60. The next year, the court appropriated $300 to cover the black home demonstration agent's salary but expected donations to cover the remainder of the black farm agent's salary. When this source seemed uncertain, the court appropriated payment out of the general fund.[12]

Interested citizens pressured Commissioners' Courts to fund positions. Tax-paying black farmers lobbied on agents' behalf, circulating petitions to pressure county commissioners to release funds to help cover agents' salaries. In 1919, W. A. Yates represented the interests of Lea Etta Lusk, the black home demonstration agent in Washington County, before the county commissioners. They deferred allotting the funds necessary to make her temporary position into a regular appointment at that time, but in 1920, they authorized $200 to support "demonstration work among the colored people." The court reviewed the agents' work in 1921 and decided to continue the appropriation for another year, based on "recommendations from a number of citizens." A representative committee of white and black citizens requested that the Gregg County commissioners fund a black home demonstration agent in 1933. The commissioners unanimously approved the request and appropriated $300 for a year of service, plus $120 to cover the rent for an office and the purchase of a typewriter. The next year, the commissioners allotted $60 to buy a cooker with attachments and directed the county judge to make the purchase for the Elderville Community, a black community in the county. Citizens in Kaufman County petitioned their commissioners in 1938 to secure the services of a black county agent. The Terrell Chamber of Commerce supported the request, noting that "we have over 11,000 Negroes that should receive all the attention it is possible for us to give them if we intend to maintain our present social standards." The court authorized $425 a year for the work but secured the services of a home demonstration agent only.[13]

Some counties became creative in how they met their allotment. In Smith County, commissioners agreed to provide $12.50 each month, $150.00 a year, for a "Negro demonstrator" if the Chamber of Commerce matched the amount. Others provided more than required. Harrison County appropriated $520.00 for a black male agent and another $540.00 for a black female agent. Such support from county commissioners was unprecedented, but Harrison and neighboring Marion County had the highest percentage of black residents and the highest percentage of black farm owners in the state. This meant that significant amounts of the tax money that Commissioners' Courts appropriated came from black farmers, and the commissioners accepted their influence in distributing the funds. Such grassroots support, however, seldom resulted in equitable pay.[14]

Even with the support provided by commissioners, several counties with a significant black population failed to provide funding to employ agents. Counties such as Austin, Burleson, Falls, Fort Bend, Polk, Robertson, Walker, and Wharton used emergency appropriations to host agents during the Great War, and in some instances local support continued into the 1920s. But many counties failed to sustain financial support until New Deal programs provided incentives during 1933. Commissioners in Walker County authorized $165 for part of the salary of a black home demonstration agent in 1919, but the agent did not continue in the position. Commissioners did not provide funding for agents again until 1934, but they exceeded the requirement, appropriating $600 for a black farm agent and $300 more for a black home demonstration agent.[15]

Obviously, black agents struggled to secure adequate resources, and this put them at a disadvantage. They had trouble getting reports from their club members, because rural families often did not have the means to keep records, and neither did the agents. Negro county agents and Negro home demonstration agents rarely had offices or office equipment to facilitate the detailed reporting expected of them. Once agents received the blank report forms, they used their own typewriters to complete the reports. Inadequate office space remained an issue as late as 1932, when district agent Henry Estelle reported on the success of a campaign to provide offices for agents. At that time, only two of forty-seven agents had offices. By 1936, at least thirty-one offices were available for Negro Division agents (Fig. 17).[16]

Home demonstration agents noted several administrative challenges, including inadequate finances and lack of equipment to help them do their

Figure 17. Office of J. V. Smith and Miss Ruby O. Phelps, McLennan County, Tex., April 1933. Opened in Sep. 1932, the office made the agents more accessible. Henderson Deckard, cotton demonstrator (left), Smith (center), and William Johnson, cotton and small grain demonstrator (right), are completing paperwork. The agents provided the office space, furniture, fixtures, equipment, and demonstration material, among other things. (Neg. S-16845-C, George W. Ackerman, photographer, FES, USDA, NA)

jobs. Most managed, however, because only two of the few who resigned listed job frustration as the reason. One agent reported that she resigned when the county failed to pay her salary, and another resigned because she could not stand the travel. Others resigned because they married or started teaching, not because they could not function with limited resources. Negro Division administrators believed that few barriers were insurmountable, and with such incentive, most agents learned to make the best of the inadequacies. Black reformers reflected a long tradition of working with limited resources and remaining mute about the disadvantages lest they indicate weakness. Such attitudes helped perpetuate the unequal system.[17]

Negro Division staff accepted inadequate salaries and expended personal funds to further their programs without hope of reimbursement. Pay inequities became worse over time because performance expectations increased despite stagnant salaries. The TAEX maintained professional standards, and legislators increased those expectations through the appropriation bill for 1919–21. That bill limited employment to trained agents with a higher education earned at a state school. It carried a rider that required all applicants to pass an examination. This made it more difficult for interested but untrained African Americans to become agents. It also motivated black professionals to raise performance standards without any hope of recompense. And it supported Prairie View A&M as a training ground for future TAEX employees. Extension leaders considered themselves "fortunate" when they hired trained workers who had received their education from Prairie View A&M. In 1921, all but two of the fourteen home demonstration agents in the state had attended the land-grant school. The two who had not graduated had still received special training at the school prior to their employment as agents. Numerous other training venues existed in black land-grant institutions across the South; graduates moved to Texas for work. By 1935, a survey of Negro home demonstration agents in Texas indicated that fewer than half of those employed (47.5 percent) held degrees from Prairie View A&M. Black agents understood the merits of professionalization, but they undertook it without the financial incentives whites received and professionals deserved.[18]

Agents tolerated inadequate pay in relation to job expectations because they gained great satisfaction from "helping people that need it." Many considered it their "life's profession." Thus, Negro Division agents tended to hold on to their positions until retirement. They knew, however, that a life of service would not result in leisure during old age. As Marjorie Bledsoe, an experienced home demonstration agent, reported: "To be in the Service for the amassing of wealth will cause one to be disappointed. The expenses connected with the work will not allow one to lay by competency for Old Age." She suggested that if agents could retire at age sixty-five instead of age seventy, they could have "a few years to enjoy a leisure life."[19]

Blacks had little influence over state appropriations that established pay scales or professional criteria, but they bore responsibility for securing funding. As Negro Division staff assumed regular duties during the 1920s, black agents had to generate matching funds from county courts. Commissioners sometimes invited agents to meetings to explain the work, but agents did not always wait for an invitation. If white friends intimated that commissioners in a county might listen favorably to a presentation on black extension work, Negro district agents or the state leader visited the Commissioners' Court. The first visit might not result in an appropriation, but the effort continued until commissioners authorized the expenditure. Mary Hunter described the strategy she developed in 1928 to cultivate interest among individuals and groups responsible for local funds. Home demonstration agents planned a "Good Will Tour" during which local agents met with members of the Chamber of Commerce or the county commissioners to acquaint them with the merits of present work and plans for future undertakings. Agents then asked the local authorities for suggestions on making the plans better, thereby ensuring that financiers bought into the program in two ways. The first attempt met with such success that the Chamber of Commerce in Nacogdoches County asked the local agents to return the next year. In 1929, black agents spoke to more than six hundred people gathered at the annual Chamber of Commerce banquet.[20]

Hunter and other district agents sought diversified funding to protect black agents from the vagaries of individual supporters. They solicited businessmen, Chambers of Commerce, and other localized special-interest groups to partially match federal appropriations for black agents' salaries. This involved contacting white and black leaders and meeting with them regularly to report on activities and solicit feedback on agent performance. Sometimes Negro Division district agents advised county agents to stay away from certain individuals or organizations intent on making trouble. For example, Calvin Waller, division head, discouraged African Americans in Texas from affiliating with the Farm Bureau because he believed blacks who joined subjected themselves to undue criticism from white bureau members. Black agents also encouraged farmers to participate in commodity-marketing associations when white leaders offered black members an equal vote, and to avoid those that did not extend equal treatment. Obviously, despite racial stratification, black agents affected decision making.[21]

Agents also benefited from largesse distributed by private foundations. The John F. Slater Fund supported six county training schools in Texas in 1919–20 and twenty-seven by 1928–29. Several of these schools maintained shops to teach vocational skills, and many supported farming projects on school acreage. General Education Board funding supported purchases of industrial equipment and other resources necessary to transform schools into "rural industrial high schools, meeting the needs of the rural communities in which they were located." The course work in home economics, agriculture, and farm shop prepared graduates for jobs as teachers in rural schools, for college course work, and for farm work. The GEB also funded summer schools for teachers at Wiley College and at Prairie View A&M. Extension agents regularly participated as instructors in these summer institutes, taking the opportunity to reach more teachers with their message. This training helped prepare a more enlightened corps of teachers to work with rural Texas youth and, in turn, the extension program itself benefited.[22]

Negro Division staff held active or honorary memberships in several all-black and interracial service organizations as a way to "sell" the work to the public at large. Memberships also fostered communication between like-minded progressive reformers, including ministers, educators, vocational education workers, women's club members, and business leaders, white as well as black. Robert Lloyd Smith and Mary Hunter both sat on the Texas Interracial Commission. Hunter participated in the State Teachers' Association, the National Teachers' Association, and the Federation of Women's Clubs. Waller held honorary memberships in "all of the church organizations" as well as the Negro Medical Association of Texas, the Elks lodge, the UBF [United Brothers of Fellowship], Odd Fellows, Knights of Pythias, and "all other Negro lodges." In this way, he believed that he could "get a hearing and 'sell' the work" by demonstrating the work "on the floor of the assembly." Waller also expected one of the supervisory staff to attend "any meeting of consequence" in Texas.[23]

Such diversified support often generated small donations that made huge differences in Negro Division programs. In 1925, merchants, bankers, and Chambers of Commerce across East Texas provided settings of eggs for poultry club girls. The eggs went to no more than two girls in each of the twelve communities in any given county. Acquiring such support required a well-orchestrated strategy. Mrs. Hunter regularly undertook these types of projects in her job as the home demonstration supervisor.[24]

Henry S. Estelle nurtured diverse contacts in counties throughout the state during his thirty-three-year tenure as a Negro District agent. He met with county officials regularly, solicited support from white residents when needed, and engaged in covert maneuvers to further extension goals. He encouraged Chambers of Commerce to help pay the salaries of secretaries and provide office space. The close contact Estelle maintained with the Chamber of Commerce in Smith County helped convince commissioners to allot funds for both a farm and a home demonstration agent and to promise use of an office. Estelle's tactics, however, did not always generate support. In June 1934, when he did not receive permission from white administrators to travel to Milam County, Negro Division staff planned to visit the county secretly.[25]

Estelle pressed for additional compensation as well. He worked to get raises for agents in Harrison, Gregg, Rusk, and Walker counties in 1934. If the county provided an increase, the black state leader could then ask for an increase in state and federal allotments. The constant effort to generate and maintain support consumed 50 to 75 percent of Estelle's time, but his advocacy for adequate support for Negro Division staff did not flag.[26]

Despite superiors' prejudices, Estelle continued to chip away at inequity. In November 1934, he talked with Seth Toney, agent in Guadalupe County, about prejudice in the service. Estelle reported that "Toney [was] under the impression that his white agent is prejudiced toward his work as is Mr. Williamson toward Negro work generally." H. H. Williamson had served the TAEX since 1912, working as vice-director, then white state leader between 1928 and 1935, and, finally, as director from 1935 through 1944. Then he became assistant director of the Federal Extension Service in Washington, DC. Williamson's resistance to black involvement in TAEX programs during the 1910s perpetuated segregation, and his racist attitudes changed little throughout his tenure.[27]

In 1945, Estelle and Edward B. Evans, Prairie View A&M principal, took it upon themselves to ask for resources for competitions involving African American participants in the Houston Fat Stock Show and for ninety passes to the show. Changes in TAEX leadership may have motivated them. Dr. Ide P. Trotter had succeeded Williamson as TAEX director, but new leaders reminded Negro Division staff of race protocol. James D. Prewit, Williamson's successor as vice-director and state agent of TAEX, wrote Trotter that Evans and Estelle "were overstepping their bounds." Previously, white TAEX staff had made all contacts with stock show officials, and Prewit believed "that relationships [would] be strained" if black extension agents took it upon themselves to make contacts. "The Negroes have made considerable progress this year in securing classes at both Houston and Ft. Worth. This should not be rushed too much." Thus, Prewit informed Trotter of the status quo and reminded black administrators not to take advantage of opportunities. The reminder, however, did not quiet Estelle's steady assertion of the need for adequate resources and opportunities for black agents and their constituents. Nor did it negatively affect Evans's status as principal of Prairie View A&M or his influence on the Conference of Presidents of Negro Land-Grant Colleges, where Negro Division advocates discussed issues related to black status.[28]

Fund-raising consumed considerable amounts of time that black agents, district agents, and even the Negro Division state leader could therefore not expend on other reform activities. Federal officials noted the public relations efforts that such fund-raising initiatives required, but they criticized rather than praised blacks for spending too much time on activities "outside of

Extension." Calvin Waller, Negro state leader, responded to the white inspectors defensively, noting that Texas had "the most complete set-up" of all the segregated divisions in the southern states. This had resulted, Waller believed, from constant interaction with residents in counties with an extension agent, as well as counties without one. He itemized the factors that made a successful county: "a live-wire Chamber of Commerce, a sympathetic Commissioners Court, an active Rotary Club or Lion's Club, with all of them working for the best interest of the county." In such a situation, an agent needed little help and could make a successful showing. The agents and farmers in counties that most needed help were those with "an unsympathetic Court, a passive Chamber of Commerce or a group of farmers, the majority of whom [were] tenants or renters." This, Waller argued, accounted for the time he and the district agents spent in counties with no agent or on work "outside" of extension.[29]

The struggle to secure salaries represented only a part of the constant effort to secure funds. Agents themselves bore the responsibility for offsetting expenses not covered by the county appropriation. Once an agent began work in a county, she or he collected dues and donations from special interest groups and individuals to cover program expenses and trips. On occasion, civic organizations such as the Kiwanis, the Lions, or the Rotary Club helped black agents. Their contributions depended on contacts made by agents and the support of influential members.

Both white and black Chambers of Commerce supported extension programming, especially when economic boosterism played a role in the plan. In 1921, a chamber cooperated with county agents to purchase a train carload of Holstein cows for distribution to deserving farmers. Part of the plan involved the development of a local creamery. Farmers agreed to ship their milk to the creamery, and the payment for the cow would come from the butter fat produced and processed each month. Farmers agreed to breed their cows to purebred stock and to shelter and feed them according to the extension agent's directions. Thus, the chamber supported local development and the perpetuation of extension programming.[30]

Blacks also created their own organizations to provide financial and moral support. African American boosters had organized fairs for black Texans since the 1880s, and agents supported the organization and operation of fair associations that awarded premiums to farmers and their families. The financial incentive helped convince youth and adults to enter their poultry, pigs, and rehabilitated clothing in competitions, but the influence extended beyond money. The competition gave farm families a reason to improve methods of tillage, cultivation, and harvesting, and to introduce purebred stock. This made the Negro agent's job easier at the same time as it increased production and furthered the extension cause of self-sufficiency. The fairs showcased accomplishments, and in doing so, they placated white sponsors' expectations that county funding would reap financial returns for the county.[31]

Limited resources expended for black extension work meant that funding came in small amounts. Not until 1937 did a group of interested citizens organize the Texas Negro Farmers' Council of Agriculture to fund significant expenses. Extension director H. H. Williamson gave Calvin Waller permission to form the council. Henry Estelle served as the liaison between the Extension Service and the nonprofit organization. The council existed for "the encouragement of agriculture and horticulture and the maintenance of public fairs and exhibitions of livestock and farm products throughout the state of Texas." It gave prizes to boys and men who participated in fairs and exhibitions and financed other activities as the board of directors recommended. Isaac Philpot served as president. It began with only $400 in the bank in Hempstead. Over the years, the council helped farmers attend regional Agriculture Adjustment Administration (AAA) meetings, paid costs associated with transporting 4-H Club boys and agents to and from radio stations, purchased government bonds during World War II, and even considered raising funds to construct a 4-H camp.[32]

Both white and black staff spent considerable energy on cultivating the right attitude among colleagues. In the mid-1920s, Oscar Baker Martin, who directed the Southern States Office of Cooperative Extension Work at the time, and then directed the TAEX until his death in 1935, indicated that "there is no field of education . . . where greater good can be accomplished by earnest, devoted agents working along the right lines." Negro Division leader Calvin Waller did much to cultivate "right line" thinking. Federal inspectors praised supervisory staff in Texas, indicating that they were "well trained negroes with the right point of view with reference to the relationship of races and to the type of education that their people should have." Waller went as far as to publish in two annual reports a philosophy that emphasized a subordinate place for blacks. He wrote that agents did "not educate their people to ideals beyond their grasp but encourage[d] and guide[d] a wholesome and homely development step by step. They render an incentive to their people for effort and perseverance at tasks which otherwise they would be unlikely to attempt."[33]

Waller articulated a stance that soothed paternalistic, racist whites who wanted their opinions about black subordination reinforced. Black supervisors were well aware of the need to express such appreciation to white supporters. Martin had indicated that "Negroes are very susceptible to commendation and praise," but, in fact, blacks used commendation and praise as moral suasion to secure and retain white support. Waller credited white district, agricultural, and home demonstration agents, and even the TAEX director, with keeping black staff informed of white sentiments toward the work. This information helped black administrators make more efficient use of their time in qualifying counties. This was part of a sustained effort to express what whites wanted to hear but then work within fairly isolated black enclaves to effect change.[34]

Protocol nonetheless affected relations in the field. Black agents found that white agents sometimes had resources and expertise that could help them do their jobs more efficiently and reach more farm families. They asked white agents to judge shows for them, help with terracing or drainage demonstrations, speak at short courses and other community meetings, or assist in project planning. Most but not all white agents took time to help.[35]

Black agents also worked with white farmers on occasion. They could not assume a white farmer wanted advice, however. Instead, the white farmer had to ask for the help, and only then could the black agent provide assistance. In 1921, the agent in Cherokee County helped white farmers terrace several acres so they could participate in Federal Farm Loan Bank programs. Also, the agent in Washington County helped white farmers build two kilns to store potatoes. At least four counties in 1920–21 employed only a black home demonstration agent. In these counties, if white farm families wanted to participate in extension programs, they had to interact with blacks. Black agents and white farmers rarely engaged in this interchange, however, because it required a role reversal that challenged traditional race relations and the foundation of the segregated bureaucracy.[36]

In general, if black agents did not breach the accepted boundaries of race relations, they retained their positions until they retired or chose to leave. Sometimes, agents in a county failed to comply with supervisor requests, ignored regulations, or overstepped race protocol. Supervisors held employees accountable for their actions, but the punishments varied significantly, ranging from mild admonition to firing. Waller instructed an outspoken agent in Houston County, John Wesley Hogg, that he should not criticize white public officials in official extension correspondence. Hogg had called the county judge a "rascal" because he had failed to turn over $150 to the county treasury, money which Hogg had raised the previous year. Waller advised him to "please hold the body of your letters strictly to business and in this way we will keep out of trouble." Waller traveled to Houston County in 1925 to explore the relationship of the county's new agriculture agent, H. C. Langrum, and the home demonstration agent, Annie G. H. Hall. His visit included a thorough inspection of Langrum's work, because he had passed "the experimental stage," and Waller intended to "keep on the force only such person[s] as were actually suited to the work." Hall left the service the next year, but Langrum served as the agricultural agent in Houston County until 1933. In 1937, Waller notified Williamson of the termination of two agents for inappropriate use of funds. Both agents assured Waller that the mistakes arose from bad record-keeping. They wrote the extension director personally explaining their mistakes and got their jobs back. Waller's rapid actions in all instances left little doubt in the minds of agents in the field: he did not tolerate behavior that jeopardized the complex patronage networks on which the Negro Division depended.[37]

Waller maintained strict discipline at all levels. When personality clashes and pressures on the job created unrest among the staff, Waller "urged unity of thought and effort in Extension Organization for good of Service." He issued oral warnings to supervisors to stop bickering and gossiping about extension business and to "avoid giving out 'inside information.'" Such information could jeopardize Negro Division goals.[38]

The frenetic pace that Negro Division staff maintained could exhaust agents and negatively affect their employment. During July 1923, for example, R. H. Hines worked twenty-seven of the thirty-one days, taking only four of the five Sundays off. He spent six days in the office and twenty-one days in the field, visited two counties without agents—Anderson and Houston—and provided general assistance to demonstrators. He qualified Montgomery County for a home demonstration agent and observed the "general progress of work" in Cherokee, Gregg, Marion, Harrison, Panola, and Dallas counties. All required his interaction with white governing bodies and funding sources as well as black constituents, many of whom had different opinions about how to conduct the work and how to relate to white Texans. The county visits occurred over a ten-day period in the middle of the month, and he traveled 450 miles in a car and 871 miles on the train to accomplish the task. Other district agents logged as many miles in any given month. Waller cautioned them to "refrain from working 'over time' and by all means avoid night driving." He stressed that "it is impossible to do ALL the work." He continued: "We want work done but not at the expense of the agents' health."[39]

New Deal–era projects increased responsibilities even more, and Waller sought greater efficiency in agent work habits. He expected them to do what they could in a timely manner, but he demanded punctuality. In 1937, he reminded the district agents that they "must do *all* phases of work satisfactorily." Someone must have missed a report deadline, because he emphasized that he would accept "no more late reports—especially ANNUAL." Professions could not be built on inefficiency.[40]

Negro Division staff accumulated copious data documenting visible signs of progress to satisfy diverse funding sources and special-interest groups, both white and black. Agents tended to accentuate the positive and concentrated on "lasting evidence" of their programming in a community. Waller believed that this "salesmanship . . . proved to be an excellent policy." The trees planted, yards beautified, outhouses constructed, windows screened, purebred pigs introduced, and canning houses constructed served as lasting reminders of Negro Division influence.[41]

Emphasizing the positive and providing evidence encouraged agents to extend their programs to only select black Texans. The rhetoric about who should receive extension services indicated class bias among both white and black staff. Each held firm convictions about the ability of tenants to utilize the materials that the Extension Service provided. As early as 1916, Clarence Ousley, TAEX director, noted that the service worked best for those black farmers in a position to govern their own farms. During the 1920s, white as well as black reformers used home ownership as an indicator of autonomy, efficiency, and potential for success as a demonstrator. By 1924, Negro Division director Calvin Waller believed that middle-class African Americans looked toward the Extension Service for assistance in community reform in general. The selectivity indicated the pressures under which black farmers operated. Farmers who owned personal property, either land or a house, exercised greater control over their resources. They became targets of promotional campaigns, because agents faced fewer barriers in convincing them of the benefits of extension work. The decision to work with property owners left few opportunities to aid tenants and sharecroppers. Non-property-holding farmers moved frequently, and they often had no time to devote to gardening or tilling any crop other than cotton. In 1937, Lea Etta Lusk, a home demonstration agent with significant experience, indicated how limited tenants were in cotton country when she reported that she "worked with farmers who were free to plant gardens."[42]

Federal officials knew that white landlords posed a problem for black agents. In 1922, two federal inspectors noted that, "where the main type of farming is on the plantation system, . . . a negro agent can be of very little help." White landlords did not appreciate black agents' disrupting their labor system, but C. H. Waller, always seeking racial harmony, noted the increased interest landlords paid to the program. One landlord commented that "no Negro could stay on his place who did not have a garden, hog, cow and raise chickens." On such a plantation, an agent could make inroads, but landlords expected to profit from the service. Tenants were encouraged to expend their resources as the landlord dictated. Waller explained: "In this way an entering wedge has been made" in the process of turning a propertyless tenant into a self-sufficient farmer.[43]

Certain tenants became demonstrators (Fig. 18). They provided evidence that the Negro Division responded to white landlords' requests to help keep black labor on the land. Waller indicated that "we are trying all we know how to help the man in the lower strata." But supervisors and county agents distinguished between those who seemed able to follow through on the advice and those who had no power to do so. Tenants inclined toward increasing their property holdings appealed to the agents, and agents enjoyed reporting their progress. In 1927, TAEX featured ex-tenant Stark Stone Sr., a club member in Washington County, whose wife first approached John M. and Lea Etta Lusk. Stone moved from the community in which he lived to the plantation on which he chopped cotton. This allowed him to save time and energy previously spent commuting. At the time of the move, January 1923, the Stones bought another team of mules and some implements on credit. John Lusk secured two Jersey cows to furnish milk and butter for the family of six, and Stone paid for all but the implements after the first fall. By early January 1927, the Stones had saved enough to buy fifty-two acres on Route 6 in Brenham with $1,050 down and the rest in long-term notes.[44]

Reaching farmers trapped in debt peonage proved challenging, not just because of the economic barriers but also because of stereotypes held by middle-class blacks and whites about poor tenants. Intelligence and land-ownership often became linked in the reports that Waller prepared, indicating that he shared class bias with other reformers who associated below-average intelligence with tenancy and sharecropping. He based his evidence on responses to a question that supervisory staff asked when assessing a county agent's performance: "Is the farming group above the average intelligence or is it the lower strata, mostly tenants and renters?" Yet, Waller believed that agents should work with the underprivileged, because "it is better to make an attempt at getting a boy or girl to start a demonstration even when we feel that they will not complete it, than not start at all." New Deal programs

Figure 18. Duroc Jersey sow with her litter, owned by tenant farmer Hathaway Goodlow, near Waco, McLennan County, Tex., Apr. 1933. Goodlow's hogs dressed at 225 pounds each, on average. (Neg. S-16862-C, George W. Ackerman, photographer, FES, USDA, NA)

provided further incentives to agents to broaden their services. In 1937, Waller admonished district agents to stop confining "demonstrations and organizations to 'well-to-do' citizens and communities."[45]

Agents used whatever means available to document "lasting evidence" of progress and strengthen the Negro Division's public image. County and state fairs provided important public relations events. Black agents reported reaching thousands through the exhibits. White boosters often donated funds to fair organizers that funded premiums for black entrants. Several counties showed their support by constructing a "Negro Building" in which they segregated the stock, produce, and domestic arts exhibited by black entrants. Mary Hunter estimated that 240,000 African Americans attended the fairs in 1929, with more than 60,000 at the fair in Marshall alone. In 1931, Waller reported that black agents and club members participated in ninety-seven community, seventeen county, and three state fairs. At least 126,620 African Americans and 86,619 Euro-Americans attended these events.[46]

During the 1920s, agents began documenting programs visually. The images conveyed important information about the conditions under which

Negro Division staff members worked and their black clients lived. Agents regularly rolled up their sleeves and helped the black farm families manage less-than-ideal situations. Extension agents learned from other black reformers how to use photographs as propaganda. Robert L. Smith told Booker T. Washington that he employed mounted pictures as "practical illustration" as early as 1897. The images provided valuable information about FIS objectives to a semiliterate population. Smith's interest in photographs as a public relations and educational tool continued during his service as the Negro Division's first director. He managed to have photographs made of himself and the other two agents on their circuit around East Texas, though most of the early records were destroyed in a fire. Regardless, he, Jake Ford, and Mary Hunter had their picture taken during a "great meeting" in Polk County. Such images provoked fond memories, but agents did not just collect them. Instead, they disseminated them widely.[47]

Photographs emerged as a promotional tool by the 1920s. The 1925 TAEX annual report includes two photographs of extension work directed toward black farmers. One depicts a black county agent walking behind a mule-drawn calcium arsenate spreader with a farmer driving the mule and learning about poisoning boll weevil. Another shows the corn exhibit installed by Negro boys' club members at the Texas State Fair. Negro Division staff members assessed these photographs during their March staff meeting and agreed that they carried such a powerful message that all agents should include snapshots of "outstanding projects" in their annual reports in the future. Waller wanted two copies of each, one to remain in the files at the Negro Division headquarters at Prairie View A&M and the other to accompany the annual report to College Station and, ultimately, Washington, DC. He stressed that the agents had to take the pictures at the "correct time . . . so as to show the project at its very best." This sanctioned the collection of photographic documentation by black extension staff and followed a pattern established by other social reformers of the era who used photographs to influence opinion.[48]

An offer to reimburse expenses, however, did not accompany the directive to photograph their constituents. Black agents produced images but received no additional funding as a result. This forced them to use inexpensive cameras that they or their club members owned and to pay for film and developing out of their own pocket with no potential for reimbursement. This placed additional burdens on agents already overworked and underpaid. Additionally, they had to learn a new skill to remain current in their jobs. But these demands apparently did not reduce their interest in the medium or their belief that it could help them do their job and get more funding.

Figure 19. Club boys butchering hogs, Kendleton Community, Fort Bend County, Tex., Dec. 1937. (J. B. Coleman Library, Special Collections/Archives Dept., Prairie View A&M University)

Images show men, women, and children dressed in their finest. Children often wore formal attire or club uniforms and put on polished shoes. Ladies donned hats and men tied their ties. Sometimes they went to studios, as did three boys who won corn competitions at the Dallas State Fair in 1924. More often, however, demonstrators and club members gathered out-of-doors, with tables and chairs arranged to facilitate discussion, despite the Texas heat.[49]

Photographs captured processes: members conducting meetings; men surveying; boys cultivating crops; women canning produce; girls tending chickens. Agents had opportunities to capture candid images that white Texans could not, including details of butchering or quiet back porches that showed the nature of black rural culture (Fig. 19). Such images gave whites access to a rural world that they rarely entered and tangible proof that the Negro program benefited black farm families without threatening the status quo. The images helped justify continued funding and helped reinforce black commitment to the division, as well.

To accomplish these tasks, agents often needed photographs of a quality that they could not capture themselves. In these instances, they called on professional photographers, both white and black. Studio photographers created aesthetically pleasing documents of race work. The Teal Studio, one of the most successful and enduring studios operated by African Americans in Texas, routinely photographed extension events. Clients praised the quality of Teal Studio photographs, particularly those taken by Elnora Teal. A

Figure 20. Miss Bankhead, Sunny Side, Tex., winner of Singer sewing machine, 1931. Photograph by Teal Studio, Houston. (J. B. Coleman Library, Special Collections/Archives Dept., Prairie View A&M University)

photograph of two girls with a sewing machine reflects her flair for composition and detail (Fig. 20). Arthur Chester Teal, Elnora's husband, documented short courses and other events at Prairie View A&M and provided visible evidence of donations from sources such as the Knights of Pythias well spent. In 1935, the Knights donated eighty-five tents for the first 4-H Girls' Camp. Images also capture the interracial aspect of some training. In late 1937, Teal photographed a subirrigation demonstration presented by TAEX specialist J. F. Rosborough at the extension agents' annual meeting at Prairie View A&M. Negro Division staff could not always afford the pleasing images, however, and this, combined with the need to placate white administrators, often caused black agents to work with TAEX photographers.[50]

USDA officials with the Federal Extension Service even traveled to Texas to document model black demonstrators. In 1933, during the weeks before Franklin Delano Roosevelt assumed the presidency, FES staff planned a tour for George W. Ackerman, senior photographer. His mission was to document material gains that some black farmers had realized despite the Great Depression. The USDA planned to use the photographs to illustrate reports and enliven educational filmstrips. Officials at the TAEX instructed Negro Division staff to schedule visits for Ackerman with agents who had undertaken worthwhile projects. White and black officials sought the images for contradictory uses: whites hoped to deflect criticism about the inadequate aid extended to black farmers; African Americans wanted recognition of their efforts and respect for families that had prospered despite racism, legalized segregation, and systemic discrimination.[51]

As members of Congress devised reform legislation during the first hundred days of Roosevelt's administration, Ackerman visited farmers who practiced soil conservation, diversification, home improvement, and community development. Residents of Beulah, a freedmen's community in Anderson County, made the most of opportunities that agents afforded. They built and outfitted a community canning center from lumber salvaged from a church and prize money they won at the county fair. Ackerman photographed the building and canning club members at work. The A. H. Echols family garnered comparable coverage from the USDA retinue. The Echolses scraped together a living from rich Jersey milk and cream Mr. Echols sold to the Borden Company, and Mrs. Echols sold to neighbors and through markets in nearby Mexia. They sent a son to college with proceeds from their cattle and peach and plum trees. They also raised hogs, chickens, and sweet potatoes. Though minority agents could interpret such visible signs of success as evidence of economic equality, TAEX officials reminded the agents of their subordinate status within the racially stratified state agency by instructing them to help Ackerman carry his bags.[52]

Jeffie Obrea Allen Conner, a member of an African American landowning family from the freedmen's community of Harrison, in McLennan County, provided access to the self-confident and affluent rural blacks the TAEX wanted to promote. Mrs. Conner had worked with the Negro Division of the

TAEX as a home demonstration agent since the early 1920s, was completing course work toward a degree in home economics from Prairie View A&M, and had recently been promoted to assistant district agent. She built her career as an educated professional woman during an era when few minority women attained such status. Yet, the photo shoot provided an opportunity for her to connect to family and community, a luxury that many professional women, including Mrs. Conner, often had to forgo. She and her husband of ten years, George S. Conner, a medical doctor who practiced in Waco, corresponded regularly to sustain their relationship, because her job required her to divide her time between the Negro Division headquarters in Prairie View and several county extension offices that she helped supervise. In helping coordinate the shoot, she visited both her husband and her mother.[53]

Other professionals involved in the display of economic resourcefulness included Miss Ruby O. Phelps, who had replaced Jeffie Conner as Negro home demonstration agent in McLennan County following Jeffie's promotion, and Mr. John V. Smith, the McLennan County Negro agricultural agent. They had their pictures taken with Jeffie's mother, Meddie L. Allen, at her home in Harrison. Ackerman photographed them surrounded by visible evidence of accomplishment. One image shows Mr. Smith posed with Mrs. Allen in front of smoked meat and canned lard. Others depict Meddie Allen in her garden and on her front porch steps with Ruby Phelps and Iola W. Rowan, the Negro district agent. Captions indicate that these rural minority progressives wielded power within their communities. Mrs. Allen had tenants, and she furnished them with smoked ham, bacon, and lard, as white landlords did in exchange for interest in crops. She parlayed her profits into a well-maintained modern home and 135 acres of productive land—no small accomplishment given the challenges that African Americans faced in acquiring and retaining property, and no small responsibility, given the taxes that counties levied on property-holding residents. She worked hard herself, maintaining a three-quarter acre garden with twenty-five varieties of vegetables and a modern house yard with foundation plantings and ornamental walkways. Mrs. Allen spoke confidently of her ability to weather financially hard times. She even planned to increase production, particularly of canned vegetables. In 1933, Meddie Allen served as a poster child for progressive black farmers across the South. She, the Echols family, and the women in Beulah each embraced various aspects of modernization, including scientific crop cultivation, selective breeding, hygienic canning, and home improvement. They allied with seasoned black professionals who advocated to white and black constituents on their behalf.[54]

Ackerman recognized some differences between Texas and the rest of the South. He remarked that Texas "offered the best material for pictures of demonstrations" when compared to Extension Service programs in Tennessee and North Carolina, the other states he toured. His photographs show educated, class-conscious, and politically connected African Americans who had parlayed their land into material prosperity. The images imply that they had attained their status due to their adoption of USDA recommendations touted by extension agents and demonstrators, not due to years of negotiation with white neighbors, cultivation of diverse crops and stock, soil management that helped make the marginal areas they cultivated sustainable, and communities that shielded them from overt scrutiny and suppression. Yet, those who benefited from the Negro Extension Service remained a relatively small number of rural southern blacks who added the government program to their arsenal to ward off the poverty, intimidation, and subjugation that framed the experiences of most rural southern blacks at the time. Many could appreciate the aesthetics of Ackerman's photographs of Mrs. Allen and others like her, but the clear composition of the photographs masked the stark inequities of gender and race discrimination that more accurately reflected the institutional culture of the TAEX and Texas society in general.[55]

Agents did not have to undertake public relations campaigns and education tasks unprepared. After 1930, they had access to training materials that described how to "keep results of the work before the public." An Extension Service circular mentions all types of publicity methods, including writing news releases and circular letters and creating promotional exhibits for display in storefronts, at fairs, or in other businesses and offices. Experts instructed agents to include a pleased customer in the photograph, to use a simple box camera, to have enlargements made, and to follow a series of steps to get the best results. They advised that photographs should tell only one thing, suggest action, and focus on the featured person or activity. For staged photographs, they advised agents to select a simple background that did not overpower the object and to photograph individuals in a natural setting. They warned against effects of shadow and shade and recommended optimum camera settings.[56]

White TAEX administrators who wanted to improve the quality of the images and clarify the messages they conveyed also created instructional materials. Louis Franke, TAEX assistant editor, in consultation with Howard Berry, the photographer with the Texas Agricultural Experiment Station, recommended equipment and techniques to improve the quality of photographs and provided examples. He reiterated that good images should tell a story and should incorporate action. They should include human interest but not focus on individuals.[57]

TAEX staff informed black agents they could request help with their images. Iola Rowan announced at a staff meeting in 1936 that Minnie Fisher Cunningham, TAEX editor, could arrange for a photographer to take pictures but that the time arranged would be "for Mrs. Cunningham's convenience." In 1939, the TAEX employed a specialist in visual instruction, C. H. Hensen. The black agents could write to him, and he would work with them for three to four days and provide instruction in "how to make pictures."[58]

Professional photographers bore the responsibility for photographing events that black and white administrators intended to use for purposes other than annual reports. Meat shows—an exhibition of preserved meats that involved agents in one or more counties—provided opportunities to extend the service's reach. Agents and club members invested considerable energy in these shows, organizing thirty-eight such events at the county level in 1938 alone. Studio photographers, including the Teals, attended and generated pictures that administrators could use for promotional purposes. The images document the involvement of white judges, often at the invitation of the black organizers. Photographs also show the involvement of dignitaries and extension administrators, who viewed the finished exhibits. Albon L. Holsey, a field agent of the Agricultural Adjustment Administration (AAA), attended the second South Texas Meat Show and surveyed the entries with John H. Williams, the district agent.[59]

Photographs needed narrative to provide context. The TAEX trained agents to write for different audiences. Negro Division staff also invited editors of two black Houston newspapers, the *Informer* and the *Defender,* to provide instruction in news writing. Waller encouraged agents to communicate with other big-city papers, and in 1938, he instructed them to send items to the *Dallas News.*[60]

Internal publications helped agents communicate with black farmers in Texas, but these were usually written for white as well as black audiences. During 1936, the district agents and supervisory staff at Prairie View A&M published a four-page mimeographed newsletter entitled "Negro Field Activities." Five hundred black farmers and their families received this monthly. The Prairie View A&M principal, W. R. Banks, first allowed the publishers of the *Prairie View Standard* to feature the black extension program in January 1937. The issue included numerous photographs and a summary of the activities undertaken. The newspaper normally served a local black audience of about two hundred, but the TAEX requested one thousand extra copies of the special edition and used it in place of the mimeographed newsletter.[61]

The 1937 issue generated the desired result in that it pleased TAEX director Williamson and vice-director Shelton. By 1939, the distribution list included presidents of black land-grant colleges, white extension agents in counties that did not employ black agents, Secretary of Agriculture Henry A. Wallace, director of the Federal Extension Service, C. W. Warburton, and others. The staff collected articles and photographs for these issues as they began accumulating materials for their annual report. Rowan, Estelle, Williams, Conner, and Waller all worked on articles in their areas of responsibility. Extension staff also requested that the *Prairie View Standard* feature the 1938 short course and include pictures, news features, the number of persons participating in the activities, and other information that the agents could then use to market their programs and influence public opinion.[62]

This increased coverage coincided with efforts at the national level to involve rural residents in New Deal offerings. The AAA sponsored a meeting with representatives from the Associated Negro Press (ANP) in 1937 and asked them how the federal government might reach a wider audience. The meeting led to an agreement between federal authorities and members of the ANP that offered broader coverage of extension activities in black newspapers. Prior to this agreement, the ANP did not publish articles unless it received payment, and the segregated Extension Service did not have funds budgeted for that purpose. Editors agreed to carry articles from other papers, and extension agents believed this would broaden their efforts to publicize their activities. Negro Division staff members further increased the distribution of stories and photographs to black magazines during the late 1930s.[63]

Agendas often clashed as black and white administrators tried to capitalize on one event. An exhibition of harness at the thirtieth annual short course at Prairie View A&M in 1937 provided an opportunity to reach a national audience. The leather specialist at TAEX, M. K. Thornton Jr., selected the winners from entries that "surpassed anything he expected." TAEX director H. H. Williamson suggested that the Negro Division staff send some winning harness, bridles, and halters from the short course to the annual meeting of land-grant college presidents in Washington, DC, in November 1937. He forwarded photographs of the exhibit to extension officials in Washington and suggested that they consider the harness for display. Dignitaries praised the representative sample of the home industry undertaken by the black farmers in Texas and exhibited it in the Agricultural Building in Washington. Wallace, Warburton, and even Pres. Franklin D. Roosevelt considered the hand-sewn harness an improvement over some commercially produced samples. Rather than criticize the condescending tone evident in the comments made by white officials, Negro Division staff members credited TAEX officials for helping them secure positive publicity and used it as the basis for further publicity. Waller instructed district agents to prepare stories for *Opportunity* in 1938, complete with photographs. Also in 1938, Williamson suggested that they put the best leatherwork in shop windows in Houston and in Dallas. Thornton even carried more harness to Washington to exhibit later that year.[64]

Events such as leather demonstrations indicated competition between Negro Divisions to secure national favor. Following the successful exhibit at Washington, DC, of harness from the 1937 Prairie View A&M short course, Tuskegee Institute officials tried to get TAEX leather specialist M. K. Thornton to come and do the same for them. Instead of accepting the invitation, Thornton recommended a black worker from Prairie View A&M to teach at Tuskegee Institute's summer school. Tuskegee officials did not favorably receive the recommendation, perhaps because school officials resented the national attention directed at Texas. They expected Thornton, the instigator of the harness project at Prairie View, to honor their request. Eventually, John H. Williams, Negro district agent, traveled to Tuskegee and conducted leather workshops for the school for several years. Photographs show Williams training men and at least one woman in making harness.[65]

Both supervisors and agents had to monitor their actions to ensure success and to protect their place within the larger bureaucracy. Each followed slightly different professional paths, however, as agents pursued programs of interest to their constituents while supervisors made decisions and implemented recommendations in ways that furthered the interests of the bureaucracy. African Americans used their positions to accomplish many things relative to rural reform and professional development. TAEX administrators, however, remained ultimately responsible for institutional hierarchies. This forced black supervisors and agents to appear as "safe Negroes" while they sought larger social, economic, and professional goals. On one level, Negro Division staff exercised a remarkable amount of self-direction. They had relative freedom to interact with white officials in county government and supervise black agents in the field. They maintained a high degree of visibility among members of white and black organizations. Yet, their visibility and relative freedom did not translate into equitable resources.[66]

5

Building Segregated Social Welfare

Texas' Negro Division and Roosevelt's New Deal

Negro Division staff had to work even harder during 1933 due to the increased expectations of New Deal programs. Though the division feared cutbacks as the southern economy staggered, federal funds from various sources helped increase the number of black and white agents. Black agents gained new responsibilities, more resources, and increased visibility as professionals. This helped them bolster the segregated division's reputation and create a niche for themselves within the largest public welfare program undertaken in the United States to date. Their participation, however, indicated the entrenched nature of race-based decision making at the national and the state levels. Implementation did not challenge legalized racial discrimination. Instead, New Deal administrators relied on Negro Division staff to reach African Americans, thus perpetuating social separation of the races, and they allowed blacks only minimal roles in planning, administration, and implementation, thus perpetuating racial discrimination. White supervisors expected much of black agents, both male and female, and the black staff obliged in their ongoing effort to negotiate equity.

Agents understood that New Deal programs offered select African Americans opportunities for relief long denied them by local and state officials. Black farmers who participated earned their place because of existing involvement in and connection with the TAEX's Negro Division. Those who gained the division's sponsorship had access to crop-reduction payments offered by the Agricultural Adjustment Administration or credit made available through the Farm Credit Act. National and state officials relied on Negro Division mediation to further these programs and others in Texas, including resettlement projects and mattress making.[1]

Despite efforts to reach black Texans, however, many did not secure much-needed relief. Farm families in the countryside that lived in counties where white authority figures did not fund black county agents found themselves marginalized and virtually prohibited from participating, whether they qualified for relief or not. Most tenants and sharecroppers likewise found themselves excluded from New Deal relief because Negro agents tended not to serve propertyless farm families. Black agents found themselves caught between continuing to serve their existing clientele—generally, landowning farm families in relatively stable communities—and reaching out to new constituents, specifically, the landless, who had little support but that which national policies provided.

Farmers, landed and landless alike, faced threats during the 1930s that exceeded those encountered previously. The debt cycle intensified as money supplies shrank during the inflationary 1920s and economically depressed 1930s. Natural forces, including drought and flood, destroyed crops, leaving farmers penniless and further indebted. Progressive farmers turned to machinery and synthetic chemicals to fight weeds and pests, and sharecroppers and tenants faced displacement as a result. Many tenants and sharecroppers had little choice but to abandon agriculture. The nonwhite farming population declined by approximately 30 percent across the South between 1930 and 1940. The drop was not as precipitous in Texas, as the number of Negro farm operators dropped only 21.3 percent. Ironically, as the number of farmers declined, the number of agents increased apace with the New Deal initiatives.[2]

Between 1930 and 1940, Negro Division staff doubled, a growth rate comparable to that enjoyed during the Great War. TAEX administrators as well as county commissioners supported the role of black staff in black communities, and this sustained funding matches at all levels. In 1930, 43 black agents served in counties throughout East Texas and reached 42,026 black Texans, at least 8.0 percent of the state's rural black population (see Map 5). By 1932, when officials boasted that the TAEX was "the largest Extension Service in the United States and that means in the world," 50 African American agents and supervisors worked in the Negro Division and accounted for one-sixth of the total number of black agents employed in the nation. More counties asked for agents than the TAEX could fund, even with federal monies available through the Capper-Ketchum Act (1928) and the Bankhead-Jones Act (1935). Federal appropriations funneled through New Deal agencies such as the Reconstruction Finance Corporation (RFC), the Federal Emergency Relief Administration (FERA), and the Agricultural Adjustment Administration all increased involvement of African American Texans. By 1935, the Negro Division employed 5 supervisors, 33 agricultural

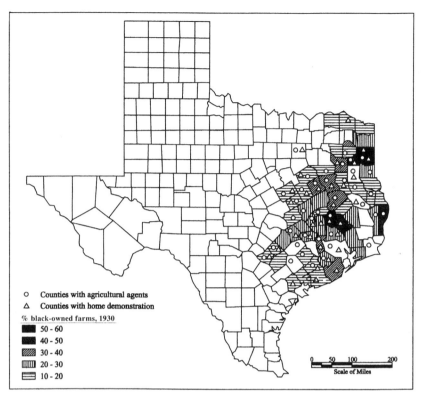

Map 5. Percentage of black-owned farms, 1930, and counties with Negro Division agents, 1925–34. (*Negroes in the United States, 1920–32*, 813–27; county personnel, TAEX Historical Files). Drawn by Chris Blakely and Ron Finger; revised by Richard Riccio.

agents, and 29 home demonstration agents, who served residents in forty counties. By 1940, 82 agents worked in forty-nine counties. They interacted regularly with 38,633 dues-paying club members, or 7.7 percent of the rural black population, a decline in the numbers they reached directly. Increased staffing, however, allowed them to publicize their programs more broadly, through curbside markets, soup kitchens, and county health campaigns. They estimated that they were reaching nearly 42 percent of all black Texans by 1940.[3]

During 1933, as the U.S. Congress passed the Agricultural Adjustment Act, TAEX administrators turned to black agents to discuss the benefits of participating in the new cotton-reduction program. The channeling of information through established lines of communication did not go unnoticed by black advocates. When TAEX decisions did not support black farmers, special-interest groups intervened. J. P. Davis, the executive secretary of the Negro Industrial League, wrote Secretary of Agriculture Henry A. Wallace requesting that the Extension Service fund an agricultural agent in Marion County, the county with the highest percentage of black residents in the state and significant numbers of black owners (62.3 percent of all farm owners) and tenants (74.7 percent of all farm tenants). County commissioners had never offered consistent support for extension agents. Davis and the members of the league believed that the farmers in the county had a right to the services of a county agent, and they asked Wallace to provide the necessary funds. Wallace responded that limited federal and state resources offered only so many opportunities to place agents in the field. Further, even if counties fulfilled their responsibilities, adding new agents was unlikely at the time. This response reflects the federal government's lack of interest in circumventing local and state authority and indicates the importance of a connection to the Extension Service. Blacks not involved in the extension system had difficulty gaining access to information and federal relief.[4]

Despite Wallace's indication that funds were limited, thirty-two Texas counties first employed black agricultural or home demonstration agents during the 1930s. These counties exhibited different characteristics from those counties that had previously sponsored agents. Prior to the 1930s, Negro Division staff worked in almost all of the counties where black landowning farmers constituted between 40 and 60 percent of the farming population and in at least half of those counties where black landowning farmers constituted between 20 and 40 percent of all farmers. Three counties hosted agents because of New Deal incentives: Hopkins, where less than 10 percent of the entire county population was black, and only 5 percent of all landowning farmers in the county were black; and Kaufman and Lamar, where black landowners represented only 8.6 percent and 12.6 percent, respectively, of all farmers. These counties, however, all lay within the Blackland Prairie, the region with the most intense cotton cultivation and dependence on tenant farming in Texas. Funding black agents in these counties increased the involvement of a few black farmers, but more important, it responded to criticisms leveled against the TAEX for not serving disadvantaged cotton farmers.[5]

Other counties that employed agents more closely fit existing patterns. Five qualifying counties lay within the Post Oak area of East Texas, a region of sandy soils, small farms, and rolling, forested hills. Five lay within the Piney Woods region of East Texas, an area dominated by the timber industry, not agriculture. These counties, particularly those in the Piney Woods, qualified as high-need counties; specifically, black residents had to tolerate a lower standard of living. New Deal initiatives sought to correct such discomfort as well as economic inequity. This indicated the broadening of extension work beyond agricultural and rural reform to larger social issues related to poverty, nutrition, and human comfort in general. Need did not guarantee support, however, and a few counties in high-need areas lost their agents either just before or during the early 1930s. Thus, white interests more than black need affected some hiring decisions. Regardless, the number of counties with agents increased throughout the New Deal, as did the money spent to further extension work among black Texans.[6]

Inequities that defined Negro Division employment during the 1920s continued into the 1930s. The percentage of money allotted to segregated staff positions did not equal the percentage of rural blacks in Texas. Furthermore, the salaries and benefits provided to black agents continued at a rate well below that offered to white agents. In 1934, Negro state leader C. H. Waller recognized the ways that racism limited black involvement. He remarked that, "as in all movements where you have a fair minded county administrator, negroes share well in all Governmental plans; where the administrator is inclined not to be fair, there is nothing that can be done to change it." He advised restraint in the face of such obvious race bias and urged all Extension Service workers "to be careful and not make any mistakes by getting involved in politics." His advice helped protect the Negro Division from repercussions and reduced funding and loss of agents. Even Thomas Campbell, the first black agent employed to undertake USDA work and a special field agent for the USDA during the 1930s, remained silent about race bias until he retired in 1953. Then he noted that "the Negro in the U.S. is more conscious than ever of the fact that he is not wholly and equably sharing in the 'American way of life.' . . . In other words the Negro knows deep down in his heart he still does not 'belong.' "[7]

During the 1930s, TAEX responses to crises that assailed farmers gave many African Americans hope for belonging. Economic conditions in Texas did not become severe immediately after the stock market crash in 1929. In fact, the Great Depression came later to Texas than to other southern states. A good cotton crop and a decent market during 1929 tempered hard times. The financial crises of 1930 also affected other states more than Texas, partially due to the oil boom around Kilgore in southern Gregg County. But natural forces, specifically drought, reduced the state's cotton harvest. Things took a turn for the worse in 1931, largely due to overproduction of the state's primary cash crop, cotton. Black and white farm operators ignored ongoing efforts by Texas legislators to reduce cotton production. As a result, Texas farmers produced a bumper crop, the second largest in the state's history. The resulting surplus drove prices down to 5.3 cents per pound. This, combined with the high prices for consumer goods, forced many into debt.[8]

Low cotton prices motivated agricultural agents, who had emphasized balanced farming through diversification, to renew their efforts to reduce farmers' dependency on cotton. In 1930 C. H. Waller advocated supplementing cash from cotton by growing other marketable crops such as corn, sweet potatoes, vegetables, and fruit or by raising hogs and maintaining dairy herds to help farmers satisfy "all living needs." In 1932 TAEX director Oscar B. Martin observed that savings and thrift "should become habitual. Then panics may come and depressions may fade but independence will go on forever." But basic needs and personal independence depended on more than thrifty habits and diversified farming.[9]

Franklin Delano Roosevelt's administration responded aggressively to the debilitated economy. In 1933, Congress standardized relief efforts with several pieces of legislation, including the Agricultural Adjustment Act and the Farm Credit Act. These represented a broad-based effort to stabilize the nation's rural economy.[10]

TAEX personnel assumed major responsibility for implementing production control authorized by the national government. Henry A. Wallace, U.S. secretary of agriculture, and Cully A. Cobb, head of the Cotton Section of the Production Division of the AAA, conceptualized and implemented the controls which depended on the participation of state-based extension programs conducted out of land-grant universities. No state proved more critical to cotton reduction than Texas. Oscar Martin did not support the concept of plowing up 30 percent of the cash crop already growing in the state, but despite his reservations, the TAEX wasted little time in following Cobb's recommendations. Martin placed H. H. Williamson, TAEX vice-director, in charge of the program in Texas and called on Calvin Waller, Negro Division leader, to further the work with black farmers. Waller also heeded the request of C. W. Warburton, director of the Federal Extension Service, who wrote to extension personnel directing them to "assist in organization and conduct of the Agricultural Adjustment Administration's programs looking to the reduction of crop acreage and production." With the authorization of officials in Washington, DC, and College Station, Waller and the black extension agents "entered whole-heartedly into the Triple-A work for Texas." Convincing black farmers to participate "required all the energy and knowledge we possessed."[11]

The magnitude of the cotton crop in Texas produced a sense of urgency during the initial sign-up campaign, scheduled to occur between June 26 and July 8, 1933. Texans had to support it, and agents had to convince farmers to destroy 4,493,700 acres, or one-third of the growing crop, in the state or the program would fail. Texas' support proved crucial because the state's acreage alone accounted for 44.9 percent of the total 10 million acres in the South required to start the plow-up campaign. White county agents administered AAA distributions in 1933. Two later acts, the Soil Conservation and Domestic Allotment Act of 1936 and the Second Agricultural Adjustment Act of 1938, changed their role from administrators to advisors, but even this did not increase black participation in decision making at the county level. Blacks remained important to the program's success but not involved in its conceptualization.[12]

White county agents took the lead in their counties, and black agents assisted them, concentrating on acquainting black farmers with the program. Farmers in two-thirds of the counties that employed black agents committed at least 40 percent of their resources to "king cotton" (Map 6). These farmers stood to benefit from cotton-reduction campaigns launched by the AAA, and Negro Division employees bore responsibility for helping them participate. Agents hosted informational meetings to recruit farmers, often involving ministers to help them spread the word. Then agents helped farmers complete paperwork, recommended them to local selection committees, and advised them on surveying so they plowed up no more acreage than their contract required. They kept white agents apprised of their efforts. This proved critical, because white agricultural agents recommended men who sat on local selection committees and made the decisions about who participated and who did not. Black agents could not jeopardize their farmers' ability to qualify for crop-reduction payments by not complying with white agents' recommendations.[13]

Brazos County agents undertook cotton-reduction efforts with relish, and their reports reflect generally believable rates of participation. C. L. Beason, the white agent, reported "throwing regular hours to the four winds'" and working every Sunday from June 26 to December 31 "to try to keep things going at the least possible expense." He did not complain, assuming that good came of the effort as he enrolled 35 percent of the county's farmers and committed 15,000 acres to the plow-under campaign. The black agent, H. K. Hornsberry, contributed by registering 11.4 percent of the county's black farm operators as a result of numerous personal visits, letters,

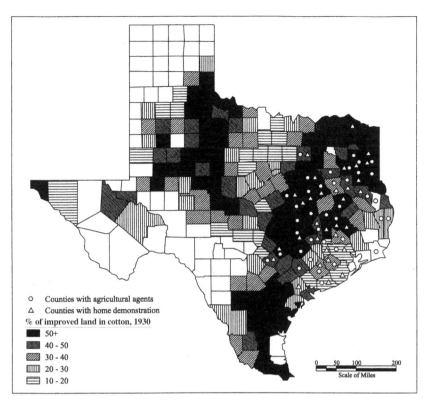

Map 6. Percentage of improved land in cotton, 1930, and counties with Negro Division agents, 1925–34. (U.S. Bureau of the Census, *Fifteenth Census of the United States, 1930, Agriculture,* vol. 2, pt. 2, *Southern States,* 1382–1401; county personnel, TAEX Historical Files). Drawn by Chris Blakely and Ron Finger; revised by Richard Riccio.

informational meetings, and explanatory articles published in local newspapers. They plowed under only 1,765 acres.[14]

The sense of urgency, however, prompted many agents, both white and black, to exaggerate their efforts. R. S. Miller, the white county agent in McLennan County, a Blackland Prairie county and home to numerous cotton farmers, claimed that two-thirds of all farmers in his county registered to plow up cotton. He believed that every farmer in the county had an opportunity to sign a contract, and hesitancy disappeared as farmers realized that "it was the first time they had ever been offered any real relief from the Government." The white agent in Walker County, D. R. Carpenter, concurred. He claimed that "no cotton grower on any of the 2,163 farms in this

county . . . failed to have the opportunity to cooperate" in the cotton reduction program, and his efforts encouraged 52 percent of the county's farmers to participate. John V. Smith, the black agricultural agent in McLennan
County, reached 2,000 farmers over the course of forty meetings and convinced 1,570 of them to sign up acreage for reduction. This number exceeded
by more than 150 the total number of black farm operators in the county as
reported on the 1930 census.[15]

Black agents took special care in educating their constituents about the
program because they had to nurture black farmers to trust in government
promises of payment. The black agent in Walker County, K. H. Malone,
worked with D. R. Carpenter in July and August 1933 to get black farmers to sign contracts. Malone read the contract thoroughly and then fielded
questions from worried farmers. Farmers expressed concern that the government would take control of their farms or that they would not get the
money promised. He assuaged their concerns by scheduling meetings in
twenty black communities in the county to explain the details. His efforts
helped convince 783 black farmers, including tenants, to plow up 5,486 acres.
Apparently, his sincerity convinced an unprecedented 61.8 percent of black
farm operators to participate. After completing the contracts, he showed
them how to measure their land so they did not plow up more cotton than
they had contracted to destroy. John Lusk, the black agent in Washington
County, convinced approximately 500 farmers, or 31.8 percent of the black
operators in the county, to participate, while R. G. Johnson, the black agent
in Gregg County, motivated 20.7 percent of black operators in his county to
plow under part of their cash crop.[16]

Black agents tried to help farmers improve their fields at the same time
as they benefited from payments for cotton not grown. They encouraged
farmers to plant replacement crops on acreage registered for cotton reduction when contracts allowed. H. K. Hornsberry, working in Brazos County,
convinced 117 of 133 farmers who retired acreage to replant. Some replacement crops, such as peas and hegari, returned nitrogen to the soil and produced a ground cover that reduced erosion, thus furthering soil-conservation
goals. Other crops, such as corn, gave farmers additional feed for stock and
family. Farmers also planted sweet potatoes and sweet sorghum, crops that
could double as cash or subsistence crops. Despite the late planting dates,
these crops apparently did well through the fall, and agents reported good
results.[17]

Black agents used their reports to celebrate their own efforts but also to
laud the government's. Lea Etta Lusk noted that the government program in

cotton reduction helped lift the spirit of farmers and produced more hope. K. H. Malone praised reduction for more concrete reasons. He reported that the program put farmers in a "much better spirit this year than they were the same time last year" because they could use their "increased earnings" to buy farm equipment and land, improve their homes, and pay back taxes and notes.[18]

The black agent in Waller County, one of the poorest farming counties in the state, presented more accurate information in his 1933 report. In fact, Jesse Wilson's truthfulness may have cost him his position. He did not mention the crop-reduction program or other New Deal initiatives. Instead, he indicated the uphill battle he fought to convince boys and their fathers of the value of using good seed, fertilizer, and proper cultivation. Few farmers he served could afford fertilizer, even though they owned farms in areas with the poorest soil in the county; they knew that the return would not offset the expenses. Wilson blamed apathy, ignorance, and even planter intervention for limiting black farmers' choices. Planters held the most fertile soil in the bottomlands and employed a "poor class of tenants," who could participate only with the permission of the landlord. County commissioners did not renew the contracts of either the black agricultural agent or the black home demonstration agent in 1933. It took more than a year to rehire for the positions. This made it difficult for black farmers to gain access to much-needed New Deal programs.[19]

Ultimately, only a select few black farmers in Texas benefited from cotton reduction. Twenty-three black agricultural agents met with 14,680 families, 17.1 percent of all black farm operators but only 3.0 percent of all farm operators in the state. Those who signed contracts plowed up 187,323 acres, 4.3 percent of the 4,350,565 acres Texans ultimately destroyed. Yet, black farm operators received only $835,529, or 2.1 percent, of the $39,225,000 paid in cotton-acreage reduction contracts to Texas farmers. This indicates that payments did not always reach those who committed to plow up their crop.[20]

Such a monumental government undertaking implemented during one crop season could not reverse generations of inequality and poverty. Studies of farm income indicate that tenants and sharecroppers earned less than their white peers. Landowners fared equally poorly in that they tended to control small amounts of poorer quality land. Of all farm operators in Texas in 1930, only 4.2 percent were blacks who owned their land; 13.2 percent were black tenants. By 1935, the percentage of owners was remaining steady, but the number of tenants had dropped to 10.2 percent, an indication that land provided some stability.[21]

These few black farmers, landholders and tenants combined, controlled a minuscule amount of Texas acreage. In 1930, blacks accounted for 17.4 percent of all farmers but operated only 3.7 percent of all farmland. By 1935, black operators had dropped to 14.3 percent of the total in the state and farmed only 2.8 percent of the land. White farmers controlled 97.2 percent of Texas' tillable acreage. The small farms blacks cultivated, their involvement with tenancy, the racism that limited their political involvement, and the TAEX concentration on the landed all conspired against the majority of black farmers and kept them trapped in poverty. The government relief program could not reverse these pernicious characteristics of southern agriculture.[22]

Agents failed to report trials and tribulations that defined the experiences of most rural blacks during the Great Depression. In combination with low prices and crop reduction, agricultural mechanization made hand labor obsolete and contributed to tenant displacement. Counties with the highest proportion of white sharecroppers experienced the highest displacement rate. Historian Keith Volanto argues that this occurred because landowners preferred black labor or whites had greater opportunities for employment. In the Blackland Prairie, land consolidation and mechanization, specifically, the use of tractors, not acreage reduction, led to black tenant displacement. Acreage reduction displaced black tenants more in other parts of East Texas, but land consolidation played a role there as well.[23]

Intimidation prevented many tenants from pursuing grievances against landlords, as they knew that county cotton committees made up predominantly of white landowners would rule against them. This did not deter some blacks from expressing their dissatisfaction to federal representatives. Sharecroppers in Fort Bend, a county with a history of involvement in FIS reform and Negro Division extension work, wrote Secretary of Agriculture Henry A. Wallace and asked for federal intervention. Cedar Walton, the black agent in Dallas County, testified before the Farm Tenancy Conference in 1937, reporting that black sharecroppers had no support in the county. The USDA, however, offered no resolution; the national government refused to question local and state authorities who remained committed to class-biased decisions that hurt farmers with no land and to race-biased decisions that hurt blacks.[24]

Nonetheless, accusations of inequity led the AAA to study the situation. Erwin H. Shinn, reporting to the secretary of agriculture for the Interdepartmental Group Concerned with the Special Problems of Negroes, noted that the majority of rural blacks did not enjoy the maximum benefits afforded by federal programs. The investigative group attributed this to failure on the part of local administrators to follow the directions provided by New Deal agencies. Black agents had little leverage for challenging inequities because they feared losing their positions. The AAA administrators capitalized on black agents' willingness to accept secondary status as proof of the efforts within the federal program to deal with race issues.[25]

Waller publicly praised actions that caused others to accuse the AAA of blatant discrimination. He justified the decisions landlords made to rent land to the government instead of tenants: "No sane person could censure the landlord for his action when he is trying to get all he can out of his investment." Waller believed displacement was "a God-send to those with a little foresight or energy to do something for themselves." He recounted a story from the Brazos Bottoms near Hearne where Italians gave up a contract on a large piece of land after contracting to reduce cotton acreage with the government. When the land appeared on the market, African Americans bought large tracts of it for settlement by select groups. Black farmers who capitalized on others' misfortunes became models of efficiency.[26]

Steady criticism prompted the AAA to increase African American involvement. Cully A. Cobb, head of the Cotton Section of the AAA's Production Division, responded to the pressure to expand the services of the AAA by calling a meeting of black state extension leaders in Washington, DC, in the fall of 1933. He used the meeting to solicit their opinions about the organization and implementation of AAA programs for 1934–35. Cobb and other staff members traveled to the Negro Division's annual meeting in Huntsville, Texas, in November 1933, as a way to meet with all black agents in the leading cotton-producing state in the nation. He asked agents to cooperate in conveying information to farmers again in the winter and spring of 1934 and encouraged them to keep 40 percent of black-operated farmland out of production. Mr. Cox, an AAA staff member in charge of crop replacement, provided some ideas about how the agents could get more involved in the program.[27]

Cobb also met with state leaders and black agents from seven southern states, including Texas, at Tuskegee Institute in December 1933. Waller and "the entire male Extension Staff" from Texas heard him explain that black agents bore the responsibility for keeping black farmers informed and for helping them complete acceptable applications and managing their participation. The agents had the opportunity to meet other administrators from Washington, DC, including Dr. J. A. Evans, chief of the work in the South, and Mr. Phil Campbell, a Washington staff member. Waller indicated that the black extension staff approved of the new contract as a means to "safe-guard and protect the fellow furtherest down." Assurances did not materialize, as the payment structure for the 1934–35 benefits provided less to sharecroppers who participated in the reduction than the 1933 program had done, and laborers got nothing at all. The lobbying efforts of the Farm Bureau and southern influence in Congress overpowered minority interests.[28]

Public opinion remained heated on the topic of race and class inequity in the distribution of federal relief. The *Dallas Morning News* considered the reform undertaken by black extension agents to be a valuable contribution to solving the "Southern white farmer's problems as well." The editor noted that many whites remained blinded to the way that the poverty of the southern black negatively affected the welfare of the southern white. But others realized that "it is impossible to maintain two widely varying standards of living for whites and blacks while they compete on equal terms in the greatest Southern industry." The *Morning News* concluded that white and black Texans should cooperate in supporting the Extension Service and its programs.[29]

Maintaining black enrollees helped the AAA avoid criticism. Cully Cobb facilitated this by appointing blacks to work in areas previously not served by black agents. The AAA borrowed Calvin Waller from Texas in 1935 to travel in Missouri and Illinois, survey black farmers, and acquaint them with the AAA relief programs. Waller resumed the task for three more months in 1936. His services pleased Cobb, who regularly asked him to continue, but Waller refused in 1937 and again in 1938.[30]

Other duties related to agricultural conservation consumed Waller's time and made it difficult for him to be away from Prairie View A&M. He bore the responsibility of conveying information about the Soil Conservation and Domestic Allotment Act to agents in Texas. Congress passed the act on the heels of the January 1936 Supreme Court decision that deemed the AAA unconstitutional. Waller and other farm leaders attended a meeting in Memphis, Tennessee, in March to hear about the new benefit program available to farmers and help them "enter into the program more intelligently and receive the benefits which they deserved." The agents had to work fast to enroll farmers before spring planting began. Farmers who replaced soil-depleting crops, specifically, cash crops such as cotton, with soil-building crops received benefits. Soil conservation had the potential to help a greater number of black farmers for several reasons. It aimed to conserve and improve depleted soils, goals important to black farmers marginalized on less fertile soils. It also supported terracing and drainage programs that black agents had advocated since the beginning of the Negro Division (Fig. 21). Commissioners in some counties even provided tractors to aid the work. Soil-conservation programs

Figure 21. Constructing terraces as part of a soil conservation demonstration at Ernest Stein's farm, Mount Enterprise Community, Rusk County, Tex., Apr. 1933. Stein owned three hundred acres of a fourteen hundred–acre tract owned by his twelve-member family. He had terraced more than half of it to increase yields and improve the look of his farm. (Neg. S-16806-C, George W. Ackerman, photographer, FES, USDA, NA)

sometimes involved tenants interested in increasing their yields, but the work also increased the value of the owner's property. Sometimes, owner and tenant cooperated in a program that could be mutually beneficial (Fig. 22).[31]

Training for the new approach to crop reduction followed the model established by the first AAA. Agents attended conferences where they heard step-by-step explanations of the program and the things farmers needed to do to participate. Several conferences in different regions of the state provided opportunities for agents to hear about the work from the federal representatives. Two meetings were scheduled at Prairie View A&M, and attendees heard Cully Cobb, chairs of the soil programs in Texas and Oklahoma, and TAEX director H. H. Williamson. The meeting drew delegates from Oklahoma, Arkansas, Louisiana, and Texas. Williamson also invited all black extension agents, male and female, to two regional meetings, in Tyler and in Wharton. These meetings "sold each agent to the program and gave him definite information to carry back to his group." Other regional meetings open to farmers occurred in Marshall, Mexia, Wharton, and Lockhart. The

Figure 22. Checking terrace elevations on R. P. Pervey's farm, Browndale Community, near Neches, Anderson County, Tex., Apr. 1933. Pervey (right) owned forty-four acres and had terraced thirty-five. Cotton yields on twelve terraced acres increased by four hundred pounds as a result. F. J. Robinson (center) instructs tenant farmer W. T. Smith (left) and Pervey in how to maintain adequate grades to reduce wind erosion and improve water retention. (Neg. S-16839-C, George W. Ackerman, photographer, FES, USDA, NA)

audiences heard lesser dignitaries, including former congressman Lafayette Patterson of Washington, DC, TAEX extension leaders, and mayors.[32]

Calvin Waller and other Negro Extension leaders gathered for a conference devoted to the topic of soil conservation at Tuskegee Institute in March 1936. They drew up a petition to support additional USDA programs for rural blacks. They called for educational conferences, more black extension agents, additional information on the new Soil Conservation and Domestic Allotment Act, the appointment of blacks to local and state boards responsible for implementation and complaints, and the involvement of women. The strategy worked, and Cully Cobb appointed four African Americans in the fall of 1936. Claude A. Barnett, president of the Associated Negro Press, became a special assistant and three others became special field agents: Albon L. Holsey, director of publicity, Tuskegee Institute; James P. Davis, president, National Federation of Colored Farmers; and Jennie Moton, wife of Robert Moton, Tuskegee Institute principal. Waller's involvement as a field agent for the AAA preceded these appointments.[33]

Negro special agents traveled regularly and talked with black and white extension staff and the general public about USDA programs. Cully Cobb informed Williamson of a trip to Texas in 1937. Williamson indicated that Calvin Waller knew of the plans and could arrange the necessary meetings. Waller escorted Holsey to a meeting with Williamson in October 1937. Williamson later informed E. A. Miller, Cobb's assistant in the Southern Division of the AAA, that he "was very much interested and much impressed" with Holsey's approach. "I believe that this type of work is going to mean much to the program as a whole. Please be assured that we will give maximum cooperation."[34]

White administrators used the visits by black special agents as opportunities to micromanage Negro Division activities. Calvin Waller had to inform AAA administrators of dates and content of the frequent meetings and had to conduct the meetings with little monetary support. Sometimes conferences overlapped, and staff in Washington made decisions about which conference Texas staff should attend. This happened in 1937, when an AAA informational meeting in Texas scheduled for January 14–15 conflicted with the Taeusch Discussion Conference at Tuskegee on January 15–16. Washington officials believed that Waller and other Texas supervisors needed to attend the Tuskegee discussion and a related conference at Petersburg, Virginia. The USDA field agent for the southern states, Charles A. Shefield, sent a telegram to H. H. Williamson requesting that he allow Waller to drive to the meeting with the other staff and that the TAEX reimburse him for mileage. Williamson authorized Waller to make the trip with four other staff members, including Iola W. Rowan, Henry S. Estelle, John H. Williams, and Jeffie O. A. Conner. The TAEX believed these five could all travel in Waller's car "without additional expense for transportation." Williamson expected Waller to attend meetings and told him "not to hesitate to come to any Agricultural meeting being called as he would always be welcome, and called on to have something to say, because of the confidence that people have in him." Of course, travel across the South posed its own set of challenges for African Americans, who had to use "colored only" walk-up windows and could not stay in most hotels.[35]

A well-trained corps of extension agents, however, did not convince farmers to reduce cotton cultivation by approximately 4.5 million acres. In fact, the 1937 season resulted in the third-largest crop in the state's history, 5,154,000 bales, and farmers across the South contributed their share to the largest crop in U.S. history, 18,946,000 bales. Prices dropped, and President Roosevelt and the southern congressional delegation struggled to come to a compromise. Roosevelt signed the second Agricultural Adjustment Act on February 16, 1938. A new wave of training sessions began, and the work of agents increased as they dealt with payments under the 1936 Soil Conservation Act as well as the administration of the 1938 act. Black agents participated in this phase of the AAA reform, as they had in the past, and partook of fall training sessions to help them understand the demands awaiting them during 1939.[36]

Training continued in 1940 and 1941 before World War II shifted attention away from production control. In 1940, E. A. Miller wrote Calvin Waller with the topics for the AAA conference planned for Texas, including the Agricultural Adjustment Act of 1938 and the details of the 1941 cotton program and crop insurance and the grant-of-aid program. African American special field agent A. L. Holsey shared information on food and feed and publicity including the use of the annual report material from extension agents. Mrs. Jennie Moton discussed the "farm woman's place in the AAA program, with particular reference to utilizing the garden payment in living at home and feed crops provided by soil-building practices for increasing the supply of dairy and poultry products." Both male and female agents attended the meeting along with "some of their key farmers." Agents came away believing that black farmers in Texas were "as well acquainted with the AAA program as any group of farmers in the southland." The frequency of the meetings, however, wore staff down, as they shouldered regular responsibilities in addition to the emergency work. The Negro district agents in Texas requested that the two district AAA meetings be consolidated into one in 1941.[37]

Black agents realized little benefit from their years of service in support of AAA programs. Their relative position compared to that of white agents and administrators within the Extension Service remained subordinate. The advisory positions they held within the AAA had little influence on white policy makers. But advisors used their position to further reform among rural African Americans. Participation in a government program provided thousands of black farmers in Texas an opportunity to affiliate with national, not just state or local, authority figures. This gave some exposure to new ideas about participation and entitlements. Supervisors and agents remained informed about the ways legislation affected black farmers and shared details with club members. Waller had a copy in his correspondence of a critique of Senate Bill 1800, introduced by Sen. John H. Bankhead in 1935 and prepared by Dr. George E. Haynes, Department of Race Relations, Federal Council of Churches. Extension staff expected and asked for increased services as a result of such well-founded criticism. Petitions submitted to the AAA to employ black specialists, circulated during the soil conservation conference at Tuskegee in 1936, prompted action. Five years later, Calvin Waller mentioned the need to have a state AAA officer located at Prairie View A&M as a way to better serve black farmers. Such comments did not fall on deaf ears, and often influenced white decision makers.[38]

Depressed commodity prices and a shrinking money supply affected traditional lines of credit in rural Texas. In 1931, Calvin Waller reported that "money was not as plentiful nor can the farmer borrow or make a loan as he has done in former years; neither can he run large store accounts to be paid for when the crop is harvested." Families that previously supplemented their meager incomes with sales of excess produce realized losses when meat sold at "the lowest price in years" and vegetables went "cheap." Families had little recourse but to fill their barns and pantries to ward off famine. Agents explained that those who preserved excess had "little suffering as to feed and food supplies" for their immediate needs, but they lacked cash. Inadequate cash made credit more appealing, but black agents discouraged farmers from taking advantage of government-supported loans "unless it was absolutely necessary." Regardless, agents told tales of farmers who had effectively managed debt owed to government sources by using the money for the purpose intended and following "the advice given by the Negro agent," thereby repaying the loans on schedule.[39]

Roosevelt's administration responded aggressively to the credit shortage assailing the rural South. Limited collateral made it difficult for poor farmers of either race to secure loans, and inflation made a loan through a lending agency almost as hazardous as the traditional debt cycle that Robert L. Smith reacted against with the FIS. The Farm Credit Act, passed in 1933, created the Farm Credit Administration (FCA) to reform farm credit. It combined all federal agencies extending credit to farmers, including Federal Land Banks, Intermediate Credit Banks, and Crop Production Offices operated by the USDA. The last had offered seed loans to black farmers since 1929, and those farmers had established an excellent repayment record. Seed loans remained a popular item for farmers even as the AAA attempted to reduce crop production. Tenants and sharecroppers had trouble securing these loans, but property-owning farmers had the collateral that facilitated their participation. Black agents helped farmers apply for these loans and helped them strategize repayment, but they reminded farmers not to become dependent.[40]

K. H. Malone reported that 212 black farmers, farming 1,050 acres in Walker County, applied for seed loans in 1933. He helped them complete their applications in March but discouraged others from applying because he did not think the loans were necessary. They received loans totaling $6,480. This meant that 17.7 percent of the black farm operators in the county participated. All "pledged themselves to work cooperatively with the county agent" to make the most of the seed loans, and by the end of 1933 all but six had repaid. R. G. Johnson in Gregg County got a greater percentage involved. He helped 325 farmers, 29.5 percent of the black farm operators in that county, obtain seed loans. Calvin Waller reported that 5,877 African Americans in Texas had received loans from the national government in 1933 and 92.6 percent had repaid their debt. The remaining 7.4 percent intended to repay when they received their option contracts from the AAA.[41]

The seed loan program provided an opportunity for farmers to meet and discuss common interests and concerns. Malone held one of these "Get Together Meetings" in late April 1933 at the "Colored High School." He wanted farmers not only to organize but also to ally themselves with "some agricultural organization." Loans to black farmers accounted for 70 percent of all seed loans in Walker County, and he believed that this high percentage meant that too many black farmers depended on these loans. Malone intended to reduce the need. The solution proposed by the white county agent, D. R. Carpenter, involved following the advice of agents and participating in the Extension Service's "Live-at-Home" program. The farmers also met Lewis E. Ball, the chair of the Relief Committee of Walker County and a member of the County Committee on Agricultural Seed Loans. He repeated Malone's advice on the need for black farmers to raise their own food. The field supervisor for the government seed loan program also spoke, providing details about the methods of payment and the qualifications for the 1934 loan. Malone took the opportunity to promote extension programs. He explained that farmers with loans should use the canning houses under construction to preserve as much produce as possible and thus make themselves more self-sufficient. The president of the local Negro Chamber of Commerce also spoke, as did several farmers.[42]

Negro agents did not make a habit of recommending that farmers take out loans; they remained committed to breaking the crop lien system by making farm families more self-sufficient. But emergency relief appealed to those who needed to refinance mortgages. The Emergency Farm Mortgage Act, passed in May 1933, helped at least four farmers in McLennan County. Others participated in the Federal Farm Loan Association. The Federal

Emergency Relief Act, also passed in May 1933, channeled aid toward black farmers as well.[43]

The idea of a special credit bureau for African Americans did not gain support from the USDA in 1933 because Secretary of Agriculture Henry A. Wallace believed that the provision of agricultural credit rested with the FCA. Black farmers continued to request consideration, however, and Negro Division supervisors discussed the need at a staff meeting in 1937, recommending "the establishment of a Credit Rating for farm people as well as agents in their respective counties." The FCA appealed to black extension agents as a means to reach more farmers. A representative of the FCA, Mr. King, explained FCA services and informed the staff of the nature of credit unions. He believed that the agents could help reduce the number of farmers who lost their farms due to foreclosure by recommending them to the FCA. This could also serve to reduce the incidents of unfair treatment based on race. King urged the agents to ask farmers about their debts and to help them avoid foreclosures. He told agents to have farmers write him directly and to provide details.[44]

As black farmers became more informed about credit and management of credit, they took advantage of opportunities. Yet, the "forgotten farmer"— the black tenant or sharecropper—had trouble qualifying for loans, and black owners shied away from loans for various reasons. County agents usually advised farmers not to secure loans. This limited black farmers' use of farm credit.

The Bankhead-Jones Farm Tenant Act of 1937 offered credit options for black farmers, otherwise dependent on landlords or merchants for credit, but it never realized its potential because so few loans reached the needy. The Farm Security Administration, a new agency, administered Bankhead funds. The agency offered rehabilitation loans to marginal farmers, stable tenants, and owners fearing the loss of their farms. It employed a black advisor specializing in race relations, Joseph H. B. Evans, as well as black personnel to work with resettlement projects. By 1938, approximately 21 percent of all families approved for FSA loans were black. Yet, some discrimination existed. The loans for black families in the South averaged $606 while those for white families averaged $659. Also, the FSA favored those with the greatest potential for rehabilitation. Detailed enrollment forms helped officials screen applicants, and only those with a good credit history and personal commitment qualified.[45]

The FSA undertook other projects, namely, the resettlement of farm families on small farmsteads. Twelve of these projects were built in Texas and included two for blacks. One, Sabine Farms in Harrison and Panola counties, offered as many as 120 farm units of eighty acres each to selected families. It included a cooperative store, a crafts building, and a community center. The other, the Texas Farm Tenant Security Project, involved the resettlement of fifty black families on lands acquired in Denton and Limestone counties. The selection process screened potential residents, and only those most capable of functioning in a communal society and making a living from the acreage designated were accepted.[46]

Inadequate funding limited the effectiveness of these programs, and they did not offer the kind of relief needed by those selected. Nor did the number of blacks involved reflect their proportion of the state's rural population. Only 10.3 percent of all resettlement families were black, but 12.6 of the rural population was black in 1940. North Carolina, South Carolina, and Virginia distributed the rehabilitation loans and the opportunity to participate in resettlement units more equitably than did Texas.[47]

The extension agent staff worked with both FSA projects. The appointment of Calvin Waller as chair of the FSA Committee for Negroes in Texas ensured the involvement of county and home demonstration agents in referring satisfactory clients. The same training process occurred with African Americans involved in the FSA as it had for the AAA. Tuskegee hosted the training meetings at which extension leaders gathered for general information. Fifty-seven black FSA workers from the South, including Waller, met there on December 12–17, 1938. This provided an opportunity for those vested in the program to meet each other, share information, and discuss problems and solutions. The FSA relied on communication between these attendees and agents in the field. Regular staff meetings at Prairie View A&M facilitated exchange as well. Henry Estelle reported to supervisory staff about the counties that the FSA planned to use to settle tenants and the process by which Negro clients would be selected. The district agents then relayed the information to the agents in their respective areas. The FSA also looked for information from agents. Extension staff members discussed topics at their meetings and made lists of "what we want from FSA," including prospective supervisors. Agents listed qualifications for supervisors and in this way established professional standards. Ultimately, a Mr. Ellerson asked that the extension staff assist in choosing farmers.[48]

Field agent B. T. Lacey talked with white agricultural and home demonstration agents about the process of selecting families for the Texas Farm Tenant Security Project. They would identify an "above average" tenant family "with sufficient funds or credit for this year's operation," while he looked for an area with good land to ensure a "good set up" and talked with companies about land they had for sale. John V. Smith, the black county agent in McLennan County, was involved in selection and relocation of tenant farmers from the county. Smith wrote Elbert E. Pace, the supervisor, on January 4, 1938, that their landlords were "anxious for them to move just as soon as possible." Moving day took on a whole new significance that year for these families. Black agents offered advice in minute detail to make the process as painless as possible. Smith asked that Taylor and Whitaker, two farmers chosen, be allowed to move first. He also asked that Taylor and the Jack Powell family be settled on adjoining land and that Whitaker and the William M. Estelle family be settled next to each other. Pace relayed Smith's requests to Cecil Johnson, rural supervisor in Limestone County. Pace thought that the farm owned by Miss Zephie Anglin, if vacant, might be a good place to start relocating the families.[49]

Even with close screening, not all clients made their payments on time. Flexible standards helped many who built homes and improved farms with FSA funds. Several of these families later appeared on the list of lease and purchase contracts for Sabine Farms, an indication that experience with one New Deal program paved the way for more involvement. The relief entered even the poorest regions, including Prairie View A&M's home county. Waller met with officials at the FSA office in Dallas in support of the Waller County project in 1940 and helped settle fourteen families there.[50]

Boosters in Harrison County likewise sought a resettlement project in the county. In January 1936, Texas governor James Allred wrote regional FSA director, D. P. Trent, about the possibilities of creating a "Negro" resettlement project in the area. Allred indicated that "the City of Marshall through the auspices of the Marshall Chamber of Commerce is desirous of obtaining a negro colony for that section." Trent responded that the FSA was "giving this project favorable consideration." The FSA placed it on the list of preferred projects and sent a project engineer to Marshall to do preliminary surveys and plan Sabine Farms' development.[51]

The Sabine Farms project benefited from extension advice. Black district extension agents and the Negro Division leader encouraged the FSA to hire experienced agents, even if it meant a loss to the Extension Service. As a result, the FSA appointed Otis Anthony Mason in 1939. Previously, the Negro agricultural agent in Lee County, Mason resigned in November 1939 after more than eight and a half years of service to work at Sabine Farms. The colony did not prosper as hoped, however, because by November 1941, it had 68 families in residence, 453 individuals, and twelve vacant dwellings waiting to be occupied, of a total of eighty planned.[52]

Even though some extension agents worked closely with FSA projects, the Extension Service cooperated less and less with the FSA over time. Generally, the Extension Service did not support the FSA's cooperative ventures nor the agency's work with farm labor during World War II. Furthermore, the FSA extended the potential for more relief toward the lower classes, and this strategy threatened the race and class hierarchy that white Texans had established. Some whites also opposed Bankhead-Jones Act loans because they did not believe the government should encourage the tenant class. Strict regulations governed the loans, however, and getting them proved difficult. Black extension agents in Texas lent their support in the hope that deserving tenants could benefit.[53]

Traditional gender relations came into question, as FSA loan applications acknowledged the importance of women to domestic economics and required as much information from the woman of the house as it did from the man. Many female applicants indicated that they worked year-round with their husbands to make the farm viable and that they took breaks only when they were sick. Extension programming also mattered; many of the women indicated that they had participated in a homemakers' or a canning club. The skill of canning positioned them well for a loan because of the role canned goods played in creating a household independent of the influence of creditors. Thus, a quest to secure an FSA loan could indicate efforts to overcome class as well as gender bias.[54]

Women routinely participated in construction and operation of canning centers, a role in keeping with their involvement in economic development begun through Negro extension work. Yet, New Deal administrators vested more responsibility in male agents to negotiate funding with local relief commissions. Canning centers offered employment to many and produced commodities that families could sell and counties could distribute to the needy. Men and women cooperated in construction, as did residents in the Beulah Community in Anderson County when they built the first "really modern canning house" in 1932. They salvaged materials from an old hall destroyed by a storm and pooled two years' worth of winnings from displays at the Anderson County Fruit Palace to complete their canning house.[55]

Extension staff featured the Beulah center at the annual agents' conference in 1932. Male and female agents left the meeting committed to the idea. They secured plans from the TAEX to help them construct centers

in their counties. Within a year, black Texans had built forty-seven kitchens in nine counties, three owned by individuals but the rest owned by
communities. Negro Division leader Calvin Waller noted that the enthusiasm "enabled the Negroes to take full advantage of the program put into
effect by the R.F.C. as in many cases they had places already prepared to
house equipment." [56]

In 1933, loans from the Reconstruction Finance Corporation and grants
from the Federal Economic Relief Administration, both distributed through
the Texas Relief Commission (TRC), created a new wave of canning centers
in the Texas countryside. County commissioners, civic organizations, and
other local or county committees helped agents purchase pressure cookers
and sealers for use in the public centers. Agents provided advice and supervised processing of vegetables and meat in this phase of emergency work.
The funds available in 1933, a total of $3,050 in Texas, helped rural blacks
construct fourteen structures and furnish others already constructed. Waller,
despite the fine showing of Beulah residents, and others believed more aid
for African Americans was justified: "We have not been able to secure much
of the R.F.C. money in building canning houses." [57]

New Deal programs provided more money but also more white influence
over black programs. Negro agents interested in having canning centers had
to gain the support of the white county agent to act as their sponsor. In
Walker County, D. R. Carpenter secured funds from the County Relief and
Improvement Committee and built eighteen canning units in 1933. He had
half of them set up in black communities. Each canner had one retort, one
twenty-nine-quart cooker, and one sealer. The relief committee collected a
fee from those who used the center and distributed money to the needy. The
black county agent, K. H. Malone, praised community extension councils
for building the canning houses. He motivated communities to raise funds
for buildings through concerts, picnics, box suppers, community sings, and
4-H Club events to create a vested interest in the work among African Americans. He located the centers so residents in each of the twenty-five black
communities in the county had an opportunity to use them. [58]

As canning centers became profit centers, men became more associated
with their management. Agents in several counties hired field workers to
help supervise canning plants. Fred D. Bates managed a plant in Robertson
County, and his wife assisted him. The plants provided formative experiences for many African Americans, and many recall these sorts of canneries
when they reminisce about their depression-era experiences. They provided
additional income to help many through lean times, but they also represent a

departure from communitarian to commercial-scale production, and a shift in gender roles.[59]

The emphasis on the commercial may have resulted from the general focus of New Deal programs on agricultural relief and other traditional male domains, namely, crops, credit, and conservation. This caused counties to hire county agents rather than home demonstration agents to help implement the programs. Regardless, home demonstration agents played an important role in promoting AAA programs, particularly in counties that did not hire male agents. Brazoria County did not employ a county agent until 1937, so the home demonstration agent, Clara J. S. Hall, worked with Calvin Waller to inform farmers about the program. Waller asked Hall to plan a meeting on Monday night and another on Tuesday morning in February 1934, and he spent that time talking with farmers about the reduction campaigns. Jessie Shelton, the home demonstration agent in Travis County, indicated that she met with farmers about the AAA, interpreted the rules for them, and monitored their performance throughout 1941. She also encouraged FSA clients to participate in training meetings and attend demonstrations and short courses. These women proved exceptions to the general rule of men presenting information on the most important New Deal program for rural Texas cotton reduction.[60]

As women found themselves involved in less responsible positions as canning projects became part of national relief efforts, they responded with other community-based relief projects that allowed them full authority. Large families needed plenty of beds with mattresses and bedding. Many made do with ticks stuffed with grass, moss, or corn shucks laid on the floor. These mattresses and ticks needed routine, regular care, so mattress making and restuffing became a regular occurrence in farm homes. Those who used moss restuffed their mattress casings, or ticks, twice each year. Few poor families could afford to stuff their mattresses or pillowcases with their cash crop, but others used lint cotton when available. Those who could afford it had mattresses made in factories and provided cotton for stuffing. Agents demonstrated the techniques of mattress making in the early days of the service, but the process did not gain significant attention until 1939, when the federal government passed legislation that distributed cotton to relief families for the purpose of making mattresses. Texans proved instrumental in the passage of this legislation and in the formation of the mattress-making program.[61]

Home demonstration agents incorporated mattress making into their bedroom-improvement campaigns. Club members constructed only a few

Figure 23. Evans Spring club women, Neches, Anderson County, Tex., refinishing a bedstead, Apr. 1933. These six women were improving their bedrooms with the help of Mrs. I. S. Kinchion. They worked cooperatively to reduce the cost and burden of physical labor. (Neg. S-16838-C, George W. Ackerman, photographer, FES, USDA, NA)

mattresses each year, but families with adequate resources bought new ones. Clara S. Hall reported that members tacked three mattresses in 1933. Ruby O. Phelps, the black agent in McLennan County, did not report any work in mattress making. Her description of one of the "outstanding" bedrooms in the county indicated the poverty that consumed even progressive black farmers. Bedrooms looked like new with repainted old furniture and tables made from cheese boxes (Fig. 23). The "winner" covered her costs by selling okra and spent $5.85 on Rit dye to tint old curtains rose pink, to varnish and wax the floor, and to frame attractive pictures to hang on the walls. In 1933, Lea Etta Lusk in Washington County reported that her club members also made dressing tables from boxes, but they had enough resources to purchase 110 mattresses, so had to make only fifty-six (Fig. 24).[62]

Home demonstration agents and women who attended the short course at Prairie View A&M in August 1935 participated in a course on mattress making. They went home and helped club members make 538 mattresses. The next year, club members made 204 mattresses at home, but in 1937, they

Figure 24. Ruby O. Phelps conducting a slipper chair–making demonstration to Harrison Community club women, McLennan County, Tex., Apr. 1933. The chair was made from old packing crates, cotton, and flour sacks, and cost thirty-five cents. (Neg. S-16853-C, George W. Ackerman, photographer, FES, USDA, NA)

made 688. Increased productivity in 1937 resulted from a slumping economy that produced a cotton surplus. Alma O. Huff, newly appointed Negro home demonstration agent in Kaufman County, defined the conditions of home life in the cotton-rich area as "poor, definitely lacking in comfort and culture." She focused on two programs: increasing the home food supply, and bedroom improvements. She began offering mattress-making schools during October, in the midst of the cotton harvest, and she encouraged women to use "some of the excess cotton grown on the farms" to cut the costs of the mattresses. Fifty-six people participated in the schools and made four mattresses. The winning mattress cost only $2.50 to make, had a value of more than $10.00, and was valuable as a public relations tool displayed in furniture stores in Terrell and Kaufman. Texas women involved in the home improvement program in 1938 made 613 mattresses at home and had 474 made in factories. Home demonstration agents concentrated on making cotton mattresses in 1939. As a result, they added 1,337 mattresses, making 681 of them at home.[63]

Cotton surplus and the number of families on relief in the rural South prompted Texas legislators Luther G. Johnson and Tom Connally to introduce bills concurrently in the House and the Senate in 1939. The bills called for the release of government-owned cotton to the Works Progress Administration for the manufacture of mattresses and other articles for families on relief. Kate Adele Hill, a white district home demonstration agent working out of the TAEX headquarters in College Station, discussed the situation with Johnson and Connally in Washington in 1939 and sent them her ideas for broadening benefits provided by the surplus-commodities bill. She recommended that cotton could also be made available to low-income families that did not qualify for relief but that still needed mattresses and did not have the funds to purchase them. Families would furnish ticking, and the home demonstration council or individual clubs would acquire the cotton. A cadre of as many as ten trained mattress makers resided in each county in Texas, so implementing the program would prove no challenge for white agents. Black agents also stood poised to undertake the government project.[64]

The cotton mattress program began in 1940 and continued through 1942, when wartime production consumed all surplus cotton. It involved agents throughout the South, the AAA, and the Surplus Commodity Corporation. Iola Rowan, the Texas black home demonstration leader, bore the responsibility for implementing the special assignment among black farm families that year. She included the cotton mattress demonstrations as part of the established home improvement program and devised ways for the male agricultural agents and men enrolled in agricultural demonstrations to participate. To complete her task, she requested authority to train WPA workers to teach mattress making. She also requested two WPA teachers dedicated to the program to work out of the Prairie View A&M office.[65]

In just over a month, Rowan reported that every county with black agents had accepted the special project, except two, Waller and Walker, both of which had large black populations. She explained that no white home demonstration agents worked in these counties, and this hindered the program's adoption, perhaps because the relief committees did not feel comfortable vesting authority in professional black women for a program that would involve poor white women. Rowan again stressed the educational nature of the demonstration, and she and other district agents discussed the best ways to approach the work in counties that employed only a black agricultural agent rather than a black home demonstration agent.[66]

The special program began in March 1940 in Austin County. Rowan proudly proclaimed that the Harvey family in the Burleigh Community had made the "first mattress in the nation" under the new system (Fig. 25). The program, undertaken by black agents among black farm families, spread rapidly in Texas as it did throughout the South. An average of twelve mattress centers existed in each county that employed a black agent, collectively producing an average of 3,645 mattresses per month. The home demonstration agent in Kaufman County, Alma Huff, continued to offer mattress-making schools, and the Home Demonstration Council undertook its first tricounty fair in 1940. The three counties, Kaufman, Van Zandt, and Rockwell, promoted a new homemade bed completely made up with sheeting, pillows, and a new mattress.[67]

In 1940, agents in Texas made 32,810 mattresses using 50 pounds of cotton per mattress. This eliminated 1,640,500 pounds of surplus cotton from the warehouses and helped make way for the 1941 crop. These mattresses required 3,281 bales and 328,100 yards of cotton ticking. Male agents in seven counties in the northern district carried the program to their constituents because the counties did not employ black home demonstration agents. These men attended a training session in Marshall under the leadership of Negro district agent Jeffie O. A. Conner. She trained them in the simple technique of cutting and sewing a tick, attaching the side panels, filling the tick with cotton, attaching the top to the sides, settling the cotton by beating it with sticks, and then tacking or tufting the mattress to hold the cotton in place. The finishing touch consisted of sewing a rolled edge around the sides of the mattress. The male agents then supervised the construction of 5,398 mattresses during 1940.[68]

Families that participated in government-supported mattress making qualified for relief. Agents recruited them by holding informational meetings and asking for applications. To qualify, families could not earn more than $400 per year, with at least half of this derived from farm income. Agents then relayed these applications to a local selection committee and awaited the decision before ordering the materials necessary for outfitting the mattress center. Agents trained assistants who staffed the centers, or agents presented instruction directly to farm families when assistants could not handle the load.[69]

The special program, added to full schedules, overtaxed agents. Jessie L. Shelton, home demonstration agent in Kaufman County, pushed herself

Figure 25. Nathan and Ellitie Harvey family, Burleigh, Austin County, Tex., with the "first mattress in the nation," constructed 1940. Children pictured (left to right): Haskell, Julia, Leon, L. V., and Vinie. (Collection of Mrs. Vera Dial Harris)

to deliver programs. She organized twenty-one adult clubs and twelve 4-H Clubs in her first full year of service and focused her normal demonstrations on increasing the quantity of vegetables grown and preserved and on improving bedrooms. The second year of the government mattress program affected her work, and she and her club leaders helped poor families produce 1,251 cotton mattresses and 1,051 cotton comforters. She presented canning demonstrations and encouraged families to prepare balanced meals. The work took eleven months and she spent 212 days in the field and 53 days in the office. This left her 69 days off, averaged over eleven months, or approximately 1.5 days each week.[70]

White and black agents in Texas produced a total of 163,197 mattresses as part of the government program in 1940 and 367,416 in 1941. This compared favorably with other states such as Alabama, where agents made 196,374 mattresses in 1940 and 289,181 in 1941, or Georgia, where they made 150,000 mattresses in 1940. The black agents in Texas alone made as many mattresses in 1940 as did all the agents in Louisiana, 33,000, and Mississippi, 40,000. The high figures in Texas and Alabama reflected the strength of the organization that coordinated the project as much as it did the abilities of those who benefited and the importance of utilizing surplus cotton.[71]

The limited relief that New Deal programs made available to rural blacks did not satisfy the desperate need. Three things contributed to the inadequacy: the federal government did not provide enough resources to meet demand; white administrators directed aid toward those with proven track records rather than the impoverished; finally, the structure that channeled information on relief and recovery programs through overextended staff within the Negro Division limited the recipients to those already involved in extension work. As a result, farmers and their families with a history of extension involvement gained an advantage in the application and selection process. Many rural blacks, as well as rural whites, unable to secure loans or participate in plow-under campaigns because they had no history of involvement with the extension program, could not reap any benefits from nationwide relief and recovery efforts. Extension agents, however, found themselves increasingly involved in visible ways beyond their community. This proved critical to the survival of the profession they were building.

6

—•◦•—

Beyond the Farm

Cultivating New Audiences and Support Systems at
Home and Abroad

During the 1930s and 1940s, Negro Division professionals justified their existence even as their traditional constituents left farming and the rural lifestyle behind. They did this through public relations campaigns that carried their message beyond rural communities and farms. Public observances of key events in Texas history, specifically, the centennial of Texas independence in 1936 and the twenty-fifth anniversary of TAEX in 1939, gave agents cause for celebration, reflection, and promotion. With the assistance of extension agents, Negro Division administrators collected data and created history lessons that emphasized African American contributions to Texas history.

World War II increased the visibility of an expanding staff. Public events and domestic mobilization helped agents broaden their networks of support and their interaction with politicized African Americans. This proved critical as black farmers, including a significant proportion of owners, left Texas during the 1950s. Negro Division agents remained in the field largely because their visibility made their employment defensible.

Negro agents strengthened their position relative to their constituents in several ways. Exclusion from white professional groups left them little choice but to form their own associations, through which they gained information, support, and increasingly rigorous professional standards. They used their positions to link farming to patriotism during the cold war. This public service increased interaction between agents and rural Texans, between agents and increasing numbers of urban Texans, and eventually with the world. A few Negro Division staff became involved in U.S. diplomacy by serving in international reform programs. Their service often took them to Third World regions, particularly Africa. Some had identified inequity in New Deal programs during their service as agents; their foreign service, theoretically, involved them in nation building abroad. But U.S. officials believed their service could deflect criticism of race-biased decision making, not reverse it. Specifically, the involvement of black public servants, it was thought, could reduce international frustration with discriminatory policies in the United States.

The variety of experiences agents gained during the first decades of the cold war coincided with the growing public struggle for civil rights. Increasing national and international opposition to discrimination and segregation drew attention to inequitable practices in national and state Extension Service employment during the 1940s and the 1950s. Agents could discuss such treatment in professional gatherings, but they did not always agree on solutions. Agents walked a fine line, because their challenge to race discrimination and inequity could compromise their position in the quasi-autonomous Negro Division. Many balanced their goals of equality with their professional interests. Others challenged legal and political inequity directly by moving beyond established lines of communication, defying TAEX policy, and demanding their rights. They sought many things, including job security, equal pay for equal work, and national and international audiences for their messages. Although equality eluded them, they made serious gains in visibility and influence.

Negro Division staff members carried their message beyond small gatherings of dues-paying members and other supporters, who represented only 7.5 percent of the black Texas population, but the division claimed to reach much greater numbers indirectly. Staff members used a variety of media to accomplish this task. Radio provided an avenue for black agents and their clients to air their opinions and offer advice. The USDA had a long relationship with radio, so the medium provided a reliable outlet for conveying information. USDA staff members broadcast market prices over the airwaves for the first time in December 1920, using a navy station in Arlington, Virginia. Radios remained scarce in rural areas because they were expensive, impossible to operate without a dependable electricity source, and frustrating because of reception problems, but in 1922, the *Daily Oklahoman* indicated the ways that radio could reduce isolation for rural Americans. By 1923, the Bureau of Agricultural Economics had the Radio Market News Service. William M. Jardine, U.S. secretary of agriculture, created a radio division to facilitate communication and information sharing between the USDA and commercial and university broadcasting stations in 1926.[1]

Ownership of radios in the South lagged behind that of all other regions. Only 1 percent of southerners reported owing a radio in 1925, and only 5 percent did in 1930. Not until 1950 did a majority of southerners have electricity in the home, so southern black farmers did not have ready access to the medium. Regardless, the introduction of an African American farm boy on National 4-H Club Radio in 1933 generated considerable enthusiasm among Negro Division staff in Texas. The black home demonstration agent in Brazoria County, Clara S. Hall, requested the assistance of individuals and businesses to ensure that those who wanted to hear George Peasant, a seventeen-year-old 4-H club member in Dallas County, Alabama, could do so. She announced the broadcast in the newspaper and informed interested blacks that they could hear the program at the home of A. D. Snow in West Columbia, or in Angleton between the Times building and the A. R. Kelley pressing shop. Mr. M. E. Bergen provided the radio for the broadcast in Angleton.[2]

In 1935, a Texan gained the national spotlight. Federal Extension Service officials selected Alvin Wilkins, Wharton County, to speak on National 4-H Club Radio to represent the work of African American boys throughout the South. Wilkins's speech aired in early May 1935 and was heard on over fifty-eight National Broadcasting Corporation (NBC) radio stations. The sixteen-year-old described his experiences with 4-H over a period of three years, specifically, the ways he grew better feed through his corn demonstrations and parlayed that success into raising better hogs with the help of pig club demonstrations. He won first prize for his corn yield of 76.64 bushels per acre in 1933, an accomplishment that earned him a trip to the Texas State Fair in Dallas. He earned $309.25 in premiums and sales of corn and pigs over several years, and he saved this for college. Wilkins recounted other experiences that showed how the Extension Service worked to broaden the perspectives of youth. He participated in a table etiquette contest, played games as a part of camps and short courses, judged hogs and dairy cattle, and made friends with like-minded youngsters in Wharton County and across East Texas. He concluded that his involvement with 4-H made him "more determined to struggle for an education and stay on the farm and take my chances with farming people."[3]

Radio became increasingly important to extension agents as more farmers purchased sets, but agents utilized motion pictures to convey their message as well. As early as 1920, the USDA had made a documentary emphasizing Negro extension work in an Alabama community and the ways it could help Negro communities develop. The film, *Helping Negroes to Become Better Farmers and Homemakers,* summarized Negro Extension work from boll weevil eradication to storing sweet potatoes. FES personnel encouraged wider use of motion pictures during the 1930s because film appealed to audiences.

Figure 26. Leigh 4-H Club girls created an educational display titled "Solve the Meat Problem by Raising Poultry," for the 1946 Central East Texas Fair. (Annie L. Barrett, "Annual Narrative Report," Harrison County, Tex., Dec. 1, 1945–Nov. 30, 1946; original in author's possession)

The Kaufman County agent showed *The Negro Farmer* at 4-H Club Day in 1940, but black agents often faced challenges when showing films as part of club meetings, because projection equipment proved difficult to acquire.[4]

Exhibits proved the most useful educational tool. Extension agents relied on information displays in a variety of formats and of different complexity to educate the general public. Exhibits served several purposes. Promotional displays in storefronts could convince white residents of how support provided to black farmers could positively affect the local economy. With such support, Negro Division administrators could qualify counties, and once a county qualified, blacks could stage exhibits to recruit members. Most African Americans in rural Texas could not take the time to tour the countryside and see the corn and the grain sorghum that demonstrators grew. Agents responded by organizing educational displays of crops in town for white and black clients to view. These exhibits, along with images of the demonstrators at work, was a way to entice more to join. Displays appeared in storefronts and at county, tricounty, regional, and state fairs (Fig. 26). Educational exhibits at the Texas Centennial Exposition in 1936, at the State Fair in Dallas in 1937, 1938, and 1939, and at the 1940 Prairie View A&M short course used pictures, graphs, and other visual aids such as dioramas to relay the message of racial uplift possible through extension work undertaken by the Negro Division.[5]

Two anniversaries during the 1930s featured exhibits developed by black extension workers that emphasized Negro Division influence over time. Venues guaranteed a wide audience. In 1932, Texans voted to observe, in 1936, the hundredth anniversary of the state's independence. State legislators authorized $3 million for the event, and national appropriations matched this amount. Congress dedicated WPA staff and other aid to the state observance. Communities received appropriations to develop commemorative events, publications, or markers. Traditional racial attitudes affected black participation initially. In 1935, the federal Texas Centennial Commission announced that African American material would be segregated into the Hall of Negro Life. Other examples of racial favoritism existed as well, from decisions about contractors to paternalistic attitudes among white organizers.[6]

Blacks challenged their marginalization but debated about how far their challenge should extend. Some believed the Hall of Negro Life, professional and well managed, could pave the way for greater expenditures in their behalf and increased responsibilities and authority. Others argued that they should seek integration into general exhibit themes. Several project planners and work team leaders had professional positions in segregated divisions. Many had come of age as advocates of industrial education and rural reform in keeping with Booker T. Washington's Tuskegee Institute. The Hall of Negro Life's general manager, Jesse O. Thomas, had matriculated at Tuskegee and was serving as southern field director for the National Urban League at the time of the fair. TAEX Negro Division personnel who bore responsibility for the exhibit on agricultural progress shared Thomas's pedigree. They had received their training at Prairie View A&M, predominantly, and depended on segregated public agencies for their professional positions. Willette R. Banks, Prairie View A&M principal, along with his faculty, bore responsibility for other exhibits in the hall. Banks and A. Maceo Smith, the hall's assistant manager, held influential positions in public education in Texas. Smith managed the business department at Booker T. Washington High School in Dallas.[7]

Ultimately, those interested in integrating the exposition gave up because no local or state appropriations allowed their inclusion. Jesse Thomas recalled that black organizers became determined "to evolve an advantage out of a disadvantage." They desegregated the hall, and white and black men and women sat on the same benches and used the same lavatories, thus facilitating an exchange uncommon in the South at the time.[8]

Though organizers debated the best response to official segregation, they faced non-negotiable time constraints. Exhibit teams had only three months to complete research, design, and installation for the six-month exposition, and Negro agents wasted no time soliciting information from retired agents as well as agents in the field. Iola Rowan wrote Robert Lloyd Smith, the first state leader, in her efforts to document the evolution of service in Texas and referred to material collected previously by Mary E. V. Hunter, particularly Hunter's 1931 compilation, "Outstanding Achievements in Negro Home Demonstration Work." District administrator John H. Williams helped produce and install the exhibit. These efforts resulted in "a very creditable exhibit at the Centennial" when it opened on Juneteenth 1936.[9]

The agricultural exhibit told a story that white Texans could appreciate. Visitors encountered a series of miniatures as they entered the hall that showed the progression of a black-owned farm in Texas over more than seventy years. Agents selected the farm after reviewing surveys collected by thirty-eight Negro Division agents. The story began in 1863, when a black farmer acquired his freedom after service in the Confederate army and secured the property three years before emancipation. The original owner conveyed the farm to his son in 1918, and the son took advantage of extension work to modernize the property. Thomas, predisposed to celebrations of agricultural progress, believed that the diorama created by Negro Division agents "represented one of the most attractive features of the Agriculture Exhibit."[10]

The juxtaposition of appeals to white Texans' sympathies, including former Confederates, and integrated public accommodations indicates why Thomas believed that the fair fundamentally changed Texans, white and black alike. He believed that "never again during the life of the white people of this generation in the State of Texas will they undertake any program of a community or state-wide character which . . . involves the interest and welfare of colored people, without first enlisting the intelligent and understanding cooperation of Negro leadership." Likewise, the exhibits helped African Americans realize that they had to "decide what degree and kind of segregation they will cooperate with or capitalize upon." [11]

Negro Division staff members did not overtly challenge the racial status quo in 1936, but their commemoration emphasized African American accomplishments despite their segregated status. In 1939 the TAEX planned events to recognize the twenty-fifth anniversary of the Smith-Lever Act, which had vested responsibility for extension work in white land-grant institutions and led to the formation of the Negro Division in Texas. Black supervisors used the anniversary as an opportunity to accomplish two things: to reflect on the growth of their profession; and to educate Texans about the benefits of extension work. As the anniversary approached, supervisors drew on staff expertise. Home demonstration agents prepared "historical appraisals" of extension work in their counties. They documented local initiatives to qualify counties and service poor Texans, including interracial cooperation that helped convince county commissioners to provide funds for Negro agents. Sometimes their stories indicated that "the financial condition of the people" constrained Negro Division work, but others attributed inequity to race discrimination. Black agents had no office help, inadequate time for professional development, unequal compensation, nonexistent travel allowances, and no retirement incentives. The local histories collected indicate awareness of race discrimination within the service from early days. [12]

Negro Division planners, however, did not want their gala to become tainted by criticism of discrimination. Agents relied on their strong support network as a buffer. Iola Rowan suggested that black agents celebrate their silver anniversary during the Prairie View A&M short course in 1940. Waller secured permission from W. R. Banks, Prairie View A&M principal, and TAEX director, H. H. Williamson. Rowan recommended inviting members of the first team of black agents, including Robert Lloyd Smith, Mary E. V. Hunter, Mrs. Jake Ford, and even Clarence Ousley, TAEX director in 1915, when the division began, to official festivities. Waller appointed Rowan to draft a program for the retrospective. He believed that the occasion warranted documenting, so he planned to request the services of a Federal Extension Service photographer to make a movie. Rowan corresponded with Hunter, who provided additional details about the segregated service's history. Jeffie Conner contacted Hunter and Smith to speak and asked the TAEX's state girls' club agent and state boys' club agent to participate. [13]

Figure 27. Lula Foreman, Limestone County, Tex., showing Henry S. Estelle her new refrigerator, July 8, 1949. (TAEX Historical Files, Cushing Memorial Library and Archives, Texas A&M University)

The 1940 short course, "Home Improvement on Texas Farms," empha-sized an enduring message, fitting for an anniversary: property ownership. Programs offered inexpensive but modern approaches to make life more pleasing—specifically mattress making. Agricultural agents remained com-mitted to the basics; they advocated soil conservation, fertilizer application, and improved breeds and seeds to increase production and stabilize the farm

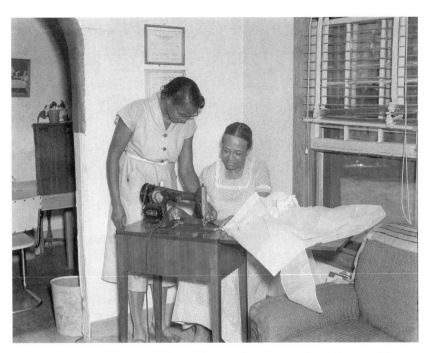

Figure 28. Mrs. R. H. Franc, home demonstration agent, Smith County, Tex., inspecting a modern electric sewing machine used by one of her demonstrators, June 5, 1955. (TAEX Historical Files, Cushing Memorial Library and Archives, Texas A&M University)

economy. After 1940, however, agents encouraged adoption of machines and labor-saving devices more frequently than before (Fig. 27). This reflected both an increase in available technology and black farm family participation in the consumer age. Home demonstration agents featured electric appliances more and linked adoption of such devices to more efficient home management and increased leisure pursuits, including beautifying homes (Fig. 28). Agents obviously remained convinced that scientific applications helped black farmers pursue the American dream of economic independence and personal security. Certainly, families that chose to spend money on refrigerators were more likely to invest in prize stock and have resources to pay 4-H Club dues for their children (Fig. 29).[14]

Negro Division staff members took their increasingly consumer-driven message beyond the farm to Chicago, Illinois, a major purveyor of mail-order catalogs and mass-produced commodities as well as home to thousands of relocated rural Texans. Organizers of the American Negro Exposition in Chicago asked for proposals for demonstrations or exhibits during May

Figure 29. Jim Foreman (center), and sons, Ervin (left) and Reives (right), with hogs they planned to show at the 1949 State Fair of Texas in Dallas. (TAEX Historical Files, Cushing Memorial Library and Archives, Texas A&M University)

1940. The Texas staff approved the idea of team demonstrations and considered a range of process-based exhibits, including mattress making, canning, and home health and sanitation. But staff members worried about securing the funds necessary "to carry the demonstration team to Chicago and to maintain the team while there." Waller and his staff suggested that "enlarged pictures of Negro Extension work" be used instead. The exhibits depicted

Figure 30. Annie L. Barrett (left) presenting purebred Barred Rock chicks to five new 4-H poultry demonstrators and 375 chicks, sponsored by Sears-Roebuck Foundation, to five girls who won prizes at the county poultry show, Marshall, Harrison County, Tex., Apr. 1946. (Annie L. Barrett, "Annual Narrative Report," Harrison County, Tex., Dec. 1, 1945–Nov. 30, 1946; original in author's possession)

black Texas farmers as model citizens, informed about modern devices and involved in economic decisions.[15]

Firms that marketed consumer goods became involved in funding Negro Division programs, an indication of African American participation in rural consumerism. Sears, Roebuck and Company, with administrative offices in Dallas and world headquarters in Chicago, furthered stock improvement goals by providing purebred pigs, chicks, and heifers to club members selected by county agents or judges at stock shows (Fig. 30). Hog shows allowed boosters, specifically, local Chambers of Commerce, to cooperate with the Sears-Roebuck Foundation and the TAEX to sponsor the shows. The 1942 eastern district show in Lufkin drew winning swine and the youth who raised them from several counties. Despite the emphasis on consumption evident in event sponsorship, however, poverty often limited participation, even though Sears gave pigs away. Agents persevered, though, as did Sears, and by 1946, the Sears Cow-Sow-Hen Program extended into poorer East Texas counties, including Houston, Newton, Harrison, Rusk, and Smith (Fig. 31).[16]

In the midst of rising interest in African American history, culture, and status, Negro Division leadership changed. Edward B. Evans assumed responsibility for the division in mid-1941, and his approach to management differed

Figure 31. Southern District Sears, Roebuck Cow-Sow & Hen Program, Gilt & Boar Show, unidentified date, location, and participants. Three white judges regularly determined winners at district shows; e.g., O. C. LaGrone, county agent; George W. Johnson, district agent; and E. M. Regenbrecht, former swine husbandman, judged at the Eastern District show in College Station, Tex., in 1942. First-place winners usually won registered Jersey heifers, and second- through tenth-place winners received cash prizes. (Clippings, J. B. Coleman Library, Special Collections/Archives Dept., Prairie View A&M University Archives; photograph, TAEX Historical Files, Cushing Memorial Library, Texas A&M University)

markedly from that of his predecessor. He supported independent actions by black agents and pursued interracial contacts aggressively. Evans had the support of Prairie View A&M principal, W. R. Banks, a former student of W. E. B. Du Bois and president of the Conference of Presidents of Negro Land-Grant Colleges. Du Bois's recognition of the influence that the land-grant presidents wielded helped them gain confidence in pursuing larger goals.[17]

Evans and Banks proved a potent combination during the 1940s, and their leadership helped several Texans secure their appointments, and helped the segregated division grow. Evans served as Negro Division leader for only five years, until 1946, when he became the first president of Prairie View A&M, recently designated a university. The renaming symbolized a step toward equity, and Evans embraced the potential. He remained concerned about and supportive of the Negro Division's needs and used his position to lobby for more funds and better facilities despite the shrinking rural black population. These actions raised concerns among white administrators, who wanted to

TABLE 9. Texas Negro Division Specialists

Headquarters	Name/Specialty	Tenure
Cameron	J. H. Williams	Jan. 15, 1932–June 30, 1934
	Boys' Club advisor; meat work	
Prairie View	Eugenia A. Woods	May 1, 1943–Nov. 18, 1945
	Food	
Prairie View	Alton E. Adams	
	Emergency war food assistant	Apr. 6–Oct. 16, 1944
	Farm & home development	Dec. 1, 1954–May 30, 1959
LaGrange	Emmett A. Randolph	
	Farm housing	Apr. 1–June 30, 1950
Prairie View	Dempsey H. Seastrunk	
	Farm & home development	July 15, 1959–Feb. 1, 1972
College Station	Dempsey H. Seastrunk	? 1967–Feb. 1, 1972
	Farm & home development	

Source: Seastrunk, "Fifty Years of Negro Extension Work in Texas, 1915–1965," TAEX Historical Files.

approach changes in race relations more slowly. Black agents provided plenty of ammunition for Evans to use to support requests made to his white peers at Texas A&M, and to his black peers across the South.

Evans led the Negro Division through World War II, a period of intense growth and influence. Prairie View A&M hosted the War Emergency Conference for Negro Local Leaders in August 1942. Erwin Shinn, representative from the Federal Extension Service, addressed attendees on the importance of local and neighborhood leadership. War appropriations prompted TAEX officials to recognize two African American agents as specialists. Ms. Eugenia A. Woods served as a food specialist from May 1943 to November 1945, and Mr. Alton E. Adams served as an emergency war food assistant briefly during 1944. They worked with a cadre of male and female emergency food assistant appointees and county agents to reach residents in fifty-one counties with the patriotic message to increase production (Table 9). The conferences, bureaucratic expansion, and increase of agents in the field heightened the visibility of the Extension Service.[18]

Woods used the radio to influence blacks to "save and share," an indication that a growing number of black Americans owned radios and that agents believed the medium provided a viable option to carry their message beyond normal constituents. Henry Estelle, Negro Division district agri-

Figure 32. Third Annual Meat Show, Tyler, Tex., Mar. 1942. Agents from twenty-two counties organized a three-day show featuring approximately 1,240 pieces of meat butchered and home-cured "the A. and M. way." Cuts included hams, shoulders, shoulder butts, bacon, Dixie square loins, and pork chops. (*Houston Defender*, clipping, Mar. 14, 1942; photograph, J. B. Coleman Library, Special Collections/ Archives Dept., Prairie View A&M University)

cultural agent, participated in the "Food for Freedom" program broadcast by Station WTAW in College Station in late March 1942. He discussed the role black farmers had assumed in domestic mobilization and praised black agents, who "put themselves unstintingly into their work in the production of food and education of the people." He reported that "no stone would be left unturned in the production of food and fiber so necessary in the winning of the war for the allies." Others used the radio to reach out to Texans, as did appointees to the Farm Labor Program, developed to alleviate labor shortages caused by increased demand from war-related industries and removal of men from the workforce due to the draft.[19]

The number of special-interest expositions increased during the war years as Negro Division agents enthusiastically displayed their members' accomplishments. Shows of cured meats drew crowds that munched on home-cured ham sandwiches as they inspected meat displays. Through such initiatives, agents believed that "farm and city residents [could study] the part livestock production [played] in the Food for Freedom campaign" (Fig. 32). Numerous Chambers of Commerce allied with the Negro Division to further this aspect of World War II mobilization.[20]

The number of farm families available to participate in rural mobilization efforts declined rapidly during and after the war. In fact, many farm families were less devoted to rural life than were Negro Division staff. Between 1940 and 1960, the number of black farmers declined by 71.6 percent, with the steepest decline occurring between 1950 and 1960, when twenty thousand left the business in Texas—a 56.3 percent drop over the decade. African Americans fled tenancy and sharecropping fastest, as their numbers declined by 92.4 percent over the same twenty-year period.[21]

Southerners with various stakes in rural life worried about the out-migration and called conferences to address the topic. In June 1945, the South-Wide Extension Conference on Work with Negroes met in Washington, DC. Iola W. Rowan served on the committee that organized the conference to address changes necessary to protect the Negro Division as black farmers fled the South. William C. David, acting state leader of the Negro Division, had directed the Farm Labor Program in Texas during the war. He chaired the report committee. The report urged Negro extension staff to solve labor shortages by educating farmers on how to use declining numbers of laborers more effectively and by encouraging farmers to use laborsaving methods and devices. David's report committee also encouraged farmers to enlist ministers to recruit labor, to define farm work as a patriotic expression, and to provide child care so mothers could work in the fields more easily. Finally, it recommended using Negro agents to appeal to Negro laborers.[22]

Other conferences drew Negro Division staff together to discuss contradictions in the division's expanding message related to labor. Black administrators convened "The Southern 'Fireside Chats'" in 1947 to encourage African Americans to keep farming, even as tractors made field labor veritably obsolete. Agents, during the 1947 chat, wondered how they could address factors that displaced agricultural laborers, including mechanization, fairly. They were not convinced that low wages forced migration. The Negro state farm labor assistant reported that pickers averaged from $4.00 to $7.00 per ten-hour day from 1944 to 1946, based on $1.25 to $2.50 per hundred pounds picked. This was comparable to the minimum wage at the time and amounted to $600.00 to $800.00 per year. The state labor expert predicted that increased demand for labor would cause wages to increase. Prognostications based on classic economic theory, however, did not materialize. Agricultural labor was not the same as most wage labor. Cotton pickers had to migrate to take full advantage of top wages. Most laborers chose not to devote themselves so completely to a lifestyle that had such low return on their labor investment, and they left the fields in droves.[23]

Despite failed efforts to reverse rural out-migration, Negro Division staff proved remarkably adept at protecting their positions. Agents created all-black organizations at the local, state, and national levels because whites excluded them. A time lag existed between white formation of professional associations and Negro equivalents at the state and national levels, but black growth occurred during periods critical to the preservation of the service. White county agents and their supervisors organized at the state level first, but by 1915, white male agents had formed the National Association of County Agricultural Agents, a cooperative composed of state associations. It existed specifically to maintain and improve standards, the traditional function of professionalizing bodies. Black county agricultural agents did not organize a comparable national association until the early 1940s, when they formed the National Negro County Agents Association (NNCAA). White home demonstration agents organized at the state level and federated nationally later than white males, forming the National Home Demonstration Association in 1933. Black home demonstration agents formed their own state associations, but limited resources seriously affected their ability to create a national organization. They did not federate into the National Association of Negro Home Demonstration Agents until 1958.[24]

The parallel organizations offered support to black club participants and agents when no other support network existed for them. Even the presidents of land-grant colleges that hosted African American extension offices responded to segregation by creating a parallel organization—the Conference of Presidents of Negro Land-Grant Colleges. These separate organizations facilitated communication, self-improvement and professional improvement, skills acquisition and honing, and self-promotion. They emerged as a result of successful local and state reform conducted within the confines of racialized rural reform, that is, rural reform developed around restrictions imposed by race-based decision making.[25]

During the 1940s, youth experienced in 4-H Club work, successful at fairs, and college educated had accumulated the credentials necessary for extension work. Agents responded to increased supplies of qualified applicants by raising criteria for employment. Iola Rowan encouraged William David to recommend that Negro home demonstration agents complete a minimum of a four-year course leading to a bachelor of science degree in home eco-nomics. The course work would include at least ten hours in rural sociology and rural economics so potential agents were prepared to "address the prob-lem" of substandard living conditions. Proposed criteria also stressed a farm background—the most competitive applicant would have been "reared on a farm or [have] a reasonable amount of farm experience." Thus, the TAEX's Negro Division remained focused on rural and farm backgrounds for agents involved in ever-widening circles of influence.[26]

Congressional appropriations for extension work in the postwar period helped agents implement more rigorous applicant screening. The Bankhead-Flannigan Act of 1945 increased total funding to the land-grant institutions by $12.5 million over three years. Consequently, the Negro Division retained administrative staff added during World War II and hired specialists and 4-H Club leaders, positions considered luxuries for the African American divisions, though they were fundamental to the white divisions. Given the higher standards for hiring, agents in the field received leave to attend ex-tension summer school, and applicants looked increasingly toward white state universities for this training. Agents generally received the assurance of county commissioners that they would be reinstated on return from their study leave. Several agents applied for leaves, and most received them. They sought degrees from institutions of higher education such as Cornell Univer-sity, Iowa State College, Hampton University, and even Prairie View A&M. Yet, offers of professional development were not supported adequately. Ex-tenuating circumstances, specifically, Jim Crow regulations that segregated public accommodations, sometimes foiled their plans. Administrators at host institutions, rather than lobbying for equal access to housing and dining ar-eas, advised agents not to attend if adequate housing and eating accommoda-tions could not be arranged. Training institutions undermined black agents' goals by refusing to admit them, and this frustrated agents, who became increasingly vocal and resistant.[27]

The size of Texas' Negro Division and its influence within the state and across the South masked inequity. By 1946, 108 agents (56 men and 52 wo-men) worked in at least fifty-six Texas counties assisting residents in plan-ning and implementing better farming practices and methods to improve ru-ral life. Only Mississippi employed more agents (110); only North Carolina, with 103 agents, distributed more total funds to support Negro extension work (Table 10). Generally, Texas allotted a disproportionately large amount of money to support the agents when compared to the number of black farm-

TABLE 10. Number of Workers in Negro Extension Service, 1941–47

State	Jan. 1, 1941				1946–47		
	Men	Women	Supervisors/ Club Work	Total	Men	Women	Total
Alabama	35	30	8	73	49	53	102
Arkansas	11	14	4	29	24	30	54
Florida	9	8	2	19	15	15	30
Georgia	22	24	4	50	51	37	88
Kentucky	4	2	1	7	5	5	10
Louisiana	12	7	1	20	24	24	48
Maryland	2	3	—	5	6	2	8
Mississippi	33	40	4	77	43	67	110
Missouri	—	—	—	—	0	1	1
North Carolina	33	18	5	56	51	52	103
Oklahoma	9	9	2	20	14	17	31
South Carolina	19	16	2	37	31	29	60
Tennessee	10	8	3	21	16	13	29
Texas	46	36	5	87	56	52	108
Virginia	25	7	3	35	32	25	57
West Virginia	1	1	3	5	3	16	19
Total	271	223	47	541	420	438	858

Source: Jan. 1, 1941, figures from Crosby, "Building the Country Home," 107. Data for 1946–47 from "1941–1947 Statement of Expenditures for Negro Extension Work," David Papers, PV.

ers in the state. In 1940, only 17.2 percent of all farmers in Texas were black, and these black farmers controlled little land, only 2.7 percent. Perhaps white Texans believed that the black farmers were numerically insignificant and not threatening to white supremacy but still important enough to cotton production to warrant an investment in their welfare. This made it possible for white administrators to support the black program without threatening white power.[28]

The Negro Division in Texas remained the largest in the nation, even though all other southern states except Kentucky had a greater proportion of blacks than whites, and all other states except Kentucky and Tennessee had a greater proportion of black farmers than white. Regardless, the TAEX received more available funds for the segregated program than did the extension services in other states.[29]

Despite the relative wealth of Extension Service resources compared to other states, salaries earned by Texas agents changed little from the middle of the depression to the end of World War II. For example, the black male agent in Cherokee County earned the same in fiscal year 1938–39 as in fiscal year 1944–45, $1,620. During fiscal year 1945–46, his pay increased to $1,680. This amounted to only 61.1 percent of the white male agent's salary, 81.8 percent of the white female agent's salary, and 124.6 percent of the African American female agent's salary for the same period. Salaries in Gregg County, while higher, still reflected the unequal status of African Americans and women of both races in the service. The black male agent in Gregg County earned 62.1 percent of the white male's salary, 75.0 percent of the white female's salary, and 138.5 percent of the black female's salary. Salary inequity prompted increasingly vocal and sustained criticism during the 1940s.[30]

As agents became increasingly dissatisfied with low pay, administrators tried to increase county appropriations by regularly lobbying the commissioners for more support. Black supervisors, hesitant to undertake salary reform except through the extension hierarchy, consistently enforced protocol. The state leader of the Negro Division during World War II, Edward B. Evans, reprimanded those who overstepped their authority and jeopardized the tenuous supplemental funding. Some counties never employed agents despite efforts on the part of administrators to secure the funding. Agents in richer counties and in counties with strong wartime economies, such as Harris, home to the growing city of Houston, fared better.[31]

By 1950, average annual salaries for Negro extension workers had improved substantially across the South, but discrepancies reflected race-bias. Black county farm agents earned approximately three-fifths of what white agents earned in all southern states except Arkansas, where the Negro farm agent actually earned more in appropriations than the white farm agent. But black agents in Virginia, North Carolina, Maryland, and Arkansas earned more than those in Texas; workers in Louisiana and Oklahoma earned nearly the same; and workers in Georgia, Florida, Tennessee, Alabama, Mississippi, and South Carolina ranked lowest in average annual salaries.[32]

Extension agents' responses to the financial inequality changed after World War II as they turned to activist political and business organizations to attain equal consideration and support. During 1945, Negro Division representatives met with Prairie View officials in hopes that they could convince TAEX officials at Texas A&M to remedy the problem. In 1948, the Texas Negro Farmers' Council of Agriculture convened a similar meeting to attempt to effect change. Neither meeting influenced pay scales. Extension agents' contracts prohibited them from "becoming involved" in political activities, but this did not stop political organizations from informing agents and administrators of issues, or of lobbying on the behalf of agents. In 1950, the Democratic Progressive Voters League of Texas, headquartered in Dallas, requested David's help to get agents to encourage rural blacks to pay their poll tax and vote. The league considered the African Americans' "failure to qualify enough voters to make our voting strength felt" as the "only hindrance to our free participation in all political affairs in our state." The league asked David, as state leader, to chair the effort to involve county agents in the campaign. Perhaps in exchange for agent support, in 1951, the Democratic Progressive Voters League and the Texas Negro Chamber of Commerce went over the heads of TAEX officials to protest unequal wages. They contacted William L. Dawson, a U.S. representative, and requested his advice and help in equalizing the distribution of federal funds appropriated to state extension work. Home demonstration agents and county farm agents increasingly resented the extra work that they had to perform for the smaller salary that they earned. Agents had to work with no assistants in the field and had to serve "a larger number of farmers who need help worse than do white county agents."[33]

Hobart Taylor, president of the Texas Negro Chamber of Commerce, and R. A. Hester, executive secretary of the Texas Democratic Progressive Voters League, claimed that neither agents nor the Chamber of Commerce nor the league had been able to secure facts about the extent of the inequities. With more evidence, the two organizations intended to pursue justice. They claimed that the work undertaken by the county agents added to the agricultural income of Texas and that they should receive equal pay for equal work.

Figure 33. Judging entries at a Negro hog show, unidentified location and judges, 1940. (TAEX Historical Files, Cushing Memorial Library, Texas A&M University)

They abandoned traditional methods of bringing about change that agents had used to some effect for the previous thirty years and went increasingly to the source. They kept W. C. David informed, as well as Cedar A. Walton, a county agent in Dallas, and G. G. Gipson, director of the TAEX.[34]

The Dallas Negro Chamber of Commerce launched other protests against unequal treatment in instances related to agricultural extension work. The chamber's board of directors expressed concern over the way the State Fair of Texas discriminated against Negroes by segregating midway rides and implying that African Americans were welcome only on designated days—"Negro Achievement Days." The agents did not boycott the fairs, however, but made the event a festive occasion for club members (Figs. 33 and 34). Equal pay proved just as elusive as equal access. The Civil Rights Act of 1964 made segregation in public accommodations illegal, but not until a class-action lawsuit was filed in 1974 did race stop being the determining factor in figuring extension agent wages in Texas.[35]

During the 1950s, media professionals allied with rural reformers. The Associated Negro Press proved particularly influential in lobbying efforts. Claude

Figure 34. Mr. Jim Foreman (center) and sons Reives (left) and Ervin (right), with ribbons they won at the 1948 State Fair of Texas in Dallas, July 8, 1949. (TAEX Historical Files, Cushing Memorial Library, Texas A&M University)

Barnett, the ANP director, had received an appointment as USDA special agent in 1942, so he had nearly ten years' experience interacting with officials. He asked David and other Negro Extension Service leaders to provide information on the agricultural situation in their states. Barnett intended for Negro presses to use the information to keep Secretary of Agriculture C. F. Brannan (1948–53), a man Barnett described as having "a fine and constructive interest in Negro farmers," informed about "our principal needs and most urgent problems." The pressure kept the USDA attentive to rural African Americans. Pressure from local agents, state associations, and black newspaper editors concerned white administrators enough that the USDA organized a seminar on "race relations" in 1952.[36]

FES officials integrated their staff in response to the growing criticism of the USDA's discriminatory practices. They promoted John W. Mitchell, a longtime regional field agent for the USDA who worked out of Hampton Institute to the position of "national leader" in September 1953. Mitchell had started with extension in North Carolina in 1917 as an emergency agent during World War I and had climbed the ladder of extension administrative positions to state leader in North Carolina before his appointment as the field agent for the eastern states. He became the "first colored Extension worker" to be promoted to national leader. The job change involved a move from his headquarters at Hampton Institute to the USDA offices in Washington, DC, where he could more effectively counsel FES staff on ways to "develop and strengthen the work with Negro farm families and 4-H club youths."[37]

The frustrations that agents felt became palpable. Dr. J. R. Otis, former state leader of the Negro Division in Alabama, spoke to a gathering of African Americans attending a conference at Tuskegee Institute in 1950. He scoffed at the Negro Division's slogan—"Live-at-Home"—compared to the white division's slogan—"Plan to Prosper"—and wondered why the "Negroes" had to be original: "By all means, let us be original. But if that originality is not just as good or better than the other fellow's slogan, let's not be original. Why two 'anythings' when one will do just as well?" His call to integration anticipated the 1954 U.S. Supreme Court decision *Brown v. Board of Education* and its ruling that the "separate but equal" doctrine established by the 1896 *Plessy v. Ferguson* decision was unconstitutional.[38]

James David Prewit, associate director of the TAEX, spoke to the Negro County Agricultural Agents' Association in Dallas in March 1960. He urged agents to direct change, not just accept it. "Accepting change implies submission, while directing it implies vision, planning and the will to action." But Prewit was talking about revolutionary transformation in agriculture over the last thirty years, not southern race relations. Did Negro agents in Texas realize that they worked within the "most rigidly segregated agency identified with the Federal government?" An institution that discriminated based on race as well as class? Prewit's presentation to Negro agents carried the ring of a canned speech written for a convention of white, not black, farm agents. He talked about the transition from a "simple type of agriculture with horse and mule power, single practice demonstrations to a highly complex enterprise system requiring a great deal of capital, organizations, and management." The transition to big farming operations brought with it a host of challenges, according to Prewit, and he used expert testimony to support his claim. He quoted Earl L. Butz, then dean of agriculture at Purdue University, who believed that "scientific and technological developments are coming at such a rapid rate that it makes the kind of economic and sociological adjustments that are required very difficult." Agents had to remain better informed than the farmers they served and aware of research findings and government policies regarding agriculture so they could help farmers make decisions that they faced for the first time. He urged them to act as professionals, working longer than 8:00 AM to 5:00 PM, to deliver accurate information, and to serve the community in church, school, and civic organizations. What Prewit did not say was that black agents had to satisfy the expectations of black as well as white supervisors, and do so with fewer resources, for less pay, and with inadequate support services and opportunities for professional development.[39]

The state prioritized services and implemented policies that privileged white capitalist farmers. Agricultural policy during the 1950s strove to manage overproduction by setting prices and selling staples abroad and to reduce production by taking land out of cultivation. Smaller farmers, regardless of race, reaped disproportionately fewer benefits than did commercial-scale producers. Small farmers functioned without a significant lobbyist bloc, as the commercial producers had. Black extension agents, well positioned to convey issues from the countryside to the highest ranking officials, tended to restrain from emphasizing the negatives. Instead, they shifted their focus to avoid addressing the grave concerns among rural Americans. They advocated the extension education ideal rather than a systematic program of intervention to stabilize small farmers. The bureaucracy had worked for nearly fifty years to promote landownership and production. The rural flight of the 1940s and the 1950s did not divert them from their emphasis; rather, it reinforced their convictions. But small black farmers, still the bulk of constituents black agents served, could not operate on the scale white agents increasingly advocated, because they lacked the capital necessary to secure credit to expand and were discriminated against, even with collateral. Nor could they take land out of production, given the small amount that they farmed. Furthermore, they faced the loss of their rural culture as the black out-migration depopulated the rural South. The Federal Extension Service did not adjust its national message and thus missed a huge opportunity to revolutionize American agriculture by supporting subsistence models in addition to commercial agriculture. Mechanization, consolidation, and government subsidies created a class of megafarmers dependent on public support, a far cry from the yeoman idea espoused by Jefferson, and followed for generations by small-scale black and white farmers alike. By 1960, only 272,541 black farmers remained on the land, and 14,994 of them (5.5 percent) lived in Texas.[40]

The struggle for civil rights that increasingly engaged black agents coincided with cold war initiatives that involved agents of both races in patriotic programs, rural economic development, and civil defense. The Negro Division strengthened services to urban residents as well, responding to the demographic shift in the African American population. This sustained Extension Service growth into the 1960s. One of the initiatives related to involving the general public, particularly veterans, in program planning. No longer did dues-paying members reap the majority of the benefits. Agents who managed strong countywide extension services became most innovative. They involved the general public, not just club members, in program planning by holding public planning meetings in courthouses and churches. They targeted veterans, specifically, because they believed that convincing them to remain in the rural South would help solve the major challenges facing rural populations, for example, the loss of residents and associated community resources. TAEX officials hoped that the agents would use new technology to help spread their message, specifically, "the 2 x 2 slide field of education."[41]

Some agents, disgruntled by the constant frustration of working with disadvantaged rural populations, found new outlets for their reform agenda through cold war–era mobilization. Goals that agricultural and home demonstration agents pursued—land acquisition and retention, crop and stock improvement, nutrition and domestic science, and organization building—gained importance abroad as opportunities to implement them at home declined. The rapid out-migration of black farmers from the rural South left the agents with a shrinking client base, and those less inclined to serve an urban clientele took advantage of new opportunities offered by the USDA's Office of Foreign Agricultural Relations (OFAR), reconstituted from its foreign relations branch during the late 1930s. The OFAR extended scientific agriculture and technical assistance to "friends from (and within) foreign lands."[42]

African American agents seeking new challenges, broadened zones of influence, and international experiences looked to the OFAR as an outlet. They believed that humanitarian aid to developing countries would make a difference. Additionally, the fear of communism helped U.S. officials justify the placement of minorities as technical experts in nations that seemed vulnerable to communist influences. Aid could sway popular opinion away from communism and toward democracy. Several African nations, unstable politically because of the wave of decolonization sweeping the continent, and parts of the Middle East and Asia seemed appropriate regions in which to station Americans of color. Finally, U.S. officials believed that, by involving Negro Division employees in the international reform effort, the citizens downtrodden by racialized decision-making could serve as proof that the

U.S. government took seriously its responsibility for eliminating race discrimination and improving race relations at home and could be trusted to do so abroad.[43]

Europeans recognized that racism existed in the United States. They criticized white Americans for their attitude of superiority as well as the laws that they passed and the actions that they took to keep black Americans subordinate and marginalized. Formation of the United Nations and the passage of the U.N. Declaration of Human Rights in 1948 created an international standard for realizing justice despite race, gender, ethnicity, religion, or class. Article 1 of the declaration states the ultimate standard quite frankly: "All human beings are born free and equal in dignity and rights. They are endowed with reason and conscience and should act towards one another in a spirit of brotherhood." Attitudes and policy decisions supported by racist legislators in the United States increasingly became targets of international criticism.[44]

In contrast, African Americans within the state worked to carry information to the world to reduce inequity and promote self-reliance and sustainability. The Negro Division's message could help citizens around the world realize the declaration's Article 17—that everyone has the right to own property—and Article 25—that everyone has a right to a healthful standard of living. Furthermore, the governmental positions that the African American agents held made it possible for them to engage in international relations that furthered the spirit of Article 22—that international cooperation can help everyone realize "economic, social, and cultural rights indispensable for his dignity and the free development of his personality." Ironically, the liberty, justice, and equality that the agents believed they could help the world realize continued to elude them and their peers at home.

African American reformers had considered African countries as outlets for their agenda for close to fifty years by the cold war era. Almost immediately after Booker T. Washington delivered his speech at the Cotton States and International Exposition in Atlanta in 1895, black nationalists sought him out for encouragement and support of their efforts to further the goals of separation and colonization. Washington either disappointed them or disassociated himself from them, because he did not believe that African American immigration to Africa would solve the race problem in the United States, nor would migration to African countries fraught with racial unrest of their own ease the burden of subjugation that African Americans bore.[45]

Nonetheless, in 1900, students and faculty from Tuskegee Institute, including agronomists skilled in cotton cultivation, traveled to the German colony of Togoland to help farmers there increase production to meet Germany's demand. Germans and Alabamans ignored a relatively stable communal economy based on matriarchal authority over farming to impose the patriarchal Tuskegee approach to modern cotton production. Such examples of undoing native culture motivated others from Africa, India, Ceylon, and elsewhere to pursue extension education.[46]

Foreigners showed great interest in learning about scientific agriculture and home economics, but they did not gravitate to the black land-grant institutions initially. Instead, students sought admission to white land-grant institutions, particularly schools such as Cornell University, the University of Illinois, Michigan State University, and other northern and Midwestern schools. Asians, especially natives of India, believed that the northern schools offered more welcoming environments for foreign students. Ultimately, however, natives of India and Africa gained admission at Tuskegee Institute as well as land-grant institutions founded in 1890 across the South, including Prairie View A&M.[47]

After foreigners accumulated data on improved stock and increased crop production, they returned home to implement their new methods, often through cooperative ventures with international corporations. An uneasy alliance developed between colonizers and international investors intent on increasing production of everything from cotton to rubber for world consumption and the native farmers who hoped that they could free their people from exploitation. This scenario played out in Liberia, a country colonized by African Americans. In 1924, W. E. B. Du Bois explained to Liberia's president, C. D. B. King, and the United States' minister to the country, Solomon Porter Hood, that the solution to Liberia's economic woes lay in a long-term plan that entailed recruiting technical assistance from black farmers, mechanics, and educators who would reside in the republic temporarily as they trained Liberians. Du Bois's proposal sounded remarkably similar to the extension work undertaken by Negro Divisions across the South at the time. Through technical assistance, the Liberians could construct demonstration farms to teach better farming methods, but these goals served business interests because training concentrated on crops key to international trade, particularly rubber.[48]

African nations colonized by the British also gained access to Extension Service ideals and adopted the models readily. The British government of South Rhodesia used vocational education based on extension work as a means of retaining power over a more educated and healthy population.

Thomas Campbell, who developed and popularized the Movable School and the demonstration model among African Americans in the late 1890s, reminisced about the influence of Tuskegee Institute and its informal educational programs, but he neglected to indicate the ways that it helped sustain white control. Rather, for Campbell and other rural blacks, the educational programs helped them strategize their way out of their subordinate status. They could gain independence through reducing dependency on a credit source, increasing their yields, and improving their nutrition so they could work harder for themselves rather than for their landlords. The African American agents believed that the programs could wrest indigenous people out of dependency, even if the colonizing powers perceived the programs as functioning otherwise, and even if the agents' approach threatened indigenous economies and cultures. International interest in the Agricultural Extension Service increased during the 1920s, and by 1936, the idea had affected reform in Albania, India, and China, as well as African nations.[49]

Private special-interest groups advocated the extension message to improve standards of living abroad as well. During World War II, the Foreign Missions Conference determined to form a study group to assess African churches and missions and their effectiveness in educating Africans in various methods to improve their conditions. In 1944, the General Education Board funneled money through the Phelps-Stokes Fund to send a team of three, including Thomas M. Campbell, then a field agent with the Federal Extension Service, to Central West Africa. Over six months they visited several countries, including Liberia, Sierra Leone, the Gold Coast, Nigeria, French Equatorial Africa, Cameroon, and the Belgian Congo. Campbell concentrated on the ways that missions and the governments could cooperate to reduce disparity in African agriculture, a contrast between traditional subsistence and exploitative plantation production. Nations attempted policies to "graft modern scientific technique on to the primitive stock of native land custom." Reversing the plantation system of agriculture required new approaches to landownership and trusteeship. Campbell and the other members of the survey team believed that success depended on "the extension and improvement of education, sanitation, health and self-direction in business and community affairs," but the changes threatened native agriculture.[50]

The USDA had granted Campbell a leave of absence to participate in the 1944 survey, but during the cold war such activities became official business of agents of the state. Campbell's position as a USDA field agent with experience in Africa ensured his involvement in programs that related to extension methods abroad. He served as a member of the Committee for African Students in North America and on a subcommittee on Africa for a conference convened by the OFAR. The meeting, held in May 1949, analyzed current efforts to develop and adapt the extension model of education in countries around the world.[51]

Typically, the white land-grant institution initially took the lead in communications with and programs for foreign delegates. The TAEX welcomed foreign dignitaries regularly. In 1945, two Haitian visitors, Gabrial Nicholas and Rodini Counte, assessed TAEX operations. This visit piqued Iola Rowan's interest, and she asked her white supervisor, Maurine Hearn, the vice-director for women and state home demonstration, to find out how Negro agents might be able to engage in the same sort of exchange and study tour. Nothing apparently came of the inquiry. The TAEX sometimes involved minority agents in study tours arranged for visitors but usually chose staff to participate based on race and ethnic similarities. For instance, in 1953 a group of Latin American women working in extension home economics met with twenty home economists from Latin American countries who visited Texas, Oklahoma, the District of Columbia, and Puerto Rico to discuss options and adapt the extension education model to suit their countries' needs. The delegation included women from Bolivia, Brazil, Cuba, Ecuador, Nicaragua, Peru, Costa Rica, El Salvador, Paraguay, Chile, Uruguay, Colombia, Mexico, and Venezuela, as well as three Pakistani women.[52]

Not until the early 1950s did Texas agents become more responsible for foreign extension work. Moses L. Davis told W. C. David, the Negro state leader, that USDA efforts to participate in international reform included technical assistance to Liberia (Fig. 35). The 1890s land-grant institutions and Negro Division agents proved important to the planning and delivery of the assistance. Davis had undertaken surveys of agriculture in East Texas with the help of African American agricultural extension agents and hoped to use the information to promote agricultural programs in Liberia. He asked for David's endorsement. C. D. B. King, no longer president of Liberia but, rather, the Liberian ambassador to the United States, might have remembered the enthusiasm he felt over Du Bois's report from nearly twenty-five years before.[53]

The cold war made officials more supportive of international work, and the promise came to fruition after 1950. Prairie View A&M's president, E. B. Evans, a veterinarian by training, a veteran of extension administration, and an astute land-grant administrator, led the six-year $3 million project to help

Figure 35. Charles E. Trout (left), former agricultural specialist in Liberia, West Africa, and Henry S. Estelle (right) watch George [White] and John H. Singleton, farmers, unload bags of cucumbers at Singleton's grading shed in Hempstead, Tex., Sep. 15, 1947. White, Singleton, and other black farmers around Hempstead raised five thousand bushels of cucumbers for pickles. ([Ed. C. Hunton], photographer, FES, USDA, NA; J. B. Coleman Library, Special Collections/Archives Dept., Prairie View A&M University)

Liberia improve its standard of living and develop its economic resources. The project resulted from a three-way partnership between the U.S. government, the Liberian government, and Prairie View A&M.[54]

The involvement of high-ranking extension and black land-grant college personnel in such visible international programs generated competition among Negro divisions. Specifically, individuals retained a state-focused bias in their efforts, and this often led them to define zones of influence internationally, as Prairie View A&M did when it took advantage of OFAR opportunities and partnered with representatives of the Liberian government. Several agencies undertook reform in Liberia at the same time, however, so Negro agents from other states also worked in that country.

Frank Pinder began his career in Florida's Negro Division, then he worked with the FSA before leading a team of specialists to Liberia to improve agricultural methods and develop an experiment station. Pinder could do in Africa what he could not do at home. Only two traditionally black universities had experiment substations in 1950, one in Virginia that received a $4,000 appropriation annually, and one at Prairie View A&M, which received $14,000 from the state coffers in 1951, mere pennies when compared to the budgets allocated to the 1862 land-grant institutions across the South.[55]

U.S. agents often became involved in institutional rehabilitation, as did Pinder. Prairie View A&M's project involved the rehabilitation of the Booker T. Washington Industrial Institute in Kakata, Liberia, founded by James L. Sibley, a reformer who had also introduced the Jeanes system of teacher enrichment to the country. In addition to modernizing the institute's physical plant, technical assistants helped educate Liberians to assume faculty positions there. The undertaking generated increased support for Prairie View A&M, and the Extension Division headquartered there afforded an international work experience for selected staff and provided an opportunity for African American agents of the government to convey their idea for racial uplift to the African continent.[56]

Departments other than the USDA supported international agricultural reform during the cold war. The Point Four program emerged as an international relief effort undertaken by the U.S. Department of State. Pres. Harry S. Truman introduced the idea as the fourth point in his inauguration address on January 20, 1949. He indicated that the United States must boldly provide technical assistance to poor people in "underdeveloped areas" who suffered because of "primitive and stagnant" economies. Secretary of State Dean Acheson bore responsibility for implementing the program, and he, along with George C. McGhee, a Texan by birth and assistant secretary for Near Eastern South Asian–African Affairs, orchestrated the effort, including the involvement of government employees of color. McGhee assumed the assistant secretary position in June 1949 and held it through December 1951. During his tenure, Point Four sought African American extension agents for two-year stints as technical experts to facilitate Liberian rural reform, raise the nation's standard of living, and develop its economic resources. W. C. David informed his agents of the opportunity and encouraged them to apply.[57]

International organizations likewise looked to African Americans for technical assistance. E. B. Evans parlayed his veterinary training and his international experience with the Liberian project into service with the State Department's Point Four program, but also with the United Nation's Food and Agriculture Organization (FAO). Rinderpest, a highly fatal viral disease that infected cattle, buffalo, sheep, goats, and other animals in many counties, did not affect stock in the United States. African American agents became involved in studies, nonetheless. In 1953, Evans worked for the FAO specifically on disease mitigation, including rinderpest. He assessed eradication programs in Pakistan, Egypt, and Ethiopia, and also inspected the Department of State's Point Four program in each country.[58]

During the 1940s and the 1950s, some African Americans realized that their technical expertise could further help them reform rural life internationally. They introduced agricultural science to several African countries, sought to reduce the debilitating effects of fatal diseases such as rinderpest, and improved opportunities for related experimentation and education. More generally, however, the opportunities to participate in international aid helped some agents realize their potential. They faced fewer restrictions placed on them by their host supervisors, even in African countries still colonized. While they still had to abide by U.S. government regulations, they believed that they could improve the lives of millions in keeping with ideals expressed in the U.N. Declaration of Human Rights.

The exhibits and engagement in media events and opportunities for public celebration did not lull anyone into thinking that Negro Division staff were happy with their status. Increasing criticism of inadequate resources and race discrimination began to galvanize public employees and their cadre of supporters. Up to the 1950s, black agents had used moral suasion and strong arguments to gain resources, inadequate though they were. After the 1950s, agents in Texas and other southern states began to use the law as leverage to secure equal rights. Black agents, realized, however, that integration into full citizenship, when it came, would come on white terms.

7

Separation Despite Civil Rights

Sustained resistance to legalized discrimination evident through grassroots activism, Supreme Court decisions, and progressive legislation combined to create a second Reconstruction that challenged a century of government compliance with race-biased decision making. In May 1954, as the nation anticipated the *Brown v. Board of Education* decision, which struck the first major blow to the separate-but-equal doctrine, Lea Etta Lusk, the Negro home demonstration agent in Washington County, Texas, won the USDA award for superior service. The award recognized "her contribution to the enrichment of rural life through successful advocacy of self-sufficiency in farm-family living, promotion of understanding of Negro problems, and her ability to train leaders and inspire youth." She earned the award for nearly thirty-five years of untiring service, having first served during the Great War thanks to an emergency appointment, and continuing full time from 1920 through 1953 with white and black support offered by Washington County residents. Such recognition should not be considered coincidental. The civil rights era raised considerable questions about the merits of segregation. Mrs. Lusk had reached the end of her long and illustrious career, but in the face of well-founded challenges to segregation, black agents wondered what fate would befall them (Fig. 36).

The ambiguity surrounding the civil rights movement's progress began after the *Brown v. Board of Education* decision. Some state Extension Services procrastinated in authorizing new Negro Division hires. The Texas Negro Division, however, continued to hire new agents. The National Negro County Agents Association, formed twenty years earlier, increased activities and opportunities for communication by publishing its first magazine in 1961, an indication that professional development continued even as agents wondered where civil rights activism would lead.[1]

Figure 36. Mrs. Lea Etta Lusk, Washington County, Tex., won the USDA award for superior service on May 15, 1954. She first held an emergency appointment in 1919, and then worked from Mar. 1920 through Nov. 1953 full time. (*Texas A&M System News,* clipping, TAEX Riverside; photograph, TAEX Historical Files.)

Extension Services across the South, however, anticipated changes to their public programs by ensuring that race distinctions would remain. They began renaming Negro Division positions. Some agents found themselves labeled as "CRD agents," code for "Negro agent" in some southern states. CRD stood for "community rural development," the primary goal of most agents, and one that Negro agents became increasingly focused on as their constituents left the countryside. Federal legislation passed in 1955, after the *Brown* decision, and in 1962, even encouraged use of the CRD euphemism.[2]

Congress modified the Smith-Lever Act in 1955 with Section 8, directing funding toward disadvantaged agricultural areas to foster development.

The funding was to be used to facilitate local studies of the potential for agricultural and industrial development and cooperation with other agencies or groups that could share information on employment opportunities. The new mandate coincided with existing Negro Division policy in many ways. Additionally, African American staff became most closely associated with the disadvantaged agricultural areas, hence the association between CRD and Negro agent.[3]

Congress authorized a rural renewal program in 1962 which offered USDA technical and financial resources to improve the rural economy. Rural Texans needed these initiatives, but the connection of Negro agents to the programs undermined their broad adoption and wide influence. African Americans, however, responded enthusiastically because CRD perpetuated the types of reform programs the agents had been undertaking for decades, and it enhanced community connections and economic vitality.[4]

By June 1964, with a congressional filibuster waning, Extension Service administrators began anticipating the Civil Rights Act. Within the USDA, FES administrator Dr. Lloyd H. Davis, Cornell University educated and a veteran extension employee, encouraged his assistant secretaries and agency heads to analyze their departments so they could act quickly to fully comply with the letter and the spirit of law. He asked each agency to determine how FES programs would be affected, to plan for the transition, and to identify program areas that could "present unusual problems in transition." He expected answers by June 19.[5]

Reports indicated that a rapid transition to integrate 4-H Clubs would "likely result in the complete destruction of the 4-H program" because of the clubs' symbiotic relationship with "the whole fabric, social structure and tradition of the community." The other unusual problem related to workspace. FES officials predicted repercussions if white and black agents had to share offices. The county governing boards would not take the national legislation lightly. FES officials advised exercising care "to avoid county government attempting to solve the problem by discharging the Negro staff."[6]

On July 2, 1964, Pres. Lyndon Baines Johnson, a Texan, signed the Civil Rights Act. It required all federally assisted programs to eliminate discrimination and prohibited job discrimination based on race, religion, national origin, or sex. The world as Negro extension employees had known it for fifty years ceased to exist after passage of the Civil Rights Act of 1964. African Americans in Texas welcomed the promise of equality, but they feared loss of position and influence. Their worst fears materialized as Texas did not abandon race inequality willingly or quickly. It took more than three years for the

Negro Divisions across the South to disappear, and much of the staff disappeared with the bureaucracy. Officials stalled compliance waiting for Negro agents to retire or resign rather than enter the workforce as equal to whites.

Integration exacerbated political divisions among African Americans, as well, because some wanted integration to guarantee equal treatment, but others regretted the demise of their distinct service. Some African Americans secured appointments in the previously white state Extension Service offices as a result of integration while others secured positions in separate and autonomous extension programs created by U.S. congressional action and housed at traditionally black public colleges, known as 1890 institutions. This was done in response to the requirement to maintain federal services for economically disadvantaged minorities.

Texas' compliance with the Civil Rights Act addressed both quests, but neither African Americans seeking integration nor those seeking an autonomous organization got what they wanted. Integration did not guarantee equality; self-segregation did not provide equitable resources for minority constituents. Instead, post–Civil Rights Act legislation ensured that the USDA could continue to marginalize economically disadvantaged and ethnically diverse rural populations and focus services on commercial, predominantly white, farmers. The 1890 institutions remained inadequately funded, staffed by African American veterans of the Negro Divisions, and increasingly involved in dealing with the consequences of modernization rather than reaping its benefits.

White Texans' compliance with the Civil Rights Act of 1964 integrated the service but incorporated African American agents at a subordinate status. This faulty compliance or incomplete integration destroyed the fifty-year-old black bureaucracy, leaving self-help proponents rudderless, without a separate organization to meet minority needs. It took a few years, but efforts to reinvigorate services to small farmers and the economically disadvantaged and ethnically diverse population resulted eventually in two approaches that appeased integrationist and self-segregationist objectives. These dichotomous approaches—integration and separation—divided resources and prevented the formation of a biracial coalition dedicated to saving the small family farm.[7]

The FES released its compliance plans on July 9, 1964. These plans indicate the complexity of the agendas involved in Title VI compliance, as well as the absence of African Americans in the process. Given the funding structure, with 36 percent appropriated by the national government, 39 percent by the state, and 23 percent coming from county or local sources, the FES proposed extension field reviews in selected counties to determine the level of access under the segregated system and the degree of discrimination. The FES remained unconvinced that discrimination in the service really existed. The plan called for the involvement of officials from the land-grant institutions as well as state extension directors and their supervisory and administrative staffs. After the meetings and review, the state Extension Services bore the burden of bringing the service into conformity and establishing a timeline for completion of the tasks. The complicated administrative structure along with the hands-off attitude adopted by the USDA ensured that compliance would stall.[8]

The equality promised by the Civil Rights Act of 1964 failed to materialize. In fact, the act worked against the black extension agents, because TAEX officials used the legislation to eliminate rather than strengthen services to African Americans. The process destroyed the bureaucracy that black agents had built over the years and forced African American agents into subordinate positions that justified lower pay. In 1964, TAEX employed 104 professional staff members working in 60 counties, figures that rivaled the peak year of 1946 (108 agents in 56 counties). The transition year began with the death of the Negro Division's state leader, Marshall V. Brown, on January 22, 1964. His assistant, Alton E. Adams, had begun as a Negro county agricultural agent (NCAA) in 1933, but the TAEX stalled in appointing him as acting Negro state leader. On March 16, 1964, anticipating the Civil Rights Act, TAEX officials exchanged the designation "Negro" for "associate." Then, on April 1, 1964, they appointed Adams, with more than thirty years' experience as a county agent and specialist, the "acting associate state leader."[9]

The U.S. Congress responded to procrastination by government agencies such as the USDA by passing Title VI of the Civil Rights Act on December 11, 1964. It required federally assisted programs such as TAEX to eliminate discrimination. TAEX officials developed a single line of administration. They accomplished this by eliminating the Negro Division and absorbing agents from that division's three districts into TAEX districts 4, 5, 8, 9, 10, and 11, all in Central and East Texas. They left the "associate district agents" stationed at Prairie View A&M and did not integrate the TAEX headquarters at Texas A&M University. They justified the decision by citing examples of white agents and supervisors who worked out of district offices. The TAEX administrators also conferred supervisory titles on the black agents, but the new position descriptions and lines of authority confirmed their subordinate status as "associates," a.k.a. "Negroes." TAEX director John Hutchison recommended the strategy because he believed it would "create fewer prob-lems." In other words, white agents would have no grounds to protest the conferring of titles equal to theirs on black agents. The merger occurred dur-ing the summer of 1965, at which point Alton became a "staff assistant" with headquarters at Prairie View University. He retired five years later.[10]

Hutchison and his peers throughout the South believed that most agents would not jeopardize their positions by challenging decisions that stalled in-tegration. They learned, however, that some agents had reached the limits of complicity. Hutchison believed that "some few . . . might try to encourage certain radical groups to put pressure on the Extension Service and Texas A&M University to be publicly critical of many programs which might be interpreted as being possibly discriminatory against Negro participants." In reality, black agents did not readily accept the separate offices, subordinate titles, lower pay and benefits. Some retired. Others tested their new equal-ity by moving into offices under their own steam, without the approval of white peers. Still others wrote letters complaining about various inequities, and these criticisms made their way to the USDA office in Washington, DC. Arthur Britton traveled from Louisiana to Washington to personally meet with FES administrators and convey the way Louisiana administrators had unjustly fired him. The FES refused to deal with the issue. Administrators cited federalism and the inability of the national government to intervene in state Extension Service hires. A few months later, they reacted differently when two women agents launched substantial complaints against the Vir-ginia compliance plan. Sara H. James, Lawrenceville, an agent with twenty-three years' experience, indicated that officials had filled vacancies with ju-nior white agents rather than veteran black agents; that black agents did not receive promotions; that all held the title of associate; that all black agents received less pay than white agents; and that no black subject matter special-ists existed. The FES forwarded her complaint and that of Delores Morse, Boydton, to the Office of the Inspector General for further investigation. The inequities continued into 1968.[11]

Ordinary citizens joined the critics. By the end of July 1964, residents of Livingston, Alabama, had written to complain about the "colored only" signs that remained. FES administrator Davis responded that the signs were defi-nitely against FES policy and that they should be eliminated, along with "all forms of discrimination." F. Peter Libassi, director of the Federal Programs Division of the U.S. Commission on Civil Rights, criticized the Louisiana Extension Service for its segregated fiftieth-anniversary observance in Au-gust 1964 of the founding of the Federal Extension Service. Louisiana's administrators had lost "a golden opportunity" to "break an old pattern and set forth on a new adventure" in race relations. Instead, the entire Negro staff remained publicly segregated. Earline G. Malone, an African American secretary, complained of discrimination in hiring practices in a white county agent's office in Hinesville, Georgia, in 1965. Even government officials criticized the FES. LeRoy Collins, Community Relations Office, U.S. Department of Commerce, asked Orville L. Freeman, secretary of agriculture, why the Department of Agriculture still sanctioned discrimination and segregation in state extension services six months after the Civil Rights Act became law.[12]

NAACP branches and other political organizations launched accusations to prompt the FES to deal with pernicious racism. The Austin, Texas, branch of the NAACP submitted a detailed questionnaire to the FES with additional documentation of the lack of integration in the TAEX in November 1965: black farmers did not receive the same services from extension that white farmers received; the 4-H Clubs were not integrated; white home demonstration club members refused to share leadership with blacks because "they just wouldn't know how to go about it." Charles Byrant, president of the Southwest Louisiana branch of the NAACP, wrote Secretary of Agriculture Freeman about the ways white extension agents ensured the segregation of the Yambilee, a sweet potato harvest festival in Opelousas. The Mississippi Freedom Democratic Party asked Joseph Y. Resnick, U.S. representative, to visit the state and survey voting irregularities. Through discussion with Extension Service personnel he learned that the Federal Housing Administration (FHA) would not lend money to Negro farmers for any crop other than cotton, that Agricultural Stabilization and Conservation Service agents perpetuated racism, and that white planters prohibited food distribution to rural blacks. The FES forwarded his extensive report to the inspector general for investigation.[13]

The compliance process became more structured as Civil Rights Office investigators began monitoring noncompliance. Southern officials had to integrate offices by December 31, 1965, one and a half years after passage of the act, and had until January 15, 1966, to produce a final report of their progress. FES officials anticipated problems in Louisiana and prepared to initiate hearings quickly after the deadline. The process included a thorough investigation by the Office of the Inspector General in concordance with the Office of the General Counsel. Problems in Mississippi included inadequate information to guide agents in integrating 4-H Clubs and nonintegrated office space. The relocation of the entire Negro staff from Tuskegee Institute to Auburn University in Alabama in October 1965 created hard feelings and frustration on the part of professionals who had been involved in the longest-running Negro Extension Service. Fred Robinson, director of the Alabama Cooperative Extension Service, continued to have his hands full with white Alabamans who resented the incorporation of black farmers into their programs, particularly in Macon County, the county left without any black staff after the Tuskegee move but with plenty of black farmers expecting service.[14]

Investigative reports documented complicated systems of racial discrimination. Communication on issues yielded contradictory information. William Seabron, assistant to the secretary, USDA, concerned about reported resignations of Negro staff in Florida and reductions in black employment in the state office, queried the FES administrators. They responded that, in fact, vacancies had occurred because of retirement, and they planned to re-hire qualified Negroes after the offices became integrated. They claimed that it was increasingly difficult to hire qualified black personnel because of the increased competition for their services.[15]

Hutchison's prediction that "some few . . . might try to encourage certain radical groups to put pressure on the Extension Service" never materialized, but "some few" used the courts when communication with the FES failed to effect change. Preston E. Poole, agricultural agent in Galveston County, Texas, dissatisfied with TAEX responses to the Civil Rights Act, challenged the Federal Extension Service to reinterpret the relationship of federal, state, and county authorities. Poole believed that the federal government should require local officials to extend equal pay and office space and require state officials to comply with the spirit of the act. Frustrated by responses, Poole launched an official complaint that the USDA forwarded to the Office of the Inspector General in June 1966.[16]

USDA officials condoned discrimination in Texas' Extension Service and refused to interfere with the TAEX decision-making and implementation process. They, in fact, did little more than field complaints from agents about continued segregation and discrimination. Lloyd Davis, FES administrator, used humanitarian reasons to justify the decision to ignore black agents' requests for mediation. He claimed that swift federal enforcement of the integration law would lead to the firing of black agents.[17]

Even though the USDA created an administrative position to assist the secretary with civil rights compliance in 1965, the wheels turned slowly and many agents, including Poole, did not resolve claims until the early 1970s. In the meantime, one of Poole's relatives was killed in Vietnam, a harsh reminder of the sacrifices made by African Americans for a country that did not protect the rights of its citizens. The failure of federal and state government to integrate justly created unstable working conditions that lasted until 1972, when most southern states finally integrated state extension headquarters. African Americans criticized the decisions regularly through editorials, political cartoons in major newspapers such as the *Washington Afro-American,* and a steady stream of letters to the FES and the USDA (Fig. 37).[18]

Efforts to correct generations of inequity backfired. Experienced agents lost their positions, many retired rather than face demotion, and very few African American agents were hired during the transition. This instability made it difficult for African American agents to continue to serve farmers. During the 1960s, the federal government documented that most black producers were unfamiliar with government farm programs. The reports supported new policies to address racial exclusion, often by creating separately funded programs to serve economically disadvantaged and ethnically diverse populations. Yet, a belief that the problems of racial inequality had been solved led to perpetual underfunding and ineffective implementation of special-needs legislation. This contributed to a new wave of out-migration of the few remaining black farmers during the late 1960s and into the 1970s, which significantly diminished rural African American influence.[19]

As the officials of the TAEX and the FES contemplated integration, an experienced Negro Division agent from Southeast Texas gained the experience and education he needed to integrate the service and provide needed programs. Seastrunk began as an agent in Jasper County in 1948, transferred to Prairie View A&M University to work as a farm and home development specialist in 1959, and continued in that position until 1972. Hutchison identified Seastrunk as a "very promising young man" during the transition in 1964, and in 1967, TAEX officials gave him an office at the headquarters in College Station. Seastrunk earned a PhD in extension administration at the University of Wisconsin-Madison in December 1972, having completed a dissertation titled "Organizational Incentives Associated with Motivation of County Extension Agents Toward Professional Development." He spent the rest of his career, after his appointment in March 1972, as TAEX's first black assistant director, managing special programs. In this capacity, Seastrunk implemented a new program designed to improve the income position of small farmers. His thoughtful approach to involving marginal-income farmers proved popular for the TAEX and farmers alike.[20]

Also in 1972, extension administrators in Texas and other southern states implemented new federal legislation, the Agricultural Act of 1971. The act vested Prairie View A&M and 1890 land-grant institutions throughout the

THE REAL POWER BEHIND THE THRONE

Figure 37. Political cartoon by Thomas Stockett, published in *Washington Afro-American,* Mar. 1965. (Courtesy of Afro-American Newspapers Archives and Research Center)

South with full authority for the new "Small Farm Program," thereby creating autonomous extension programs to serve economically disadvantage and ethnically diverse populations throughout the South, separate from the bureaucracies at white land-grant colleges.[21]

On April 1, 1972, the TAEX selected a Prairie View University–trained extension agent, Hoover Carden, to administer the new project. Carden began as an agricultural agent in Marion County and then worked in Montgomery and Jefferson counties, where he created some concern among TAEX officials and white participants because he motivated farm youth and integrated 4-H shows at the state level. Special-needs legislation made it possible to promote him to a position administering an autonomous program, but one effectively segregated from the resources that the TAEX possessed. He directed the Prairie View Cooperative Extension Program for twenty-three years, until his retirement on March 31, 1995.[22]

The Cooperative Extension Program at Prairie View A&M University received additional support on September 29, 1977, when the Cooperative Extension Work Act was passed. It increased funding through the USDA and the Federal Extension Service to institutions established in the 1890s. Thereafter, extension work conducted at 1890 land-grant institutions across the South, including Prairie View A&M, became popularly known as the 1890 Cooperative Extension Program. It served low-income rural and urban African Americans and other ethnic groups but followed equal employment opportunity requirements and did not discriminate on the basis of socio-economic level, race, color, religion, national origin, sex, or disability. Some black agents found positions within the 1890 Program while others worked out of TAEX headquarters on the Texas A&M campus at College Station. As black agents retired from the TAEX, white agents generally replaced them.[23]

African American farmers did not find their needs served by the new program, and the decline in the number of black agents working for the "integrated" TAEX operating out of College Station made many leery of seeking advice and assistance from white agents. Frustrated by the hesitancy to provide equal resources, experienced county extension agents took further action. In 1974, eight years after his initial complaint, Preston E. Poole, the Galveston County agent, launched a class action suit that charged the TAEX with discrimination in employment. Poole believed that two groups of people suffered because of the chronic discrimination: the black employees of the TAEX, and "those blacks who receive[d] the services provided . . . to the agricultural community." A consent decree resulted which satisfied the complaints of the black employees, because the TAEX voluntarily adjusted the pay scale to reflect merit and service, not race. The interests of the second group, the African Americans seeking the services of the TAEX, remained unaddressed.[24]

Other African American agents filed similar suits. Willie L. Strain, who had worked as a specialist at Tuskegee Institute prior to integration, filed a class action lawsuit against the Alabama Cooperative Extension Service alleging unequal hiring and retention practices. The consent decree, issued in 1971, required the service to reformulate its Civil Rights Act compliance plan. Over the following decade, African Americans gained higher-ranking positions and more service delivery to black clientele. Strain managed to retain his position with the Alabama service despite the suit, and when he retired in 1999, Alabama representatives awarded him a commendation for outstanding public service. Charlie F. Wade, along with two other agents employed by the Mississippi Cooperative Extension Service (MCES), LaVerne Y. Lindsey and Athaniel H. Moody, filed a class action lawsuit on April 29, 1970, and the U.S. District Court for the Northern District of Mississippi, Eastern Division ruled on February 15, 1974. The class action suit included, in addition to the agents, the minor children of Ms. Lindsey and of Ms. Odell Durham, who were 4-H Club members; a home demonstration club member; and a farmer. The class represented the employees of the service, the youth clientele, and the members of segregated home demonstration clubs. The court ruled for affirmative remedial relief to combat racial discrimination in Mississippi Extension Service hiring practices. Rather than instituting a quota system to ensure equity, the court ruled that Mississippi officials should hire qualified blacks in substantial numbers at all levels of the MCES and station them throughout the state without delay.[25]

Some African Americans managed to hold onto their farms despite the preferential treatment afforded to white farmers. The inequities not resolved in *Poole v. Williams* continued, and eventually more southern black farmers charged the USDA with discrimination documented between 1981 and 1996. *Timothy C. Pigford et al. v. Dan Glickman, Secretary, the United States Department of Agriculture* was settled by consent decree in January 2001, with the USDA agreeing to offer restitution to African American farmers who could prove that the USDA did not respond to their applications for loans and other services on the basis of race. The Federation of Southern Cooperatives/Land Assistance Fund and other black farm-support organizations have criticized the government, however, for delaying decision making regarding claims and denying nearly 40 percent of the claims. Finally, the Associated Press published a series on black land loss in December 2001 that brought the inequities to a larger audience. These articles indicate that black farmers can claim chronic discrimination on the part of the USDA, originating with the department's founding in 1862.[26]

The effect of the *Pigford* a.k.a. *Venable* a.k.a. *Johanns* decision will not be known for a while, but settlement has not been hasty, and many farmers believe it has been unfair. Though it stands, theoretically, as a major challenge to institutionalized racism, the settlement has lacked deliberate speed. More must be done to undermine the inherent bias against small-scale U.S. farmers of all races to make small-scale farming a viable life choice. Minority farmers in Texas managed to persevere throughout the 1980s and the 1990s. In fact, the number of full and part owners and tenants increased modestly but significantly, from 3,292 in 1982—10.5 percent of all black-operated farms in fifteen southern states—to 3,462 in 1997, 20.2 percent of the southern total. Increased attention to the injustice of discriminatory practices, the viability of less intensively capitalized farming, and laws that protect inherited property will help protect the interests of African Americans in the countryside.[27]

Ending legalized segregation of TAEX proved problematic. Complying with national legislation addressed decades of inequality but did not create historical amnesia. Memories of mistreatment remained, but so did recollections of accomplishments realized through all-black community efforts. Integration reinvigorated an old debate about the advantages and disadvantages of integration and separation.

CONCLUSION

Measuring Greater Harvests

African Americans in twentieth-century Texas adopted various strategies to sustain their rural lifestyle. Those who became agents and supervisors in TAEX's Negro Division played a visible public role. They directly affected the people whom they served as well as the bureaucracy that employed them and the local officials who supplemented the meager resources that TAEX provided.

These African American professionals engaged in sophisticated negotiation as they tried to convince skeptical constituents and racist administrators, educated and uneducated alike, of the need to treat rural black Texans fairly. They did so by defying racist assumptions at every opportunity. They gained the highest level of education available to them, they embraced progressive rationality and efficiency, and they refused to tolerate poverty. They reasoned with black farmers as well as with white officials at the local, state, and national levels and expected change in fields, farm homes, and society.

Limitations existed. Some proved less astute at negotiating than others, but larger issues, specifically, race, class, and gender bias, constrained the agents' opportunities to negotiate and prompt change.

The agents of the Negro Division facilitated exchange of ideas in the countryside. They built communities around canning centers, offered rural blacks the opportunity to govern themselves through clubs, and addressed grave inadequacies in rural life, including limited education and unsanitary living conditions.

African Americans concentrated their efforts on black landowning farmers and successful tenants to accomplish these things because they had to pacify white authority figures with measurable accomplishments. Working with prosperous or at least independent farmers furthered that agenda. The efforts of the agents in the countryside combined with the professional bureaucracy that the black agents created prompted white officials to sustain support of the organization. The Negro Extension Service's growth continued through the New Deal and World War II and the cold war, even as the number of black farmers in the United States declined precipitously. The agents accomplished this by working with new public reform programs directed toward rural Americans generally, and less toward farmers and their families.

The profession that the agents created helped sustain them as they negotiated bias. Whites acquiesced to the organizational structure that the black agents worked within, a structure that linked individuals to clubs and community networks. But white officials ensured their racial hegemony by segregating the agents, regulating activities, and providing inadequate funding.

The segregated agency offered blacks an opportunity to organize at the local level, often within black communities, and therefore somewhat removed from the watchful eye of white Texans. Also, the programs made rural blacks, particularly the youth, more conscious of and confident in their abilities and their entitlements as citizens. The public recognition of club members, agents, and administrators at the local, state, and national levels energized the service. Newspapers published the names of club members and activities, and this public attention helped make violence obsolete as a tool of white hegemony. Black property owners also paid county taxes, and this gave black farmers legitimate influence at the local level. County commissioners often failed to provide adequate support, but minority agents maintained their momentum. Black agents managed to maintain club work while earning less than half what white agents earned and receiving none of the benefits accorded to whites.

Several things made it difficult for blacks to realize the same degree of success that whites enjoyed. Many African Americans did not own their own time, and white landlords who controlled the labor of tenants and sharecroppers prevented many from participating. Black agrarians ignored their plight in many instances, but the exodus of talent concerned them. Many realized that life existed beyond the confines of their small communities and chose to leave instead of stay. This undermined the intended purpose of the agrarian reforms: to strengthen rural communities as the rightful locus of independent black citizens. African Americans watched powerless as rural youth chose emigration and town life in their struggle to attain a better life.

The nature of extension programming also undermined the agents' effectiveness. Agents implemented programs within the private networks of family and community, and even though agents shared accomplishments through newspapers and other public media, the recognition often remained within black circles of influence. Black administrators did what they could to give these private victories greater significance, but most white recipients refused to hear of or acknowledge the efforts. Those administrators who responded often reminded blacks of their place as second-class citizens, not authorized to act independently of white authority figures.

The number of college-educated African Americans who remained in the country increased steadily until World War II. They became educators, clergy, and extension agents. Some even remained farmers. As a group, they became more involved in public reform, particularly as employees or beneficiaries of New Deal programs. The increased visibility in public presentations and media releases made it possible for white administrators to claim that they serviced rural blacks. Black agrarians benefited, but this concentration on the deserving hurt the needy. The decline in the number of black farm operators resulted from the out-migration of poorer farmers; the number of landowners remained relatively stable, particularly in the "new" South, throughout the 1930s. The black farmers who persevered benefited from public education, public agricultural reform, community activism, and private initiative. The disadvantages of rural life remained, however, because black farmers still could not control the market nor the government.

Nor did the self-sufficient lifestyle that reformers advocated make farmers independent. The political power of whites became increasingly concentrated in urban areas, and country folk in general became more isolated. The small number of rural blacks, regardless of the amount of influence they wielded at the county, state, or national level, controlled too few resources to elicit a radical change in race relations.

World War II and the cold war provided another opportunity for the agents to expand their influence, and they met the challenges willingly. As agents of the state, the Negro Extension Service staff began to act as recruiters selling the potential of rural uplift. They used various media, including exhibits at fairs and expositions, radio, and even television, to convey their message. They took advantage of other opportunities to promote their work and the profession. They began to participate as technical experts in foreign nations, particularly Liberia. The agents found that what they could not receive in the United States—appointments as experts or specialists in their field—they could find to some degree if they became involved in the foreign reform efforts. These visible positions, and the building movement for civil rights reform, prompted many of them to challenge discrimination and segregation vocally, or to enlist the aid of others to help them secure the equality that they deserved.

The Civil Rights Act of 1964 had deleterious consequences for the public service and the professional structure that the extension agents had created over fifty years but at least in theory gave them equal opportunity. The Negro agents had no role in designing the process by which the state extension services integrated their divisions. All delayed as long as possible, at least until December 31, 1965, before integrating offices, and many refused to confer equal titles or equal pay on African American agents with seniority. Discrimination in hiring and promotion continued into the 1970s until class action law suits helped eliminate outdated pay ratios that denied equal pay for equal work. The professional organizations that agents had created and nurtured also evaporated under the mandate to integrate.

Eventually, public policy responded to requests to reinstitute a service to focus on rural minority and economic development. The Cooperative Extension Program of Prairie View A&M University today serves Texans of diverse ethnic and socioeconomic levels in thirty-four counties, the result of Texans' ambiguous compliance with the Civil Rights Act of 1964 and of a long heritage of proud service on the part of rural blacks. In some ways, it exists as a legacy of the impressive work the Negro Division undertook. It reflects the philosophy of self-help and self-segregation that always characterized the program. It indicates the real, if limited, political power that black agents of the state wielded throughout the twentieth century as they protected their sphere of authority within TAEX. Most troubling, however, is the durability of race and class bias despite the Negro Division's accomplishments. Individual success stories abound, but no structural changes of consequence emerged from fifty years of Negro Division efforts to secure equal access for rural black Texans. As a result, advocates of rural southern minority rights still struggle to effect change.[1]

NOTES

ABBREVIATIONS

A&M President's Records	Texas A&M University President's Office Records, Cushing Memorial Library and Archives, Texas A&M University, College Station.
AHC	Austin History Center, Austin, Tex.
Annual Reports	Annual Narrative and Statistical Reports of the Cooperative Extension Work Demonstration Program, Federal Extension Service, Record Group 33, National Archives and Records Administration, Microfilm Series (T-845-T-895), Texas (1909–45), T-890. Abbreviated in text as Annual Reports, state, year, reel number, T number. Agents completed these reports to document activities in their county and submitted them to the Negro state leader, who submitted them to TAEX headquarters. TAEX administrators submitted them to FES officials. The reports for all states were microfilmed in 1951 and destroyed. All 182 Texas reels are housed at Texas Agricultural Extension Service headquarters, Texas A&M University, College Station.
Brown Papers	Marshall Vernon Brown, Correspondence, 1941–61, Prairie View A&M University Archives, Prairie View, Tex.
BTW Papers	Louis R. Harlan and Raymond W. Smock, eds. *The Booker T. Washington Papers,* 14 vols. Urbana: University of Illinois Press, 1972–89.
BU	The Texas Collection, Baylor University, Waco, Tex.
CAH	Center for American History, University of Texas, Austin.

CC	Commissioners' Court Minutes. Abbreviated in text as county, date, book, page.
Conner Papers	George S. and Jeffie O. A. Conner Papers, The Texas Collection, Baylor University, Waco, Tex.
David Papers	William Cullen David Papers, 1937–47, 1951–59. Prairie View A&M University Archives, Prairie View, Tex.
ES, RG 33, NA	Records of the Federal Extension Service, Record Group 33, National Archives and Records Administration II, College Park, Md.
FES Photos NA	Photographs, Federal Extension Service, S-series (1920–54) and SC-series (1920–45). National Archives and Records Administration II, College Park, Md.
FHA, RG 96, NA-FW	Farmers' Home Administration, Record Group 96, National Archives and Records Administration, Southwest Region, Fort Worth, Tex.
FSA, RG 96, NA	Farmers' Home Administration and Predecessor Agencies [Farm Security Administration], National Archives and Records Administration II, College Park, Md.
NA-FW	National Archives and Records Administration, Southwest Region, Fort Worth, Tex.
NARA II	National Archives and Records Administration II, College Park, Md.
Negro Division	Negro Division of the Texas Agricultural Extension Service.
OSA, RG 16, NA	Records of the Office of the Secretary of Agriculture, Record Group 16, National Archives and Records Administration II, College Park, Md.
PV	University Archives, John C. Coleman Library, Prairie View A&M University, Prairie View, Tex.
SCFP	Smith-Cobb Family Papers, The Texas Collection, Baylor University, Waco, Tex.
SHRLRC	Sam Houston Regional Library and Research Center of the Texas State Library and Archives Commission, Liberty.
Seastrunk A&M	Dempsey H. Seastrunk file, Cushing Memorial Library and Archives, Texas A&M University, College Station.
Seastrunk's History PV	Negro Extension History, comp. D. H. Seastrunk, May 1986, Prairie View A&M University Archives, Prairie View, Tex.

Staff Minutes	Staff Conference Minutes, 1925–40, in Calvin H. Waller Papers, Prairie View A&M University Archives, Prairie View, Tex.
TAEX Annual Report	Serial publication, *Annual Report of the Extension Service of the Agricultural and Mechanical College of Texas;* also titled *Texas Extension Work* [year], *Extension Work in Texas* [year], published by Extension Service, A. and M. College of Texas, and U.S. Department of Agriculture, Cooperating. The 1933 and 1934 reports appeared in *Extension Service Farm News.*
TAEX Historical Files	Texas Agricultural Extension Service Historical Files, 1914–70, including Farmers' Cooperative Demonstration Work, Historical Notes and Staff Lists, Personnel Records, and County Files. Some items predate 1914. Cushing Memorial Library and Archives, Texas A&M University, College Station.
TAEX-PS	Salary Register, Payroll Services, Texas Agricultural Extension Service, College Station. Abbreviated in text as, e.g., SR [Salary Register], county (year), reel, TAEX-PS.
TAEX Riverside	Texas Agricultural Extension Service Archives, Texas A&M University, Riverside Campus, Bryan.
TDA	Permanent Records, Texas Department of Agriculture, Austin.
TSA	Texas State Library and Archives Center, Austin.
Waller Correspondence	Calvin Hoffman Waller Correspondence, 1922–42. Prairie View A&M University Archives, Prairie View, Tex.
Waller Papers	Calvin Hoffman Waller Papers, 1880–35. Prairie View A&M University Archives, Prairie View, Tex.

INTRODUCTION

1. Elizabeth Sanders, *Roots of Rural Reform: Farmers, Workers, and the American State, 1877–1917* (Chicago: University of Chicago Press, 1999), 1–4.

2. I use the term *Negro* when it reflects contemporary use by the U.S. or state governments. For example, Texans segregated African American professionals in the Negro Division of the Texas Agricultural Extension Service. The employees in that division were officially identified as "Negro" home demonstration agents or "Negro" county or farm agents. I use the term *Division* to provide consistency. Contemporary publications used "Negro Division," "Negro Extension," "Negro Work," "Negro Demonstration Division," and "Negro Extension Work" interchangeably.

3. W. E. Burghardt Du Bois, "The Negro Farmer," *Negroes in the United States,* Bureau of the Census, Bulletin 8 (Washington, DC: Government Printing Office, 1904), 69–98, 91 (quotation), 301, 307; David Levering Lewis, *W. E. B. Du Bois: Biography of a Race, 1868–1919* (New York: Henry Holt, 1993), 3–4, 142–46.

4. Du Bois, "Negro Farmer," 72–73, 75, 81, 84, 90, 95, 98; *Negroes in the United States,* 301, 307.

5. Du Bois, "Negro Farmer," 81; Steven Hahn, *A Nation under Our Feet: Black Political Struggles in the Rural South from Slavery to the Great Migration* (Cambridge, Mass.: Belknap Press of Harvard University Press, 2003), 9 (quotation), 457–62.

6. W. E. B. Du Bois, "Of the Wings of Atalanta," in *The Souls of Black Folk,* by W. E. B. Du Bois (New York: Dover, 1994), 47–54; idem, "Of Mr. Booker T. Washington and Others," *Souls of Black Folk,* 30–31.

7. A "corps of Negro clerks" directed by three African American civil servants, Robert A. Pelham, Charles E. Hall, and William Jennifer, transcribed data and tabulated 1910 census returns ([U.S. Bureau of the Census], *Negro Population in the United States, 1790–1915* (1918; reprint 1968), 14 ("corps" quotation), 554 ("agriculture" quotation), 555, 559, 565.

8. Du Bois, "Negro Farmer," 82, 98 (quotation). Eight states had a higher percentage of black landownership than Texas, but only Virginia and North Carolina had more black landowners. Debra A. Reid, "African Americans and Land Loss in Texas: Government Duplicity and Discrimination Based on Race and Class," *Agricultural History* 77, no. 2 (Spring 2003): 258–92; Neil Foley, *The White Scourge: Mexicans, Blacks, and Poor Whites in Texas Cotton Culture* (Berkeley & Los Angeles: University of California Press, 1997), 62–63.

9. Du Bois, "Negro Farmer," 82, 98. Blacks operated 18.6 percent (65,472 of 352,190 farms) of all Texas farms in 1900 and 56,190 of these (85.8 percent) reported cotton as their principal source of income. A total of 57,055 black farmers grew cotton (87.1 percent of all black farmers), and they tilled 1,204,670 of the 6,960,367 acres (17.3 percent) in cotton in Texas during 1899. Whites operated 81.4 percent of all farms in Texas in 1900 (286,654 of 352,190 farms) and 236,933 (67.3 percent of all white farmers) grew cotton. *Negroes in the United States,* 301, 307; *Census Reports,* vol. 6, *Twelfth Census of the United States, 1900, Agriculture,* Pt. II: *Crops and Irrigation* (Washington, DC: U.S. Census Office, 1902), 419.

10. Roy V. Scott, *The Reluctant Farmer: The Rise of Agricultural Extension to 1914* (Urbana: University of Illinois Press, 1970), 212–18; Douglas Helms, "Revision and Reversion: Changing Cultural Control Practices for the Cotton Boll Weevil," in *Science and Technology in Agriculture,* ed. C. Clyde Jones and Homer E. Socolofsky (Washington, DC: Agricultural History Society, 1985), 108–25.

11. J. A. Evans, *Recollections of Extension History,* Extension Circular no. 224 (Raleigh: North Carolina State College of Agriculture and Engineering and North Carolina Agricultural Extension Service, 1938), 7–8; Scott, *The Reluctant Farmer,*

218–36; Pete Daniel, *Breaking the Land: The Transformation of Cotton, Tobacco, and Rice Cultures since 1880* (Urbana: University of Illinois Press, 1986), 9–12.

12. Larry D. Hill and Robert A. Calvert, "The University of Texas Extension Services and Progressivism," *Southwestern Historical Quarterly* 86 (1982): 230–54.

13. Scott, *The Reluctant Farmer*, 302–13; J. A. Evans, *Extension Work Among the Negroes: Conducted by Negro Agents, 1923*, USDA Circular 355 (September 1925), 1–24; O. B. Martin, *A Decade of Negro Extension Work, 1914–1924*, Miscellaneous Circular no. 72 (Washington, D.C.: U.S. Department of Agriculture, 1926), 28–29.

14. Reid, "African Americans and Land Loss," 266; Robert Carroll, "Robert Lloyd Smith and the Farmers' Improvement Society of Texas" (MA thesis, Baylor University, 1974), 28–34; Thad Sitton and James H. Conrad, *Freedom Colonies: Independent Black Texans in the Time of Jim Crow* (Austin: University of Texas Press, 2005), 18–45.

15. Belinda Robnett, *How Long? How Long?: African-American Women in the Struggle for Civil Rights* (New York: Oxford University Press, 1997), 6–7; Mary S. Hoffschwelle, *Rebuilding the Rural Southern Community: Reformers, Schools, and Homes in Tennessee, 1900–1930* (Knoxville: University of Tennessee Press, 1998); Lu Ann Jones, *Mama Learned Us to Work: Farm Women in the New South* (Chapel Hill: University of North Carolina Press, 2002); Rebecca Sharpless, *Fertile Ground, Narrow Choices: Women on Texas Cotton Farms, 1900–1940* (Chapel Hill: University of North Carolina Press, 1999); Melissa Walker, *All We Knew Was to Farm: Rural Women in the Upcountry South, 1919–1941* (Baltimore, Md.: Johns Hopkins University Press, 2000).

16. Adolph Reed Jr., *Stirrings in the Jug: Black Politics in the Post-Segregation Era* (Minneapolis: University of Minnesota Press, 1999), 15–27, 46.

17. William E. Nelson Jr., "Black Rural Land Decline and Political Power," in *The Black Rural Landowner—Endangered Species: Social, Political, and Economic Implications*, ed. Leo McGee and Robert Boone (Westport, Conn.: Greenwood Press, 1979), 83–96; *Timothy C. Pigford et al. v. Dan Glickman, Secretary, the United States Department of Agriculture* (1999; the district court's consent decree appears at www .dcd.uscourts.gov/97cv1978.pdf).

CHAPTER 1

1. Robert Lloyd Smith, "Village Improvement among the Negroes," *Outlook* (Mar. 31, 1900): 734, quoted in Carroll, "Smith and the FIS," 21, 28–34; "An Act Concerning Rents and Advances," Apr. 4, 1874, *General Laws of the State of Texas Passed at the Session of the Fourteenth Legislature begun and held at the City of Austin, January 13, 1874* (Houston: N.p., 1874), 55–59; Farmers' Improvement Society of Texas, Smith-Cobb Family Papers, The Texas Collection, Baylor University, Waco, Tex. (hereafter SCFP).

2. William H. Isaac[s] household, Tenth Census of the United States (1880), Colorado County, Texas, Schedule 1, 358–59; William H. Isaacs household, Twelfth

Census of the United States (1900), Colorado County, Texas, Schedule 1, Enumeration District 17, p. 16; "About Middleton's Inlaws," in Dr. Nathaniel Hill Middleton vertical file, Nesbitt Memorial Library, Columbus, Tex.; Merline Pitre, *Through Many Dangers, Toils and Snares: Black Leadership of Texas, 1870–1890*, 2nd rev. ed. (Austin, Tex.: Eakin Press, 1997), 197; Marriage Record, R. L. Smith and Francis Isabella Isaacs, Nov. 10, 1890, Book I: 355, Colorado County Court House, Columbus, Tex.; "Hon. Robert L. Smith," in *The National Encyclopedia of the Colored Race,* ed. Clement Richardson (Montgomery, Ala.: National Publishing, 1919), 1: 383; "Robert Lloyd Smith," in *Who's Who in Colored America, 1928–1929,* 2nd ed. (New York: Who's Who in Colored America, n.d.), 341–42; Carroll, "Smith and the FIS," 16.

3. Debra A. Reid, "African Americans, Community Building, and the Role of the State in Rural Reform in Texas, 1890s–1930s," in *The Countryside in the Age of the Modern State,* ed. Catherine McNichol Stock and Robert D. Johnston (Ithaca: Cornell University Press, 2001), 41–45; Du Bois, "Negro Farmer," 95–98; Manning Marable, "The Land Question in Historical Perspective: The Economics of Poverty in the Blackbelt South, 1865–1920," in *The Black Rural Landowner,* ed. McGee and Boone 3–24; Orville Vernon Burton, "African American Status and Identity in a Postbellum Community," *Agricultural History* 72, no. 2 (Spring 1998): 213–40; Valerie Grim, "African American Landlords in the Rural South, 1870–1950: A Profile," *Agricultural History* 72, no. 2 (Spring 1998): 399–416; Sitton and Conrad, *Freedom Colonies,* 18–42.

4. Robert B. Campbell, *Grass-Roots Reconstruction in Texas* (Baton Rouge: Louisiana State University Press, 1997), 29; Carroll, "Smith and the FIS," 28–40.

5. Carroll, "Smith and the FIS," 37–38.

6. Pitre, *Through Many Dangers,* 202, 214–16; Jack Temple Kirby, *Darkness at the Dawning: Race and Reform in the Progressive South* (Philadelphia: J. B. Lippincott, 1972), 176. Kirby believed that Smith did not pose "a threat of substantive change in the basic scheme of southern affairs" (176).

7. Pitre, *Through Many Dangers,* 69, 75–77, 199; Barry A. Crouch, "Hesitant Recognition: Texas Black Politicians, 1865–1900," *East Texas Historical Journal* 31, no. 1 (1993): 41–58; Maceo D. Dailey Jr., "Neither 'Uncle Tom' nor 'Accommodationist': Booker T. Washington, Emmett Jay Scott, and Constructionalism," *Atlanta History* 38 (Winter 1995): 20–33; E. M. Beck and Stewart Tolnay, "The Killing Fields of the Deep South: The Market for Cotton and the Lynching of Blacks, 1883–1930," *American Sociological Review* 55 (Aug. 1990): 526–39. Beck and Tolnay do not include Texas statistics.

8. "Republican State Convention, 1900," in *Platforms of Political Parties in Texas,* ed. Earnest William Winkler (Austin, Tex.: The University, [1916]), 433, 435; Lamar L. Kirven, "A Century of Warfare: Black Texans" (PhD diss., Indiana University, 1974), 82–90; Pitre, *Through Many Dangers,* 201 (quotation), 202–204.

9. B. Youngblood, "Report of Director of Experiment Stations," *Nineteenth Biennial Report of the Board of Directors of the Agricultural and Mechanical College of Texas, for the fiscal year ending August 31, 1913 and August 31, 1914* (Austin, Tex.: A. C. Bald-

win & Sons, 1915), 32–33 (quotation, 33). The Texas legislature accepted Morrill Land-Grant College Act funds in 1866 and established a permanent fund to operate a college to teach agricultural and mechanical arts. A site was selected in 1871, south of Bryan, Tex. (Henry Dethloff, *A Centennial History of Texas A&M University, 1876–1976,* 2 vols. [College Station: Texas A&M University Press, 1976], 1: 3, 10–18).

10. E. R. Kone, "Our State Department of Agriculture," *General Sessions of the Farmers' Congress,* Texas Department of Agriculture Bulletin, 1909 (Austin, Tex.: Von Boeckmann-Jones, 1909), 40–41.

11. "Edward Reeves Kone," *Texas and Texans,* clipping, TDA, 1285; Ed R. Kone, member, Committee on Platform and Resolutions, 21st Senatorial District, Democratic State Convention, Fort Worth, Aug. 18–19, 1896, in Winkler, *Platforms of Political Parties,* 388; Kone, member, Committee on Platform and Resolutions, 21st Senatorial District, Democratic State Convention, Houston, Aug. 2–3, 1904, in Winkler, *Platforms of Political Parties,* 466; George Ruble Woolfolk, *Prairie View: A Study in Public Conscience, 1878–1946* (New York: Pageant Press, 1962), 27–28, 44, 68, 102–3, 104; "Agricultural and Mechanical College for Colored Youths, at Alta Vista," *Reports on the Agricultural and Mechanical College of Texas and Alta Vista College for Colored Youths* (Jan. 1878–79): 12; Thomas S. Gathright, "Report on Alta Vista College," *Reports on the Agricultural and Mechanical College of Texas and Alta Vista College for Colored Youths* (Dec. 1878): 13, Annual Reports, 1878–1924, Agricultural and Mechanical College of Texas, Cushing Memorial Library and Archives, Texas A&M University, College Station.

12. Scott, *The Reluctant Farmer,* 212; Wayne D. Rasmussen, *Taking the University to the People: Seventy-five Years of Cooperative Extension* (Ames: Iowa State University Press, 1989), 24, 34–36; Helms, "Revision and Reversion," 108–9; Daniel, *Breaking the Land,* 7–9; C. Vann Woodward, *Origins of the New South, 1877–1913* (Baton Rouge: Louisiana State University Press, 1951; reprint 1971), 410–11.

13. Roy V. Scott, "American Railroads and Agricultural Extension, 1900–1914: A Study in Railway Developmental Techniques," *Business History Review* 39, no. 1 (Spring 1965): 74–98, esp. 91. The *Terrell Times-Star* (Feb. 5, 1904), printed an advance release of the USDA bulletin describing the work. O. B. Colquitt, the railroad commissioner in Texas at the time, happened to be from Kaufman County (Winkler, *Platforms of Political Parties,* 447; Scott, *The Reluctant Farmer,* 206–36, esp. 211; Dethloff, *Centennial History,* 2: 386–88). Dewey Grantham, *Southern Progressivism: The Reconciliation of Progress and Tradition* (Knoxville: University of Tennessee Press, 1983), 320–48. See also *Silver Anniversary Cooperative Demonstration Work, 1903–1928,* Proceedings of the Anniversary Meeting Held at Houston, Tex., Feb. 5–7, 1929 (College Station: Extension Service, Agricultural and Mechanical College of Tex., [1929]), 40; O. B. Martin, *The Demonstration Work: Dr. Seaman A. Knapp's Contribution to Civilization* (San Antonio, Tex.: Naylor, 1941), 33; *Acco Press* 31, no. 2 (Feb. 1953): 8; John E. Hutchison, "The Texas Agricultural Extension Service: A Historical Overview," in *Southwestern Agriculture:*

Pre-Columbian to Modern, ed. Henry C. Dethloff and Irvin M. May Jr. (College Station: Texas A&M University Press, 1982), 123–35, esp. 128.

14. Bradford Knapp, Seaman Knapp's son, and others believed that black tenants had an advantage over white tenants because the former followed directions routinely. Agents reported to Knapp that "the negro farmer lends himself readily to instruction. He is adept at doing things the way he is told to do them." See Bradford Knapp, "The Negro as Farmer," TMs, Bradford Knapp Papers, Southwest Collection, Texas Tech University, Lubbock; *Terrell Times-Star* (Jan. 29, 1904).

15. Evans recalled that he enrolled black farmers at Livingstone, though he likely meant Livingston, seat of Polk County (*Recollections,* 12). See also W. B. Mercier, *Extension Work among Negroes, 1920,* USDA circular 190 (Washington, DC: Government Printing Office, 1921), 3; Scott, *The Reluctant Farmer,* 213, 232; *Negro Population in the U.S., 1790–1915,* 567, 588, 624.

16. Everett W. Smith, "Raising a Crop of Men," *Outlook* 89 (July 18, 1908): 603.

17. Martin, *The Demonstration Work,* 22 (quotation).

18. For criticism of Knapp's philosophy, see "Dr. Knapp Finds Another Scapegoat Place for the Negro," *Colored American Magazine* 12 (May 1907): 329–30, quoted in Earl William Crosby, "Building the Country Home: The Black County Agent System, 1906–1940" (PhD diss., Miami University, 1977), 29.

19. Scott, *The Reluctant Farmer,* 219; Sanders, *Roots,* 324; John Wesley Payne Jr., "David F. Houston: A Biography" (PhD diss., University of Texas at Austin, 1953), 21, 56–57, 78; David Franklin Houston, *Eight Years with Wilson's Cabinet, 1913–1920,* 2 vols. (Garden City, N.Y.: Doubleday, Page, 1926), 1: 203–4.

20. The first official lecture trains carrying USDA demonstration agents ran in Texas in February 1904; see G. W. Orms, "History of Agricultural Extension Work in Texas," in *Silver Anniversary,* 66; W. D. Bentley, "Early Experiences in the Demonstration Work," in *Silver Anniversary,* 87; Scott, *The Reluctant Farmer,* 219, 223–24; Raymond B. Fosdick, *Adventure in Giving: The Story of the General Education Board, a Foundation Established by John D. Rockefeller* (New York: Harper & Row, 1962), 40–41 (Fosdick incorrectly identifies College Station as College Park, 43); Jackson Davis, "An Experiment in Agricultural Education," in *Silver Anniversary,* 41.

21. Woodward, *Origins of the New South,* 411; Scott, *The Reluctant Farmer,* 224–34; Lewis W. Jones, "The South's Negro Farm Agent," *Journal of Negro Education* 22, no. 1 (Winter 1953): 38–45; Earl Crosby, "The Roots of Black Agricultural Extension Work," *The Historian* 39, no. 2 (Feb. 1977): 228–47; Allen W. Jones, "Thomas M. Campbell: Black Agricultural Leader of the New South," *Agricultural History* 53, no. 1 (Jan. 1979): 44.

22. Scott, *The Reluctant Farmer,* 223–34; Crosby, "Building the Country Home," 30–34, 55–56; General Education Board, *The General Education Board: An Account of Its Activities, 1902–1914* (New York: General Education Board, 1915), 26–27, 55; [University of Texas], "The Educational Conference," *Bulletin of the University of Texas,* no. 91; *The Work of the Fall and Winter Terms* [*University Record,* vol. 7, no. 3] (Austin: University of Texas, Mar. 15, 1907), 212 (quotation).

23. J. B. Cauthen, Huntsville, Tex., Walker County, in W. F. Procter, State Agent, "Farmers' Cooperative Demonstration Work, Tyler, Tex., September [?], rec'd October 6, 1909," report prepared for Dr. S. A. Knapp, USDA, Bureau of Plant Industry, Washington, DC, Annual Reports, Tex. (1909), reel 1, T-890. Agents' reports were microfilmed as Federal Extension Service, Annual Narrative and Statistical Reports of the Cooperative Extension Work Demonstration Program, Record Group (RG) 33, National Archives and Records Administration, Microfilm Series (T-845–T-895), Texas (1909–44), T-890 (hereafter Annual Reports, state [year], reel number, and T number, e.g., Annual Reports, Tex. [1909], reel 1, T-890). Copies of all reels in series T-890 are housed in Payroll Services, Texas Agricultural Extension Service. Blacks operated 56.3 percent of all farms in Walker County in 1910. Of these, 30.1 percent owned their farms, 69.9 farmed as tenants and sharecroppers (U.S. Bureau of the Census, *Thirteenth Census, 1910*, vol. 7, *Agriculture*, 653, 676).

24. C. E. Allen, Mineola, Tex., Wood and Rains counties in Procter, "Farmers' Cooperative Demonstration Work," 8, Annual Report, Tex. (1910), reel 1, T-890. Allen served as agent for both Wood and Rains counties in Northeast Texas. Only 11.1 percent of all owners were black, and only 17.1 percent of tenants were black in Wood County in 1910. This percentage was even lower in Rains County, with only 7.8 percent of all owners being black, and 10.9 percent of all tenants in 1910.

25. Scott, *The Reluctant Farmer*, 238; Dethloff, *Centennial History*, 2: 385, 388.

26. J. L. Quicksall, "History of the Movement of Organizing Boys' Corn Contest Clubs in Texas," Jan. 1909, in Texas Agricultural Extension Service Historical Files, Cushing Memorial Library and Archives, Texas A&M University, College Station (hereafter TAEX Historical Files); E. P. Elrod, special agent, Sherman, Tex., Oct. 28, 1910, reporting on his work in Lee County, Annual Reports, Tex. (1910), reel 1, T-890.

27. Carroll, "Smith and the FIS," 70; Letter, Trustees, D. N. McCoy et al., Giddings, Tex. [Lee County], "To all concerned," n.p. , Sep. 23, 1910, Annual Reports, Tex. (1910), reel 1, T-890.

28. Concerning Williamson, see Dethloff, *Centennial History*, 2: 392–93; H. H. Williamson, College Station, to Clarence Ousley, campus, Apr. 23, 1915, TAEX Historical Files; Farmers' Cooperative Demonstration Work, 1913, TAEX Historical Files.

29. Williamson to Ousley, Apr. 23, 1915, TAEX Historical Files. See also Kate Adele Hill, *Home Demonstration Work in Texas* (San Antonio, Tex.: Naylor, 1958), 194.

30. See P. C. Parks, "Conditions among Negro Farmers," *Southern Workman* 40 (Feb. 1911): 100–104; letter, Ed R. Kone to Bradford Knapp, Oct. 19, 1910, Annual Reports, Tex. (1910), reel 1, T-890. Kone welcomed the influx of European immigrants into Texas as a way of reducing the percentage of blacks in the population (*TDA Bulletin, 1909*, 39–40).

31. The son of slaves, Blackshear was born in Montgomery, Alabama, and attended school in Alabama and Iowa before moving to Texas to teach (May Schmidt,

"Edward Lavoisier Blackshear," *New Handbook of Texas* (Austin: Texas State His-torical Association, 1996), 1: 573; Mrs. M. E. V. Hunter, "Outstanding Achieve-ments in Negro Home Demonstration Work," Aug. 1931, TMs, TAEX Historical Files; Crosby, "Building the Country Home," 20–23). The university employed E. B. Evans, a doctor of veterinary medicine, to tend the stock in 1918 (Evans, "Down Memory Lane: The Story of Edward Bertram Evans, Sr., and the Early History of Prairie View A&M University," 11, PV). See also June 6–7, 1915, Board Minutes, June 1909–Mar. 1917, p. 73, Prairie View Normal and Industrial College, PV; *Prairie View Standard* (Sep. 18, 1915): 1, 4; *Prairie View Standard* (Dec. 11, 1915).

32. The *Prairie View Standard* printed Farmers' Congress programs and discussions in depth, as did major city newspapers; see *San Antonio Daily Express* (July 20, Aug. 8, 1908), *Dallas Express* (Aug. 28, Sep. 11, 1920), and *Dallas Morning News* (Aug. 11, 1921).

33. For Blackshear's quotation on farmer improvements, see *Prairie View Stan-dard* (Aug. 5, 1916), N. p.

34. Karen J. Ferguson, "Caught in 'No Man's Land': The Negro Cooperative Demonstration Service and the Ideology of Booker T. Washington, 1900–1916," *Ag-ricultural History* 72, no. 1 (Winter 1998): 33–54.

35. Ibid.

36. For Washington's tour, see Louis R. Harlan, *Booker T. Washington: The Wiz-ard of Tuskegee 1901–1915* (New York: Oxford University Press, 1983), 265; Louis R. Harlan and Raymond W. Smock, ed. *The Booker T. Washington Papers,* 14 vols. (Ur-bana: University of Illinois Press, 1972–1989), 11: 322–30, 11: 331–43 (hereafter *BTW Papers*). Washington thanked the Texas State Negro Business League, R. L. Smith, president, for extending an invitation to tour the state (*BTW Papers,* 11: 326) and credited Smith for his work with the FIS (*BTW Papers,* 11: 325). For the influence of Washington on the formation of industrial institutes, see Ada Simond, "Looking Back," *American-Statesman Neighbor* (Jan. 27, 1983).

37. *General Laws of the State of Texas Passed by the Thirty-Second Legislature, Regu-lar Session 10 January–11 March 1911* (Austin, Tex.: Austin Printing Co., 1911), 105–6; [Kate Adele Hill], "Highlights in the History of the Texas Agricultural Extension Service," TAEX Historical Files, n.d.; Mrs. Lillie G. Bryan, *The Story of Demonstra-tion Work in Texas: A Sketch of the Extension Service of the Texas A. and M. College,* B-93 rev. (College Station: Extension Service, Agricultural and Mechanical College of Texas and the USDA, 1938), 4, 9. The agent in Brazoria County noted that the tax base supported demonstration work. Nearly one-third of Brazoria County farm owners were black. See Texas Agricultural Extension Service, A. and M. College of Texas and U.S. Department of Agriculture Cooperating, *Annual Report of the Exten-sion Service of the Agricultural and Mechanical College of Texas 1918* (College Station, 1918), 65 (hereafter *TAEX Annual Report 1918*).

38. In Walker County, blacks owned 39.5 percent of all farms. Commissioners au-thorized $750 for a county agricultural agent in November 1911 (Minutes, Commissio-ners' Court, Walker County, Nov. 13, 1911, vol. G, 351; Feb. 19, 1915, vol. H, 110).

39. For the relationship of railway lines and public reform, see Roy V. Scott, *Railroad Development Programs in the Twentieth Century* (Ames: Iowa State University Press, 1985), 36–57. A photograph shows a mixed-race audience gathered at Glen Flora in Wharton County to listen to the lectures delivered from the Extension Educational Train in 1911 (photo with caption, TAEX Historical Files); see also *Negro Population, 1790–1915*, 834. Three issues of the Wharton *Spectator* that might have mentioned these lecture trains do not exist among the issues at the Center for American History, University of Texas, Austin (hereafter CAH); these are vol. 24, nos. 1, 2, and 3 (Dec. 15, 22, 29, 1911). See also *Nineteenth Biennial Report of the Board of Directors of the Agricultural and Mechanical College of Texas for the Fiscal Years Ending 31 August 1913 and 31 August 1914*, 13.

40. The Adams Fund supported Experiment Station research. See Youngblood, "Report of Director," 34, 43; C. H. Waller, professor of agriculture, Prairie View Normal and Industrial College Teachers Salary List for January 1915, *Journal of the House of Representatives of the First Called Session, Thirty-fourth Legislature, April 29, 1915–May 28, 1915* (Austin, Tex.: Von Boeckmann-Jones, 1915), 81. Waller earned $108.33 per month and was one of the five highest-paid employees at the school. E. L. Blackshear, principal, earned the most per month, at $150.00. See Evans, "Down Memory Lane," 41.

41. Dethloff, *Centennial History*, 2: 392–93. The selection of Texas A&M as the cooperating institution did not occur without a fight. See Hill and Calvert, "The University of Texas Extension Services," 238–39.

42. Marie Cromer received a temporary appointment as the first white female to organize girls' clubs in Aiken County, SC, in 1910 (Lynne Anderson Rieff, "'Rousing the People of the Land': Home Demonstration Work in the Deep South, 1914–1950" [PhD diss., Auburn University, 1995], 45); Hill, *Home Demonstration Work*, 5–14, 15–28; Farmers' Cooperative Demonstration Work, 1913, in TAEX Historical Files. The USDA organized the 2,241 comments received into *Social and Labor Needs of Farm Women*, Bulletin no. 103; *Domestic Needs of Farm Women*, Bulletin no. 104; *Educational Needs of Farm Women*, Bulletin no. 105; and *Economic Needs of Farm Women*, Bulletin no. 106; all published in 1915 by the Government Printing Office. Responses also provided evidence to justify the inclusion of home economics instruction under the Smith-Lever Act. Reports submitted by those involved with girls' work in 1912 document a lack of support. See also Annual Reports, Tex. (1912), reel 1, T-890; (1915), reel 1, T-890.

43. Hill and Calvert, "The University of Texas Extension Services," 238–39; Judith N. McArthur, *Creating the New Woman: The Rise of Southern Women's Progressive Culture in Texas, 1893–1918* (Urbana: University of Illinois Press, 1998), 48–53; Kathleen C. Hilton, "'Both in the Field, Each with a Plow': Race and Gender in USDA Policy, 1907–1929," in *Hidden Histories of Women in the New South*, ed. Virginia Bernhard et al. (Columbia: University of Missouri Press, 1994), 114–33.

44. Jeannie Whayne, "'I Have Been through Fire': Black Agricultural Extension

Agents and the Politics of Negotiation," in *African American Life in the Rural South, 1900–1950,* ed. R. Douglas Hurt (Columbia: University of Missouri Press, 2003), 152–88. States with more black farmers than Texas in 1910 included Mississippi, Georgia, Alabama, and South Carolina: *Negro Population,* 588; Crosby, "Building the Country Home," 34–46; idem, "The Roots," 228–47; idem, "Limited Success against Long Odds: The Black County Agent," *Agricultural History* 57, no. 3 (July 1983): 277–88; and idem, "The Struggle for Existence: The Institutionalization of the Black County Agent System," *Agricultural History* 60, no. 2 (Spring 1986): 123–36. See also General Education Board, *The General Education Board,* 26–27, 55. Approximately 608,009 black farms operated in the states that hosted black agents. Based on an average black farm family size of 6.65 in 1910, the sixty-six black agents served approximately 4,043,200 men, women, and children on black-operated southern farms (Du Bois, "Negro Farmer," 70). Stewart E. Tolnay, *The Bottom Rung: African American Family Life on Southern Farms* (Urbana: University of Illinois Press, 1999), 76, estimates southern farm family averages.

45. Letter, Chicago Branch, NAACP, to David A. Houston, secretary of agriculture, Sep. 12, 1913; letter, acting secretary to Judge Edward Osgood Brown, president, Chicago Branch of the NAACP, Oct. 14, 1913, General Correspondence, Negroes, 1913, Records of the Office of the Secretary of Agriculture, Record Group 16, National Archives and Records Administration II, College Park, Md. (hereafter OSA, RG 16, NA); Memoranda between O. B. Martin, assistant in charge of demonstration club work, and Bradford Knapp, special agent in charge, Office of Farmers' Cooperative Demonstration Work, Washington, DC, Dec. 1 and 2, 1913, General Correspondence, 1908–17, Records of the Federal Extension Service, Record Group 33, National Archives and Records Administration II, College Park, Md. (hereafter ES, RG 33, NA).

46. Rasmussen, *Taking the University to the People,* 24, 46–54, 56, 67–68; Dethloff, *Centennial History,* 2: 382–404. Contemporary sources commented on the professed equity of demonstration work (E. Smith, "Raising a Crop of Men," 608).

47. Alfred Charles True, *A History of Agricultural Extension Work in the United States, 1785–1923,* Misc. Publication no. 15 (Washington, DC: Government Printing Office, 1928; reprint 1969). True favored activities undertaken by white farmers. Roy V. Scott's more scholarly approach (*The Reluctant Farmer*) incorporates African Americans, especially their efforts related to the Colored Farmers National Alliance, their involvement in farmers' institutes offered by Tuskegee, and as agents and participants in extension activities. Rasmussen summarizes the history of the extension service in *Taking the University to the People.* He comments on Wilson's enthusiasm for the progressive legislation but ignores the racist heritage of the bill (48). The exchange between Sen. Wesley L. Jones of Washington State and Sen. Hoke Smith of Georgia appears in R. Grant Seals, "The Formation of Agricultural and Rural Development Policy with Emphasis on African-Americans: II. The Hatch-George and Smith-Lever Acts," *Agricultural History* 65, no. 2 (1991): 22–23, 30; Hilton, "'Both in the Field,'" 114–33.

48. H. H. Williamson, College Station, to Clarence Ousley, [A&M] Campus [College Station], Apr. 24, 1915, TAEX Historical Files.

49. Williamson to Ousley, Apr. 24, 1915, TAEX Historical Files. White boys competing at the Texas Cotton Palace received the following premiums: first place, $10.00; second, $7.00; third, $4.00; fourth, $3.00; and fifth, $2.00. Only one division was open to black youth enrolled in clubs in Texas. They exhibited their white dent corn in the hopes of winning the following premiums: first place, $4.00; second, $3.00; third, $2.00; and fourth place, $1.00 (*Special Catalogue and Premium List, Fifth Annual Texas Cotton Palace Exposition, Waco, Texas, 31 October through 15 November 1914,* 74, The Texas Collection, Baylor University, Waco, Tex. (hereafter BU). The discrepancy was narrower in 1927 at the Texas State Exposition in Austin, when African Americans competed for awards that were one-fifth to one-sixth lower than white awards. The winner in the community exhibit in the "colored" division won $25.00 instead of the $30.00 premium the white community winner received. Black winners took home from $1.50 to $3.00, depending on the division they entered, whereas white winners took home $2.00 to $5.00 for the same produce (*Premium List, Rules and Regulations, Texas State Exposition, Austin, Texas, 4–8 October 1927,* 16–17, 71, Austin History Center, Austin, Tex. [hereafter AHC]).

50. For Washington's use of farmers' letters, see Crosby, "The Struggle," 129–30. Crosby describes Washington's strategy to secure funding from the Smith-Lever Act through Auburn University in ibid., 132. Crosby argues that the Smith-Lever Act expanded the black demonstration program in Alabama and led Texans to follow suit (ibid., 133), but that the elimination of GEB funding retarded program expansion in Virginia, North Carolina, South Carolina, and Georgia and depleted the number of black agents in Arkansas and Mississippi ("Building the Country Home," 55–56). Case studies shed light on the role Washington played in expanding the black service. See Gary Zellar, "H. C. Ray and Racial Politics in the African American Extension Service Program in Arkansas, 1915–1929, *Agricultural History* 72, no. 2 (Spring 1998): 429- 45; Trustees, D. N. McCoy et al., Giddings, Tex. [Lee County], "To all concerned," n.p., Sep. 23, 1910, Annual Reports, Tex. (1910), reel 1, T-890; *Prairie View Standard* 5, no. 26 (Sep. 18, 1915): 1, 4; *Prairie View Standard* (Dec. 11, 1915). Of all blacks over ten years of age in Texas in 1920, 17.8 percent were illiterate: *Negroes in the United States,* 813.

51. Winkler, *Platforms of Political Parties in Texas,* 504; "Clarence N. Ousley," *Handbook of Texas Online* [accessed Jan. 25, 2006]; [Clarence Ousley], *Biennial Report of the Director of Extension Service Agricultural and Mechanical College of Texas, 1915–17,* Bulletin of the Agricultural and Mechanical College of Texas (in cooperation with the U.S. Department of Agriculture), No. B-33 (College Station: A. and M. College of Texas, Nov. 1916), 2 (hereafter *Biennial Report, 1915–17*); C. Vann Woodward, *Thinking Back: The Perils of Writing History* (Baton Rouge: Louisiana State University Press, 1986), 26; idem, *The Strange Career of Jim Crow,* 3rd rev. ed. (New York: Oxford University Press, 1974).

52. Louis R. Harlan provides the most comprehensive study of Washington's ideology and influence in *Booker T. Washington: The Making of a Black Leader, 1856–1901* (New York: Oxford University Press, 1972) and idem, *Booker T. Washington: The Wizard of Tuskegee.* For a counterpoint, see David Levering Lewis's two-volume biography, *W. E. B. Du Bois: Biography of a Race,* and *W. E. B. Du Bois: The Fight for Equality and the American Century, 1919–1963* (New York: Henry Holt, 2000).

CHAPTER 2

1. Mary Evelyn V. Hunter, "History of Extension Service among Negroes in Texas, Brief Summary," attachment to "History of Extension Work among Negroes in Texas from August 1, 1915 to Semptember [*sic*] 15, 1931," TMs, TAEX Historical Files; see also R. L. Smith, Wolf City, Texas, to I. W. Rowen [*sic*], Prairie View, "History of the Negro Extension Service in Texas," Apr. 19, 1936, TMs, TAEX Historical Files; Dempsey H. Seastrunk, "Black Extension Service, *New Handbook of Texas,* 1: 567. Hunter spent her career in public service. After years with the segregated division of the TAEX, she moved to Iowa and earned a graduate degree at Iowa State College in Ames then founded and directed the Division of Home Economics at Virginia State College for Negroes, now Virginia State University (Sherilyn Brandenstein, "Mary Evelyn V. Edwards Hunter," *New Handbook of Texas,* 3: 788; Ruthe Winegarten, *Black Texas Women: A Sourcebook* [Austin: University of Texas Press, 1996], 253–54; and Hill, *Home Demonstration Work in Texas,* 132–43). For manuscript materials on Hunter, see TAEX Historical Files, and the archives at the Johnson Library, Virginia State University, Petersburg, Virginia. In 1930, Mrs. Hunter compiled materials from agents documenting the first twenty-five years of the Negro Extension Service. Ford had cooperated with Wharton County's white agent, J. F. Bagwell, for several years prior to 1915. Ford worked until his death on June 12, 1921.

2. William Procter, College Station, to Bradford Knapp, Washington, DC, Sep. 23, 1915, General Correspondence of the Extension Service and Its Predecessors, June 1907–June 1943, ES, RG 33, NA. (Hunter, "History of Extension Service.") See also Historical Notes and Staff Lists, TAEX Historical Files; [Ousley], *Biennial Report, 1915–17,* 4, 9.

3. For quotations, see "A. & M. Extension to Be Enlarged," [*Bryan*] *Eagle* (Sep. 16, 1915), Texas Agricultural Experiment Station, Special Subject Backfiles, Early to 1978, Cushing Memorial Library and Archives, Texas A&M University, College Station; Procter to Knapp, Sep. 23, 1915, General Correspondence, ES, RG 33, NA; Mrs. M. E. V. Hunter, Petersburg, Va., to Mrs. I. W. Rowan, Prairie View, Tex., Feb. 13, 1940, TAEX Historical Files; Historical Notes and Staff Lists, TAEX Historical Files.

4. The assistant chief of the Federal Extension Service explained franking privileges to Procter (Sep. 27, 1915, General Correspondence of the Extension Service and Its Predecessors, June 1907–June 1943, ES, RG 33, NA). See also [Clarence Ousley], "Annual Report of the Director of Extension, Agricultural and Mechanical College of Texas, for the Calendar Year, 1915," TMs, TAEX Historical Files; idem, *Biennial Report, 1915–17*, 2–3, 4; *Annual Report of the Director of Extension Service Agricultural and Mechanical College of Texas 1917*, Bulletin of the Agricultural and Mechanical College of Texas (in cooperation with the U.S. Department of Agriculture), no. B-45 (College Station: A. and M. College of Texas, Jan. 1918), 23 (hereafter *TAEX Annual Report 1917*); *TAEX Annual Report 1918*, 65, 91; *Annual Report of the Extension Service of the Agricultural and Mechanical College of Texas [1919]* (College Station: Extension Service, A. and M. College of Texas and U.S. Department of Agriculture Cooperating, 1920), 116 (hereafter *TAEX Annual Report 1919*); *Annual Report of the Extension Service of the Agricultural and Mechanical College of Texas [1920]*, 57 (College Station: Extension Service, A. and M. College of Texas and U.S. Department of Agriculture Cooperating, 1921) (hereafter *TAEX Annual Report 1920*); *Annual Report of the Extension Service of the Agricultural and Mechanical College of Texas [1921]* (College Station: Extension Service, A. and M. College of Texas and U.S. Department of Agriculture Cooperating, 1922), 75 (hereafter *TAEX Annual Report 1921*). The percentage increased to 7.89 in 1937 (Gladys Baker, *The County Agent* [Chicago: University of Chicago Press, 1939], 198). For the number of office staff, see *TAEX Annual Report 1918*, 93; *TAEX Annual Report 1920*, frontispiece. Pinkie Rambo may have been related to Mildren Isaacs-Rhombo [Rambo], one of Smith's four adopted children ("Smith Is Laid to Rest Obsequies Held for Hon. Robt. L. Smith," *Waco Messenger* [July 17, 1942], 1).

5. Mrs. M. E. V. Hunter, Petersburg, Va. to Mrs. I. W. Rowan, Prairie View, Tex., Feb. 13, 1940, TAEX Historical Files. Historical Notes and Staff Lists, TAEX Historical Files. The first appointees in Texas held degrees and had middle-class status and a relatively stable source of income.

6. R. L. Smith, Wolfe City, Texas, to Mrs. Rowan, Apr. 19, 1936, attached to Smith, "History of the Negro Extension Service," Ms, TAEX Historical Files; [Ousley], "Annual Report, 1916," TMs, 14, TAEX Historical Files; *Prairie View Standard* (Nov. 13, 1915). By 1917, two agents were working full time in the field and two more were working nine months. A leader and a stenographer brought the number of staff in the Negro Division to six. They traveled 48,796 miles in 1917 to satisfy demand. The *TAEX Annual Report 1917*, 37, recounts that agronomists visited eighteen counties regularly, and the home economics demonstrators visited twenty. Combined, they organized corn and canning clubs in nineteen counties and visited demonstration corn plats in seventeen counties and demonstration gardens in ten counties; see [Ousley], *Biennial Report, 1915–17*, 9; [T. O. Walton], *TAEX Annual Report, 1917*, 37.

7. Sitton and Conrad, *Freedom Colonies*, 24–25, 29–30, 191–98.

8. Smith to Rowan, Apr. 19, 1936, TAEX Historical Files; Walton, "Annual Report, 1918–1919," 6, TMs, TAEX Historical Files; Hattie R. Green, "History of Extension Work in Smith County among Negro Farm Families [1939]," TMs, TAEX Historical Files.

9. Ousley, *Biennial Report, 1915–17*, 2–3.

10. Green, "History of Extension Work in Smith County among Negro Farm Families," TAEX Historical Files; Hunter, "History of Extension Service among Negroes in Texas"; and R. L. Smith, "History of the Negro Extension Service in Texas," Ms, TAEX Historical Files. Smith's history does not reflect the same degree of analysis as Hunter's, perhaps because he lost records when lightning struck a garage where they were stored. Also, Smith does not present specialist information. Ford died in 1921 and did not reflect on his career. Karen Ferguson documents resentment among black farmers toward the extension agents and their message in "Caught in 'No Man's Land.'"

11. The best descriptions of the "Ford System" appear in surviving copies of *The Helping Hand,* the newspaper of the FIS. See "Prof. J. H. Ford Outlines Plans for Sure Corn Crop," *The Helping Hand* (Nov. 1918), SCFP. Smith recalled that Ford instructed farmers to select good seed from "a good parent stalk" of corn, to test the seed to document fertility, and to prepare a seedbed. He recommended planting two rows of corn and a row of peas and to cultivate repeatedly. See Smith to Rowan, Apr. 19, 1936, TAEX Historical Files; and [Ousley], "Annual Report, 1916," TMs, 14, TAEX Historical Files. Information on Ford appears in Procter to Knapp, Sep. 23, 1915, General Correspondence, ES, RG 33, NA. See flyer R. L. Smith, "Great Food and Feed Campaigns," Waco, Tex., Jan. 26, 1918, SCFP.

12. [Hunter], "History of Extension Work," TAEX Historical Files.

13. [Ousley], "Annual Report, 1916," TMs, 13–14, TAEX Historical Files.

14. Hill, *Home Demonstration Work,* 132–36 (quotation, 135); *TAEX Annual Report 1918,* 82; *TAEX Annual Report 1919,* 110–11; E. A. Miller and Madge J. Reese, "Report of the Annual Visitation to the Texas Agricultural and Mechanical College, College Station, Texas, as Provided for in the Smith-Lever Act of 8 May 1914, 1920–1921," [visited] Aug. 1–8, 19–20, 1921, Annual Inspection Reports of Cooperative Extension Work in the Field, ES, RG 33, NA; Ronald R. Kline, "Ideology and Social Surveys: Reinterpreting the Effects of 'Laborsaving' Technology on American Farm Women," *Technology and Culture* 38, no. 2 (1997): 355–85.

15. Letter, M. E. V. Hunter to Mildred Horton, Apr. 9, 1929, requesting the appointment of Irene Sanders; and [Irene Sanders], "Historical Appraisal, Anderson County," TAEX Historical Files.

16. Limestone County officials did not create a position for a black male agent until 1927 or for a black female agent until 1928 (TAEX Historical Files).

17. TAEX directors during the time with which we are concerned include Clarence N. Ousley (1914–17), Thomas Otto Walton (acting director 1917–19; director 1919–25), Charles H. Alvord (1925–27), Oscar Baker Martin (1928–35), Howard H.

Williamson (1935–43), Ide Trotter (1944–49), George G. Gibson (1949–57), John E. Hutchison (1957–76). For titles and tenure of TAEX administrators, see Agents and Specialists: Appointments, Transfer Changes (Men, Women), TAEX Historical Files; Dethloff, *History of Texas A&M*, 2: 394–403; Hutchison, "The Texas Agriculture Extension Service," 134. Edward B. Evans recalls Bizzell's address to Prairie View students and faculty in Evans, "Down Memory Lane," 69. Woolfolk describes the administrations of Bizzell and his Prairie view principal, J. Granville Osborne, as a "revolution" (*Prairie View,* 178–85); Presidents and chancellors of Texas A&M during the existence of the Negro Division include William Bennett Bizzell (president 1914–25), Thomas Otto Walton (president 1925–43), Gibb Gilchrist (president 1944–48; chancellor 1948–53), Marion Thomas Harrington (chancellor 1953–59), David Hitchens Morgan (president 1953–56), and James Earl Rudder (president 1959–70).

18. See E. Evans, "Down Memory Lane," 70 (quotations). Walton held the presidency of Texas A&M until the board did not rehire him in August 1943 (Dethloff, *Centennial History,* 1: 395–96). Principals and presidents of Prairie View A&M during the existence of the Negro Division include Edward Lavoisier Blackshear (1895–1915), I. M. Terrell (1915–18), J. Granville Osborne (1918–25), P. E. Bledsoe (acting 1925), Willette Rutherford Banks (1926–46), Edward Bertram Evans (1946–48; president 1948–66), and Alvin I. Thomas (1966–82). See also Seastrunk, "Fifty Years of Negro Extension Work in Texas, 1915–1965," TMS, Negro Extension History, PV.

19. *TAEX Annual Report 1917,* 37; E. Evans, "Down Memory Lane," 64–65 (quotation on 65).

20. Kirby describes "Bookerism" in *Darkness at the Dawning,* 175. See also Lewis, *Du Bois: Biography of a Race,* 466–68; Whayne, " 'I Have Been through Fire.' "

21. For dates of appointment and positions held, see Historical Notes and Staff Lists, 1916, 1917, 1918, 1919, TAEX Historical Files. Also see *TAEX Annual Report 1917,* 37.

22. After 1915, in addition to the "Negro" designation, Federal Extension Service reporting forms included a special attachment to the standard narrative report, "Special Report by White Agents on Work with Negro Farmers." This allowed white agents to describe work with black clients.

23. *Chicago Defender* (Oct. 30, 1915). The identity of the lynched men and the location of the lynching remain a mystery. Nothing on the lynching appears in [NAACP], *Thirty Years of Lynching in the United States, 1889–1918* (New York: NAACP, 1919; reprint 1969). Successful minority farmers suffered a similar fate across the South during the early 1900s (Leon F. Litwack, *Trouble in Mind: Black Southerners in the Age of Jim Crow* [New York: Knopf, 1998], 160, 308–12).

24. Beck and Tolnay, "The Killing Fields."

25. *Chicago Defender* (Apr. 3, 1915).

26. Letter, E. L. Blackshear, Prairie View, Tex., to colleagues, Mar. 23, 1919, General Correspondence, Negroes, 1919, OSA, RG 16, NA. Whayne, "I Have Been through Fire," 166–67.

27. Blackshear to colleagues, Mar. 23, 1919, and memorandum, Bradford Knapp to Mr. Secretary [of Agriculture], Apr. 25, 1919, General Correspondence, Negroes, 1919, OSA, RG 16, NA. Whayne, "I Have Been through Fire," 167–69.

28. Blackshear to colleagues, Mar. 23, 1919, General Correspondence, Negroes, 1919, OSA, RG 16, NA.

29. Charles E. Hall [résumé], n.d.; letter, Charles E. Hall, Division of Agriculture, Bureau of the Census, Washington, DC, to Hon. Henry C. Wallace, secretary of agriculture, Washington, DC, Apr. 25, 1921; letter, Hall to Wallace, May 7, 1921 (White, Bailey, Caldwell quotations, p. 1; Polk quotation p. 2); letter, Hall to W. A. Jump, secretary to Mr. Wallace, USDA, Washington, DC, May 6, 1921; all in General Correspondence, Negroes, 1921, OSA, RG 16, NA. See also Gilbert T. Stephenson, "The Segregation of the White and Negro Races in Rural Communities of North Carolina," *South Atlantic Quarterly* 13, no. 2 (Apr. 1914): 107–17; Clarence Poe, "Rural Land Segregation between Whites and Negroes: A Reply to Mr. Stephenson," *South Atlantic Quarterly* 13, no. 3 (July 1914): 207. Clarence Poe edited the *Progressive Farmer*. He, with the support of the North Carolina State Farmers' Union, had proposed legislation in 1914 that would have allowed voters in a district to prohibit land sales to "a person of a different race" if justified "by considerations of the peace, protection and social life of the community." Poe's proposal allowed for review by a judge or board of county commissioners.

30. Memorandum, A. C. True, director, USDA State Relations Service, to Mr. Jump, June 25, 1921, General Correspondence, Negroes, 1921, OSA, RG 16, NA; C. H. Alvord and E. A. Miller, "Annual Visitation to Texas Agricultural and Mechanical College, College Station, Texas, May 20–25, July 22–25, 1918," Annual Inspection Reports of Cooperative Extension Work in the Field, July 1914–June 1947, Other Regular Reports Concerning Field Extension Work, ES, RG 33, NA.

31. *TAEX Annual Report 1917*, 37 (quotation); *TAEX Annual Report 1918*, 91; Rieff, "'Rousing the People,'" 90. Mary Evelyn Hunter supervised one agent in 1916, thirteen in 1918, and fifteen in 1919. Three held year-round positions, but the others received their employment through the emergency appropriations and worked only during the canning season, May through June. Men appointed to permanent positions in counties without a female emergency agent encouraged women to can meat and surplus garden produce to fill their pantries (Alvord and Miller, "Annual Visitation, 1918," Annual Inspection Reports of Cooperative Extension Work in the Field, ES, RG 33, NA; Walton, "1918–1919 Annual Reports," TMs, TAEX Historical Files; *TAEX Annual Report 1918*, 82). For a list of counties and agents, see TAEX Historical Files.

32. *TAEX Annual Report 1918*, 1, 5, 37; [Ousley], *Biennial Report, 1915–17*, 2 (Ousley quotations), 3, 9. For statistics on the early extension effort in other states, see Crosby, "Building the Country Home," table II, 107.

33. E. L. Blackshear to T. O. Walton, Dec. 31, 1918, in Annual Reports, Tex. (1918), reel 4, T-890; *TAEX Annual Report 1918*, 3, 91. Crosby explains the influence

of World War I on the work of county agents in "Building the Country Home," 59–63. Lynne Rieff does the same for home demonstration agents in "'Rousing the People,'" 90–97. Rieff describes the role women played in curbside markets in other parts of the South in "'Rousing the People,'" 93. See also Crosby, "Building the Country Home," 60–62, and Rieff, "'Rousing the People,'" 97, where both discuss the role agents played in Saturday Service Leagues.

34. Memo, [Knapp] to True, Sep. 28, 1918, General Correspondence, ES, RG 33, NA.

35. Ibid.

36. The white agent in Brazos County, C. L. Beason, worked with 100 black farmers to produce a majority of their home food and feed in 1918 (Annual Report, Brazos County, Tex. [1918], reel 4, T-890). At least 244 blacks owned their farms and 944 rented on the share in Brazos County in 1910. Thus, Beason reached 8.4 percent of his county's black operators (U.S. Bureau of the Census, *Thirteenth Census of the United States, 1910,* vol. VII, *Agriculture, 1909–1910* [Washington, DC: Government Printing Office, 1913], 657). Interest on the part of black farmers in Lee County continued, and the white agent worked with at least three black demonstrators, two concentrating on cotton and one on corn, see map, Lee County, Texas, 1919–20, Material Submitted with Annual Narrative and Statistical Reports, 1914–44, Other Regular Reports Concerning Field Extension Work, ES, RG 33, NA. Knapp outlined the qualifications of three "very able, upright and conscientious negroes who are devoted to their service and to the Government": John B. Pierce, Hampton Institute; Thomas M. Campbell, Tuskegee Institute; and Edward L. Blackshear, Prairie View Institute. He proposed the expansion of their responsibilities with only a modest increase in expenditures, approximately $8,000. He intended to use emergency funds to offset their traveling expenses, and perhaps their salaries, and their offices were to remain the same to ensure access to the territory they covered (Memo, [Knapp] to True, Sep. 28, 1918, General Correspondence, ES, RG 33, NA). As a special agent for the USDA's States Relations Service, Blackshear was responsible for Texas, Oklahoma, Louisiana, and Arkansas. Knapp admitted that he did not know Blackshear personally, and he was vague about his education and background, incorrectly stating that Blackshear graduated from Tuskegee. He actually matriculated at Tabor College in Iowa in 1881 and completed his MA at Tabor in 1902 (Schmidt, "Edward Lavoisier Blackshear," *New Handbook of Texas,* 1: 573). Blackshear possibly received consideration because Secretary of Agriculture David Houston "knew him well and favorably" (memo, [Bradford Knapp] Chief to Dr. True, Sep. 28, 1918, General Correspondence, ES, RG 33, NA). Upon Blackshear's death, the State Relations Service of the USDA eliminated the field agent position and reassigned responsibilities to the two remaining agents, Campbell and Pierce. Kirby mentions John B. Pierce's appointment in *Darkness at the Dawning,* 174. See also Crosby, "Building the Country Home," 64. Baker, *County Agent,* 195, enumerates Campbell's responsibilities as supervisor of Texas, Oklahoma, Alabama, Mississippi, Georgia, and Florida, and Pierce's as supervisor

of Virginia, Maryland, North Carolina, South Carolina, West Virginia, Kentucky, Tennessee, and Arkansas. She ignores Blackshear's appointment. Whayne, "I Have Been through Fire," 155.

37. *TAEX Annual Report 1918*, 82–84. The two black urban agents who are listed among the staff in 1918 are Miss Harrison and Miss E. Maynard. No first names appear, but they did earn courtesy titles (Alvord and Miller, "List of Salaries Paid from All Sources," in "Annual Visitation, 1918," Annual Inspection Reports of Cooperative Extension Work in the Field, ES, RG 33, NA).

38. W. D. Bentley and F. M. McLaughlin, "Report of Annual Visitation to the Texas Agricultural and Mechanical College at College Station, Texas, 15–17 May and 30 July–4 August; and an inspection of Smith-Lever Accounts on 18–20 October, 1917," 5, Annual Inspection Reports of Cooperative Extension Work in the Field, ES, RG 33, NA. Miller and Reese, "Report of the Annual Visitation, 1920–1921," [visited] Aug. 1–8, 1921, 19–20, Annual Inspection Reports of Cooperative Extension Work in the Field, ES, RG 33, NA.; *Proceedings of the Seventh Meeting Texas State Farmers' Institute 1917*, Texas Department of Agriculture Bulletin no. 57 (Nov.–Dec. 1917): 34, 78.

39. "Joseph Elward Clayton," *Who's Who in Colored America*, Thomas Yenser, ed., 3rd ed. (New York: Garrett and Massie, [1932], 97); David L. Bearden, "Clayton Vocational Institute, a Superior School," TMs, 11, Clayton Vocational Institute Papers, AHC; Reid, "African Americans, Community Building," 55–59; Sitton and Conrad, *Freedom Colonies*, 197. Clayton held his commission from 1917 until the Negro Farmers' Institutes ceased operation on August 31, 1921: *General Laws of the State of Texas*, 37th Legislature, First Called Session, 1921 (Austin: A. C. Baldwin & Sons, 1921), 197–98. Clayton first addressed Texas State Farmers' Institute attendees in 1917: "The Negro and the South," *Proceedings Texas Farmers' Institute, 1917*, 34–35; *San Antonio Express* (June 27, July 2, 1917), 34 (quotation). He conducted two institutes for black farmers, in Manor and Elgin. Each selected the same officers and elected Clayton their special representative: "Professor J. E. Clayton's Address," *Proceedings of a Joint Meeting of State Farmers' Institute (in Eleventh Annual Meeting) and Texas Pecan Growers' Association 1921*, State Department of Agriculture Bulletin, no. 69 (July–Aug. 1921): 97.

40. Clayton, "The Negro and the South," *Proceedings Texas Farmers' Institute 1917*, 34; "Colored Division," *Preeceedings of the Ninth Annual Meeting Texas State Farmers' Institute 1919*, Texas Department of Agriculture Bulletin, No. 67 (July–Aug. 1919): 8, 11. "Professor J. E. Clayton's Address," *Proceedings State Farmer's Institute and Pecan Growers' Association 1921*, 96–99; *General Laws of the State of Texas*, 36th Legislature, Second Called Session, June 23–July 22, 1919 (Austin: A. C. Baldwin & Sons, 1919), 435.

41. *TAEX Annual Report 1920*, 53–56. The 1920 federal census reported 518,444 rural blacks.

42. "Conferring Powers upon Commissioners Courts to Appropriate Money for

Canning Demonstration Work," H.B. 58, *General and Special Laws of the State of Texas,* 35th Legislature, First Called Session (Austin: A. C. Baldwin & Sons, 1917), 56–57.

43. *Proceedings Texas Farmers' Institute, 1919,* 109–10. Clayton's recommendations prompted black farmers in Brazoria County to buy a tract of 2,200 acres near Sandy Point in 1921; and another group in Gregg County bought 1,900 acres at Easton, an established freedman's colony. Both colonies developed close to railroads to facilitate marketing (Reid, "African Americans, Community Building," 58–59; Sitton and Conrad, *Freedom Colonies,* 193).

44. Steven A. Reich, "Soldiers of Democracy: Black Texans and the Fight for Citizenship, 1917–1921," *Journal of American History* 82, no. 4 (Mar. 1996): 1490–92. Farmers constituted the majority of members in NAACP branches in Falls, Milam, Polk, Robertson, and Wharton counties. This rural membership was concentrated in the Brazos River bottoms of Central Texas. See map in ibid., 1495. "The time has come" quotation from J. E. Turner, secretary, Mumford, Texas, branch, to John R. Shillady, Mar. 25, 1919, Mumford Branch File, NAACP Papers, Manuscript Division, Library of Congress, Washington, DC, quoted in Reich, "Soldiers of Democracy," 1492. Agents employed by the segregated TAEX or regular or emergency appointments worked in all of these counties during the war years but were not retained in any of them after the war, probably because commissioners failed to appropriate funds (County Files, TAEX Historical Files).

45. Smith asked for prayers for R S. Boone of Courtney, Tex., who lost two of his children, one of whom was murdered (*The Helping Hand* [Aug. 18, 1918]: 3, 4; [Nov. 1919]: 1). Smith later served as a member of the Texas Committee on Interracial Violence, organized in 1928. Letter, Blackshear, Prairie View, Texas, to colleagues, Mar. 23, 1919, General Correspondence, Negroes, OSA, RG 16, NA.

46. There were 69,816 Negro farm operators in Texas in 1910, and 78,597 in 1920 (*Negro Farmer in the United States,* 30, 50); *TAEX Annual Report 1917,* 25; *TAEX Annual Report 1918,* 93.

47. *TAEX Annual Report 1919,* 5, 105, 110; *TAEX Annual Report 1920,* 53. Also see TAEX Historical Files; Martin, *A Decade of Negro Extension Work,* 12. Six out of twenty-three black employees of the TAEX were receiving monetary support from counties in 1918 (Alvord and Miller, "Annual Visitation, 1918," Annual Inspection Reports of Cooperative Extension Work in the Field, ES, RG 33, NA). Blacks expressed disappointment at the lack of response after the war to their service during it (Reich, "Soldiers of Democracy," 1478–1504). Emmett Scott noted that "I confess personally a deep sense of disappointment, of poignant pain that a great country in time of need should promise so much and afterward perform so little" (quoted by Jane Lang Scheiber and Harry N. Scheiber, "The Wilson Administration and the Wartime Mobilization of Black Americans, 1917–1918," *Labor History* 10 [1969]: 458, in David M. Kennedy, *Over Here: The First World War and American Society* [New York: Oxford University Press, 1980], 284).

48. "Commissioners Courts—Providing That They May Prescribe and Appropri-

ate and Use Any Sum or Sums of Money Not Exceeding $1,000 per Year for Farmers Cooperative Demonstration Work," S.B. 225, *General Laws of the State of Texas,* 32nd Legislature, 1911, 105–6. No record exists for the amount paid Jacob H. Ford in 1915 (Assistant chief to Mr. W. F. Procter, College Station, Texas, Sep. 28, 1915, General Correspondence, ES, RG 33, NA; Alvord and Miller, "Annual Visitation, 1918," Annual Inspection Reports of Cooperative Extension Work in the Field, ES, RG 33, NA). A discrepancy exists between the amount entered on the 1918 inspection form for Blackshear's salary and the amount Bradford Knapp, chief of extension, believed Blackshear earned as assistant state leader. Knapp indicated that Blackshear's salary of $1,620.00 compared favorably with that of his peers in other states. Other district agents in charge of the segregated extension program in their states in 1918 included John B. Pierce, who earned $1,800.00, and Thomas M. Campbell who earned $1,600.00 (memo, [Bradford Knapp] Chief to Dr. True, Sep. 28, 1918, General Correspondence, ES, RG 33, NA). By 1919, Blackshear was earning $1869.96 as the person "in charge of Negro work." Smith still earned $1,260.00, and Ford and Hunter both still earned $1,020.00 (Charles H. Alvord, "Report of Annual Visitation to the Texas Agricultural and Mechanical College, College Station, Texas, as Provided for in Smith-Lever Act of 8 May 1914," 13, Annual Inspection Reports of Cooperative Extension Work in the Field, ES, RG 33, NA).

49. Brazoria was in TAEX's District Seven areas, one of the largest and most rural in the Gulf Coast. It included "the largest percentage of colored farming population of any county in the district." See *TAEX Annual Report 1918,* 65; Brazoria County, TAEX Historical Files.

50. State district agents expressed pride in the number of agents earning college degrees. Iola W. Rowan reported on the number of agents and their degrees in "Negro Home Demonstration Agents in Texas, July 1915–July 1935," TAEX Historical Files. See also McArthur, *Creating the New Woman,* 5, 48, 149; Julia Kirk Blackwelder, *Now Hiring: The Feminization of Work in the United States, 1900–1995* (College Station: Texas A&M University Press, 1997), 65–66, 84–85.

51. Martin, *A Decade,* 12. Other states with significant programs included Alabama, Mississippi, Virginia, and Georgia. Reports submitted by the state leader and the state agent for home demonstration work appear annually in the published annual reports between 1915 and 1941, variously titled. Only 1917, 1918, and 1919 prove exceptions, but each of these does include a report on Negro home demonstration work. Woolfolk discusses the Extension Service in *Prairie View,* 248–54, 340–42.

CHAPTER 3

1. There were 78,597 black farm operators in Texas in 1920, and 85,940 black farm operators in 1930 (*Negro Farmer in the United States,* 37, 50, 51).

2. Quotation from John I. Donaldson, Annual Report, Washington County, Tex. (1919), reel 11, T-890.

3. *Annual Report of the Extension Service of the Agricultural and Mechanical College of Texas 1928* (College Station: Extension Service, A. and M. College of Texas and U.S. Department of Agriculture Cooperating, [1929]), 63 (hereafter *TAEX Annual Report 1928*).

4. Jeffie O. A. Conner, "My Experiences as an Extension Worker," Waco, 1925, George S. and Jeffie O. A. Conner Papers, The Texas Collection, Baylor University, Waco, Tex. (hereafter Conner Papers), quoted in Winegarten, *Black Texas Women*, 157. See also *Annual Report of the Extension Service of the Agricultural and Mechanical College of Texas 1926* (College Station: Extension Service, A. and M. College of Texas and U.S. Department of Agriculture Cooperating, 1927), 2–3 (hereafter *TAEX Annual Report 1926*); Robert A. Calvert and Arnoldo De León, *The History of Texas*, 2nd ed. (Wheeling, Ill.: Harlan Davidson, 1996), 225. Keith J. Volanto, *Texas Cotton and the New Deal* (College Station: Texas A&M University Press, 2005), 12–25. See also *Texas Extension Work in 1930* (College Station: The Extension Service, Agricultural and Mechanical College of Texas and the United States Department of Agriculture, [1931]), 4 (hereafter *TAEX Annual Report 1930*). For Ford's attendance at training, see *Prairie View Standard* (Jan. 8, 1916); [Ousley], *Biennial Report, 1915–17*, 2–3; Hines, Annual Report, McLennan County, Tex. (1919), reel 10, T-890.

5. *TAEX Annual Report 1921*, 79, 83; *Annual Report of the Extension Service of the Agricultural and Mechanical College of Texas [1924]* (College Station: Extension Service, A. and M. College of Texas and U.S. Department of Agriculture Cooperating, 1925), 14–15 (hereafter *TAEX Annual Report 1924*). Some bulletins include E. J. Kyle et al., *Money Crops in Place of Cotton*, Agricultural and Mechanical College of Texas Bulletin no. 2 (College Station, 1914); and Agricultural and Mechanical College of Texas, *Sweet Potatoes for Profit*, Agricultural and Mechanical College of Texas Bulletin no. 6 (College Station, 1915).

6. Hines, Annual Report, McLennan County, Tex. (1919), reel 10, T-890.

7. *TAEX Annual Report 1926*, 71.

8. John M. Lusk, Annual Report, Washington County, Tex. (1933), reel 71, T-890.

9. Hines, Annual Report, McLennan County, Tex. (1919), reel 10, T-890.

10. C. H. Waller, State Agent, Annual Report, Tex. (1928), reel 52, T-890, quoted in Crosby, "Building the Country Home," 143.

11. J. M. Lusk, Annual Report, Washington County, Tex. (1924), reel 35, T-90; idem, Annual Report Washington County, Tex. (1930), reel 71, T-890; "Negro Agents Work toward Farm Ownership," *Texas Extension Service Farm News* 20, no. 9 (May–June 1934): 8.

12. Smith, Annual Report, McLennan County, Tex. (1924), reel 33, T-890.

13. W. H. Isaacs, Annual Report, Colorado and Lavaca counties, Tex. (1919), reel 8, T-890.

14. Claire Strom, "Texas Fever and the Dispossession of the Southern Yeoman Farmer," *Journal of Southern History* 66, no 1 (Feb. 2000): 70–71, 74 (quotation).

15. TAEX administrators described the model of organization that Waller borrowed as similar to the county farm bureau structure. White agents organized a county council of agriculture or home economics following this model as early as 1920. See *TAEX Annual Report 1920*, 12; *Annual Report of the Extension Service of the Agricultural and Mechanical College of Texas [1922]* (College Station: Extension Service, A. and M. College of Texas and U.S. Department of Agriculture Cooperating, 1923), 71 (hereafter *TAEX Annual Report 1922*).

16. Hunter, "History of Extension Work," 5–6, TAEX Historical Files; *Twelfth Annual Report of the Agricultural Extension Service, A. and M. College of Texas 1925* (College Station: Agricultural and Mechanical College of Texas and United States Department of Agriculture Cooperating, 1926), 68 (hereafter *TAEX Annual Report 1925*); *Annual Report of the Extension Service of the Agricultural and Mechanical College of Texas 1927* (College Station: Extension Service, A. and M. College of Texas and U.S. Department of Agriculture Cooperating, [1928]), 63 (hereafter *TAEX Annual Report 1927*); *TAEX Annual Report 1929*, 48; R. H. Hines, "County Organizations," Annual Report, McLennan County, Tex. (1919), reel 10, T-890; R. G. Johnson, Annual Report, Gregg County, Tex. (1923), reel 27, 1923; Sitton and Conrad, *Freedom Colonies*, 193–94; Darlene Clark Hine, "Black Professionals and Race Consciousness: Origins of the Civil Rights Movement, 1890–1950," *Journal of American History* 89, no. 4 (2003): 1279–95.

17. *TAEX Annual Report 1924*, 16.

18. [Marshall], "Historical Appraisal, Colorado County, 1939," TAEX Historical Files; [Irene Sanders], "Historical Appraisal, Anderson County, 1939," TAEX Historical Files.

19. *TAEX Annual Report 1925*, 68.

20. Isaacs, Annual Report, Colorado and Lavaca counties, Tex. (1919), reel 8, T-890, Colorado County, TAEX Historical Files. He worked alone in the county from January 1, 1918, until his retirement on July 31, 1933. Then the county commissioners hired Mary E. Bledsoe, and she worked alone from January 2, 1935, until another agricultural agent received an appointment on August 16, 1936.

21. L. E. Lusk, Annual Report, Washington County, Tex. (1923), reel 29, T-890. A total of 60 former club members enrolled in college in 1923 (*Annual Report of the Extension Service of the Agricultural and Mechanical College of Texas [1923]* [College Station: Extension Service, A. and M. College of Texas and U.S. Department of Agriculture Cooperating, 1924], 29 [hereafter *TAEX Annual Report 1923*]). In 1926, 163 former club boys enrolled but no number for girls appears in the report (*TAEX Annual Report 1926*, 67). Agents reported that girls' clubs prepared 267 girls for high school and college in 1928 (*TAEX Annual Report 1928*, 62).

22. J. M. Lusk, Annual Report, Washington County, Tex. (1923), reel 29, T-890. Bennie Elliott won first place at the Dallas State Fair for red dent corn in 1930. J. M. Lusk, Annual Report, Washington County, Tex. (1930), reel 71, T-890.

23. J. M. Lusk, Annual Report, Washington County, Tex. (1930), reel 71, T-890.

24. J. M. Lusk, Annual Report, Washington County, Tex. (1923), reel 29, T-890.

25. Fair for Negroes at Grapeland, Tex., Nov. 21–23, 1923, broadside, Agricultural Extension Service, PV. J. M. Lusk, Annual Report, Washington County, Tex. (1930), reel 71, T-890.

26. Mrs. M. E. V. Hunter, "Negro Home Demonstration Work," *TAEX Annual Report 1928*, 62–64; C. H. Waller, "Negro County Agent Work," *TAEX Annual Report 1928*, 58–61; *TAEX Annual Report 1929*, 48.

27. See Evans, "Down Memory Lane," 30.

28. Tolnay *The Bottom Rung*, 19, 96–97. R. L. Smith reported that the death rate among FIS members had dropped below that of blacks as a whole by 1899, with only 2.5 deaths per 1,000 in 1900 ("Village Improvement," 736, quoted in Carroll, "Smith and the FIS," 55). Smith reports 2.5 deaths per 1,000 in *The Farmers' Improvement Society . . . an Interesting Dialogue about Its Origins and Methods* (Victoria, Tex.: [Farmers' Improvement Society], [c.1900]), 18), SCFP. Members paid monthly dues to the FIS endowment that provided death insurance to members (*Constitution and By-Laws of the Farmers' Improvement Society of Texas Organized 20 December 1890; Chartered 8 July 1901* [N.p.: n.p., n.d.], 2, SCFP).

29. Lu Ann Jones, *Mama Learned Us to Work*, 154–56; Gibbons and Armentrout, *Child Labor among Cotton Growers in Texas: A Study of Children Living in Rural Communities in Six Counties in Texas* (New York: National Child Labor Committee, 1925), 96–106; J. M. Benton, Marshall, to C. H. Waller, Prairie View, Aug. 17, 1923, with a press release and two unidentified newspaper clippings attached, Waller Correspondence, PV; Lea Etta Lusk, Annual Report, Washington County, Tex. (1930), reel 71, T-890.

30. Lea Etta Lusk, Annual Report, Washington County, Tex. (1930), reel 71, T-890. Lu Ann Jones describes the importance of milk in babies' diets in *Mama Learned Us to Work*, 155.

31. *TAEX Annual Report 1920*, 53; *TAEX Annual Report 1921*, 79.

32. Staff Conference Minutes, 1925–40, in Waller Papers (hereafter Staff Minutes, date, PV). *TAEX Annual Report 1921*, 79 (quotation); James M. Smallwood, "The Black Community in Reconstruction Texas: Readjustments in Religion and the Evolution of the Negro Church," *East Texas Historical Journal* 16 (Fall 1978): 16–28; unidentified news-paper clipping attached to Benton to Waller, Aug. 17, 1923, Waller Correspondence, PV.

33. *TAEX Annual Report 1921*, 79; James Butler, "James Harrison and the Development of Harrison Switch" (MA thesis, Baylor University, 1989), 95–99. Communities improved fourteen church buildings in 1925 (*TAEX Annual Report 1925*, 68).

34. Extension officials in November 1915 spoke on topics related to the Rural High School Department. See "Program of State Colored Teachers' Association," *Prairie View Standard* (Nov. 20, 1915). Extension agents again presented in 1921, and by then the proceedings were reaching six hundred teachers who paid dues. See *TAEX Annual Report 1921*, 79.

35. [Sanders], "Historical Appraisal, Anderson County, 1939," TAEX Historical Files. Communities built twenty-three schools during 1925 alone (*TAEX Annual Report 1925,* 68). Anna T. Jeanes gave $10,000 to both Tuskegee Institute and Hampton Institute in 1902 for the purpose of helping rural schools. Booker T. Washington and Hollis B. Frissel, presidents of the recipient institutions, convinced Jeanes to increase her gift to extend the work to small schools serving African Americans throughout the South. Robert L. Smith served on the Jeanes Foundation board per Washington's recommendation ("Smith Is Laid to Rest," *Waco Messenger* [July 17, 1942], clipping in SCFP; Darryl Stevens, "Reform without Change: The Motivation behind the Involvement of the General Education Board and the Southern Education Board in Black Southern Education, 1900–1915" [MA thesis, University of Houston–Clear Lake, 1992], 13–14; Hoffschwelle, *Rebuilding,* 28). By 1907, Jeanes teachers were working in Virginia, organizing tomato and canning clubs for rural girls. They were working in four counties in Tennessee in 1909 and thirteen counties in North Carolina by 1913. For relations between Jeanes teachers and home demonstration in other states, see Rieff, "'Rousing the People,'" 46; Ann Elizabeth McCleary, "Shaping a New Role for the Rural Woman: Home Demonstration Work in Augusta County, Virginia, 1917–1940" (PhD diss., Brown University, 1996). Lu Ann Jones, *Mama Learned Us to Work,* 143–44, mentions the appointment of a Jeanes teacher in 1911 in North Carolina; see also Glenda Elizabeth Gilmore, *Gender & Jim Crow: Women and the Politics of White Supremacy in North Carolina, 1896–1920* (Chapel Hill: University of North Carolina Press, 1996), 161. The Texas counties served by Jeanes teachers in 1919 included Atascosa, Houston, Lee, Milam, Navarro, Travis, and Victoria. In 1920, fifteen counties were being served: Atascosa, Brazos, Burleson, Cherokee, Fayette, Fort Bend, Freestone, Jasper, Lee, Montgomery, Navarro, Travis, Victoria, Washington, and Williamson. Houston and Milam counties did not participate after the first year because "satisfactory" teachers could not be employed. Counties provided funds to assist in this work. In 1920, the Jeanes Fund provided $6,828.20 and the fifteen counties appropriated an additional $3,936.80. See Texas State Department of Education, *Historical and Statistical Data as to Education in Texas, 1 January 1919–1 January 1921,* Bulletin 133 ([Austin]: Department of Education, 1921), 83. Of these counties, emergency agents had worked in eight during World War I, but only Victoria employed a home demonstration agent full time in 1920. Three others—Brazos, Burleson, and Washington—employed seasonal agents. See county files, TAEX Historical Files. In 1924, fourteen counties in Texas employed Jeanes teachers: Bastrop, Camp, Cass, Cherokee, Fort Bend, Harris, Harrison, Limestone, Marion, Milam, Morris, Smith, Travis, and Washington. Again, only one of these counties, Washington, employed a home demonstration agent full time in 1924 (Texas State Department of Education, *The Twenty-third Biennial Report State Department of Education 1922–24* [Austin: Von Boeckmann-Jones, (1924)], 181).

36. Lu Ann Jones, *Mama Learned Us to Work,* 143–44, 147; Texas State Depart-

ment of Education, *Historical and Statistical Data,* 82; idem, *Twenty-second Biennial Report of the State Superintendent of Public Instruction State of Texas School Sessions of 1920–21 and 1921–22* (Austin: State Board of Education, [1922]), 138–39. Counties with both extension and Jeanes appointees in 1927–28 included Cherokee, Harris, Harrison, Houston, and Washington. Three counties, Cherokee, Harris, and Harrison, discontinued their Jeanes teachers in 1928–29, but two other counties with home demonstration agents added a Jeanes teacher, so residents in Houston, Limestone, Waller, and Washington counties benefited from both services for brief periods. See Texas State Department of Education biennial reports for respective years; Staff Minutes, May 6, 1936, PV; Staff Minutes, Sep. 1, 1937, PV. Jeanes teachers remained active in Texas into the 1930s. Travis County hired a Jeanes teacher in 1937. She worked out of the office of the county school superintendent and provided teacher training, new ideas, and materials to poor schools (Ada Simond, "Jeanes Teacher 'Aladdin's Lamp,'" *American-Statesman Neighbor* [Aug. 4, 1983]).

37. *TAEX Annual Report 1919,* 110; *TAEX Annual Report 1921,* 84.

38. [J. W. Hogg], "Form of Organization," attachment to Annual Report, Houston County, Texas, 1923, Waller Papers, PV; "Fair for Negroes at Grapeland, Texas, 21, 22, and 23 November 1923," broadside, Agricultural Extension Service, PV; Houston County, TAEX Historical Files.

39. T. C. Richardson, "Building His Own Monument: Negro Teacher Spends Lifetime Building a School around Which Grows a Prosperous Community," *Farm and Ranch* 46 (Apr. 2, 1927): 3–16; Sitton and Conrad, *Freedom Colonies,* 193.

40. Gregg County, TAEX Historical Files; T. C. Richardson, "Building His Own Monument," 16. Studies of property ownership among blacks as slaves and freedmen include Loren Schweninger, *Black Property Owners in the South, 1790–1915* (Urbana: University of Illinois Press, 1990); Philip D. Morgan, "Work and Culture: The Task System and the World of Lowcountry Blacks, 1700–1880," *William and Mary Quarterly,* 3rd series, 39, no. 4 (Oct. 1982): 563–99, esp. 587–94. For the significance of property accumulation by rural women, see Sharon Holt, "Making Freedom Pay: Freed People Working for Themselves, North Carolina, 1865–1900," *Journal of Southern History* 60, no. 2 (May 1994): 229–62. Studies of the development of black communities concentrate on freedmen's towns or the exodus to Kansas in 1879 and do not consider the significance of the black-led back-to-the-land movements in the early-twentieth century (Nell Irvin Painter, *Exodusters: Black Migration to Kansas after Reconstruction* [New York: W. W. Norton, 1976]; Robert G. Athern, *In Search of Canaan: Black Migration to Kansas, 1879–1889* [Lawrence: Regents Press of Kansas, 1978]).

41. Hunter to Rowan, Feb. 13, 1940, TAEX Historical Records; Hattie R. Green, "History of Extension Work," Smith County, TAEX Historical Files.

42. Hines, Annual Report, McLennan County, Tex. (1919), reel 10, T-890.

43. J. V. Smith, Annual Report, McLennan County, Tex. (1924), reel 33, T-890.

44. Hunter, "History of Extension Work," TAEX Historical Files; M. E. V.

Hunter, Petersburg, Va., to I. W. Rowan, Prairie View, Feb. 13, 1940, TAEX Historical Files. Hunter remembered that the meeting occurred in a rural church in the Wellingham community, a switch where the train stopped, but Smith County residents remembered it in the home of the Williams family in Blackjack. See Hattie R. Green, "History of Extension Work, Smith County," TAEX Historical Files; Vista K. McCroskey, "Blackjack, Texas," *New Handbook of Texas* (Austin: Texas State Historical Association, 1996), 1: 569. T. G. Simpson was encouraging market gardeners to invest in canning by 1908. Canning culled tomatoes from the first shipment could pay shipping costs for the fresh crop for the rest of the season (*Texas Department of Agriculture Yearbook 1908* [Austin: Texas Department of Agriculture], 98–100). White extension agents began canning clubs for girls in Texas in 1912. The TAEX published a leaflet to facilitate club formation: Laura F. Neale, *Girls' Canning Clubs, Garden Clubs and Poultry Clubs,* Agricultural and Mechanical College of Texas Bulletin no. B-43 (College Station, 1918). In 1914, Bernice Carter, the assistant state leader for girls' clubs, spoke to the Texas State Farmers' Institute about the benefits of canning clubs and having a home canner on the farm (Bernice Carter, "The Home Canner on the Farm," *Proceedings of the Fourth Meeting Texas State Farmers' Institute 1914* [Austin: Von Boeckmann-Jones, 1914], 47–50). By 1914, the Texas Federation of Women's Clubs also encouraged canning clubs through its Rural Life Committee, established that year and chaired by Mrs. Mamie Gearing (Texas Federation of Women's Clubs, *Annual 1914–1915, Sixteenth Convocation held in Galveston, 17–20 November 1914* [N.p.: Printing Committee, (1915)], 60–61).

45. Families could meet demand with modified equipment (C. E. Hanson, *Household Conveniences and How to Make Them,* Agricultural and Mechanical College of Texas Bulletin no. B-8 [College Station, 1915]). Specialists were describing the "open-kettle method" as "old" by the 1910s (E. M. Barrett, *Canning and Preserving* [Austin: Texas Department of Agriculture, 1916?], 10, in the Katherine Golden Bitting Collection on Gastronomy, Library of Congress, Washington, DC).

46. Both Blackjack (Smith County) and Stump Toe (Gregg County) were freedmen's communities (Sitton and Conrad, *Freedom Colonies,* 194, 197); Hunter to Rowan, Feb. 13, 1940, TAEX Historical Files (quotation p. 1); Hunter, "Outstanding Achievements," TAEX Historical Files. Rebecca Sharpless summarizes the importance of canning and the numbers of rural women of different races involved in the process in the Blackland Prairie in *Fertile Ground,* 126–31. See also *TAEX Annual Report 1922,* 75–76.

47. *TAEX Annual Report 1918,* 82, 83–84; "Conferring Powers upon Commissioners Courts to Appropriate Money for Canning Demonstration Work," H.B. 58, *General and Special Laws of the State of Texas,* (1917), 56–57; Lea Etta Lusk, "Historical Appraisal, Washington County, 1939," TAEX Historical Files; Robert Hines, Annual Report, McLennan County, Tex. (1919), reel 10, T-890. During World War I, two black agents certified at least three other black women, who then supervised

community canners in urban areas and taught neighborhood groups. See *TAEX Annual Report 1918*, 82–84. Agents' memories present a more bucolic situation than Ruth Allen documents in her study of tenancy in the Blackland Prairie (*The Labor of Women in the Production of Cotton*, University of Texas Bulletin no. 3134 [Sep. 1931]).

48. Hunter, "Outstanding Achievements," TAEX Historical Files. Early instruction manuals include James Frank Breazeale, *Canning Vegetables in the Home*, USDA Farmers' Bulletin no. 359 (Washington, DC: Government Printing Office, 1909), located in the Katherine Golden Bitting Collection on Gastronomy, Library of Congress, Washington, DC; *Canning, Preserving, Pickling*, Agricultural and Mechanical College of Texas Bulletin no. B-26 (College Station, 1916); and Cornelia Simpson, *Food Saving in Texas: Drying, Brining, Canning, Curing*, Agricultural and Mechanical College of Texas Bulletin no. B-38 (College Station, 1917). Federal inspectors commented on M. E. V. Hunter's enthusiasm for canning work in 1922. See Schaub and Goddard, "Annual Visitation to the Texas State Agricultural College, College Station, Texas, 4–14 October 1922," Annual Inspection Reports of Cooperative Extension Work in the Field, ES, RG 33, NA; *TAEX Annual Report 1922*, 76. Efforts to fill pantries as an act of domestic mobilization did not stop with canned goods. Agents also encouraged club members to raise 104 chickens each so they could eat chicken twice each week, year-round, and to pickle other foods to satisfy their families' needs. The agents asked them each to preserve thirteen jars of pickles and thirteen bottles of catsup, one for each month and an extra for Christmas, and to can as much jelly and preserves as the family would eat. See *TAEX Annual Report 1919*, 110–11; *TAEX Annual Report 1921*, 84; *TAEX Annual Report 1922*, 75.

49. *TAEX Annual Report 1924*, 16 (quotation). *TAEX Annual Report 1925*, 68.

50. John M. Lusk, Annual Report, Washington County, Tex. (1924), reel 35, T-890; [Brenham, Tex.] *Press Banner* (Aug. 7, 1925), quoted in Thad Sitton and Dan K. Utley, *From Can See to Can't: Texas Cotton Farmers on the Southern Prairies* (Austin: University of Texas Press, 1997), 60.

51. *The Helping Hand* (Oct. 1919). Maggie Lee worked in Polk County on a regular appointment from April 1, 1918, to January 31, 1922, TAEX Historical Files. As an emergency agent, Mary Dixon worked in Fort Bend and Wharton counties, May 21, 1918, to June 30, 1918; in Waller County from April 16, 1919, to August 15, 1919; and in Brazoria County from March 1, 1920, to June 30, 1921. See TAEX Historical Files. Several references document the work of the Parish sisters. *The Helping Hand* (Nov. 1919), describes their work and mentions a photograph that appeared in the *Dallas Daily News* on September 10, 1919. The Dallas editor praised it as one of the best of its kind in the state. The Parish sisters came from a large family in Robertson County. Hunter first began working with them before 1916, and that fall the family exhibited the best display of vegetables at the county fair. See Hill, *Home Demon-*

stration Work, 135–36. Smith also described the accomplishments of the Parish sisters and the appearance of the photograph that Mary Evelyn Hunter took of them and their canned goods at the FIS school. It appeared in the *County Gentleman:* R. L. Smith, "History of the Negro Extension Service," TAEX Historical Files. Cleo Parish worked as the home demonstration agent in Robertson County from May 16, 1920, to June 30, 1920, and then in Matagorda County; see TAEX Historical Files.

52. Walton Peteet, Chauncey Merwin, and Cornelia Simpson, *Community Canning Plants,* Agricultural and Mechanical College of Texas Bulletin no. B-48 (College Station, 1919). This includes an undated photograph of the first community canner, probably for white extension members, located in Smith County; see *TAEX Annual Report 1925,* 68; *TAEX Annual Report 1929,* 49; Hunter, "Outstanding Achievements," TAEX Historical Files; *TAEX Annual Report 1930,* 31.

53. C. H. Waller, Annual Report, Tex. (1933), reel 84, T-890.

54. Clubs bought thirty-eight canners in 1924 and as many sealers to finish the work (*TAEX Annual Report 1924,* 15–6; *TAEX Annual Report 1925,* 68; Hunter, "Outstanding Achievements," TAEX Historical Files; *TAEX Annual Report 1922,* 75–76; R. G. Johnson, Annual Report, Gregg County, Tex. [1923], reel 27, T-890). Cooperative purchasing continued into the 1930s as clubs pooled premiums from fairs and purchased equipment. See district agent reports quoted in Crosby, "Building the Country Home," 143; C. H. Waller, Annual Report, Tex. (1933), reel 84, T-890. For contemporary descriptions of methods and regulations, see Barrett, *Canning and Preserving,* 10, 14. Mary E. Creswell and Ola Powell, *Home Canning of Fruits and Vegetables* (Washington, DC: Government Printing Office, 1917), 26, includes standards for 4-H canned goods. One photograph in the 1930 *TAEX Annual Report* (pp. 30–31) shows the distinctive 4-H label affixed to cans that met the home demonstration standards and another shows a black girl standing next to shelves of canned goods including tin cans with different labels.

55. *TAEX Annual Report 1929,* 49. Crosby discusses the limited credit available to rural blacks in the 1920s and limited landownership in "Building the Country Home," 134–44. This supports the notion that more prosperous black farmers participated in extension.

56. Ruth Dawson-Batts recalls that her father shared his syrup mill with neighbors in Wortham, Freestone County, and assisted at the canning center; see *Reflective Years, Reflective Moments: My Memories, a Vivid Story Told in Words and Photographs* (Waco, Tex.: Ruth Dawson-Batts, 1996), 44. Staff Minutes, Feb. 2, 1937, PV.

57. Hunter, "History of Extension Work," TAEX Historical Files; *TAEX Annual Report 1925,* 68; Hunter, "Outstanding Achievements," TAEX Historical Files.

58. In 1930, Lea Etta Lusk was still "striving to have every club member cut out the annual yearly account run at the stores, by producing and conserving the food supply for the family" (Lusk, Annual Report, Washington County, Tex. [1930], reel 71, T-890; Reich, "Soldiers of Democracy," 1487–89).

59. Lea Etta Lusk, Annual Report, Washington County, Tex. (1924), reel 35, T-890.

60. D. E. Colp, "The Value of Good Roads to the Farmer," *Proceedings of the Fifth Meeting of the Texas State Farmers' Institute 1915* (Austin: A. C. Baldwin & Sons, 1916), 91–92; Calvert and De León, *The History of Texas,* 269–70.

61. Crosby, "Limited Success," 287.

62. Hogg to Waller, Mar. 12, 1923, Waller Correspondence, PV.

63. Ibid.

64. W. Hogg, "Form of Organization, Distinctive Features," Annual Narrative Report, Houston County, 1923, Waller Papers, PV.

65. *Negroes in the United States,* 591. There was an average of 2.0 white farmers per automobile compared to an average of 4.7 black farmers per automobile in the South in 1930. In Texas, there was an average of 3.9 black farmers per automobile compared to Arkansas (7.1), Louisiana (6.7), Mississippi (5.5), Alabama (7.5), and Oklahoma (3.2) (*Negro Farmer in the United States, Fifteenth Census, 1930,* 49; Jack Temple Kirby, *Rural Worlds Lost: The American South, 1920–1960* [Baton Rouge: Louisiana State University Press, 1987], 55).

66. Benton to Waller, Apr. 17, 1923, Waller Correspondence, PV; *The Helping Hand* 21, no. 10 (Nov. 1918) (Smith quotation).

67. Only the May 2, 1925, minutes exist prior to 1933, and 1933 is incomplete. Minutes for most meetings held during the 1930s exist. See Staff Minutes, 1925–40, PV; C. H. Waller, State Leader (Negro), Annual Report (1940), reel 140, T-890 (quotation); Waller to Williamson, Mar. 15, 1937, Waller Correspondence, PV.

68. Staff Minutes, May 1, 1934, PV; Staff Minutes, Sep. 4, 1935, PV.

69. Hunter, "History of Extension Work," 5–6, TAEX Historical Files; *TAEX Annual Report 1927,* 63. Only six of the nine home demonstration agents worked twelve months of the year; two worked ten months, and one worked only afternoons and Saturdays (*TAEX Annual Report 1922,* 75). Staff Minutes, 1925–40, PV; Evans, *Extension Work,* 22–23; Baker, *County Agent,* 199–201; Crosby, "Building the Country Home," 168–75.

70. *TAEX Annual Report 1925,* 68; *TAEX Annual Report 1927,* 63.

71. Stephanie J. Shaw, *What a Woman Ought to Be: Black Professional Women Workers during the Jim Crow Era* (Chicago: University of Chicago Press, 1996), 3, 247n8.

CHAPTER 4

1. J. A. Evans, one of the first USDA special agents in Texas in 1904, and the agent who signed up four black demonstrators on his first day on the job, was serving as chief of the Office of Extension Work in the South in 1921, when the first circular appeared. Evans wrote the preface to W. B. Mercier, *Extension Work among*

Negroes, 1920, USDA Circular 190 (1921), 2 (quotation), 9. Mercier misidentifies Prairie View as Prairie Grove, Texas (9).

2. Mercier, *Extension Work among Negroes, 1920,* 11, 19.

3. Evans, *Extension Work,* 2 (quotation), 3; Martin, *A Decade,* 1, 2, 11.

4. Martin, *A Decade,* quotations on 1, 2, 11.

5. Black district agents and the state leader agreed to approach Waller and Montgomery county officials to discuss the placement of male and female agents and Fayette and Caldwell county officials about placement of a female agent (Staff Minutes, Jan. 11, 1934, PV; County files, TAEX Historical Files). Mr. Estelle received direction to visit Trinity County and "use his judgement" in the matter of that county's obtaining a black agent (Staff Minutes, Mar. 2, 1934, PV). "Commissioners Courts—Providing That They May Prescribe and Appropriate and Use Any Sum or Sums of Money Not Exceeding $1,000 per Year for Farmers Cooperative Demonstration Work," *General Laws of the State of Texas,* 1911, 105–106; "County Demonstration Work," S.B. 82, *General and Special Laws of the State of Texas, 40th Legislature, Regular Session* [Austin: N.p., 1927], 9–10. In 1937, black supervisors recommended that TAEX administrators accept not less than $400 for black agents and that the increase take effect on July 1, 1937 (Staff Minutes, June 3, 1937, PV).

6. *TAEX Annual Report 1920,* 53–54; *TAEX Annual Report 1921,* 79.

7. *TAEX Annual Report 1925,* 67.

8. Crosby, "Building the Country Home," 166–68; *TAEX Annual Report 1920,* 53.

9. "Brief History of Extension Work among Negroes in Texas, 1915 to 1948," TMs, TAEX Historical Files. The salary register of county agents and some administrative staff resides in the TAEX Payroll Services Office, Texas A&M University, College Station (hereafter SR, county [year], reel, TAEX-PS). The register is organized chronologically starting in fiscal year 1922–23, in alphabetical order, by the agent's last name. See Miss Margaret Moore, SR, McLennan County (1924), reel 1, TAEX-PS; Mrs. Jeffie Allen Conner, SR, McLennan County (1924), reel 1, TAEX-PS; E. R. Eudaly, SR, McLennan County (1924), reel 1, TAEX-PS; J. V. Smith, SR, McLennan County (1923–24), reel 1, TAEX-PS; Mayme Lou Parr, SR, McLennan County (1930), reel 3, TAEX-PS; Mrs. Jeffie A. Conner, SR (1930), reel 2, TAEX-PS; R. S. Miller, SR, McLennan County (1930), reel 3, TAEX-PS; J. V. Smith, SR, McLennan County (1930), reel 3, TAEX-PS.

10. [Vera S. Dial], "Historical Appraisal," Austin County, 1939, TAEX Historical Files.

11. Schaub and Goddard, "Annual Visitation," Annual Inspection Reports of Cooperative Extension Work in the Field, ES, RG 33, NA; *TAEX Annual Report 1924,* 16 (quotations).

12. Minutes, Commissioners Court (hereafter CC), McLennan County, Jan. 28, 1918, book O, 401; Jan. 27, 1919, book O, 519; Feb. 10, 1919, book O, 522. See also Robert H. Hines, Annual Report, Tex. (1919), reel 10, T-890; Minutes, CC, Colorado County, Nov. 28, 1934, book 12, 454–55; Nov. 15, 1935, book 12, 585, [July 13]

1936, book 13, 136–37. M. E. Bledsoe began as the home demonstration agent in Colorado County on January 2, 1935. She brought with her more than eight years of experience in Jasper County (Colorado County, TAEX Historical Files; Colorado County Historical Commission, comp., *Colorado County Chronicles: From the Beginning to 1923* [Austin, Tex.: Nortex Press, 1986], 439; "Colored Demonstration Agent Comes to County" [Jan. 3, 1935], unidentified newspaper clippings, Other Regular Reports Concerning Field Extension Work, ES, RG 33, NA).

13. Minutes, CC, Washington County, Feb. 10, 1919, book E, 272; Feb. 9, 1920, book E, 339; Mar. 22, 1921, book E, 397; Feb. 13, 1922, book E, 460. Washington County continued to provide $200 to partially offset the salaries of the black agents, but it provided the white agents fourteen times that amount. In 1927, county commissioners appropriated $200 for the two black agents and $2,800 for the two white agents (CC, Washington County, July 25, 1927, book F, 182; Nov. 14, 1927, book F, 197). See also Minutes, CC, Gregg County, May 8, 1933, book F, 271; May 8, 1934, book F, 429; Minutes, CC, Kaufman County, June 13, 1938, book 14, 579–80.

14. Minutes, CC, Smith County, Sep. 11, 1922, book 10. G. W. Crouch began on November 1, 1922 (Smith County, TAEX Historical Files). Crouch worked with both men and women and boys and girls until he retired in 1930 (James M. Smallwood, *Born in Dixie: Smith County from 1875 to Its Centennial Year. The History of Smith County, Texas* [Austin, Tex.: Eakin Press, 1999], 2: 607–9; Minutes, CC, Harrison County, Apr. 8, 1929, book H, 561; Apr. 22, 1929, book H, 565).

15. Ford used Wharton as the Southern District headquarters from 1918 to 1921. During these years, Wharton County did not support a separate agent. Other counties that served as district headquarters did employ agents. G. W. Crouch served as county agent in Cherokee County, and a home demonstration agent received an appointment during the canning season from 1918 to 1922. Brenham, in Washington County, served as the headquarters for the Southern District, under the supervision of Henry Estelle, from 1921 to 1924. R. H. Hines served as district agent with headquarters in Waco (McLennan County) from 1923 to 1924. Both Washington and McLennan counties sponsored county and home demonstration agents (County files, TAEX Historical Files; Minutes, CC, Walker County, Sep. 17, 1919, book I, 21; Jan. 22, 1934, book K, 215; Oct. 22, 1934, book K, 320).

16. H. S. Estelle, Prairie View, to I. W. Rowan, Prairie View, May 1, 1936, TAEX Historical Files; *Extension Work in Texas 1932* (College Station: The Extension Service, Agricultural and Mechanical College of Texas and The United States Department of Agriculture, [1933]), 37 (hereafter *TAEX Annual Report 1932*). Administrative staff members benefited from their relationship to Prairie View, which provided office and storage space (*TAEX Annual Report 1920*, 53).

17. Iola W. Rowan, "Negro Home Demonstration Agents in Texas," TAEX Historical Files.

18. *TAEX Annual Report 1920*, 53; *TAEX Annual Report 1921*, 84; Iola W. Rowan, "Negro Home Demonstration Agents in Texas, July 1915 to July 1935," report and

summary of a questionnaire distributed to thirteen of the nineteen former home demonstration agents and twenty-seven of the current agents in Texas in 1935, TAEX Historical Files; "Appropriation Bill for 1919–1921," *General Laws of the State of Texas,* 36th Legislature, 1919, 336.

19. The survey of home demonstration agents in the state in 1935 indicates that the women stayed with the service once hired. If they left, most either entered the teaching profession or got married (Rowan, "Negro Home Demonstration Agents in Texas," TAEX Historical Files; [Mrs. Marjorie "Margie" E. Bledsoe], "Historical Appraisal, Colorado County, 1939," TAEX Historical Files).

20. Crosby, "Building the Country Home," 74–75; Waller to Williamson, Mar. 15, 1937, Waller Correspondence, PV; Hunter, "Outstanding Achievements," 3, TAEX Historical Files. Federal inspectors described Mrs. Hunter as "unusually effective," a leader, and more successful at securing county funding than the male agents (E. A. Miller, "Report of Annual Visitation to the Texas Agricultural and Mechanical College, College Station, Texas, as Provided for in Smith-Lever Act of 8 May 1914, [visited] 21 July and 6 August 1920," Annual Inspection Reports of Cooperative Extension Work in the Field, ES, RG 33, NA).

21. Crosby, "Building the Country Home," 74–75; Staff Minutes, Mar. 30, 1934, PV. For Waller's feelings about the Farm Bureau, see Crosby, "Limited Success," 286–87; *TAEX Annual Report 1925,* 65.

22. The Slater Fund began in 1882, when John F. Slater donated money to develop educational facilities for African Americans in the South. This fund provided more support for a longer period of time than any other fund directed toward African American education. It established and provided operational funds to normal schools, denominational schools, and academies exclusively for black students, and it emphasized vocational training and summer teacher institutes. See Stevens, "Reform without Change," 11, 14; Texas State Department of Education, *The Twenty-fifth Biennial Report State Department of Education 1926–1928,* 5, no. 1 (Jan. 1929), 135; *Historical and Statistical Data as to Education in Texas, 1919–21,* 83. Counties included Camp, Guadalupe, Lavaca, Travis, Trinity, and Walker. Robert L. Smith served on the Slater Fund board at the behest of Booker T. Washington ("Smith Is Laid to Rest," *Waco Messenger* [July 17, 1942], clipping in SCFP).

23. Martin, *A Decade,* 13–14; Hill, *Home Demonstration Work,* 134; *TAEX Annual Report 1921,* 79; Waller to Williamson, Mar. 15, 1937, Waller Correspondence, PV.

24. *TAEX Annual Report 1925,* 67.

25. Estelle worked as the farm superintendent at Prairie View and as the first teacher of vocational agriculture at Prairie View prior to joining the Extension Service (Evans, "Down Memory Lane," 25, 29). A. T. Wood resigned in July 1920 and Estelle succeeded him as district agent for the southern region. Estelle maintained a district office at Brenham, Washington County, from 1920 until 1924, when the southern office was transferred to Waco, McLennan County. On September 1, 1935, the southern district headquarters moved to Prairie View. Estelle remained active

until 1953 (Historical Notes and Staff Lists, TAEX Historical Files; Henry S. Estelle, Correspondence, 1922–35, PV; Staff Minutes, May 1, 1934; Dec. 3, 1934; June 6, 1934, PV; C. H. Waller, state agent, and H. S. Estelle, district agent, Annual Report, Tex. [1932], reel 78, T-890).

26. Staff Minutes, Dec. 3, 1934, PV.

27. Staff Minutes, Nov. 1934, PV; Hill, *Home Demonstration Work,* 146, 194, 195.

28. Memo, J. D. Prewit to I. P. Trotter, Mar. 26, 1945, Texas Agricultural Extension Service Archives, Prairie View, 1915–71, Texas A&M University, Riverside Campus (hereafter TAEX Riverside); Dr. E. B. Evans, TAEX Riverside.

29. [C. L. Chambers], "Partial Analysis of Study of Negro Supervision for C. H. Waller, of Texas. 1934," attachment, Chambers, In Charge, Southern States, to H. H. Williamson, College Station, Mar. 11, 1937, Waller Correspondence, PV; C. H. Waller, Prairie View, to H. H. Williamson, College Station, Mar. 15, 1937, Waller Correspondence, PV. Waller lamented that rural blacks did not have such civic organizations (Waller, State Leader [Negro], Annual Report, Tex. [1940], reel 140, T-890).

30. *TAEX Annual Report 1920,* 53; Waller, State Leader (Negro), Annual Report, Tex. (1940), reel 140, T-890; *TAEX Annual Report 1921,* 81.

31. *TAEX Annual Report 1924,* 14. Examples of efforts to start black fairs include the Colored Lone Star State Fair and the Texas Colored State Fair.

32. Staff discussed the formation of the association at the monthly meetings. See Staff Minutes, Oct. 29, 1937; Nov. 30, 1937; Jan. 14, 1938; Feb. 1, 1938; Feb. 2, 1938; and Apr. 1, 1938, PV. The council organized on July 20, 1937 (letter with attachments, Isaac Philpot, President, Texas Negro Farmers' Council of Agriculture, to Dr. Ide P. Trotter, Director, Cooperative Extension Service, College Station, Texas, June 13, 1946, TAEX Riverside).

33. Miller, "Report of Annual Visitation, 1920," Annual Inspection Reports of Cooperative Extension Work in the Field, ES, RG 33, NA; *TAEX Annual Report 1925,* 66; *TAEX Annual Report 1926,* 67; Martin, *A Decade,* 27.

34. Martin, *A Decade,* 11 (quotation). One white agricultural agent refused to work in a county that did not also hire a black agent if the population warranted it. Waller used this to help qualify that county (Waller to Williamson, Mar. 15, 1937, Waller Correspondence, PV).

35. Crosby, "Building the Country Home," 167–68, quotes Erwin H. Shinn, *A Survey of the Manner of Procedure Followed in Developing County Programs of Negro Extension Work in Agriculture and Home Economic,* Misc. Extension Publication 11 (mimeographed) (Mar. 1933), Waller Papers, PV. Shinn reported that 53.3 percent of black agricultural agents and 47.4 percent of black home demonstration agents did not receive help from their white peers.

36. Newspaper clippings and annual reports mention the help white agents provided. Less frequent are mentions of black agents working with white agents or white farmers. See *TAEX Annual Report 1921,* 83. Federal inspectors mentioned that four

counties employed only black home demonstration agents (Miller and Reese, "Report of the Annual Visitation, 1921," 17, Annual Inspection Reports, ES, RG 33, NA).

37. J. W. Hogg, Crockett, to C. H. Waller, Mar. 6, 1923; C. H. Waller, Prairie View, to J. W. Hogg, Crockett, Mar. 12, 1923; both in Waller Correspondence, PV. District agent Robert H. Hines convinced Waller to retain Hogg despite these breaches and Hogg's accusing Waller of wanting him to fail. See C. H. Waller, Prairie View, to R. H. Hines, Waco, Apr. 3, 1923, Waller Correspondence, PV. Regardless, Hogg's personnel record indicates he was terminated on January 31, 1924. H. C. Langrum replaced him (Houston County, TAEX Historical Files; Staff Minutes, May 2, 1925, PV). The agents accused of malfeasance—Sherman M. Merriwether, Limestone County, and Jessie C. Bradford, Cherokee County—had long extension careers. Merriwether served from January 1, 1927, until he died on December 30, 1942 (Limestone County, TAEX Historical Files). Bradford served from July 1, 1922, to December 31, 1957 (Cherokee County, TAEX Historical Files). See C. H. Waller, Prairie View, to H. H. Williamson, College Station, May 5, 1937; Waller to Williamson, May 12, 1937; J. C. Bradford, Alto, to H. H. Williamson, Prairie View, May 13, 1937; S. M. Merriwether, Mexia, to H. H. Williamson, May 13, 1937; all in Waller Correspondence, PV.

38. See Staff Minutes, June 4, 1934; Feb. 2, 1937, PV.

39. R. H. Hines, Statistical Report for the Month, July 1923, Waller Papers, PV. Waller's preoccupation with health appeared first in Feb. 1937, when he cautioned district agents to "keep fit" and to place social engagements and other activities secondary to their remaining physically fit (Staff Minutes, Feb. 2, 1937, PV). See also Staff Minutes, Apr. 29, 1938, PV.

40. Staff Minutes, Feb. 2 ,1937, PV; original emphasis.

41. *TAEX Annual Report 1925,* 66; *TAEX Annual Report 1926,* 67 (quotation).

42. Schaub and Goddard, "Annual Visitation, 1922," 30, Annual Inspection Reports of Cooperative Extension Work in the Field, ES, RG 33, NA; Ousley, "Negro Work," in Annual Report of the Director of Extension, Agricultural and Mechanical College of Texas, for the Calendar Year, 1916, TMs, 14, TAEX Historical Files; Lea Etta Lusk, "Historical Appraisal," Washington County (1939), TAEX Historical Files.

43. Schaub and Goddard, "Annual Visitation, 1922," 30, Annual Inspection Reports, ES, RG 33, NA; *TAEX Annual Report 1921,* 82–83. Hunter also comments on the increased interest in the segregated extension program on the part of white landlords (*TAEX Annual Report 1924,* 16).

44. Waller to Williamson, Mar. 15, 1937, Waller Correspondence, PV. Crosby considers tenancy and the relationship of tenants to the Extension Service in "Building the Country Home," 129–36. See also A. W. Buchanan, Annual Report, Brazos, Tex. (1915), reel 1, T-890; *TAEX Annual Report 1927,* 62.

45. Waller to Williamson, Mar. 15, 1937, Waller Correspondence, PV. See also Staff Minutes, Feb. 2, 1937, PV.

46. *TAEX Annual Report 1927*, 60; *Extension Work in Texas 1931* (College Station: The Extension Service, Agricultural and Mechanical College of Texas and the United States Department of Agriculture, [1932]), 32 (hereafter *TAEX Annual Report 1931*).

47. Smith to Washington, *BTW Papers*, 4: 297; Smith stored records in a garage that was "struck by lightening [*sic*] and destroyed" Smith to Rowan, Apr. 19, 1936, TAEX Historical Files. Hunter suggested that Rowan contact the wife of Mr. Church Banks of Houston, who had a "very good representation." (Hunter to Rowan, Feb. 13, 1940, TAEX Historical Files).

48. *TAEX Annual Report 1925*, 65, 66. David N. N. Jones, a photographer in Dallas, took the image of the exhibition at the state fair (Staff Minutes, May 2, 1925, PV). Other scholars have studied photographs taken by extension agents as evidence and illustration, e.g., D. Clayton Brown, "Leadership among Rural Women: The Arkansas Extension Service, Women's Division, 1911–1945," paper presented at the annual meeting of the Southern Historical Association, Birmingham, Ala., Nov. 1998; Valerie Grim, "The First African-American Woman Extension Agent in Mississippi," paper presented at the Sixth Conference on Rural and Farm Women in Historical Perspective, Waco, Tex., Sep. 1997; Alan Govenar, *Portraits of Community: African American Photography in Texas* (Austin: Texas State Historical Association, 1996); Maren Stange, *Symbols of Ideal Life: Social Documentary Photography in America, 1890–1950* (Cambridge: Cambridge University Press, 1989).

49. In 1923, James M. Benton, Harrison County, attached portraits of Reuben Anderson, Armelia Marsh, and Elijah McConey, who won prizes for their corn exhibits at the Dallas State Fair to his annual report (Harrison County—Negro Agent, 1924, Material Submitted with Annual Narrative and Statistical Reports, 1914–1944, Other Regular Reports Concerning Field Extension Work, ES, RG 33, NA). One undated photograph depicts a 4-H Club meeting at the home of Bobbie Jean Fisher, a poultry demonstrator in the Piney Grove community in Harrison County. Bobbie Jean served as the club secretary, and Martha Brewster served as president. See Photos, PV.

50. Teal Portrait Studio took images of events throughout the state, and its mark appears on many but not all extant photographs of the Prairie View A&M short courses and extension agent annual meetings. See TAEX Historical Files, the files of the Extension Service and University Archives at Prairie View A&M, and the Houston Metropolitan Research Center. See also Dannehl M. Twomey, "Into the Mainstream: Early Black Photography in Houston," *Houston Review* 9, no. 1 (1987): 47; Kendall Curlee, "Teal Portrait Studio," *New Handbook of Texas*, 6: 231–32. One of the earliest documented photographs taken by the Teals for Negro Division use features the home of Mr. and Mrs. Daniel Edwards of Westfield, Texas, remodeled by them in 1930 (Pictures, TAEX Historical Files). Negro Division supervisors believed Teal prices were too high (Staff Minutes, Sept. 1, 1933, PV). For Waller's role in securing photographers, see Staff Minutes, Nov. 16, 1936, PV; "4-H Girls' Camp," TAEX Historical Files; "Farm and Home Demonstration Agents receive instruc-

tions in making and laying tile for sub-irrigation. Mr. J. F. Rosborough, Extension Specialist, A. and M. College, gave the method demonstration" (Teal Studio, Houston, Pictures, TAEX Historical Files). For C. A. Teal's work with short courses, see Staff Minutes, July 3, 1935; Sep. 4, 1935, PV. Photographs identified as being by the Teal Studio appear in *Extension Work in Texas 1931,* 35 (4-H Club members in front of an exhibit of canned goods); *Extension Work in Texas 1932,* 33 (4-H Club girls with an exhibit of canned goods), and *Extension Work in Texas 1932,* 35 (girls at a sewing demonstration). The Teal Studio did not respond promptly at least once, in 1936, when TAEX director H. H. Williamson and vice-director Shelton requested images. Regardless of the delay, the TAEX administrators indicated that they "were pleased with the pictures" (Staff Minutes, Sep. 2, 1936, PV).

51. "Notes of Conference at College Station, Texas, Feb. 27, 1933, with Mr. Darrow and Mrs. Cunningham Relative to an Itinerary for the Extension Photographer from Washington DC," in Staff Minutes, Feb. 27, 1933. PV; Phelps, Annual Report, McLennan County, Tex. (1933), reel 88, T-890. George W. Ackerman took more than 50,000 photographs during his forty-year career with the USDA (*Picturing the Century: One-Hundred Years of Photographs from the National Archives* [Washington, DC: National Archives and Records Commission, 1999], 66–69). He photographed Negro Division staff and constituents in Anderson, Limestone, McLennan, and Rusk counties in April 1933. Photographs were published in the 1933 annual report "Negro Agents Work toward Farm Ownership," *Texas Extension Service Farm News* 20, no. 9 (May–June 1934): 8. Ackerman visited in 1936 to photograph white projects (Lester A. Schlup, Washington, to Minnie Fisher Cunningham, College Station, Mar. 4, 1936, Texas, General Correspondence, ES, RG 33, NA). Mr. E. C. Hunton toured during 1947 ("Photographs of the Federal Extension Service, 1920–1954 [S Series]," M 1146, 13 reels; "Photographs of the Federal Extension Service, 1920–1945 [SC Series], M 1147, 11 reels (hereafter FES Photos NA).

52. The Echols family lived in a freedmen's settlement, Woodland, also known as Bethlehem, in Limestone County (Sitton and Conrad, *Freedom Colonies,* 191, 195; Beulah Community Canning House, neg. nos. 33-SC-16832-C, 33-SC-16833-C, 33-SC-16834-C (FES Photos NA). For photo captions, see Anderson County, TAEX Historical Files. See also A. H. Echols, neg. nos. 33-SC-16840-C, 33-SC-16841-C, 33-SC-16842-C, 33-SC-16843-C (FES Photos NA); for captions, see Limestone County, TAEX Historical Files. Staff Minutes, Feb. 27, 1933, PV.

53. George S. Conner Personal Materials, Correspondence—J. O. A. Conner, 1923–1935; Conner Correspondence, 1936–37; Conner Correspondence, 1937–1939, Conner Papers. See also Jane Johnson, "Mrs. Jeffie Connor [*sic*], Long-time Educator: Gentle Advocate of the Education Report," *Waco News-Tribune* (Jan. 13, 1969), Conner Papers; George S. Conner Personal Materials: Biographical Records, Conner Papers; Virginia Lee Spurlin, "The Conners of Waco: Black Professionals in Twentieth Century Texas" (PhD diss., Texas

Tech University, 1991); Patricia Wallace, *A Spirit So Rare: A History of Women of Waco* (Austin, Tex.: Nortex Press, 1984), 195–204, 288; Butler, "James Harrison."

54. Meddie L. Allen and John V. Smith with smoked meat, neg. nos. S-16846-C and S-16847-C; M. L. Allen in her garden, neg. no. S-16848-C; M. L. Allen on her porch with Iola Rowan and Ruby O. Phelps, neg. no. S-16849-C (all in FES Photos NA). For prints of the images, see J. O. A. Conner Personal Materials: Photographs, Conner Papers. For descriptions, see McLennan County, TAEX Historical Files.

55. Lester A. Schlup, acting chief of the Federal Extension Service's Visual Instruction and Editorial Section, orchestrated Ackerman's trip from Washington, DC, to Texas and then to Tennessee and North Carolina (Schlup to Cunningham, Mar. 4, 1936, Texas, General Correspondence, ES, RG 33, NA). Minnie Fisher Cunningham, TAEX editor, arranged Ackerman's schedule for work in eleven counties over eleven days, with a one-day break midway through the project. Agents provided housing. See Cunningham to Schlup, May 2, 1936, Texas, General Correspondence, ES, RG 33, NA; Waller to Williamson, Mar. 15, 1937, Waller Correspondence, PV; *Picturing the Century*, 66–69.

56. C. L. Chambers, *How the Supervisor Aids the County Agent*, Extension Service Circular 126 (Washington, DC: USDA, July 1930), 9–14.

57. Memorandum, Louis Franke to Minnie May Grubbs, Aug. 6, 1937, Pictures 1937, TAEX Historical Files.

58. Staff Minutes, Nov. 3, 1936, PV; Staff Minutes, May 3 and Aug. 8, 1938, PV; Staff Minutes, June 29, 1939, PV.

59. For discussions of meat shows and a list of counties participating, see Staff Minutes, Mar. 29, 1938, PV. Forty-three counties held meat shows in 1939. Two district shows in 1940, one held in Houston on Mar. 20–21 and the other in Longview on Apr. 5–7, included two thousand pieces of home-cured meats and twenty-four hundred exhibits of sausage, lard, and eggs. Agents in forty counties planned exhibits. See *Prairie View Standard* (Feb. 1940): 7, 8. For the photograph of Holsey and Williams in front of the Fayette County exhibit c.1940, see loose photographs, Smoke Meat folder, PV. For an image of the 1942 District Meat Show taken by the Teal Studio, see Photos, PV. This lists the Teal Studio address at 500 Louisiana St., Houston, Tex.

60. The agents at the staff meeting planned to invite C. F. Richardson, editor of the Houston *Informer*, for Monday, and J. Alston Atkins, Houston *Defender*, for Tuesday, to present at the twenty-eighth annual Prairie View short course in 1935. See Staff Minutes, May 28, 1935, PV. Richardson agreed, but Atkins proposed that the Extension Service enter into a publicity bargain with his paper, and the extension staff did not favor the offer. See Staff Minutes, July 3, 1935, in County Extension Service Administrative Records, PV. Concerning the *Dallas News*, see Staff Minutes, Sep. 30, 1938, PV.

61. *Prairie View Standard* (Jan. 1937). The staff discussed the need to print 1,000 more of the special edition, Jan. 1937. See Staff Minutes, Mar. 2, 1937, PV.

62. Concerning Williamson and Shelton, see Staff Minutes, Apr. 1, 1937, PV. For the distribution list, see Staff Minutes, Mar. 2, 1939, PV. The agents planned for the report scheduled to appear in the February 1938 issue by assigning responsibilities in Nov. 1937. See Staff Minutes, Nov. 30, 1937, PV. Also see *Prairie View Standard* (Feb. 1938), 1.

63. "Negro Editors Promise Free Publicity in 1938," *Prairie View Standard* (Feb. 1938), 1; Theodore Saloutos, *The American Farmer and the New Deal* (Ames: Iowa State University Press, 1982), 183–84.

64. "Negro Editors Promise Free Publicity in 1938," *Prairie View Standard* (Feb. 1938), 4. For the request to extend the coverage of the *Prairie View Standard,* see Staff Minutes, May 31, 1938, PV. For discussion of the role of photographs in acquainting white administrators with the black agents' work, see Staff Minutes, Sep. 1, 1937, PV. At the meeting, Mr. Waller reported on a "very fine conference" with Texas A&M president T. O. Walton. Waller showed him the photographs of harness and feed exhibits taken at the short course completed in August 1937. Walton asked that Waller send the pictures to Warburton and Wallace. Pictures were also shown to Mr. Snyder and Mr. Thornton, TAEX staff members. Waller reported that Mr. Thornton was "highly pleased." Waller reported that Williamson "made it possible to exhibit at the Land Grant College Meeting" (*Field Activities of Negro Farm and Home Agents* [Oct. 1937], mimeographed newsletter, Extension Work File, General Correspondence of the Office of the Secretary, 1906–1970, USDA, RG 16, NA). For mention of *Opportunity,* see Staff Minutes, Sep. 30, 1938, PV. Waller instructed Henry Estelle and John Williams to write articles on leather and syrup making and for Iola Rowan and Jeffie Conner to write and select photographs. For the 1938 displays, see on Staff Minutes, May 24, 1938, PV.

65. For discussions of the Tuskegee school, see Staff Minutes, May 3, 24, 1938, PV. Thornton hauled more harness to Washington for display in the summer of 1938 (Staff Minutes, May 31, July 1, 1938, PV). Waller shared Thornton's positive comments about the exhibition of harness during the July staff meeting. TAEX director Williamson commented on Williams's trip to Tuskegee (Staff Minutes, June 29, 1939, PV). The Louisiana director, Bateman, also wrote and asked for Williams's services the first week in September to work with agents in Louisiana (Staff Minutes, June 29, 1939, PV). Williams received another invitation from Tuskegee in 1940 to work there between May 27 and June 15 (Staff Minutes, Feb. 27, 1940, PV). See also "Making Mule Gear" folder, n.d., loose photographs, PV; photograph with caption that reads "A Class in Leather Crafts and Harness Making, Tuskegee Institute, Ala., Taught by J. H. Williams, District Agent, Extension Service, Prairie View, Texas, May 1941," TAEX Historical Files.

66. Pierce and Campbell continued as liaisons between black agents working in the segregated programs in southern states and white administrators in the

federal office into the 1940s. See Crosby, "Building the Country Home," 67–68. C. L. Chambers informed Williamson that "it was impossible to use the material we had last year at our conference with Pierce and Campbell. We are planning to have them in here on the 31st, and we are getting the material ready for the purpose of going over it with them" (Chambers to Williamson, Mar. 11, 1937, Waller Correspondence, PV). Chambers does not explain why it took three years to prepare the report.

CHAPTER 5

1. Saloutos, *The American Farmer*, 179–91; Raymond Wolters, *Negroes and the Great Depression: The Problem of Economic Recovery* (Westport, Conn.: Greenwood, 1970), 3–82. Harvard Sitkoff devotes a few pages to the inequity of the crop-reduction program of the AAA, but the AAA modified its procedures to make more black tenants eligible; see *A New Deal for Blacks: The Emergence of Civil Rights as National Issues: The Depression Decade* (New York: Oxford Univ. Press, 1978), 52–54. See also Crosby, "Building the Country Home," 180–97; David Eugene Conrad, *The Forgotten Farmers: The Story of Sharecroppers in the New Deal* (Urbana: University of Illinois Press, 1965); Douglas Hurt, *American Agriculture: A Brief History* (Ames: Iowa State University Press, 1994), 327.

2. A total of 854,964 blacks lived in Texas in 1930. Of these, 329,829 (38.6 percent) lived in urban areas and 525,135 (61.4 percent) in rural (*Negroes in the United States,* 813). The number of rural blacks declined from 525,135 in 1930 to 504,281 in 1940 (a 4.0 percent drop). In 1930, 409,922 lived on farms, but this number decreased to 354,485 in 1940 (a 13.6 percent drop) (U.S. Bureau of the Census, *Sixteenth Census of the United States: 1940,* vol. 2, *Population,* pt. 6, 763). There were 85,940 black farm operators in Texas in 1930 (*Negro Farmers in the United States,* 50) and 67,597 in 1940 (Foley, *White Scourge,* 66–67). See also Keith J. Volanto, "Leaving the Land: Tenant and Sharecropper Displacement in Texas during the New Deal," *Social Science History* 20, no. 4 (Winter 1996): 533–51, esp. 539; Donald H. Grubbs, *Cry from the Cotton: The Southern Tenant Farmers' Union and the New Deal* (Chapel Hill: University of North Carolina Press, 1971).

3. Rieff, "'Rousing the People,'" 112–58; *TAEX Annual Report 1929,* 44, 17, 66–67; *Texas Extension Work in 1930,* 31; *Extension Work in Texas, 1931,* 32; *Extension Work in Texas, 1932,* 4; *Extension Work in Texas, 1935,* 28; *Texas Extension Work, 1940,* 41, 43, 44. In 1930, twenty-two counties sponsored agricultural agents, and twenty-one counties sponsored home demonstration agents. The 1930 and 1935 annual TAEX reports list the counties with black agents, but the 1940 annual report does not. Negro Division archives and payroll records indicate that forty-six county agents and thirty-six home demonstration agents worked in the Negro Division in 1940. In 1937, black county agents reached 166,720 persons in 12,695 meetings. Of this total, 80,532 attended 6,311 adult demonstrations, 28,397 visited result demonstrations, and 8,512 boys attended

extension meetings. Home demonstration agents reached 14,417 women and girls enrolled as club members (H. H. Williamson, Jack Shelton, and Mildred Horton, Annual Report, Tex. [1937], reel 110, T-890; *Texas Extension Work, 1940,* 41–44).

4. Saloutos, *The American Farmer,* 181.

5. Texas counties that began employing either agricultural or home demonstration agents between 1930 and 1940 include Angelina, Austin, Bowie, Brazoria, Brazos, Caldwell, Cass, Colorado, Falls, Fayette, Fort Bend, Freestone, Greg, Grimes, Hopkins, Jasper, Jefferson, Kaufman, Lamar, Liberty, Madison, Matagorda, Milam, Montgomery, Newton, Red River, Rusk, San Augustine, Shelby, Trinity, Wharton, and Wood. The growth of the Texas force coincided with the expansion of black extension services throughout the South. Agents increased from 335 in 1930 to 524 by 1940 (a 36.1 percent increase); see A. Jones, "Thomas M. Campbell," 50–52.

6. Counties that lost agents include Burleson, Henderson, Marion, Nacogdoches, Panola, and Upshur.

7. In 1935, the federal and state appropriations for annual salaries increased from $1,100 to $1,200 for Negro agricultural agents, and from $900 to $1,000 for Negro home demonstration agents. In addition, each received at least $300 from other sources. Black agents received no travel allowance. White county agents earned $1,600 annually, and white home demonstration agents earned $1,200 annually from state and federal funds. Additionally, each of the white agents received no less than $1,000 from other sources as a supplement, and they received a travel allowance. See W. H. Conway and Ola P. Malcolm, "Report of Examination of Cooperative Extension Work in Agriculture and Home Economics in the State of Texas for the Fiscal Year Ended 30 June 1935," 3, Texas Inspection Reports, vol. 2, 1935–1939, Annual Inspection Reports of Cooperative Extension Work in the Field, Other Regular Reports Concerning Field Extension Work, ES, RG 33, NA; C. H. Waller, Prairie View, to Samuel E. Warren, Madison, Wis., Nov. 7, 1934, Waller Correspondence, PV; *Extension Work in Texas, 1932,* 31; "Negro Agents Work," *Texas Extension Service Farm News* (May–June 1934): 8; Staff Minutes, Feb. 1, 1938, PV. For Campbell quotation, see Jones, "Thomas M. Campbell," 58.

8. Volanto, *Texas,* 13–26; Ben Procter, "The Great Depression," *New Handbook of Texas,* 3: 302; Calvert and De León, *The History of Texas,* 292–311; William Joseph Brophy, "The Black Texan" (PhD diss., Vanderbilt University, 1974), 220–52. Brophy argues that African Americans often received a greater percentage of the aid than their proportion of the state population, but they endured inferior living conditions and needed greater support. Thus, New Deal programs fell short of satisfying need.

9. *Texas Extension Work in 1930,* 31; *Extension Work in Texas, 1932,* 1.

10. Selected Texans active at the national level include John Nance Garner, "Cactus Jack" to his Texas friends, who ran as Roosevelt's vice-president in the 1932 election, and others who chaired congressional committees, including Sam Rayburn, eventually speaker of the U.S. House of Representatives; James P. Buchanan, House

Appropriations Committee; Marvin Jones, chairman of the House Agriculture Committee and the person most responsible for the Agricultural Adjustment Act's passage (according to Volanto, *Texas*, 31); and Thomas T. Connally, Senate Public Buildings and Grounds Committee. A Texan eventually held the national relief purse strings as well. By 1938, Jesse H. Jones headed the RFC. Legislation such as the Bankhead-Jones Act of 1935 more directly affected TAEX services by increasing allocations; see Dethloff, *Centennial History*, 2: 396.

11. Volanto, *Texas*, 35, 39–41; Waller to Williamson, Mar. 15, 1937, Waller Correspondence, PV.

12. Volanto, *Texas*, 41. Henry Dethloff discusses the role Texans and the TAEX played in the passage of farm recovery acts in 1936 and 1938 (*Centennial History*, 2: 396). Few studies of black farmers and the AAA exist and most underestimate the involvement of black owners and extension agents. See C. C. Yancy, "Negro Participation in the Agricultural Adjustment Agency Program in Texas" (ME thesis, Colorado A&M College, 1946), cited in Alwyn Barr, *Black Texans: A History of Negroes in Texas, 1528–1971* (Austin, Tex.: Jenkins, 1973), 155–56, 246.

13. Volanto, *Texas*, 42–45. Cedar A. Walton, Negro agricultural agent, Dallas County, asked ministers to announce informational meetings scheduled for African American farmers (Annual Report, Dallas County, Tex. [1933], reel 85, T-890).

14. C. L. Beason (Annual Report, Brazos County, Tex. [1933], reel 85, T-890) generated 897 contracts for 15,000 acres. As of 1930, 1,255 white farmers operated in the county (H. K. Hornsberry, Annual Report, Brazos County, Tex. [1933], reel 85, T-890). Per the 1930 census, 191 black farmers owned or partially owned their farms in Brazos County in 1930 while 1,045 farmed as sharecroppers or share renters (U.S. Bureau of the Census, *Fifteenth Census of the United States: 1930*, vol. 2, *Agriculture*, pt. 2, *The Southern States*, 1383).

15. R. S. Miller, Annual Report, McLennan County, Tex. (1933), reel 88, T-890; D. R. Carpenter, Annual Report, Walker County, Tex. (1933), reel 90, T-890; J. V. Smith, Annual Report, McLennan County, Tex. (1933), reel 88, T-890. Per the 1930 census, 6,641 operated farms in McLennan County, including 214 black owners or part owners and 1,207 black tenants, a total of 1,421 black farmers (U.S. Bureau of the Census, *Fifteenth Census of the United States: 1930*, vol. 2, *Agriculture*, pt. 2, *The Southern States*, 1394).

16. K. H. Malone, Annual Report, Walker County, Tex. (1933), reel 90, T-890. In Walker County during 1930, 370 blacks owned or partially owned their farms and 896 farmed as tenants (U.S. Bureau of the Census, *Fifteenth Census of the United States: 1930*, vol. 2, *Agriculture*, pt. 2, *The Southern States*, 1400; J. M. Lusk, Annual Report, Washington County, Tex. [1933], reel 90, T-890). Black farmers owned or partially owned 397 farms, and 1,176 more farmed as tenants in Washington County as of 1930 (R. G. Johnson, Annual Report, Gregg County, Tex. [1933], reel 86, T-890). In Gregg County, 426 blacks owned or partially owned their land and 793

farmed as tenants in 1930 (U.S. Bureau of the Census, *Fifteenth Census of the United States: 1930,* vol. 2, *Agriculture,* pt. 2, *The Southern States,* 1389, 1400).

17. H. K. Hornsberry, Annual Report, Brazos County, Tex. (1933), reel 85, T-890; R. G. Johnson, Annual Report, Gregg County, Tex. (1933), reel 86, T-890.

18. L. E. Lusk, Annual Report, Washington County, Tex. (1933), reel 90, T-890; K. H. Malone, Annual Report, Walker County, Tex. (1933), reel 90, T-890.

19. Jesse Wilson, Annual Report, Waller County, Tex. (1933), reel 90, T-890; U.S. Bureau of the Census, *Fifteenth Census of the United States: 1930,* vol. 2, *Agriculture,* pt. 2, *The Southern States,* 1400.

20. Waller to Warren, Nov. 7, 1934, Waller Correspondence, PV. For statistics, see C. H. Waller, Annual Report, Tex. (1933), reel 84, T-890. Volanto indicates that Texans received $42,970,646.63 in cash and options for 738,095 bales of cotton (*Texas,* 54). See also Crosby, "Building the Country Home," 185. Several sources document the flawed payment structure (Wolters, *Negroes,* 27–28; Saloutos, *The American Farmer,* 188–89). The AAA's Cotton Plow-up Campaign discriminated against tenants regardless of race. Landlords received payments for land they removed from production but did not satisfy the part of the contracts that stipulated that they turn over the entire amount for land rented to cash tenants; 50 percent to sharecroppers, and 75 percent to share tenants. This placed white and black tenants at a disadvantage. The parity payment system accompanying the 1934–35 program worked against the tenant to a greater degree and forced the poor tenant off the land; see Brophy, "The Black Texan," 236–37.

21. U.S. Bureau of the Census, *Fifteenth Census of the United States: 1930,* vol. 2, *Agriculture,* pt. 2, *The Southern States,* 35, 1382; U.S. Bureau of the Census, *United States Census of Agriculture: 1935,* vol. 1, *Reports for States with Statistics for Counties and a Summary for the United States* (Washington, DC: Government Printing Office, 1936), 742, 764.

22. Ibid. The percentage of black owners increased slightly to 4.8 percent of all farm operators in 1940, while black tenants declined to 7.8 percent. These black operators controlled only 2.2 percent of all farmland in Texas in 1940 (U.S. Bureau of the Census, *Sixteenth Census, 1940, Agriculture,* 188). For information on the inequity of black farm income, see Wolters, *Negroes,* 7–8.

23. Volanto, "Leaving the Land," 540–41, 547.

24. Foley, *White Scourge,* 164–72.

25. Crosby, "Building the Country Home," 187–88; Saloutos, *The American Farmer,* 185.

26. Waller to Warren, Nov. 7, 1934, Waller Correspondence, PV.

27. Saloutos, *The American Farmer,* 181. For a summary of Cobb's attempts to inform black agents, see Crosby, "Building the Country Home," 183. See also C. H. Waller, Annual Report, Tex. (1933), reel 84, T-890. Correspondence between Waller and black agents documents black assistance to white agents during the 1934 cam-

paign. See [Mrs.] L. B. Austin, Richmond, Tex., to C. H. Waller, Prairie View, Feb. 19, 1934; B. F. Hudson, Texarkana, to C. H. Waller, Feb. 28, 1934; B. T. Price, Madisonville, to C. H. Waller, Feb. 28, 1934; and O. A. Mason, Giddings, to C. H. Waller, Feb. 1934; all in Waller Correspondence, PV.

28. C. H. Waller, Annual Report, Tex. (1933), reel 84, T-890. Wolters offers a good summary of the differences in the cotton acreage reduction programs in *Negroes,* 9–16. Waller spent so much time on the AAA program during 1934 that he received criticism from extension officials in Washington. Mr. C. L. Chambers, responsible for the southern section of extension activities, said he spent too much time with the AAA and questioned why he spent twenty-nine days in counties without agents. See [Chambers], "Partial Analysis," attachment, Chambers to Williamson, Mar. 11, 1937, Waller Correspondence, PV. For Waller's response, see Waller to Williamson, Mar. 15, 1937, Waller Correspondence, PV; Staff Minutes, Apr. 1, 1937, PV. Chambers later apologized to Waller when they encountered each other on business in Washington, DC. See Staff Minutes, Nov. 29, 1937, PV.

29. Wolters, *Negroes,* 21–22; "Negro Farm Programs," *Dallas Morning News* (Feb. 11, 1936), clipping attached to C. H. Waller, Annual Report, Tex. (1936), reel 103, T-890.

30. Crosby, "Building the Country Home," 184; Saloutos, *The American Farmer,* 183–84. Crosby indicates that Waller worked in Missouri and Illinois in 1935 and in Missouri, Illinois, Tennessee, and Arkansas in 1936. Waller reported that he spent a little more than four months as a field agent in the lower southern cotton states in 1936. The work began in 1935 but ended abruptly after Jan. 6, 1936, when the Supreme Court deemed the AAA's processing tax unconstitutional. This cut short a work tour of the Gulf Coast from Texas to the Atlantic seaboard then north through Virginia to Washington, DC. See Staff Minutes, Jan. 6, 10, 30, 1936, PV. District agent Henry Estelle acted as state leader during Waller's absence, per Staff Minutes, Dec. 3, 1935, PV. Waller returned to AAA duty in Aug. 1936, when he accepted reappointment as a field agent. See Waller, Annual Report, Tex. (1936), reel 103, T-890. "Mr. Cobb requested Mr. Waller back on the AAA—Since he could not be spared at this time, he has been definitely withdrawn from the AAA" (Staff Minutes, May 3, 1937, PV). Mr. Waller was again requested to "assist with AAA work during July and August" (Staff Minutes, June 28, 1937, PV). "Mr. Waller will probably be requested to render services to AAA but does not desire to serve in that capacity" (Staff Minutes, July 1, 1938, PV). Waller's hesitancy to remain active as a field agent for the AAA may have related to his 1937 appointment as chair of the Farm Security Administration Committee for Negroes in Texas. See "Professor Calvin H. Waller," *Prairie View Standard* (May 1941).

31. Waller, Annual Report, Tex. (1936), reel 103, T-890. The Memphis meeting for the Soil Conservation and Domestic Allotment Act occurred on March 5–7, 1936. See Staff Minutes, Mar. 2 ,1936, PV; *Extension Work in Texas, 1935,* 23. See Keith J.

Volanto, "Ordered Liberty: The AAA Cotton Programs in Texas, 1933–1940," PhD diss., Texas A&M University, 1998," 165, for a discussion of the Memphis meeting, 157–75 for a summary of the act and its ramifications in 1936 and 1937.

32. At least sixteen hundred farmers attended the Marshall meeting, with a few hundred at the other regional meetings. See Waller, Annual Report, Tex. (1936), reel 103, T-890. The first of the two Soil Conservation Service conferences held at Prairie View involved black extension agents as well as vocational agricultural workers, Jeanes supervisors, and teachers of agriculture and students enrolled in agriculture at Prairie View. They met on May 13–14, 1936. See Staff Minutes, May 6, 1936, PV.

33. A similar effort in 1918, supported through a meeting at Tuskegee Institute and a petition instigated by President Moton, convinced Bradford Knapp to include more African Americans in the Extension Service. Thomas Campbell, John Pierce, and E. L. Blackshear gained appointments as USDA field agents as a result. Campbell and Pierce each played a role in the 1936 petition. For biographical information on Jennie Moton, see Lu Ann Jones, "In Search of Jennie Booth Moton, Field Agent, AAA," *Agricultural History* 72, no. 2 (Spring 1998): 446–58, esp. 451–52, 453 (Moton spoke at the Texas State Interracial Commission, presenting "How Interracial Cooperation Can Advance the Program of Agricultural Conservation and the National Association of Colored Women").

34. Holsey visited Texas on more than one occasion, meeting with Williamson in Oct. 1937 and attending the supervisory staff meeting at Prairie View on June 1, 1939 (H. H. Williamson to C. A. Cobb, Mar. 30, 1937, Waller Correspondence, PV; Williamson to E. A. Miller, Oct. 22, 1937, Waller Correspondence, PV; Staff Minutes, June 1, 1939, PV).

35. Staff minutes, Sep. 2, 1936, PV; Chas. A. Shefield, Washington, to H. H. Williamson, College Station, Dec. 29, 1936, Agricultural Extension Service, PV; Williamson to Sheffield, Dec. 30, 1936, Agricultural Extension Service, PV; Williamson to Dr. C. W. Warburton, Dec. 10, 1936, Waller Correspondence, PV. For Williamson's invitation, see Staff Minutes, Feb. 1, 1938, PV.

36. Volanto, *Texas,* 102–103. The act included price stabilization policies for cotton, corn, wheat, rice, and tobacco and allowed all farmers already enrolled in the soil conservation program to continue receiving payments. For discussion of the act, criticism of it in Texas, and the outcome in 1938, see ibid., 118–22; for 1939, see 122–24. For mention of three concurrent training meetings scheduled for Nov. 10, 11, and 12 in Marshall, Mexia, and Columbus, see Staff Minutes, Oct. 29, 1938, PV.

37. Staff Minutes, Mar. 29, 1939, PV; E. A. Miller to C. H. Waller, Feb. 8, 1940, with Staff Minutes, Feb. 5, 1940, PV; C. H. Waller, Annual Report, Tex. (1940), reel 140, T-890. For the request to hold one meeting in 1941, see Staff Minutes, Nov. 30, 1940, PV. E. A. Miller scheduled the AAA meeting for black county agents on March 3–4, 1941, "if Prairie View can take care of it." See Staff Minutes, Jan. 28,

1941, PV. For the meeting dates, see Staff Minutes, Feb. 19, 1941, PV. That meeting occurred at Prairie View A&M on February 24–25, 1941.

38. Memorandum, George E. Haynes to members of the Economic Life Committee, n.d., Waller Correspondence, PV; Staff Minutes, Jan. 29, 1941, PV.

39. *Extension Work in Texas, 1931,* 30–32; *Extension Work in Texas, 1932,* 30–31.

40. Saloutos, *The American Farmer,* 181; Wolters, *Negroes,* 24–27. The Wilson administration began seed loans with a wartime fund in 1918. The Extension Service administered them but opposed them. Only small amounts were loaned, $150 to $200, and collateral was normally a crop lien. The Federal Farm Loan Board continued loans in the 1920s, and the Reconstruction Finance Corporation increased the loans available when it was approved by Pres. Herbert Hoover after the 1929 stock market crash. See David E. Hamilton, *From New Day to New Deal: American Farm Policy from Hoover to Roosevelt, 1928–1933* (Chapel Hill: University of North Carolina Press, 1991), 154–62.

41. C. H. Waller, Annual Report, State Leader, Tex. (1933), reel 84, T-890; K. H. Malone, Annual Report, Walker County, Tex. (1933), reel 90, T-890; R. G. Johnson, Annual Report, Gregg County, Tex. (1933), reel 86, T-890; U.S. Bureau of the Census, *Fifteenth Census of the United States: 193,* vol. 2, *Agriculture,* pt. 2, *The Southern States,* 1389, 1400.

42. "Negro Farmers of County Hold a Special Meeting," unidentified newspaper clipping attached to K. H. Malone, Annual Report, Walker County, Tex. (1933), reel 90, T-890.

43. J. V. Smith, Annual Report, McLennan County, Tex. (1933), reel 88, T-890; "Negro Farmers Have Short Course," *Brenham Banner Press* (Nov. 19, 1934), Texas 1927–37, Other Regular Reports Concerning Field Extension Work, ES, RG 33, NA.

44. Saloutos, *The American Farmers,* 181; Staff Minutes, Sep. 29, 1937, PV; Staff Minutes, June 2, 1939, PV.

45. For a history of the FSA, see Sidney Baldwin, *Poverty and Politics: The Rise and Decline of the Farm Security Administration* (Chapel Hill: University of North Carolina Press, 1968); Saloutos, *The American Farmer,* 185, 186. Between the start of the allocations in 1937 and June 30, 1940, only 162 black families received these loans in Tex. (Brophy, "The Black Texan," 237–38, 247; Foley, *White Scourge,* 181; applications completed by residents of Brazoria County, Farmers' Home Administration Rehabilitation Loan Cases, Rural Rehabilitation Loan Case Files, 1934–44, Records of the County Offices, Record Group 96, Farmers Home Administration, National Archives and Records Administration, Southwest Region, Fort Worth, Tex. [hereafter FHA, RG 96, NA-FW]).

46. On resettlement projects in the West, see Brian Cannon, *Remaking the Agrarian Dream: New Deal Rural Resettlement in the Mountain West* (Albuquerque: University of New Mexico Press, 1996); and for parts of the South, see Donald Holley,

Uncle Sam's Farmers: The New Deal Communities in the Lower Mississippi Valley (Urbana: University of Illinois Press, 1975). A photograph of residents at Sabine Farms appears in Procter, "The Great Depression," 3: 307. See also RR-TX-22, Texas Farm Tenant Security Project, Records of the Resettlement Division, Project Records, 1936–42, FHA, RG 96, NA-FW; RR-TX-24, Sabine Farms Project, Records of the Resettlement Division, Project Records, 1936–42, FHA, RG 96, NA-FW. For the quota of farm families to participate in the Texas Farm Tenant Security Project, see "The Farm Tenant-Purchase Project," TMs, TX 22–160, Records of the Resettlement Division, Project Records, 1936–42, FHA, RG 96, NA-FW. It allowed for 265 total families—215 white and 50 black, figures based on the 1930 census.

47. For blacks and the FSA in Texas, see Brophy, "The Black Texan," 239, 247–48.

48. Waller's obituary indicates that he received the appointment in 1937, but he more likely was named on April 30, 1938. See "Professor Calvin H. Waller," *Prairie View Standard* (May 1941); Staff Minutes, Feb. 1, 1938, PV, and Staff Minutes, Apr. 30, 1938, PV. See also "Selected Activities of Negro Farm and Home Demonstration Agents, December 1938," attached to C. H. Waller, Annual Report, Tex. (1938), reel 119, T-890. Waller read a letter at the Apr. 30 Staff Minutes from Mr. M. C. Wilson relative to the appointment of an FSA committee: Mr. Waller, Mr. McShan, and Mr. Pemberton; see Staff Minutes, Apr. 1 and 2, 1938, PV. For Ellerson's request, see Staff Minutes, Sep. 30, 1938, PV.

49. B. T. Lacey, Ft. Worth, to H. A. Graham, Dallas, Mar. 5, 1936, TX-22–060, Records of the Resettlement Division, Project Records, 1936–42, FHA, RG 96, NA-FW. Some heads of families selected for Limestone County included Priest R. H. Carr, William McKinley Estelle, Willie Jackson, Jack Powell, James Taylor, and John Whitaker. See Elbert E. Pace, Dallas, to Carder D. McKenzie, Groesbeck, Feb. 16, 1938, TX 22–912, Records of the Resettlement Division, Project Records, 1936–42, FHA, RG 96, NA-FW. Some of those settled near Lake Dallas in Denton County included Lue D. and Betsy Taylor Sanders, George W. and Leomy S. Mohair, James and Laura Butler Lewis, Vera Nichols and Sam McKenzie, Milton and Opal Holley Scott, and Otis H. and Ora D. Holley. See Raymond A. Klein, Dallas, to W. A. Canon, Dallas, Apr. 4, 1938, TX-22–912, Records of the Resettlement Division, Project Records, 1936–42, FHA, RG 96, NA-FW. The records in the TX-22 file include additional names but do not always note the "Negro" or "Colored" tenants (J. V. Smith, Waco, to Elbert E. Pace, Dallas, Jan. 4, 1938; Elbert E. Pace, Dallas, to Cecil Johnson, Groesbeck, Jan. 5, 1938; Elbert E. Pace, Dallas, to Cecil Johnson, Groesbeck, Dec. 22 1937, TX-22–912, Records of the Resettlement Division, Project Records, 1936–42, FHA, RG 96, NA-FW). Letters indicate that the farmers had to move into old structures on the Anglin farm because they had to move before construction on the new buildings was finished.

50. Families listed with lease and purchase contracts as clients of Sabine Farms Projects include Priest R. H. Carr, Jewel N. Crow, William McKinley Estelle, James Tayloe, John Whitaker, and Jack Powell (C. M. Evans, Dallas, to W. W. Alexander,

Washington, DC, July 22, 1938, TX-22–912, Records of the Resettlement Division, Project Records, 1936–42, FHA, RG 96, NA-FW). For the information on Smith County, see "Selected Activities of Negro Farm and Home Demonstration Agents, December 1938," attached to C. H. Waller, Annual Report, Tex. (1938), reel 119, T-890. For Ellisor's request in 1939, see Staff Minutes, Nov. 27, 1939, PV. Waller's obituary mentions the Prairie View settlement ("Professor Calvin H. Waller," *Prairie View Standard* [May 1941]). For reports on the project, see Staff Minutes, Jan. 19, 1940; Feb. 27, 1940, PV. Iola Rowan also reported on a proposed FSA project on the Menke Farm (Staff Minutes, Mar. 26, 1940, PV).

51. E. B. Hayes, president, Marshall Chamber of Commerce, Marshall, Tex., to Morris Sheppard, Senate Office Building, Washington, DC, Dec. 11, 1935, TX-24–000–900, Project Records, 1935–40, Farmers Home Administration and Predecessor Agencies (Farm Security Administration), National Archives and Records Administration II, College Park, Md. (hereafter FSA, RG 96, NA). These files also include letters from white residents opposing the "black colonization project." See Barret Gibson, Marshall, to Tom Connally, Morris Sheppard, and Wright Patman, Mar. 2, 1936; memorandum, G. C. Ellisor, to Dan Scoates, Aug. 14, 1936; both in TX-2 4–028, Records of the Resettlement Division, Project Records, 1936–42, FHA, RG 96, NA-FW. See also James Allred, Austin, to D. P. Trent, Dallas, Jan. 10, 1936, TX-24–028; and D. P. Trent to James Allred, Jan. 23, 1936, TX-24–028; both in Records of the Resettlement Division, Project Records, 1936–42, FHA, RG 96, NA-FW.

52. The extension agents expressed their support of the appointment of agents (Staff Minutes on March 2, 1939, PV). They also discussed Sabine Farms. (Staff Minutes, May 1, 1939, PV). Lee County, TAEX Historical Files. See also M. M. Thayer to H. H. Williamson, Oct. 10, 1939; D. L. Weddington to M. M. Thayer, Oct. 10, 1939; "Colored County Agent Continued," clipping attached to "Appropriating Funds for Cooperative Extension Work in Agriculture and Home Economics," Lee County, June 1933, Prairie View, 1915–71, TAEX Riverside; C. H. Waller, Annual Report, Tex. (1940), reel 140, T-890; J. D. Reagan, Dallas, to Mr. Jesse L. Owens, community mng., Sabine Farms, Marshall, Tex., Jan. 6, 1942, TX 24–183; all in Records of the Resettlement Division, Project Records, 1936–42, FHA, RG 96, NA-FW.

53. Daniel, *Breaking the Land,* 243; Foley, *White Scourge,* 180–81. The United States Army and the War Department selected Sabine Farms as a location for War Department maneuvers in the South, effective early Aug. 1941 (Jesse L. Owens, community manager, Marshall, Tex., to Mr. W. A. Canon, asst. regional dir. FSA, Dallas, July 28, 1941, TX 24–071, Records of the Resettlement Division, Project Records, 1936–42, FHA, RG 96, NA-FW).

54. Women in families that qualified for FSA loans completed an "Annual Home Business Statement and Home Management Plan" and a canning budget that complied with "Resettlement Diet and Food Conservation Standards" required by the FSA. They also had to complete quarterly reports that indicated what they did in

food production, food conservation, clothing and bedding construction and rehabilitation, home and farm improvements, management, and education. Only limited records of these loan case files exist. Texas county records at the Southwest
Regional National Archives in Fort Worth include Brazoria, Dallas, Dawson, El
Paso, Hamilton, Haskell, Jeff Davis, Kendall, La Salle, Leon, Nueces, Randall, San
Jacinto, Throckmorton, Willacy, and Wise. For example, see Bobie Baugh, Brazoria County, FHA Rehabilitation Loan Cases, Rural Rehabilitation Loan case Files,
1934–44, Records of County Offices, FHA, RG 96, NA-FW.

55. Anderson County, TAEX Historical Files; neg. S-16833, FES Photos NA.

56. "Negro Agents Work," *Texas Extension Service News* (May–June 1934): 8;
C. H. Waller, Annual Report, Tex. (1933), reel 84, T-890. Agents helped construct
seventy-eight more canning houses in 1934. See H. S. Estelle to I. W. Rowan, May 1,
1936, TAEX Historical Files.

57. Calvert and DeLeón, *The History of Texas,* 300. Gov. Miriam Ferguson cre-
ated the TRC to distribute RFC funds, and the Texas legislature renamed it the
Texas Rehabilitation and Relief Commission (Rieff, " 'Rousing the People,' " 124–27;
"Relief Canning Directed by Home Agents," *Texas Extension Service News* 20, no. 9
[May–June 1934]: 3; C. H. Waller, Annual Report, Tex. [1933], reel 84, T-890).

58. K. H. Malone, Annual Report, Walker County, Tex. (1933), reel 89, T-890.

59. Waller to Warren, Nov. 7, 1934, Waller Correspondence, PV; C. H. Waller,
Annual Report, Tex. (1933), reel 84, T-890. Ruth Dawson-Batts recalls that her fa-
ther-in-law, Fred Douglas Batts, coordinated the canning center in Hammond,
Robertson County, in the 1930s and that his wife, Eunice Love Batts, assisted in
the center (Dawson-Batts, *Fred Douglas Batts Sr.: A Family with a Mission . . . to
Educate, to Serve in the School, Church, and Community* [N.p.: Ruth Dawson-Batts,
1994], 19–20; idem, *Reflective Years,* 44).

60. Waller to Clara S. Hall, Angleton, Feb. 5, 1934, Waller Correspondence, PV;
Jessie L. Shelton, Annual Report, Travis County, Tex. (1941), reel 158, T-890. See
also correspondence between Ludia B. Austin and Waller, Feb. 19, 1934, Waller Correspondence, PV.

61. Sharpless, *Fertile Ground,* 80. Professor J. H. Johns, Crockett, demonstrated
mattress making at the first black Houston County fair in Grapeland, Tex., on
Thursday, November 22, 1923. See "Fair for Negroes," broadside, Agricultural Extension Service, PV; Rieff, " 'Rousing the People,' " 142.

62. Clara S. Hall, Annual Report, Brazoria County, Tex. (1933), reel 85, T-890;
Ruby O. Phelps, Annual Report, McLennan County, Tex. (1933), reel 88, T-890;
Lea Etta Lusk, Annual Report, Washington County, Tex. (1933), reel 90, T-890.

63. *Extension Work in Texas, 1935,* 25; *Texas Extension Work, 1936* (N.p.); *Texas Extension Work, 1937,* 61; Alma O. Huff, Annual Report, Kaufman County, Tex. (1937),
reel 115, T-890; *Texas Extension Work, 1938,* 55, 58; "Bed Room Improvement in 1938,"
Prairie View Standard (Feb. 1939); *Texas Extension Work, 1939,* 29; "Statistical Summary of Home Demonstration Work," *Prairie View Standard* (Feb. 1940).

64. Hill, *Home Demonstration Work,* 96–98, 201.

65. Rieff, "'Rousing the People,'" 139; Staff Minutes, Mar. 26, 1940, PV. Rowan gave a presentation on the program to district agents at a staff meeting and distributed a memo about the training dates. See Staff Minutes, Apr. 1, 1940, PV. Rowan prepared a list of WPA supervisors and distributed it to staff. See I. W. Rowan, Prairie View, to Extension Service staff members, with list of supervisors attached, Waller Correspondence, PV; Staff Minutes, July 30, 1940, PV.

66. Staff Minutes, May 6, 1940, PV.

67. Iola W. Rowan and Jeffie O. A. Conner, Annual Narrative Report, Tex. (1940), reel 140, T-890.

68. Northern Division, Annual District Report, Tex. (1940), reel 140, T-890. This report lists Angelina, Bowie, Cass, Marion, Red River, Robertson, and San Augustine as counties with black county agents but not black home demonstration agents.

69. Rieff, "'Rousing the People,'" 141–42. The process is illustrated but not described in Hill, *Home Demonstration Work,* insert between 96–97.

70. Jessie L. Shelton, Annual Report, Travis County, Tex. (1941), reel 158, T-890.

71. *Texas Extension Work, 1940,* 58; Rieff, "'Rousing the People,'" 142; *TAEX Annual Report 1941,* 16.

CHAPTER 6

1. Reynold M. Wik, "The USDA and the Development of Radio in Rural America," *Agricultural History* 62, no. 2 (1988): 177–88.

2. George Peasant appeared on April 1, 1933 (Clara S. Hall, Annual Report, Brazoria County, Tex. [1933], reel 85, T-890). Ronald R. Kline, *Consumers in the Country: Technology and Social Change in Rural America* (Baltimore, Md.: Johns Hopkins University Press, 2000), 287.

3. Alvin Wilkins, "What 4-H Club Work Has Taught Me," TMs, Waller Correspondence, PV.

4. Agents produced radio skits as part of *Farm and Home House,* broadcast by Station WTAW at College Station (Staff Minutes, Nov. 29 1938, and Feb. 2, 1939, PV; Mercier, *Extension Work among Negroes, 1920,* 18–19). Supervisory agents discussed the value of a "motion picture tour." See Staff Minutes, Oct. 2, 1936, PV; Iola W. Rowan and Jeffie O. A. Conner, Annual Report, 1940, Tex. (1940), reel 140, T-890.

5. H. H. Williamson, Jack Shelton, and Mildred Horton, Annual Report, Tex. (1937), reel 110, T-890. Iola Rowan encouraged the use of educational exhibits at most annual meetings and special extension programs at Prairie View. She usually bore the responsibility for accumulating the information for captions and images. She planned an extension exhibit featuring local industry for a special summer school at Prairie View in 1938. See Staff Minutes, May 31, 1938, PV. For mention of

the exhibits at the State Fair, see Staff Minutes, Sep. 29, Dec. 16, 1937; Sep. 21, 1938, PV. Discussions about what the Extension Service hoped to accomplish through its exhibits at the State Fair continued into the 1940s. Rowan reported on participation in 1940—1,091 entries—but itemized the inadequacies, including lack of space and other needs. She asked the staff "to decide on what we would like to have for the Fair" (Staff Minutes, Nov. 2, 1940, PV). For the discussion of the exhibit commemorating the silver anniversary of the segregated Extension Service, see Staff Minutes, June 27, 1940, PV.

6. Calvert and De León, *The History of Texas,* 314; Jesse O. Thomas, *Negro Participation in the Texas Centennial Exposition* (Boston: Christopher Publishing House, 1938).

7. Banks served as Prairie View A&M principal for twenty years (1926–46). Negro Division staff sought involvement in the Centennial in early April 1936. Calvin Waller made Jeffie O. A. Conner responsible. Conner reported her findings at the next staff meeting (Staff Minutes, Apr. 6, 1936, PV; "Narrative Report, Historical Appraisal of Extension Work, District: Northern, County: McLennan," pp. 2–3, TAEX Historical Files). Banks assembled exhibits on the mechanical arts (Thomas, *Negro Participation,* 8, 28, 41, 45, 144–50).

8. Thomas, *Negro Participation,* 146 (quotation).

9. Staff Minutes, May 15, 1936, PV. Estelle prepared a "progress" list for the Negro Division (H. S. Estelle to I. W. Rowan, May 1, 1936; Smith to Rowan, Apr. 19, 1936; both in TAEX Historical Files). See also Hunter, "Outstanding Achievements," Aug. 1931, TAEX Historical Files. Staff minutes do not indicate the content of the agents' exhibit (Staff Minutes, July 1, 1936, PV).

10. Alonzo J. Aden, "Educational Tour through the Hall of Negro Life," *Southern Workman* 65, no. 11 (Nov. 1936): 337; Frederick D. Patterson, Tuskegee Institute, coordinated agricultural exhibits. A photograph of the miniatures of the three stages of farm development appears in Thomas, *Negro Participation,* 41 (quotation), insert; see also 42–43, 144–50. Thomas secured leave as southern field director of the National Urban League to manage the hall.

11. Thomas, *Negro Participation,* 149, 150.

12. "Historical Appraisal of Extension Work in Dallas County," 1939; "Historical Appraisal of Extension Work in Colorado County," 1939; both in TAEX Historical Files. Many historical appraisals carry significant comments; see TAEX Historical Files.

13. Staff Minutes, May 1, 1939, PV; Hunter to Rowan, Feb. 13, 1940, TAEX Historical Files; Staff Minutes, May 6, 1940, PV.

14. Staff Minutes, May 6, 1940, PV.

15. Staff minutes, May 1, 1940, PV. The exposition occurred between July 4 and September 2, 1940.

16. Counties in the Colorado and Brazos river bottoms most frequently participated in the Sears Cow-Sow-Hen Program. See unidentified newspaper clipping

describing the 1942 hog exhibit in Lufkin, PV; photographs in TAEX and PV collections; letter, W. C. David, Prairie View, to E. M. Regenbrecht, College Station, Apr. 10, 1944, David Papers, PV; letter, E. M. Regenbrecht, College Station, to W. C. David, Prairie View, Feb. 20, 1947, David Papers, PV; report, W. C. David, "Cow-Hog-Hen Project with Negro 4-H Club Boys in Swine Demonstrations, Texas," Nov. 1945–Nov. 1946, David Papers, PV.

17. Memo, J. D. Prewit to I. P. Trotter, Mar. 26, 1945, Dr. E. B. Evans, TAEX Riverside. Prairie View became a university in 1945 (Lewis, *Du Bois: The Fight for Equality,* 480, 491; George Ruble Woolfolk, "W. R. Banks: Public College Educator," in *Black Leaders: Texans for Their Times,* Alwyn Barr and Robert A. Calvert, eds. [Austin: Texas State Historical Association, 1981], 128–54).

18. Only one African American had served as a specialist before Woods and Adams; J. H. Williams served as Boys' Club advisor for the Negro Division and specialist in meat work between January 1932 and June 1934 ("State Leaders of Negro Extension Work," comp. D. H. Seastrunk, May 1986, in Negro Extension History folder, Prairie View A&M University Archives, Prairie View, Texas [hereafter Seastrunk's History, PV]). For Shinn's presentation, see Marshall Vernon Brown Papers, Prairie View A&M University Archives, Prairie View, Texas (hereafter Brown Papers, PV). For agent appointments, see County Files, TAEX Historical Files.

19. "Dist. Ag. Agent Broadcasts at College Station," unidentified newspaper clipping [Mar. 1942], H. S. Estelle folder, PV; letter, Jeffie Conner, Prairie View, to Prairie View staff, July 7, 1943, with attached Revised Schedule Radio Broadcasts–1943, David Papers, PV; letter, T. A. Mayes, Austin, Tex., to W. C. David, Hempstead, Tex., Mar. 7, 1944, David Papers, PV; letter, Laura Lane, College Station, to W. C. David, Prairie View, May 27, 1944, with attached edited radio script, David Papers, PV; letter, C. C. Randall, Little Rock, Ark., to W. C. David, Prairie View, June 16, 1944, David Papers, PV. David served as agricultural agent in Madison County and then district agent. He also served as Negro state farm labor leader. Subsequently, he led the Negro Division until 1959.

20. "Third Annual Meat Show at Tyler, March 24," *Houston Defender* (Mar. 14, 1924), clipping, PV.

21. There were 52,648 black farm operators in Texas in 1940, including 32,610 sharecroppers and tenants, and only 15,432 in 1959, including 3,138 sharecroppers and tenants (Calvin L. Beale, "The Negro in American Agriculture," in *The American Negro Reference Books* [Englewood Cliffs, N.J.: Prentice-Hall, 1966], 171; Barr, *Black Texans,* 196–97). Only 628 African Americans remained tenants in Texas in 1970, the last year non-owners were enumerated. Only 6,978 African Americans were farming in Texas in 1990; see Reid, "African Americans and Land Loss," 284.

22. Memo, Committee Representing Negro State and District Supervisors in Attendance at the South-Wide Conference, to M. L. Wilson, director of Extension Service, June 28, 1945, David Papers, PV; memo, Meredith C. Wilson, Washington,

DC, to extension directors in southern states, July 4, 1945, copied to state Negro leaders, with attachment ("Report of Committee on Mobilization of Negro Labor to Produce and Harvest Agricultural Products Necessary to the Prosecution of the War," 1053 [7–45], David Papers, PV).

23. Letter, C. A. Walton, Dallas, to W. C. David, Prairie View, Jan. 29, 1947, with attached program for "The Southern 'Fireside Chats,'" David Papers, PV; letter, "W. C. David, Prairie View, to R. A. Sanders, Seguin, Feb. 20, 1947, David Papers, PV; letter, Harry V. Richardson, Tuskegee Institute, Ala., to W. C. David, Prairie View, Feb. 5, 1947, David Papers, PV; letter, J. V. Smith, Prairie View, to Harry V. Richardson, Tuskegee Institute, Ala., Feb. 19, 1947, David Papers, PV.

24. Rasmussen, *Taking the University to the People,* 11.

25. Hine, "Black Professionals," 1279–81; Lewis, *Du Bois: Fight for Equality,* 490–91.

26. Letter, Ide P. Trotter to W. C. David, Nov. 20, 1945; memo, Maurine Hearn to Ide P. Trotter, Nov. 12, 1945, Prairie View, 1915–71, TAEX Riverside.

27. Marguerite Merriwether could not attend Colorado A. and M. College in 1946 after extension summer school administrators discouraged "Negro Workers" because "no satisfactory living or eating accomodations [*sic*]" were "available to them." The late notice prevented Merriwether from arranging other training (letter, W. C. David, Prairie View, to J. D. Prewit, College Station, May 14, 1947, David Papers, PV). Additional requests appear in David Papers, PV.

28. Joel Schor, "The Black Presence in the U.S. Cooperative Extension Service Since 1945: An American Quest for Service and Equity," *Agricultural History* 60, no. 2 (Spring 1986), 143; "1941–1947: Statement of Expenditures for Negro Extension Work," David Papers, PV; TAEX Historical Files.

29. In 1940, Mississippi had the highest proportion of black to white farmers in the nation; North Carolina ranked fifth, and Texas ranked seventh. By 1950, Mississippi remained first, North Carolina had moved up to second, and Texas remained seventh (U.S. Bureau of the Census, *Sixteenth Census, 1940, Agriculture,* 188; Orville Vernon Burton, "Race Relations in the Rural South since 1945," in *The Rural South since World War II,* R. Douglas Hurt, ed. [Baton Rouge: Louisiana State University Press, 1998]: 56–58). Negro Division staffing across the South increased during the war years, from a total of 541 black staff members in 1941 to 858 in 1947, a 36.9 percent increase).

30. Salary register, reels 1, 2, 3, 4, and 5, Texas Agricultural Extension Payroll, TAEX-PS.

31. Edward Bertram Evans (state leader, 1941–46), later Prairie View A&M principal/president (1946–66), reprimanded Jesse James Adams, the agent in Van Zandt County, because he "about ruined an opportunity for us to place an agent" in Jackson County on a permanent basis (letter, E. B. Evans, Prairie View, to J. J. Adams, Canton, May 20, 1944, David Papers, PV). Jackson County never employed African American agents, and Adams was transferred from Van Zandt to Austin

County in September 1944 (letter, L. G. Luper, Houston, to W. C. David, [Prairie View], n.d., David Papers, PV).

32. "1941–1947 Statement of Expenditures for Negro Extension Work," David Papers, PV.

33. TAEX director H. H. Williamson reminded agents of the policy prohibiting A&M College of Texas and USDA Extension Service employees from engaging in political activities. See "A Message Now and Then to Extension Employees," Apr. 14, 1942, David Papers, PV; letter, R. A. Hester, secretary, Democratic Progressive Voters League of Texas, Dallas, to W. C. David, Prairie View, Dec. 13, 1950, David Papers, PV; letter, Hobart T. Taylor and R. A. Hester to William L. Dawson, U.S. House of Representatives, Washington, DC, May 16, 1951, David Papers, PV.

34. Letter, Taylor and Hester to Dawson, May 16, 1951, David Papers, PV. Walton left the Negro Extension after twenty-four years and seven months of employment.

35. After World War II, extension administrators realized some success in increasing the number of opportunities for African American youth to exhibit pigs, poultry, and other livestock at the State Fair. The shows—Junior Negro Pig Show (Oct. 4–7, 1947) and Junior Negro Poultry Show and Turkey Show (Oct. 8–11, 1947)—segregated participants. Yet, agents received invitations to pass along to farmers and 4-H Club boys to exhibit breeding hogs and other livestock in the Open Livestock Show (Oct. 8–17, 1947). The fair also designated Monday, Oct. 13, 1947, as Negro Rural Youth Day (Minutes, meeting of Negro Rural Youth Committee, State Fair of Texas, May 1, 1947, David Papers, PV). Report, Dallas Negro Chamber of Commerce Board of Directors meeting, Aug. 7, 1951, David Papers, PV. *Poole v. Williams, Individually and as President of Texas A&M University System et al.,* no. 72-H-150, Jan. 26, 1974, as corrected Jan. 28, 1974, U.S. District Court, Southern District of Texas, *Fair Employment Practice Cases,* vol. 7 (Washington, DC: Bureau of National Affairs, 1974), 102–104.

36. Claude A. Barnett, Chicago, to W. C. David, Prairie View, Mar. 27, 1951, David Papers, PV; Schor, "The Black Presence," 138, 141.

37. Press release, "Negro Extension Field Agent Promoted to National Leader," USDA Office of Information, Washington, DC, Sep. 7, 1953, David Papers, PV.

38. L. W. Jones, "South's Negro Farm Agent," 41 (quotation).

39. Talk given by J. D. Prewit to the Negro County Agricultural Agents' Association Annual Meeting, Dallas, Tex., Mar. 18, 1960, TAEX Historical Files. Extension Service quotation from L. W. Jones, "South's Negro Farm Agent," 41.

40. R. Douglas Hurt, *Problems of Plenty: The American Farmer in the Twentieth Century* (Chicago: Ivan R. Dee, 2002), 112–13, 171–73. Some examples indicate the emphasis that the TAEX Negro Division placed on commercial farmers. John W. Mitchell, USDA field agent, praised David for a press release that featured a successful African American watermelon farmer. See letter, John W. Mitchell, Hampton, Va., to W. C. David, Prairie View, July 28, 1947, David Papers, PV. David

was asked to speak on the increasing number of owner-operated farms at the 1951 Professional Agricultural Workers Conference and the Farmers' Short Course, Tuskegee Institute. Two Texas farmers, Mr. Willie Melton, Kendleton (Fort Bend County), and Mr. Hulen T. Rigsby, Dickinson (Galveston County), were invited to represent the Negro Extension Service (letter, L. A. Potts, Tuskegee Institute, Ala., to W. C. David, Prairie View, Dec. 11, 1950, David Papers, PV; letter, L. A. Potts, Tuskegee Institute, Ala., to W. C. David, Prairie View, Nov. 27, 1950, David Papers, PV).

41. Letter, W. C. David, Prairie View, to J. L. Matthews, College Station, May 2, 1947, David Papers, PV; letter, Ide P. Trotter, College Station, to W. C. David, Prairie View, May 13, 1947, David Papers, PV; *Farm and Family Life of the Texas Negro Veteran,* Bulletin 498, State Board for Vocational Education, Austin, Tex. (Nov. 1949), David Papers, PV; letter, Louis Franke, College Station, to W. C. David, Prairie View, May 16, 1947, David Papers, PV.

42. John D. Hyslop, "USDA Has Long History in Overseas Agricultural Development," *AgExporter* (Nov. 1995).

43. Schor, "The Black Presence," 138; Brenda Gayle Plummer, *Rising Wind: Black Americans and U.S. Foreign Affairs, 1935–1960* (Chapel Hill: University of North Carolina Press, 1996).

44. Thomas Borstelmann, *The Cold War and the Color Line: American Race Relations in the Global Arena* (Cambridge, Mass.: Harvard University Press, 2001); Mary L. Dudziak, *Cold War Civil Rights: Race and the Image of American Democracy* (Princeton, N.J.: Princeton University Press, 2000), 6; United Nations Declaration of Human Rights, available at http://www.unhchr.ch/udhr/lang/eng_print.htm, accessed Apr. 20, 2006.

45. Harlan, *Booker T. Washington: Wizard of Tuskegee,* 274–80, 284–88.

46. Andrew Zimmerman, "A German Alabama in Africa: The Tuskegee Expedition to German Togo and the Transnational Origins of West African Cotton Growers," *American Historical Review* 110, no. 5 (Dec. 2005): 1362–98.

47. Ian Petrie, "Practical Agriculture for the Colonies: Cornell and Asian Uplift, c1905–1945," paper presented at "A Century of Scientific Outreach," 2005 Agricultural History Society Symposium, Cornell University, Sep. 11, 2004.

48. Lewis, *Du Bois: Fight for Equality,* 122–23.

49. South Rhodesia received its independence and became Zimbabwe. See Thomas Monroe Campbell, *The Movable School Goes to the Negro Farmer* (Tuskegee, Ala.: Tuskegee Institute Press, 1936; reprint 1969), 145–46.

50. Jackson Davis, Thomas M. Campbell, and Margaret Wrong, *Africa Advancing: A Study of Rural Education and Agriculture in West Africa and the Belgian Congo* (New York: Friendship Press, 1945), 97, 101, 107.

51. Thomas M. Campbell, "Succinct Statement on Negro Extension Work, 1948–1949," n.d., David Papers, PV.

52. Memo, Maurine Hearn to Dr. Ide P. Trotter, Mar. 6, 1945, Prairie View Per-

sonnel, TAEX Riverside. Haiti's secretary of agriculture, François Georges, visited Biloxi, Miss., in Nov. 1947 as an invited attendee at the conference of the National Association of Commissioners, Secretaries and Directors of Agriculture. The conference hotel refused him a room in the hotel proper and insisted that he have meals in his room. Needless to say, he left the conference and had no interest in returning after experiencing race relations American style (Dudziak, *Cold War Civil Rights,* 40); press release, Texas A&M College Extension Service, for release Jan. 22, 1953, David Papers, PV.

53. Letter, Moses L. Davis, Washington, DC, to W. C. David, Prairie View, Tex., Dec. 24, 1950, David Papers, PV.

54. E. Evans, "Down Memory Lane," 58.

55. Frank E. Pinder, II, *Pinder: From Little Acorns* (Tallahassee: Florida Agricultural and Mechanical University Foundation, 1986). Charles L. "Chicken" Davis, the first black poultry specialist in North Carolina introduced poultry and egg production to West Africa during the early 1950s; see Schor, "Black Presence," 143–144. For information on experiment stations, see L. Jones, "South's Negro Farm Agent," 41.

56. E. Evans, "Down Memory Lane," 58; Virginia Lantz Denton, *Booker T. Washington and the Adult Education Movement* (Gainesville, Fla., 1993), 230n128.

57. Thomas G. Paterson, *Meeting the Communist Threat: Truman to Reagan* (New York: Oxford University Press, 1988), 147–48; "Ambassador George C. McGhee," *Georgetown University Library Associates Newsletter* (October 1984), online at http://www.library.georgetown.edu/advancement/newsletter/16/mcghee16.htm, accessed Apr. 20, 2006; Richard D. McKinzie, "Oral History Interview with George C. McGhee," June 11, 1975, transcript online at http://www.trumanlibrary.org/oralhist/mcgheeg.htm, accessed Apr. 20, 2006; letter, R. A. Sanders, Seguin, Tex., to W. C. David, Prairie View, Feb. 8, 1951; letter, S. P. Walton, Corsicana, Tex., to W. C. David, Feb. 8, 1951; letter, Prewit to David, Feb. 8, 1951; letter, S. E. Chase, Colorado County, to W. C. David, Feb. 10, 1951; letter, C. A. Walton, Dallas, Tex., to W. C. David, Feb. 11, 1951; Leonidas Watson, Anderson, Tex., Feb. 12, 1951; letter, S. P. Walton, Navarro County, to W. C. David, Feb. 20, 1951; letter, Reed M. Bradley, Longview, Tex., to W. C. David, Feb. 22, 1951; all letters in David Papers, PV.

58. E. Evans, "Down Memory Lane," 58–60.

CHAPTER 7

1. Schor, "The Black Presence," 145; Personnel Files, TAEX Historical Files; letter, A. S. Bacon, assistant to the assistant administrator, Programs, to D. P. Lilly, president, NNCAA, Apr. 10, 1961; letter, D. P. Lilly to Dr. E. T. York, administrator, FES, Washington, DC, May 8, 1961, General Correspondence, ES, RG 33, NA. Hesekiah Lee Hubbard, agent in Brazoria County, served as the first vice-president for the NNCAA in 1961, an indication of Texans' participation in professional development.

2. Schor, "The Black Presence," 145–46.

3. Rasmussen, *Taking the University to the People,* 192–93.

4. Rasmussen, *Taking the University to the People,* 193.

5. Memo, from secretary, USDA, to assistant secretaries and agency heads, June 15, 1964; General Correspondence, ES, RG 33, NA.

6. Memo, from Lloyd H. Davis to Joseph Robertson, administrative assistant secretary, June 19, 1964; both in General Correspondence, ES, RG 33, NA.

7. Press release, Feb. 29, 1972, Agricultural Extension Service, College Station, Tex., in Dempsey H. Seastrunk file, Cushing Memorial Library and Archives, Texas A&M University, College Station (hereafter Seastrunk A&M). For a discussion of changes in segregated extension programs and compliance with the Civil Rights Act in other states, see Schor, "The Black Presence"; Jeannie M. Whayne, "Black Farmers and the Agricultural Cooperative Extension Service: The Alabama Experience, 1945–1965," *Agricultural History* 72, no. 3 (Summer 1998): 523–551; Douglas Helms, "Eroding the Color Line: The Soil Conservation Service and the Civil Rights Act of 1964," *Agricultural History* 65, no. 2 (Spring 1991): 35–53, esp. 37.

8. Memo, from Lloyd H. Davis to Joseph Robertson, administrative assistant secretary, June 19, 1964; memo, from Davis to Robertson, July 9, 1964; both in General Correspondence, ES, RG 33, NA.

9. Biography, Marshall Vernon Brown, Seastrunk's History, PV; letter, John E. Hutchison, College Station, Tex., to Earl Rudder, College Station, Dec. 30, 1964, p. 3, Texas A&M University President's Office Records, Cushing Memorial Library and Archives, Texas A&M University, College Station (hereafter A&M President's Records); "State Leaders of Negro Extension Work, Seastrunk's History, PV.

10. Letter, Hutchison to Rudder, Dec. 30, 1964, pp. 3–4, A&M President's Records; letter, John E. Hutchison, College Station, to Earl Rudder, College Station, Mar. 2, 1965, A&M President's Records; TAEX Salary Register, TAEX-PS, reels 1, 2, 3, 4, and 5.

11. Letter, Hutchison to Rudder, Dec. 30, 1964, pp. 3–4, A&M President's Records; letter, John E. Hutchison, College Station, to Earl Rudder, College Station, Mar. 2, 1965, A&M President's Records; TAEX Salary Register, TAEX-PS, reels 1, 2, 3, 4, and 5; letter, Arthur Britton, Arcadia, La., to Davis, n.d., both in ES, RG 33, NA; letter, Davis to Britton, Jan. 19, 1965, General Correspondence, ES, RG 33, NA. See also letter, Sara H. James to Davis, FES administrator, Sep. 21, 1965; Joseph P. Flannery, acting asst. admin., FES, to Frank J. Brechenser, Office of the Inspector General, Oct. 4, 1965; all in General Correspondence ES, RG 33, NA. See also memo, Davis to sec. of agriculture, Feb. 20, 1968, General Correspondence, ES, RG 33, NA.

12. Letter, Thomas R. Hughes, exec. asst. to the sec., USDA, to Lloyd Davis, administrator, FES, July 31, 1964; memo, Davis to Hughes, Aug. 7, 1964; letter, Libassi, to Davis, Aug. 3, 1964; all in General Correspondence, ES, RG 33, NA. See also letter, Malone to Orville Freeman, secretary of agriculture, Aug. 10, 1965, General

Correspondence, ES, RG 33, NA; letter, Collins to Freeman, Dec. 3, 1964, General Correspondence, ES, RG 33, NA.

13. Questionnaire, Austin, Tex., branch, NAACP, n.d.; memo, Seabron to agency civil rights coordinators, Nov. 5, 1965; General Correspondence, OSA, RG 16, NA. See also letter, Bryant to Freeman, Dec. 13, 1965; letter, Resnick to Freeman, Dec. 4, 1965, both in General Correspondence, OSA, RG 16, NA.

14. Memo, Davis to Hughes, Compliance with Title VI of Civil Rights in Louisiana, Dec. 21, 1965; Robert J. Pitchell, deputy administrator, FES, to George L. Mehren, asst. sec., Dec. 15, 1965; letter, Fred R. Robertson, to Lloyd Davis, Aug. 2, 1965; all in General Correspondence, ES, RG 33, NA. See also B. D. Mayberry, *The Role of Tuskegee University in the Origin, Growth and Development of the Negro Cooperative Extension System, 1881–1990* (Tuskegee, Ala.: Tuskegee University Cooperative Extension Program, 1989), 121–22.

15. Memo, Seabron to Speidel, assistant to the administrator, FES, Oct. 5, 1965; memo, Davis to Seabron, Oct. 15, 1965; both in General Correspondence, ES, RG 33, NA.

16. Letter, P. E. Poole, La Marque, Tex., to William M. Seabron, assistant to the secretary [USDA], Oct. 1965, General Correspondence, OSA, RG 16, NA; letter, William M. Seabron, assistant to the secretary [USDA] to Ralph W. Yarborough, U.S. Senate, June 30, 1966, with attachments including the complaint filed June 15, 1966, by Thomas H. Dent, attorney, Galveston, Tex., for associate county agents, OSA, RG 16, NA.

17. USDA officials justified their refusal to interfere by citing the doctrine of federalism, a concept as old as the U.S. Constitution. It recognizes the authority of a state to care for its citizens without interference from the national government, a right vested in states via the Tenth Amendment. See memo, In Reply to the Secretary's Memorandum of June 15 on Implementation of the Civil Rights Bill, from Lloyd H. Davis, Administrator, Federal Extension Service [USDA], to Joseph M. Robertson, Administrative Assistant Secretary [USDA], June 19, 1964, General Correspondence, ES, RG 33, NA. This memo stresses the authority of states in complying with Title VI of the Civil Rights Act and the process by which the FES would assist. FES responses to claims of discrimination sometimes reminded agents that state extension directors were responsible for employment and other administrative functions, and that many claims did not fall "within the responsibility" of the FES in Washington, DC . For example, see letter, Lloyd H. Davis, FES administrator, to Mr. Arthur Britton, Arcadia, La., Jan. 19, 1965, General Correspondence, ES, RG 33, NA.

18. Otha Lensey Poole, Hempstead, Texas, Captain, U.S. Army, declared dead Feb. 5, 1969 in "U.S. Military personnel who died as a result of the Vietnam Conflict, 1957–95," National Archives and Records Administration, http://www.archives.gov/research/vietnam-war/casualty-lists/tx-alpha.html (accessed May 31, 2006).

19. Valerie Grim, "Black Participation in the Farmers Home Administration and Agricultural Stabilization and Conservation Service, 1964–1990," *Agricultural History* 70, no. 2 (Spring 1996): 321–36.

20. Letter, Hutchison to Rudder, Dec. 30, 1964, A&M President's Records. Press releases announcing Seastrunk's appointment as an assistant director and his retirement indicate that he assumed a specialist position at TAEX headquarters in 1967 (press release, Agricultural Extension Service, College Station, Tex., Feb. 29, 1972; "Assistant Director of Ag Extension to Retire," press release, [1986], Seastrunk A&M). Records created by Seastrunk note the location of his service as a specialist from July 15, 1959 to Feb. 1, 1972, at Prairie View ("Negro Extension Specialist," Seastrunk's History, PV; Seastrunk, "Black Extension Service," *The New Handbook of Texas* 1: 567; Hutchinson, "The Texas Agricultural Extension Service," 132). The registrar, University of Wisconsin–Madison, confirmed that Seastrunk completed his PhD in Dec. 1972 (communication with author, June 7, 2001).

21. Public Law 92–73, 10 Aug. 1971, *United States Statutes at Large, 1971,* vol. 85 (Washington, DC: Government Printing Office, 1972), 186.

22. Personnel Records, TAEX Historical Files. Gloria Mosby, "Funeral Services Saturday for Hoover Carden, Former Cooperative Extension Head," *Texas A&M Agriculture News* (Sept. 24, 1998) [http://agnews.tamu.edu/stories/AGPR/Sep2498a .htm; accessed May 30, 2006.] Unrecorded interview with author, Dr. Alfred Poindexter, veterinarian, Prairie View A&M University, May 13, 1999, notes in author's possession. See also *Impact* 1, no. 1 (Mar. 1984): 4, newsletter of the Cooperative Extension Program, Prairie View A&M University.

23. Public Law 95–113, Food and Agriculture Act of 1977, Sec. 1444, ensured a certain level of funding to 1890 institutions to conduct extension work. See Rasmussen, *Taking the University to the People,* 265.

24. *Poole v. Williams, Individually and as President of Texas A&M University System et al.,* no. 72-H-150, Jan. 26, 1974, as corrected Jan. 28, 1974, U.S. District Court, Southern District of Texas, *Fair Employment Practice Cases,* vol. 7 (Washington, DC: Bureau of National Affairs, 1974), 102–4.

25. *Strain and the United States v. Philpott,* Civil Action no. 840-E (M.D. Ala., 1971), consent decree, Sep. 1, 1971, cited in Schor, "The Black Presence," 148–49. See also HR 242 by Representative Ford (J), RFD Rules, RD 1 08-Apr-1999 (copies in author's possession); "Congratulatory Resolution, House of Representatives of the Legislature of Alabama," Mar. 31, 1999; *Charlie F. Wade et al. and United States of America et al. v. Mississippi Cooperative Extension Service et al.,* no. EC 70-29-K, Feb. 15, 1974. Litigation continued into the 1980s in *Charlie F. Wade et al. and United States of America et al. v. Mississippi Cooperative Extension Service et al.,* no. EC 70-29-K, with the court reviewing MCES performance evaluation instruments in this case on Aug. 29, 1985. I thank Robert Jones, Heifer Project International, for bringing these cases to my attention.

26. "A New Season: Black Farmers in Texas Form Group to Take Control of Their Own Destinies," *Dallas Morning News,* April 6, 1999, D1, D14. Salim Muwakkil, "Grapes of Wrath," *In These Times* 21, no. 14 (May 26, 1997), 23–25; idem, "Too Little, Too Late for Black Farmers," *In These Times* 23, no. 6 (February 21, 1999), 10–11. "Resolution of Black Farmer Law Suit passed by the Members of the Federation of Southern Cooperatives/Land Assistance Fund at their Annual Meeting in August 2001," Epes, Ala. [http://www.federationsoutherncoop.com/resolute.htm: accessed May 2, 2006]. The settlement fell far short of the damages done according to representatives of the Black Farmers & Agriculturalists Association, Tillery, N.C., "*Pigford v. Glickman* & the Consent Decree: Why so Many are Losing," *BFAA on the Move* 7, no. 1-A [May 2001], 2. Charlene Gilbert and Quinn Eli, *Homecoming: The Story of African American Farmers* [Boston: Beacon Press, 2000], 162–67). Todd Lewan and Dolores Barclay, "Torn from the Land," a multiple part Associated Press investigative series (2001) [http://wire.ap.org/APpackages/torn/; accessed May 2, 2006] explores the importance of property ownership to rural African Americans and the ways racism destroyed their land holdings and influence.

27. Spencer D. Wood and Jess Gilbert, "Returning African American Farmers to the Land: Recent Trends and a Policy Rationale," *Review of Black Political Economy* 27 (Spring 2000): 43–64, esp. 46; *1997 Census of Agriculture, United States Summary and State Data,* vol. 1: *Geographic Area Series,* pt. 51, 524–25.

CONCLUSION

1. George Ruble Woolfolk, "Extension: A Comment," in Dethloff and May, *Southwestern Agriculture,* 146–47.

BIBLIOGRAPHIC ESSAY

Summaries of cooperative demonstration work and extension service development appeared early in the twentieth century, including Seaman A. Knapp's reflections in "The Farmers' Cooperative Demonstration Work" (in U.S. Department of Agriculture [USDA] *Yearbook of Agriculture 1909* [Washington, DC: Government Printing Office, 1909], 153–70). Other early studies include W. B. Mercier, *Status and Results of Extension Work in the Southern States, 1903–1921,* USDA Circular 248 (Washington, DC: USDA, 1922); Alfred Charles True, *A History of Agricultural Extension Work in the United States, 1785–1923,* Misc. Publication no. 15 (Washington, DC: Government Printing Office, 1928; reprint 1969); and *Silver Anniversary Cooperative Demonstration Work, 1903–1928,* Proceedings of the Anniversary Meeting held at Houston, Texas, February 5–7, 1929 (College Station: Extension Service, Agricultural and Mechanical College of Texas, [1929]). Florence E. Ward produced *Home Demonstration Work under the Smith-Lever Act, 1914–1924,* USDA circular no. 43 (Washington, DC: Government Printing Office, 1929).

A second wave of general histories appeared, written by authors not directly involved in the origin of the service, but these authors were usually affiliated with extension service work at the federal level. An example includes Gladys L. Baker, *The County Agent* (Chicago: University of Chicago Press, 1939). Other histories compiled by social scientists provide more critiques of the social program. An example includes Edmund de S. Brunner and E. Hsin Pao Yang, *Rural America and the Extension Service: A History and Critique of the Cooperative Agricultural and Home Economics Extension Service* (New York: Bureau of Publications, Teachers College, Columbia University, 1949). The most serious analysis of the early years of government involvement in informal farmer education remains Roy V. Scott, *The Reluctant Farmer: The Rise of Agricultural Extension to 1914* (Urbana: University of Illinois Press,

1970). The most comprehensive history remains Wayne D. Rasmussen, *Taking the University to the People: Seventy-five Years of Cooperative Extension* (Ames: Iowa State University Press, 1989).

Some early authors had direct experience with the Texas Agricultural Extension Service. O. B. Martin, an early TAEX administrator, synthesized earlier histories into *The Demonstration Work: Dr. Seaman A. Knapp's Contribution to Civilization* (San Antonio, Tex.: Naylor, 1941). James A. Evans, one of the first cooperative demonstration agents in Texas, reflects on early extension work in *Recollections of Extension History,* Extension Circular no. 224 (Raleigh: North Carolina State College of Agriculture and Engineering and North Carolina Agricultural Extension Service, 1938).

Even Texas women told their stories. Lilla Graham Bryan wrote *The Story of the Demonstration Work in Texas: A Sketch of the Extension Service of the Texas A. and M. College,* B-93 revised (College Station: Extension Service, Agricultural and Mechanical College of Texas, and USDA, 1938). Kate Adele Hill, longtime TAEX home demonstration agent and administrator, wrote a comprehensive but celebratory history, *Home Demonstration Work in Texas* (San Antonio, Tex.: Naylor, 1958).

Early publications often emphasized the work done with African Americans. These include three overviews of Negro Divisions established across the South. The first, by W. B. Mercier, *Extension Work among Negroes, 1920,* USDA Circular 190 (Washington, DC: Government Printing Office), appeared in 1921. James A. Evans wrote *Extension Work among Negroes: Conducted by Negro Agents, 1923,* USDA Circular 355 (Washington, DC: Government Printing Office, 1925). O. B. Martin wrote *A Decade of Negro Extension Work, 1914–1924,* Miscellaneous Circular no. 72 (Washington, DC: USDA, 1926). During the 1930s, Erwin H. Shinn prepared *A Survey of the Manner of Procedure Followed in Developing County Programs of Negro Extension Work in Agriculture and Home Economics,* Misc. Extension Publication 11 (Washington, DC, March 1933, mimeographed) to facilitate expansion of the service. Interest in Negro Division efforts continued into the World War II era, when Doxey A. Wilkerson wrote *Agricultural Extension Services among Negroes in the South* (Washington, DC: Conference of Presidents of Negro Land-Grant Colleges, 1942).

Some of the early studies focus on work undertaken at Tuskegee Institute, the institutional home of the first agents. Thomas M. Campbell reflected on his work in *The Movable School Goes to the Negro Farmer* (Tuskegee, Ala.: Tuskegee Institute Press, 1936; reprint, 1969). Allen W. Jones·critiqued Tuskegee's influence in "Thomas M. Campbell: Black Agricultural Leader of the New South" (*Agricultural History* 53, no. 1 [Jan. 1979]: 42–59); idem, "Improving Rural Life for Blacks: The Tuskegee Negro Farmers' Conference, 1892–1915" (*Agricultural History* 65, no. 2 [1991]: 105–14); and idem, "The Role of Tuskegee Institute in the Education of Black Farmers" (*Journal of Negro History* 60, no. 2 [April 1975]: 252–67). See also B. D. Mayberry, *The Role of Tuskegee University in the Origin, Growth and Development of the Negro Cooperative Extension System, 1881–1990* (Tuskegee, Ala.: Tuskegee University Cooperative Extension Program, 1989).

Scholars who take seriously political expressions voiced by disfranchised minorities realize the need to understand the range of attitudes among black farmers toward demonstration work. Farmers frustrated with the inadequacy of black agrarian goals speak out in Karen J. Ferguson, "Caught in 'No Man's Land': The Negro Cooperative Demonstration Service and the Ideology of Booker T. Washington, 1900–1916" (*Agricultural History* 72, no. 1 [Winter 1998]: 33–54). Obviously, the Negro Division did not speak for all black farmers. For a case study, see Gary Zellar, "H. C. Ray and Racial Politics in the African American Extension Service Program in Arkansas, 1915–1929," *Agricultural History* 72, no. 2 (Spring 1998): 429–45.

As the Negro Division stabilized, the forced segregation created dual bureaucracies and accompanying mounds of race-specific paperwork that indicate the complex nature of the Negro Divisions and the independence that each state exercised in hiring, funding, and administering the program, and in reporting their work to the national government. Most histories of the segregated extension service begin with evidence drawn from paperwork generated from within the bureaucracy, as do the summaries by Mercier, Evans, and Martin. Primary evidence from county agents, compiled in annual reports and summarized by their supervisors each year, conveys different sorts of interactions between black agents, the clientele they served, and the white administrators with whom they negotiated. These reports, in conjunction with correspondence between black and white administrators and minutes of meetings conducted by black supervisors, indicate the organizational culture of the segregated service and its relationship with white bureaucrats. These sources also reflect the ways that the biracial bureaucratic chain of command conveyed the expectations of white supervisors but responded to the interests and agendas of minority male and female employees at the same time.

Some historians have focused on rural African American experiences with agricultural extension services across the South, for example, Allen W. Jones, "The South's First Black Farm Agents" (*Agricultural History* 50 [Oct. 1976]: 636–44). Others believe that the agents promoted unrealistic solutions

to black capitalist farmers' needs because agents' solutions outstripped the re-
sources of most other black farmers. See Lewis W. Jones, "The South's Negro
Farm Agent" (*Journal of Negro Education* 22, no. 1 [Winter 1953]: 38–45), and
a dissertation and series of articles by Earl Crosby, including "Building the
Country Home: The Black County Agent System, 1906–1940" (PhD diss.,
Miami University, 1977), and idem, "Limited Success against Long Odds:
The Black County Agent" (*Agricultural History* 57, no. 3 [July 1983]: 277–88).
Crosby and Jones both argue that black agents pursued antiquated goals in
an increasingly capitalist society. Only Crosby considers the role of agents in
Texas, and he concentrates on reports submitted by district and state leaders,
not the grassroots work of county agents. Jeannie Whayne has synthesized
data on male agents in "'I Have Been through Fire': Black Agricultural Extension Agents and the Politics of Negotiation" (in *African American Life in
the Rural South, 1900–1950,* ed. R. Douglas Hurt [Columbia: University of
Missouri Press, 2003], 152–88).

Neither Crosby nor Whayne presents the black professionals as agents
of their own destiny. Whayne argues that the middleman position that the
black male agents occupied forced them to respond to farmers' needs but
also to respect the limitations imposed by whites. She contends that the agricultural extension agents furthered goals set by the white administrators,
specifically, reducing black farmers' economic dependence on the plantation
system. By doing so, they challenged the racial status quo, but only to a limited degree. Earl Crosby argues that the goals of black county agents were
rarely realized because of the poverty that trapped their constituents and the
mismatch between the goal of diversification that the demonstration program pursued and the quest for large-scale, mechanized production that the
mainstream Extension Service celebrated.

Few scholars have ventured to study African American agents during or
after World War II. Notable exceptions include Joel Schor, "The Black Presence in the U.S. Cooperative Extension Service Since 1945: An American
Quest for Service and Equity" (*Agricultural History* 60, no. 2 [Spring 1986]:
137–53); and Jeannie Whayne, "Black Farmers and the Agricultural Cooperative Extension Service: The Alabama Experience, 1945–1965" (*Agricultural
History* 72, no. 3 [Summer 1998]: 523–51). Douglas Helms analyzes integration in another USDA program in "Eroding the Color Line: The Soil Conservation Service and the Civil Rights Act of 1964," *Agricultural History* 65,
no. 2 (1991): 35–53. Valerie Grim considers the consequences of integration in
"Black Participation in the Farmers Home Administration and Agricultural

Stabilization and Conservation Service, 1964–1990," *Agricultural History* 70, no. 2 (Spring 1996): 321–36.

More recent studies of home demonstration agents contribute to our understanding of rural women and reform but none analyze their role in Texas. Lynne A. Rieff considers the ways progressives preached both tradition and modernization through home demonstration clubs in Alabama, Georgia, Florida, Louisiana, and Mississippi. She argues that the southern reformers who strove to improve rural conditions failed. Instead of relieving poverty, inadequate living conditions, poor health, and dependency on one-crop agriculture, they perpetuated divisions based on race, gender, and class and thus did not effect the change they optimistically envisioned. See Lynne Anderson Rieff, "'Rousing the People of the Land': Home Demonstration Work in the Deep South, 1914–1950" (PhD diss., Auburn University, 1995). Lu Ann Jones devotes a chapter to the work of black home demonstration agents in North Carolina in *Mama Learned Us to Work: Farm Women in the New South* (Chapel Hill: University of North Carolina Press, 2002). Jones argues that black women overcame the racism which limited them and gained public services for black communities through self-help. Melissa Walker, in *All We Knew Was to Farm: Rural Women in the Upcountry South, 1919–1941* (Baltimore, Md.: Johns Hopkins University Press, 2000), recounts how black women shaped the programs they administered as much as their superiors did.

Separating the histories of male and female agents and their experiences in the segregated Extension Service makes it difficult to realize the combined influences of race and gender on the bureaucracy that developed in each state. The research from which this manuscript emerged, "Reaping a Greater Harvest: African Americans, Agrarian Reform, and the Texas Agricultural Extension Service" (PhD diss., Texas A&M University, 2000), sought to produce a gendered history of the largest extension service in the southern United States to understand how black agents of both sexes negotiated the power structure.

Few other state-based studies of African American Extension Service programs exist. Examples include a rich analysis of South Carolina by Carmen Veneita Harris, "'A Ray of Hope for Liberation': Blacks in the South Carolina Extension Service, 1915–1970" (PhD diss., Michigan State University, 2002), and Barbara R. Cotton, *The Lamplighters: Black Farm and Home Demonstration Agents in Florida, 1915–1965* (Tallahassee: USDA in cooperation with Florida Agricultural and Mechanical University, 1982).

For further information, bibliographic essays appear in Walker, *All We Knew*, 321–31; Marilyn Irvin Holt, *Linoleum, Better Babies & the Modern Farm Woman, 1890–1930* (Albuquerque: University of New Mexico Press, 1995, 233–40); and Ronald R. Kline, *Consumers in the Country: Technology and Social Change in Rural America* (Baltimore, Md.: Johns Hopkins University Press, 2000, 355–62).

MANUSCRIPT AND ARCHIVAL SOURCES

MANUSCRIPT ARCHIVES

Bitting, Katherine Golden. Collection on Gastronomy. Library of Congress, Washington, DC.

Blackshear, E. L. Clippings File. Agricultural Extension Service Records. Archives, John C. Coleman Library, Prairie View A&M University, Prairie View, Tex.

Brown, Marshall Vernon, Papers. Prairie View A&M University Archives, Prairie View, Tex.

Brown, Pauline R. Correspondence, 1942–61 and undated. Archives, John C. Coleman Library, Prairie View A&M University, Prairie View, Tex.

Civilian Conservation Corps. Records, RG 35. National Archives II, College Park, Md.

Clayton Vocational Institute Papers. Austin History Center, Austin, Tex.

Colored Lone Star State Fair, 1887. Charter. Texas Department of State. Austin.

Colored Teachers' State Association and Principals' Division. Proceedings, 1895–1904. Archives Division, Texas State Library, Austin.

Commission of Control for Texas Centennial Celebrations (Record Group [RG] 057), 1934–38. Archives Division, Texas State Library, Austin.

Commission on Interracial Cooperation. Papers, 1919–44. Ann Arbor, Mich.: University Microfilms International, 1984. Microform. Library of Congress, Washington, DC.

Commissioner Court. Minutes, 1901–40. Waller County Court House, Hempstead, Tex.

———. Minutes, 1911–40. Smith County Court House, Tyler, Tex.

———. Minutes, 1911–40. Washington County Court House, Brenham, Tex.

———. Minutes, 1911–40. Walker County Court House, Huntsville, Tex.

Commissioners Court. Minutes, 1909–40. Colorado County Court House, Columbus, Tex.

———. Minutes, 1911–40. Harrison County Court House, Marshall, Tex.

————. Minutes, 1915–40. McLennan County Court House, Waco, Tex.

————. Minutes, 1917–40. Gregg County Court House, Longview, Tex.

————. Minutes, 1918–40. Kaufman County Court House, Kaufman, Tex.

Conner, George S. and Jeffie O. A. Papers. The Texas Collection, Baylor University, Waco, Tex.

Conner, Jeffie O. Correspondence, 1934–48. Archives, John C. Coleman Library, Prairie View A&M University, Prairie View, Tex.

County Extension Service. Administrative Records. Archives, John C. Coleman Library, Prairie View A&M University, Prairie View, Tex.

David, William Cullen. Papers, 1937–47, 1951–59. Archives, John C. Coleman Library, Prairie View A&M University, Prairie View, Tex.

Easton, Tex. Clippings File. Longview Public Library, Longview, Tex.

Ellis, Alexander Caswell. Papers, 1871–1960. Center for American History, University of Texas, Austin.

Estelle, Henry S. Clippings File. Agricultural Extension Service Records. Archives, John C. Coleman Library, Prairie View A&M University, Prairie View, Tex.

————. Correspondence, 1922–53. Archives, John C. Coleman Library, Prairie View A&M University, Prairie View, Tex.

Evans, E. B. "Down Memory Lane: The Story of Edward Bertram Evans, Sr., and the Early History of Prairie View A&M University." TMs. Archives, John C. Coleman Library, Prairie View A&M University, Prairie View, Tex.

Farmers' Alliance, 1874–93. Fort Worth Public Library, Fort Worth, Tex.

Farmers Home Administration. Records, Region 8, RG 96. National Archives, Southwest Region, Fort Worth, Tex.

Farmers' Home Administration and Predecessor Agencies (Farm Security Administration). Records, RG 96. National Archives II, College Park, Md.

Farmers' Improvement Society of Texas. Smith-Cobb Family Papers. The Texas Collection, Baylor University, Waco, Tex.

Farm Security Administration–Office of War Information Collection. Library of Congress, Washington, DC.

Federal Extension Service. Annual Narrative and Statistical Reports of the Cooperative Extension Work Demonstration Programs. RG 33, National Archives and Records Administration Microfilm Series, (T-845–T895); Texas (1909–45) T-890. Housed in Payroll Services, Texas Agricultural Extension Service, College Station.

————. 1920–45 (SC Series), M 1147. Photographs. Microform. National Archives II, College Park, Md.

————. 1920–54 (S Series), M 1146. Photographs. Microform. National Archives II, College Park, Md.

————. Records, RG 33. National Archives II, College Park, Md.

Greenville Community Project. Clippings File. Longview Public Library, Longview, Tex.

Hill, Kate Adele. Papers, 1929–83. Cushing Memorial Library and Archives, Texas A&M University, College Station.

Houston, David F. File. Cushing Memorial Library and Archives, Texas A&M University, College Station.

Hunter, M. E. V. Papers, 1931–63. Johnson Memorial Library, Virginia State University, Petersburg.

Kerley, Lillian Gregg. Biography Clippings File. Austin History Center, Austin, Tex.

Knapp, Bradford. Papers, 1870–1940. Southwest Collection, Texas Tech University, Lubbock.

Knapp, Seaman Asahel. File. Cushing Memorial Library and Archives, Texas A&M University, College Station.

———. Papers, 1869–1929. Southwest Collection, Texas Tech University, Lubbock.

Manor, Travis County. Cities and Towns Clippings File. Austin History Center, Austin, Tex.

Marriage Records. Colorado County, 1890–1920. Colorado County Court House, Columbus, Tex.

———. Travis County. Austin History Center, Austin, Tex.

Middleton, Dr. Nathaniel Hill. Vertical File. Nesbitt Memorial Library, Columbus, Tex.

Minutes, Board of Directors, Prairie View State Normal and Industrial College, June 1909–Mar. 1917. Archives, John C. Coleman Library, Prairie View A&M University, Prairie View, Tex.

Negro Extension Service. Photo Inventory. Archives, John C. Coleman Library, Prairie View A&M University, Prairie View, Tex.

New Deal Agencies and Black America in the 1930s, ed. John B. Kirby. Frederick, Md.: University Publications of America, 1983. Microform. Library of Congress, Washington, DC.

Panther, The. Prairie View College, 1940. Archives, John C. Coleman Library, Prairie View A&M University, Prairie View, Tex.

Prairie, The. Prairie View State Normal and Industrial College, 1917, 1926. Archives, John C. Coleman Library, Prairie View A&M University, Prairie View, Tex.

President's Office, Texas A&M University, 1948–72. Records. Cushing Memorial Library and Archives, Texas A&M University, College Station.

———. University of Texas. Records, 1907–68. Division of Extension, 1918–29. Center for American History, University of Texas, Austin.

———. General Subject Files, Texas Rural Communities. Center for American History, University of Texas, Austin.

———. Rural Education, 1913–29, School of Education. Center for American History, University of Texas, Austin.

———. Texas Commission on Interracial Cooperation, 1925–31. Center for American History, University of Texas, Austin.

Purple & Gold, Prairie View University, 1946. Archives, John C. Coleman Library, Prairie View A&M University, Prairie View, Tex.

Rowan, Iola W. Correspondence, 1932–46. Archives, John C. Coleman Library, Prairie View A&M University, Prairie View, Tex.

"Rural Texas Women at Work, 1930–60." Exhibit. Texas Humanities Resource Center, Texas Council for the Humanities, Austin.

San Antonio Light Collection. Institute of Texan Cultures, San Antonio, Tex.

Seastrunk, Dempsey H. File. Cushing Memorial Library and Archives, Texas A&M University, College Station.

Smith-Cobb Family. Papers. The Texas Collection, Baylor University, Waco, Tex.

———. Personal Materials. The Texas Collection, Baylor University, Waco, Tex.

Soil Conservation Service. Records, Region 4, RG 114. National Archives, Southwest Region, Fort Worth, Tex.

State Board of Control, Texas Relief Commission Division (RG 303), 1933–35. Archives Division, Texas State Library, Austin.

Tax Records, Travis County, 1900–09. Austin History Center, Austin, Tex.

Texas Agricultural Experiment Station. Special Subject Backfiles, early to 1978. Cushing Memorial Library and Archives, Texas A&M University, College Station.

Texas Agricultural Extension Service. Agricultural Extension Service Records. Archives, John C. Coleman Library, Prairie View A&M University, Prairie View, Tex.

———. Historical Files, 1914–70. Cushing Memorial Library and Archives, Texas A&M University, College Station.

———. Historical Records, Historical Notes and Staff Lists, 1903–43. Kate Adele Hill, comp. Microform. Cushing Memorial Library and Archives, Texas A&M University, College Station.

———. Payroll Register, 1922–23, 1938–39. Microform. Texas Agricultural Extension Service headquarters, College Station.

———. Personnel. Archives, Texas A&M University, Riverside [temporary location; processing in progress].

———. Prairie View, 1915–71. Archives, Texas A&M University, Riverside [temporary location; processing in progress].

———. Special Subject Backfiles, 1900–. Cushing Memorial Library and Archives, Texas A&M University, College Station.

Texas Colored State Fair Company, 1888. Charter. Texas Department of State. Austin.

Texas Cotton Palace. Papers. The Texas Collection, Baylor University, Waco, Tex.

Texas Department of Agriculture. Permanent Records. Austin.

Texas State Exposition. Premium List, Rules, and Regulations. Austin History Center, Austin, Tex.

"Toward a Better Living for Rural Texas Blacks." Exhibit. Texas Humanities Resource Center, Texas Council for the Humanities, Austin.

U.S. Bureau of the Census. Census, 1880, 1900, 1910. Population Schedule. Microform. Sterling C. Evans Library, Texas A&M University, College Station.

U.S. Department of Agriculture. Records, RG 16. National Archives II, College Park, Md.

Waller, Calvin Hoffman. Clippings File. Agricultural Extension Service Records. Archives, John C. Coleman Library, Prairie View A&M University, Prairie View, Tex.

———. Correspondence, 1922–42. Archives, John C. Coleman Library, Prairie View A&M University, Prairie View, Tex.

———. Papers, 1880–1935. Archives, John C. Coleman Library, Prairie View A&M University, Prairie View, Tex.

Williams, John Henly. Correspondence, 1932–43. Archives, John C. Coleman Library, Prairie View A&M University, Prairie View, Tex.

———. Papers, 1943–47. Archives, John C. Coleman Library, Prairie View A&M University, Prairie View, Tex.

Works Progress Administration. Inventory of the County Archives of Texas. Center for American History, University of Texas, Austin.

———. Newspaper Index. Fort Worth Public Library, Fort Worth, Tex.

———. Record Photographs, c. 1937–38. Center for American History, University of Texas, Austin.

INTERVIEWS WITH AUTHOR

Harris, Mrs. Vera Dial, Houston, Tex., 2001

Harrison, Mr. Eddie, Brenham, Tex., 2001

Hill, Mrs. Lovie M., Hempstead, Tex., 2001

Lockett, Mr. Benny L. Houston, Tex., 2001

Mosley, Mrs. Arveta F., Livingston, Tex., 2001

Poindexter, Dr. Alfred, Prairie View, Tex., 1999

Porter, Mr. William A., Terrell, Tex., 1999

Pryor, Mr. B. J., Tyler, Tex., 2001

Robinson, Mrs. Ida, Jefferson, Tex., 2001

Seastrunk, Mrs. Vernice, College Station, Tex., 2001

Talbot, Mrs. Dorothy V., Waco, Tex., 2001

Washington, Mrs. Eddie P., Brenham, Tex., 2001

Williams, Mr. Donald, Marshall, Tex., 2001

INDEX

Acheson, Dean, 175
Ackerman, George W., 108–10, 232n51
Adams, Alton E., 24, 157, 181, 182
Adams, Jessie James, 248n31
Adams Fund, 205n40
advocacy/lobbying, xx, xxiv, xxvi, xx-
    viii, xxix, 16, 17, 39, 89, 97, 109, 116,
    126, 149, 156, 163, 164, 165, 168, 177
Africa, xxviii, 145, 169–73, 175, 251n55;
    Belgian Congo, 172; Cameroon, 172;
    Egypt, 176; Ethiopia, 176; French
    Equatorial Africa, 172; the Gold
    Coast, 172; Liberia, 171, 172, 173–75,
    176, 193; Liberian ambassador to
    U.S., 173; Nigeria, 172; Sierra Leone,
    172; South Rhodesia/Zimbabwe,
    172, 250n49; Togoland, 171
Agricultural Act of 1971, 185, 187
Agricultural Adjustment Act/Admin-
    istration (AAA), 99, 111–15, 127–32,
    134, 138, 141, 236n10; Agricultural
    Adjustment Act of 1938 (Second
    Agricultural Adjustment Act),
    120, 130; Cotton Section of the
    Production Division, 119, 125; crop-
    reduction program/payments, xxvii,
    114, 116, 119–27, 129–31, 138, 144,
    238n20; and discrimination, 124–26,
    238n20; Southern Division, 129;
    unconstitutional, 126

Agricultural and Mechanical College
    of Texas (Texas A&M University),
    xxiii-xxiv, 1, 5, 10, 12, 13, 16, 34, 50,
    157, 164, 182, 187; all male, 16–17;
    educational trains, 15–16; headquar-
    ters of TAEX, xxiv, 16, 19, 22, 181;
    presidents, 9, 17, 22, 33, 35; relations
    with University of Texas, xxiv, 17, 41;
    relationship to Prairie View A&M,
    33; as white land-grant college, 16,
    36, 41
Agricultural Stabilization and Conser-
    vation Service, 183
Aiken County, South Carolina, 205n42
Alabama, 10, 13, 14, 22, 39, 56, 147, 164,
    167, 171, 205n44, 207n50, 213n36,
    216n51, 261; Alabama Cooperative
    Extension Service, 184, 188; Auburn
    University, 184; and automobile
    ownership, 225n65; and civil rights
    compliance, 182, 183–84, 188; Dallas
    County, 147; first Negro Extension
    agent, 87; Livingston, 182; Macon
    County, 184; and mattress making,
    143; number of extension workers,
    162; and roads, 79. See also Tuskegee
    Institute
Albania, 172
Allen, C. E., 11, 203n24
Allen, Meddie L., 109, 110

269

Allred, James, 135
Alvord, Charles H., 210n17
American Negro Exposition in Chicago, 153–55
Ames, Iowa, 208n1
Anderson, Reuben, 231n49
Anderson County, Tex., 32, 56, 75, 101, 108, 128, 136, 139, 232n51
Angelina County, Tex., 236n5, 245n68
Angleton, Tex., 147
Anglin, Zephie,135
Anna T. Jeanes Foundation, 65–66, 220n35; Jeanes teachers, 65–66, 175, 220n35, 221n36, 226n5, 226n12, 228n22, 229n31, 230n37, 233n59, 236n5, 240n32, 245n68; Jeanes Foundation board, 220n35
Antioch Community, Tex., 57, 58
Arkansas, 48, 56, 127, 164, 207n50, 213n36, 239n30; and automobile ownership, 225n65; black agents earning more than white agents, 163; number of extension workers, 162; and roads, 79
Arlington, Va., 146
Asia, 169–71, 175–76; China, 172. See also India
Associated Negro Press (ANP), 112, 128, 165–66
Associated Press, 188–89
Atascosa County, Tex., and Jeanes teachers, 220n35
Atkins, J. Alston, 233n60
Atlanta, Ga., 170
Atlanta University, xx
Auburn University, 184, 207n50
Austin, Tex., 11, 17, 41, 183, 207n49, 236n5
Austin County, Tex., 82, 90, 92, 142, 143, 248n31
automobiles, 28, 77, 78, 80, 101; Ford cars, 77; opposition to ownership, 78; ownership, 78, 225n65; truck and tractor ownership, 78; race, 225n65

Bagwell, J. F., 208n1
Bailey, William A., 38
Baker, Gladys L., 257
Ball, Lewis E., 132
Bankhead-Flannigan Act, 161
Bankhead-Jones Farm Tenant Act (Bankhead-Jones Act), 115, 133, 136, 236n10. See also Farm Security Administration
Bankhead, Miss, 107
Bankhead, Sen. John H., 130
Banks, Church, 231n47
Banks, Willette R., 111, 150, 151, 156, 211n18
Barnett, Claude A., 128, 165–67
Barrett, Annie L., 54, 155
Bastrop County, Tex., and Jeanes teachers, 220n35
Bates, Fred D. and wife, 137
Batts, Fred Douglas and Eunice Love, 244n59
Bearden, Ira, 59, 60
Beason, C. L., 120, 213n36, 237n14
Benton, James Morgan, 63–65, 231n49
Bergen, M. E., 147
Biloxi, Miss., 251n52
Berry, Howard, 110–11
Beulah Community, Tex., 75, 108, 109, 136, 137
Bishop College, 67
Bizzell, William B.: and race relations, 33; Texas A&M president, 22, 35, 210n17
Black Farmers & Agriculturalist Association, 255n26
Blackjack, Tex., 68–69, 222n44, 222n46
black nationalists, 170–71
Blackshear, Edward Lavoisier, 13–14, 15, 24, 25, 40–41, 42, 45, 203n31, 211n18, 213n36, 216n48, 240n33; director of Negro Division, 35; Prairie View A&M principal, 22, 205n40; and race relations, 37–38, 44
Bledsoe, Marjorie, 94

Bledsoe, Mary E., 218n20, 226n12
Bledsoe, P. E., 211n18
Blodgett, F. H., 16
boll weevil, xxii, 7, 10, 11, 31, 36, 49, 105, 147
Bolton, Tommie, 59
Booker, J. A., 11
Booker T. Washington Industrial Institute, Kakata, Liberia, 175
Boone, R. S., 215n45
Borden Company, 108
Bowie County, Tex., 236n5, 245n68
Boydton, Va., 182
Bradford, Jessie C., 230n37
Brannan, C. F., 166–67
Brazos River Bottoms, Tex., (Brazos Bottoms), 27, 125
Brazos County, Tex., 27, 83, 120, 122, 213n36, 237n14; and Jeanes teachers, 220n35, 236n5
Brazoria County, Tex., 24, 45, 138, 147, 204n37, 215n43, 216n49, 223n51, 236n5, 251n1
Brenham, Tex., 51, 62, 77, 82, 103, 227n15, 228n25
Brewster, Martha, 231n49
Britton, Arthur, 182
Brown, H. L., 73
Brown, Pauline Rosalind Mason, 32, 84
Brown, Marshall V., 24, 181
Browndale Community, Tex., 128
Brunner, Edmund de S., 257
Bryan, Lillia Graham, 258
Buchanan, James P., 236n10
Bureau of Agricultural Economics, Radio Market News Service, 146
Bureau of the Census, xx, 38; census, xx–xxii, 9
Burks, Robert, 62
Burleigh Community, Tex., 142, 143
Burleson County, Tex., 92, 226n5; and Jeanes teachers, 220n35, 226n5
Butler, Laura, 242n49
Buttrick, Wallace, 10

Butz, Earl L., 167
Byrant, Charles, 183
Byrd, Callie, 71

Caldwell County, Tex., 226n5, 236n5
Cameron, Tex., 82, 157
Campbell, Phil, 125
Campbell, Rev. J. E., 64–65
Campbell, Thomas M., 10, 39, 87, 118, 172, 173, 213n36, 216n48, 240n33, 258
Camp County, Tex., and Jeanes teachers, 220n35, 228n22
canning: xxv, 18, 32, 36, 41–44, 71, 106, 109, 212n31, 222n44, 223n51, 224n54, 243n54, 244n59; canned goods, 32, 56; canning as defense, 70–71, 76, 77, 131; canning fruit/berries, 69, 70, 71, 75; canning meat, xxv, 69, 73, 75, 76, 137; clubs, 16, 17, 18, 42, 58–59, 69, 70, 72, 73, 75, 76, 108, 136, 154, 209n6, 222n44, 230n44; commercial canning, 68–70, 73, 76, 137–38; community canning centers, xxvi, 48, 66, 77, 132, 136–37, 191; and community cooperation, 70–71, 72–76; constructing community canning centers, xxvii, 41, 67, 68, 70, 72, 73, 75, 76, 102, 108, 136–37; in counties without agents, 70; demonstrations, 66, 68, 69, 72, 143; and economic independence, 50, 69, 70, 136, 224n58; exhibits, 71; financing/funding, 69, 75, 136, 137; first community canning center (white), 224n52; gender division of labor, 72, 75–76, 136, 137–38; and government regulations, 73; markets/marketing, 76, 77; modern canning house, 136; number of canneries, 69, 72, 137; and nutrition/health, 70; pickling, 223n48; public centers, 137; quantities canned, 70, 75; reintroducing, 71; Texas Home Canners Association, 68; urban, 222n47; white agents, 222n44

Capper-Ketchum Act, 115
Carden, Hoover, 187
Cardwell, Mr., 38
Carpenter, D. R., 121–22, 132, 137
Carter, Bernice, 23, 222n44
Carr, Priest R. H, 242n49, 242n50
Cass County, Tex., and Jeanes teachers,
    220n35, 236n5, 245n68
cattle. See cows, cattle and beef
Cauthen, J. B., 11
centennial of Texas independence, 145,
    149–51
Ceylon, 171
chambers of commerce, 77, 89, 91, 92,
    95, 96, 98, 135, 155, 159; Dallas Negro
    Chamber of Commerce, 165; Negro,
    132; Texas Negro Chamber of Com-
    merce, 164
Chappell Hill, Tex., 59
Cherokee County, Tex., 100, 101, 163,
    227n15; and Jeanes teachers, 220n35,
    221n36, 230n37
Chicago, Ill., 153–55
China, 172
cholera, 53
churches, xxvi, 65, 66, 168, 169; building
    and repair, 65, 87, 219n33; church
    organizations, 96; competition
    and disunity between, 76; Federal
    Council of Churches, 130; Federal
    Council of the Churches of Christ
    in America, 65; old church building
    as canning house, 75, 108, 136; and
    sanitation, 64; Sunday school, 65; as
    traditional gathering spot used by
    agents, 25, 64. See also religion
citizenship, xxi, xxii, xxviii, 62, 70, 80,
    87, 89, 155, 170, 176, 185, 192; second-
    class citizenship, 20, 84, 193; separate
    and unequal status as citizens, 86
civic service and fraternal organizations,
    xxv, 64, 96, 98–99, 107, 137, 168,
civil rights, xxi, xxii, xxv, xxviii, 4, 65,
    146, 169, 177, 194; Civil Rights Act
    and compliance, xxviii, 165, 179–89,

194, 252n7; Civil Rights Office, 183;
    Federal Programs Division of the U.S.
    Commission on Civil Rights, 182
Civil War, 27
Clark, William Benjamin, Jr., 83
class, xxi, xxv, 15, 44, 103, 108, 110,
    123, 124, 136, 169, 170, 194, 209n5;
    middle class, xxiv, 2, 20, 36, 39, 47,
    102–103; middle-class bias, xxvii,
    32, 45, 102–104; white, middle-class
    progressivism, 22
Clayton, Brittie, 42
Clayton, Joseph Elward, 42–43, 45,
    214n39
clothing, 56, 106
clubs/club members, xxvii, 12–13, 16, 19,
    20, 34, 46, 49, 59, 98, 116, 130, 138,
    139, 146, 147, 160, 165, 169, 183, 188,
    192, 218n21, 220n35, 224n54; 4-H
    clubs, xxvii, 68, 99, 107, 137, 143, 147,
    148, 153, 155, 160, 161, 167, 179, 183,
    187, 188, 224n54; boys' clubs, 12–13,
    16, 18, 19, 51, 58, 59, 62, 65, 68, 80, 99,
    105, 106, 151, 157; canning 16, 17, 18,
    42, 58–59, 69, 70, 72, 73, 75, 76, 108,
    136, 154, 209n6, 222n44, 230n44;
    community-based, 65; coopera-
    tive clubs, 27; corn, 12, 13, 19, 20,
    58, 209n6; Federation of Women's
    Clubs, 96, 140; gaining leadership
    experience through, xxvi, 48, 80,
    83–84, 143, 191; General Federation
    of Women's Clubs, 17; girls' clubs,
    12–13, 16, 18, 57–58, 59, 62, 65–66,
    67, 68, 77, 78, 80, 81, 83, 90, 92, 103,
    104, 105, 106, 111, 116, 151; as govern-
    ing body, 14, 53, 56; "Home Making
    Clubs," 18; Homemaker's Clubs in
    North Carolina, 66; Lion's Club, 98;
    meetings, 29; member influence, 54,
    83, 143, 169; pig, 51, 147; potential
    members, 26; poultry, 59, 96; Rotary
    Club, 98; and schools, 66, 67, 68;
    sewing clubs, 67; state organization
    of girls' clubs, 83–84; Texas Associa-

tion of Colored Women's Clubs, 17;
Texas Federation of Women's Clubs,
96, 222n44; women's clubs, 67, 75,
136

Cobb, Cully A., 119, 125, 126, 127, 128,
129

cold war, xxvii, 145, 146, 169, 170, 172,
173, 175, 192, 193

collective security, 2

College Station, Tex., xxviii, 80, 81, 105,
119, 141, 156, 157, 158, 185, 187

Collins, LeRoy, 183

Colorado, A&M College, 248n27

Colorado County, Tex., 3, 27, 53, 56, 59,
91, 226n12, 236n5

Colored Farmers National Alliance and
Cooperative Union, 3, 206n47

Colored Teachers State Association of
Texas, 65

commercial-scale farming, xxviii-xxix,
167–69, 180, 249n40; bias against
small-scale farmers, xxix, 189

communism, 169–70

communities, 27, 171, 173, 179. See also
communities, African-American

communities, African American, xxiii,
xxvi, 2, 15, 19, 48, 63, 72, 73, 74, 80,
90, 108, 110, 115, 122, 127, 128, 137,
141, 142, 143, 147, 168, 179, 189, 191,
192, 193, 221n40, 222n44, 261; Back
to the Land Movement, 215n43,
221n40; community clubs, 53–54,
65, 68, 75, 81; community gathering spots, 28, 64, 65; freedmen's
colonies/settlements, 54, 67, 68, 69,
75, 91, 106, 108, 109, 136, 137, 215n43,
ch3 n 44, 222n46, 232n52; and Jeanes
teachers, 66; and Negro Division,
23, 48

Community Council of Agriculture, 53

Confederacy/Confederates, xxiv, 150

Connally, Thomas T., 141, 236n10

Conner, Jeffie Obrea Allen, 50, 65, 66,
71, 84, 108–109, 112, 129, 142, 151,
233n54, 246n7

Conner, George S., 109

Consumerism, 153, 155

Cooperative Demonstration Work,
(Farmers'), xxiii, xxiv, xxv, 7–18,
23; with African American farmers,
7–19, 22; history, 257; international
applications, 171–72; opposition, 259;
as model for Negro Division, 25, 29;
see also Negro Division

Cooperative Extension Work Act,
187; 1890 Cooperative Extension
Programs, xxviii, 187; Cooperative
Extension Program at Prairie View
A&M University, 187

cooperative purchasing, 2, 3, 69, 73, 76,
224n54

corn, 7, 11, 12, 20, 29, 30–31, 50, 59, 105,
119, 122, 138, 149, 231n49; canning,
69; clubs, 12, 13, 19, 20, 58, 209n6;
competitions, 106; demonstrations,
147, 149; Ferguson's Yellow Dent,
59, 62; kafir corn, 7; milo maize, 7;
quality of, xxvi, 59–62, 210n11; red
dent corn, 218n22; Sure Cropper, 62;
white dent, 207n49

Cornell University, 161, 171, 179

Coss, Albert, 73

cotton, xxii-xxiii, xxv, xxvi, 7, 10, 11,
13, 20, 27, 30, 31, 49, 59, 70–71, 90,
93, 103, 117, 121, 125, 126, 128, 140,
163, 171, 183, 198n9; county cotton
committees, 124; income from to
subsidize home improvement, 57;
market/prices, xxi, 4, 20, 39, 50, 78,
118–19, 129; and mattress-making
and bedding, 138–43; as principal
source of income, xx, xxiii, 8–9, 29,
39, 50, 52, 69, 102, 119, 198n9; reduction program, xxvii, 114, 116, 119–26,
127, 129–31, 138, 144, 238n20; as
source of tension/violence, 36, 37, 50;
surplus/overproduction, 118–20, 129,
140, 141,142, 143. See also AAA

Cotton, Barbara, 261

Counte, Rodini, 173

county agricultural agents/work, 23, 24, 32–35, 45–46, 48, 50, 51, 53–56, 58–59, 62, 65–66, 68, 70–73, 75, 77, 78, 80–81, 82, 84–85, 86–113, 115–38, 141–44, 145–46, 167–70, 172–73, 175–76, 177–85, 187–88, 191–94, 260; black agents serving white farmers, 100; counties without agents 39; and health and sanitation, 63–64 (see also nutrition, health and sanitation); National Association of County Agricultural Agents, 160; National Negro County Agents Association (NNCAA), 160, 177, 251n1; Negro County Agricultural Agents' Association, 167; number of black farmers to serve, 205n44; and schools, 65–68; white agents, 23, 100, 112, 120–22, 132, 134–35, 137, 141, 143, 160, 181, 182, 183; white agents serving black farmers, xxiii, 1, 7, 9, 11, 12–13, 15, 40, 89, 112, 211n22; working alone/promoting home demonstration work, 67, 89, 142, 212n31, 218n20, 245n68. See also Cooperatives Demonstration Work; District Agricultural Agents; resistance
county commissioners courts, 15, 42, 45, 69, 78, 88–89, 90–91, 92, 98, 115, 117, 123, 126, 137, 151, 161, 163, 192, 204n38, 216n48, 218n20; pressure to fund agents, 91, 92, 94–95, 96
county councils, 53–56, 81
county superintendents, 12, 65, 66, 67
court cases. See lawsuits, court decisions and consent decrees; U.S. Supreme Court
Courtney, Tex., 215n45
cows, cattle and beef, 51, 52, 53, 103, 108; canning beef, 73, 75, 76; canning to prevent loss, 70–71; cattle and rinderpest, 176; dairy animals, 50, 52, 71, 76, 77, 98, 108, 119, 147; Holstein cows, 98; Jersey cows, 103, 156; purebred, 155

Cox, Mr., 125
credit/debt, xxi, 1, 29, 52, 103, 114, 119, 123, 131–36, 138, 144, 224n55; bank financing, 52, 77; bias against African Americans, 168, 183, 188; credit incentives, 77; credit system, 2, 52, 65, 87; credit unions, 133; crop lien, 35, 50, 51, 55, 132; debt peonage/cycle, 103, 115, 131; ending/reducing/avoiding debt, 68, 70, 76, 77, 131, 132, 136, 172; Farm Credit Act/Administration, 114, 119, 131, 133; lien law, 2; management, xxvii, 43, 55, 62, 131, 133; seed loans, 131–32
Cromer, Marie, 205n42
crop production offices, 131
crops, xix, 7, 50–51, 106, 138, 149, 171, 183; cash crops, 16, 50, 119, 122, 126, 138; cover crops, 43, 122; encouraging/growing feed and food crops, 2, 26, 29, 37, 39, 50, 62, 87, 122, 130, 131, 132, 140, 143, 147, 158; grain sorghum, 149; hegari, 122; increasing yields, xxiii, 11, 171, 172; quality of, 62, 169 (see also judging contests); replacement crops, 122, 125; small grain, 93; soil-depleting/-building crops, 126, 130; wheat, 50. See also corn; cotton; garden/ing; soil
Crosby, Earl, 260
Crow, Jewel N., 242n50
Crouch, G. W., 227n14, 227n15
cultivation. See soil
Cuney, Norris Wright, 3
Cunningham, Minnie Fisher, 111, 233n55

dairy, 2, 14, 51, 52, 75, 77, 98, 103, 130; dairies/creameries, 51, 77, 98; and improving health/diet, 64; marketing, 50, 98, 108
Dallas County, Ala., 147
Dallas County, Tex., 101, 124, 237n13
Dallas, Tex., 16, 41, 113, 135, 147, 149, 155, 164, 165, 167, 231n48, 249n39; Booker T. Washington High School, 150;

Dallas Negro Chamber of Commerce, 165; Dallas State Fair, 59, 61, 106, 149, 154, 166, 218n22, 231n49; State Teachers' Association conference, 83

David, William Cullen, 24, 72, 82, 159, 160, 164, 165–66, 173, 176, 247n19

Davis, Ben H., 91

Davis, Charles L. (Chicken), 251n55

Davis, J. P., 117, 128

Davis, Lloyd H., 179, 182, 184

Davis, Moses L., 173

Dawson, William L., 164

Dawson-Batts, Ruth, 224n56, 244n59

Deckard, Henderson, 93

Democracy, 7, 43, 170

Democratic Progressive Voters League of Texas, 164

Democrats, xxi, xxv, 1, 3, 4–5, 9, 20, 38–39, 41

demonstration work. See Negro Division; county agricultural agents/work; home demonstration agents/work

demonstrators, 7, 8, 9, 11, 12, 102, 106, 108, 110, 127, 149, 153, 155; tenants as, xxiii, 7, 8, 103. See also Negro Division; county agricultural agents/work; home demonstration agents/work

Denton County, Tex., 134, 242n49

Department of Experimental Agronomy, bulletin of seed corn selection, 20

Dial, Vera, 90

Dickinson, Tex., 249n40

dipping tanks (tick fever/Texas fever), 53

diseases, 70, 176; infectious, 5, 63; pellagra, 70; plant and animal, xix, 5, 53, 16, 176; preventing the transmission of, 67; tick fever, 53, 70; tuberculosis, 63; typhoid fever, 64; venereal disease, 63

discrimination, 18, 20–21, 108, 123, 124–25, 126, 130, 146, 164, 165, 179, 181–82, 183, 189, 194; after the Civil

Rights Act, xxv, xxviii, xxix, 180–85, 187–89, 194; class and gender, 136; gender, 17, 33, 89–90, 110, 163, 179, 187, 191; opposition to, xxvii, xxviii, 13, 146, 167, 170, 176, 177, 194; race, xix, xx, xxi, xxii, xxiii–xxvi, 1, 2, 3, 9, 13, 18, 48, 85, 86, 89–90, 92–94, 108, 110, 114, 118, 125, 129, 133, 134, 137, 146, 149, 151, 163, 168, 170, 176, 179, 187, 188, 212n29, 248n27; race and class, xix, xx, 5, 18, 126, 133, 136, 167, 181, 187, 191. See also Civil Rights Act

district agricultural agents, 80, 81, 82, 84–85, 101, 102, 104, 111, 113, 130, 134, 135, 142, 158, 226n5; "associate" agents, 181; and qualifying counties, 88, 101, 236n4; raising funds, 94–95, 97–98; white, 100, 156

district headquarters (Negro Division), 181, 227n15

district home demonstration agents, 72, 80, 81, 84–85, 101, 102, 104, 109, 111, 113, 130, 134, 135, 142, 209n5; "associate" agents, 181; and qualifying counties, 88; raising funds, 94–95, 97–98; white, 100, 141

diversified/ing farming, 2, 14, 29, 35, 36, 37, 39, 48, 50, 52, 81, 108, 110, 119

Dixon, Mary A., 71, 223n51

Doctors, 2, 63, 65, 109

Drought, 49, 70–71, 115, 118

Du Bois, W. E. B., xx-xxii, 9, 156, 171, 173

Durham, Odell and children, 188

Echols, A. H. and family, 108, 109, 232n52

economy, xxvi, 49, 50, 81, 118; downturn 44, 49, 114, 115, 119, 131, 140; entrepreneurship, xxvi, 48

education, xxi, xxvi, 2–3, 10, 14, 16, 17, 19, 31, 62, 81, 86, 88, 99, 105, 110, 141–42, 147, 149, 150, 151, 158, 159, 171, 172, 173, 175, 176, 191, 193; college-

educated African Americans, 22, 47,
160, 185, 191, 193, 210n9; exhibitions
112–13; exhibits, xxvii, 20, 245n5;
farm children attending college, 59,
80, 95, 108, 147, 160, 218n21; higher
education, xxiv, 16, 41, 94, 97, 161,
175, 180; inadequate, xxviii, 32, 70,
191; rural industrial high school,
95; teachers' institute, 67. See also
educators/teachers; land-grant col-
leges/universities; schools
educators/teachers, 2, 7, 10–14, 35,
48, 84, 93, 96, 171, 175; agents as
instructors at summer institutes, 95;
encouraging farming as a profession,
63, 95; future, 62–63, 95–96, 193;
industrial supervising teachers, 66;
Jeanes teachers, 65–66, 175, 220n35,
221n36, 226n5, 226n12, 228n22,
229n31, 230n37, 233n59, 236n5,
240n32, 245n68; National Teachers'
Association, 96; State Teachers' Association, 83, 96; teachers promoting
extension work, 65, 67, 68, 95–96;
WPA teachers, 141
Edwards, Daniel and wife, 231n50
Elderville Community, Tex., 67, 91
Elks lodge, 96
Ellerson, Mr., 134
Elliott, Bennie, 218n22
Elrod, R.P., 12
Elysian Fields, Tex., 61
Emergency Farm Mortgage Act, 132
equality/inequality, xxi, xxii, xxv, xxvi,
xxviii, 9, 13, 17, 18, 43, 76, 86, 93, 95,
108, 114, 118, 123, 125, 126, 145–46, 151,
156, 161, 163, 164, 170, 176, 179–89,
194; equal access/opportunity, xxvii,
161, 181, 187, 194; protests against
inequality, 165, 167
Estelle, Henry S., 52, 82, 92, 96–97, 112,
129, 134, 152, 157, 174, 227n15, 228n22,
234n64, 237n30, 242n49, 242n50;
and Texas Negro Farmers' Council
of Agriculture, 99

Estelle, William M., 135
European nations, people, and colonies,
170–72
Evans, Edward Bertram, 24, 63, 97,
155–57, 163, 173–75, 176, 203n31,
210n17, 211n18, 248n30; first Prairie
View president, 156; Prairie View
A&M principal, 97
Evans, J. A., 7, 125, 225n1, 258–59
Evans, Joseph H. B., 133
experiment stations (agricultural), xix,
xxiii, 1, 5, 53, 175
exodusters, 67, 221n40

fairs and expositions, xxvii, 11, 20, 29,
87, 98–99, 104, 110, 160, 176, 182,
183, 187, 224n54; Anderson County
Fruit Palace, 75, 136; award inequality, 20, 207n49; Central East Texas
Fair, 148; community, 104; corn club
show, 12; Cotton States and International Exposition, 170; county,
20, 25, 59, 67, 104, 108, 149, 223n51;
Dallas State Fair, 59, 61, 106, 149,
154, 166, 218n22, 231n49; exhibits,
193; fair associations, 98; fair for Negroes at Grapeland, 219n25, 244n61;
first "fair for negro[e]s" in Houston
County, 62; FIS, 12, 20, 71; Hall of
Negro Life, Texas Centennial Exposition, 149–51; Houston Fat Stock
Show, 97; Junior Negro Pig Show,
249n35; Junior Negro Poultry Show
and Turkey Show, 249n35; livestock,
111; local, xxvi; meat shows, 233n59;
Mineola Corn & Cotton Show, 11;
"Negro Achievement Days," 165; Negro Rural Youth Day, 249n35; Open
Livestock Show, 249n35; prizes and
premiums, xxvi, 11, 12, 20, 59, 98,
108, 155, 156, 207n49; regional, 149;
South Texas Meat Show, 111, 233n59;
state, 59, 61, 104, 105, 106 147, 149,
154, 165, 166, 245n5, 249n35; Texas
Cotton Palace, 207n49; Texas State

Exposition, 207n49; Texas State Fair, 105, 147, 165; tricounty fairs, 142, 149; see also livestock and shows

Falls County, Tex., 27, 83, 84, 92, 215n44, 236n5

farm agent. See county agricultural agents/work

Farm Bureau, 95, 126, 218n15

Farm Credit Act/Administration (FCA), 114, 119, 131, 133

farm mechanization, 124, 159, 167–69; tractors, xix, 26, 78, 124, 159

Farm Security Administration (FSA), 133–36, 138, 175; FSA Committee for Negroes in Texas, 134, 239n30. See also Bankhead-Jones Farm Tenant Act

Farm Tenancy Conference, 124

Farmers Alliance, 3

Fannin County, Tex., 27

Farm Labor Program, 158, 159

Farmer Boys' and Girls' League, 12

farmers' cooperative demonstration work. See cooperative demonstration work

Farmers' Improvement Society of Texas (FIS), xxv, 1–3, 12, 13, 15, 23, 27, 29, 35, 43, 71, 124, 131; Colorado County Union, 59; convocations, 25; death insurance, 219n28; encampments and fairs, 71; goals, 87, 105; Gold Standard Branch, 71; Juvenile Branch, 12; as model for Negro Division, xx, 35, 44; newspaper, 30; president, 13, 22, 35–36; school garden, 71; school students/private school, 27, 71, 223n51; trustees of the Giddings (Lee County) FIS branch, 12, 21; Women's Barnyard Auxiliary, 2

Fayette County, Tex., 226n5; and Jeanes teachers, 220n35, 233n59, 236n5

Federal Council of Churches, Department of Race Relations, 130

Federal Council of the Churches of Christ in America, bulletins, 65

Federal Emergency Relief Act/Administration (FERA), 115, 132–33

Federal Extension Service (FES), xxiii, 37, 39, 40, 97, 108, 112, 117, 147, 151, 157, 168, 172, 187; creation of, xxiii, xxiv; director, 119; first African American national leader, 166; history, 257; inspectors, 39, 41, 90, 97–98, 99, 102–103, ch3 n 48, 228n20, 229n36; and integration/compliance with the Civil Rights Act, 167, 179–87, 189, 194; special agents, 40–41; white agents serving black clients, 211n22. See also Federal Extension Service (FES) circulars

Federal Extension Service (FES) circulars, 86–87, 110; Civil Rights Act compliance, 253n17; A Decade of Negro Extension Work, 1914–1924, 87; Extension Work Among Negroes, 1920, 86; Extension Work Among Negroes, Conducted by Negro Agents, 1923, 87

Federal Farm Loan Association, 132

Federal Farm Loan Bank, 100

Federal Farm Loan Board, 241n40

Federal Housing Administration (FHA), 183

Federal Land Banks, 131

Federation of Southern Cooperatives/ Land Assistance Fund, 188

Federalism: definition, 253n17; federal/ state government interaction, 53, 182, 184

Ferguson, Miriam, 244n57

financial management (farm), xxvii, 31–32, 168

Fisher, Bobbie Jean, 231n49

Floods, 49, 115

Florida, 164, 175, 184, 213n36, 261; number of extension workers, 162

Flynn Community, Tex., 72

Fodice, Tex., 78

Food and Agricultural Act of 1977, 254n23

Food Control Act, 39

food preservation, 31, 243n54. See also canning

Ford, Jacob H. "Jake," 22–23, 25–31, 39, 45, 50, 82, 105, 208n1, 210n10, 216n48, 227n15; Ford System of raising corn, 31, 210n11; early employee of TAEX, 22, 151

Foreign Missions Conference, 172

Food Production Act, 39

Foreman, Lula, 152

Foreman family (Jim, Ervin, and Reives), 154, 165

Fort Bend County, Tex., 24, 27, 92, 106, 124, 223n51, 249n40; and Jeanes teachers, 220n35, 236n5

Fort Worth, Tex., 82, 97

Franc, R. H., 153

Franke, Louis, 110–11

Franklin, Joe, Jr., 59

Fredonia, Tex., 69

Freedmantown, Tex., 2. See also Oakland

Freeman, Orville L., 183

Freestone County, Tex., 83, 224n56; and Jeanes teachers, 220n35, 236n5

Frissel, Hollis B., 220n35

fruit. See orchards, fruit and berries

funding, xxiv, xxvi, xxviii, 10, 15–19, 80, 115, 157, 175; Anna T. Jeanes Foundation, 65–66, 220n35; Bankhead-Jones Act, 236n10; companies, 155; competition for, 41–43; Emergency Fund/appropriations (WWI), 39, 41, 44, 92, 212n31; federal, xxiv, xxviii, 15, 22, 39, 41, 45, 47, 95, 96–97, 114, 115, 117, 161, 164, 179, 180, 187; GEB, 10–11, 16, 17, 65, 95; "Good Will Tour," 95; Hunter as fund raiser, 228n20; John F. Slater Fund 95, 228n22; local government, 18, 25, 42–43, 45, 47, 88, 89, 90–91, 92, 94–95, 96–99, 115, 117, 151, 163, 179, 180, 216n48; local aid, 55, 90, 91, 92, 95, 96, 98, 107, 123; misuse, 101;

private foundations and philanthropists, xxv, 10, 11, 95–96; public subscriptions, 91; raising funds, xxvi, 86, 88, 89, 94–95, 96–99, 105, 106; state, 47, 96–97, 115, 117, 175, 180; TAEX, 35, 49, 163; taxes, 91, 92, 204n37; Texas Negro Farmers' Council of Agriculture, 99; underfunding of 1890 institutions and special needs programs, 180, 185; underfunding of Negro Division, 18, 25, 36, 44, 47, 81, 89, 92–94, 97, 99, 105, 108, 113, 117, 118, 129, 154, 176, 192. See also Anna T. Jeanes Foundation

furniture, xxi, 93, 138–41; bedroom, 56, 58, 138, 139; chair, 140; cheese boxes, 139; milk/ packing crates, 56, 140; rehabilitation, 56, 57, 139; stores, 140–41; tables, 139. See also mattress making

Galveston County, Tex., 16, 184, 187, 249n40

garden/ing, 2, 14, 31–2, 52, 55, 65, 67, 69–70, 74, 75, 103, 109, 130, 222n44; canning tomatoes, 16, 69; canning sweet potatoes, 69; canning vegetables, xxv, 69–70, 71, 73, 75, 137, 143; cucumbers, 174; freedom to plant gardens, 102; green beans, 75; okra, 139; peas, 7, 31, 122; pickles, 174; potatoes, 100; and schools, 67, 71; sweet potatoes, 7, 20, 108, 119, 122, 147, 183; sweet sorghum, 7, 122; vegetables, 42, 52, 109, 119, 131, 143, 223n51; watermelon, 16

Garner, John Nance (Cactus Jack), 236n10

Garrett, Myrtle Elwyn, 84

Garwood, Tex., 91

Gay Hill, Tex., 59, 60

Gearing, Mamie, 222n44

gender, xxv, xxvi, 16–17, 170, 261; biased decision making 23; black masculinity, xxvii, 23, 90; discrimination, 33, 89–90; division of labor, 57–59,

72, 75–76, 138; male agents working alone, 67, 89, 142; traditional gender relations, 136, 138; youth training, 62

General Education Board (GEB): 10–11, 16, 17, 172; and Anna T. Jeanes Foundation, 65–66; and Phelps-Stokes Fund, 172

Georges, Francois, 251n52

Georgia, 11, 19, 164, 205n44, 207n50, 213n36, 216n51, 261; and civil rights compliance, 183; number of extension workers, 162; and mattress making, 143; Atlanta, 170; Hinesville, 183

Gibson, G. G., 165, 210n17

Gilcrist, Gibb, 210n17

Glen Flora, Tex., 205n39

Goodlow, Hathaway, 104

Goodrich, Tex., 71

government, federal, xix, xxi, xxiii, xxvi, 11, 12, 17–19, 40, 43, 53, 96, 112, 115, 117, 124, 131, 132, 136, 138, 144, 170, 175, 177, 182, 185, 193

government, local, xxi, xxiii, xxvi, 25, 42, 45, 53, 77, 95–96, 113, 118, 124, 179, 191, 192, 193

government, national/state/local relations, 3, 12, 18, 19, 53, 95–96, 117, 124, 182, 184

government, state, xix, xxi, xxiii, xxvi, 10–12, 18, 43, 53, 86, 93–94, 96, 108, 168, 182, 185, 193

Grapeland, Tex., 219n25, 244n61

Graves, Minnie O., 32

Great Depression, xxvii, 68, 108, 118, 124, 137, 163

Great War. See World War I

Green, E. H. R., 7

Gregory, Ezelle M., 84

Gregg County, Tex., 27, 32, 54, 67, 68, 73, 84, 91, 96, 101, 118, 122, 132, 163, 215n43, 222n46, 236n5, 237n16

Grim, Valerie, 260

Grimes County, Tex., 32, 236n5

Guadalupe County, Tex., 51, 82–83, 97, 228n22

Haiti, 173

Hall, Annie G. H., 67, 70, 101

Hall, Charles E., 38, 198n7

Hall, Clara J. S., 138, 138, 147

Hall of Negro Life, Texas Centennial Exposition, 149–51

Hammond, Tex., 244n59

Hampton Institute, Virginia, 10, 87, 167, 220n35

Hampton University, 161

hares, raising, 59

Harrington, Marion Thomas, 210n17

Harris, Carmen Veneita, 261

Harris County, Tex., 77, 163; and Jeanes teachers, 220n35, 221n36

Harrison, Tex., 108, 109, 140

Harrison County, Tex., 9, 54, 63, 64, 77, 92, 96, 101, 155, 231n49; and Jeanes teachers, 220n35, 221n36; St. John Church, 64–65; and Sabine Farms, 134, 135

Harrison Switch, McLennan County, Tex., 65

Harvard University, xx

Harvey family (Ellitie, Haskell, Julia, Leon, L.V., Nathan, and Vinie), 142–43

Hatch Act of 1887, 5

Haynes, George E., 130

Haynie, Houston, 7

health. See nutrition, health and sanitation

Hearn, Maurine, 173

Hearne, Tex., 125

Helms, Douglas, 260

Hempstead, Tex., 99, 174

Henderson County, Tex., 236n6

Hensen, C. H., 111

Hester, R. A., 164–65

Hill, Kate Adele, 141, 258

Hine, Darlene Clark, 55

Hines, Robert H., 50, 51, 52, 68, 69–70, 82, 91, 101, 227n15, 230n37

Hinesville, Georgia, 183

Hogg, John Wesley, 62, 67, 100–101, 230n37
hogs, pigs, sows, gilts, and pork, xxvi, 9, 14, 50, 51, 52, 53, 59, 76, 98, 102, 103, 108, 109, 119, 147, 154, 165; boys and girls raising pigs, 58, 59, 155; boys butchering hogs, 106; Duroc-Jersey sow, 59, 104; pig club demonstrations, 147; Poland China, 59; purebred, 155; sow and litter demonstration, 62
Hollaway, Fannie, 71
Holley, Ora H., 242n49
Holsey, Albon L., 111, 128–30, 240n34
Holt, Marilyn Irvin, 262
home demonstration agents/work, 23, 32–34, 44–47, 48, 50, 51, 54–56, 58–59, 63–64, 65–72, 77, 78, 80–81, 84–85, 86–113, 115, 116–44, 145–65, 167–70, 172–73, 175–76, 177–84, 188, 191–94, 258, 261; black agents serving white farmers, 100, 141; concurrent appointment with Jeanes teachers, 66, 220n35, 221n36; home demonstration councils, 141, 142; leader, 141; National Association of Negro Home Demonstration Agents, 160; National Home Demonstration Association, 160; and schools, 65–68; similarity to work of Jeanes teachers, 66, 220n35, 221n36; state leader for Negro home demonstration agents, 90; supervisors/Home Demonstration Supervisor, 32, 84, 96, 173; temporary appointments, 33, 39, 44; urban, 214n37; white, 23, 39, 100, 112, 134–35, 141, 143, 160, 181, 182, 183, 222n44; white agents serving blacks, xxviii, 7, 9, 11, 12–13, 15, 89, 112, 211n22; women/men working alone, 67, 89, 138, 142, 218n20. See also county agricultural agents/work; district home demonstration agents; resistance; nutrition, health and sanitation
Hood, Solomon Porter, 171

Hoover, Herbert, 241n40
Hopkins County, Tex., 117, 236n5
Hornsberry, H. K., 120–21, 122
horses and harnesses, 53, 78, 112–13, 167, 234n65
household improvements and conveniences, xix, xxi, xxiii, 1, 9, 14, 18, 36, 50, 55–57, 58, 73, 87, 90, 108, 109, 123, 139–41, 152–53, 243n54; electric appliances, 153; electricity/electric lights, 56, 146–47; plumbing, 56; refrigerators, 152; telephones, 56; yard improvement, 109
Houston, David, 9–10, 17, 37
Houston, Tex., 10, 15, 42, 97, 113, 231n47, 233n59; Houston Fat Stock Show, 97; Teal Studio, 106–108, 231n50, 233n59; newspapers, 111
Houston County, Tex., 3, 62, 67, 70, 100–101, 155, 163; first "fair for negro[e]s" in Houston County, 62, 244n61; and Jeanes teachers, 220n35, 221n36; and roads, 77, 78
Hubbard, Hesekiah Lee, 251n1
Huff, Alma O., 140, 142
Hunter, Dr., 65
Hunter, Mary Evelyn V., 22–23, 25–28, 31–33, 39, 45, 51, 54, 55, 67–71, 76, 81, 90, 104, 105, 223n48, 223n51; biography, 208n1, 212n31; first employee of the Negro Division, 22, 151; home demonstration supervisor, 96; and membership in service organizations, 96; and "Outstanding Achievements in Negro Home Demonstration Work," 150; and raising funds, 94–95, 228n20; and state organization for girls' clubs, 83–84
Huntsville, Tex., 125
Hutchison, John, 181–82, 184, 185, 210n17

Illinois, 126, 153, 171, 239n30; Chicago, 153–55; University of Illinois, 171
independence, xxi, xxii, xxviii, 29, 39, 81, 87, 119, 136, 153, 172, 192, 193

India, 171, 172

insurance: crop, 130; death, 219n28

integration/desegregation, 165, 167, 176, 179; and the Civil Rights Act, xxv, xxviii, xxix, 179–89, 194; and the Texas Centennial Exposition, 150

Interdepartmental Group Concerned with the Special Problems of Negroes, 124–25

intermediate credit banks, 131

international reform programs/opportunities, 145, 169–76

Iowa, 213n36; Iowa State College, 161, 208n1

Isaacs family (Catherine, Francis Isabella "Belle," William H., William, Jr.,), 2, 53, 59

Jack County, Tex., 12

Jacksboro, Tex., 12

Jackson, Willie, 242n49

Jackson County, Tex., 248n31

James, Sara H., 182

Jardine, William M., 146

Jasper County, Tex., 185; and Jeanes teachers, 220n35, 226n12, 236n5

Jeanes, Anna T., 220n35. See also Anna T. Jeanes Foundation

Jeanes teachers. See Anna T. Jeanes Foundation

Jefferson, Thomas, 168

Jefferson County, Tex., 187, 236n5

John F. Slater Fund, 95, 228n22

Johns, J. H., 244n61

Johnson, Cecil, 135

Johnson, George W., 156

Johnson, Luther G., 141

Johnson, Lyndon, 179

Johnson, Rufus G., 54, 67–68, 122, 132

Johnson, William, 93

Jones, Allen W., 258–59

Jones, David N., 231n48

Jones, Jessie, 236n10

Jones, Lewis W., 260

Jones, Lu Ann, 261

Jones, Robert, 254n25

judging contests, 62, 147

justice, xxii, xxviii, xxix, 164, 170

Kansas. See Exodusters

Kaufman, Tex., 141

Kaufman County, Tex., 8, 9, 91, 117, 140, 142, 148, 236n5

Kelley, A. R., pressing shop, 147

Kemp, Tex., 7

Kendleton Community, Tex., 106, 249n40

Kentucky, xxiv, 163, 213n36; number of extension workers, 162

Kilgore, Tex., 73, 74, 118

Kinchion, I. S., 139

King, C. D. B., 171, 173–74

King, Mr., 133

kinship, xxi, 48, 109, 127, 193

Kiwanis, 98

Kline, Ronald R., 262

Knapp, Bradford, 18, 37, 40, 202n14, 213n36, 216n48

Knapp, Seaman A., xxiii–xxiv, 6–7, 9–10, 12, 20, 37, 257, 202n14, 202n18

Kone, Edward R., 13, 203n30, 203n31

Knights of Pythias, 96, 107

laborers, 9, 43, 78, 90, 103, 126, 136, 159–60; displacement, 124, 159; labor problem, 40; shortage, 158, 159

Lacey, B. T., 134–35

LaGrange, Tex., 157

LaGrone, O. C., 156

Lake Dallas, Tex., 242n49

Lamar County, Tex., 117, 236n5

land-grant colleges/universities, xix, xxiii, xxiv, xxviii, 4, 5, 10, 13, 16, 19, 33, 84, 94, 119, 151, 161, 171, 173, 174, 175, 180, 181, 185, 187–88; 1890 institutions, 180, 185, 187–88; Conference of Presidents of Negro Land-Grant Colleges, 97, 155, 160; headquarters of rural reform xxiv, 36, 41, 80, 81; presidents/principals 33, 37, 97, 112, 156, 160

Landlord and Tenant Act of 1874, 4

landlords, xx, xxi, 4, 7, 9, 14–15, 40, 43,
102–103, 109, 123, 124, 125, 127, 135,
172, 192; black, 109, 125; reducing
dependency on 31, 133

landowners/ship, African American
(Black), xxi, xxii, xxiii, xxv, xxvii, 2,
7, 13, 15, 23, 26, 31, 52, 58, 65, 67, 87,
108, 115, 124, 125, 145, 150, 152, 168, 189,
191, 192, 193, 198n8, 221n40, 224n55;
and economic stability and security,
44, 90, 123, 255n26; farm owners, 38,
59, 62, 63, 70, 116, 117, 133; freedom to
manage, 31–32, 69, 102; and influence,
xx–xxi, 2–3, 15, 21, 76–77, 92, 109;
"land poor" 32–33; in Texas, 235n2

Langrum, H. C., 101

Latin American countries, 173

Lavaca County, Tex., 82–83, 228n22

Lawrence, Eddie, 62

Lawrenceville, Virginia, 182

lawsuits, court decisions and consent
decrees, 165, 184; class action suits,
187, 188, 194; consent decrees,
187–88; Poole v. Williams, 188;
Timothy C. Pigford et al. v. Dan
Glickman, Secretary, the United
States Department of Agriculture,
188–89; U.S. District Court for the
Northern District of Mississippi,
Eastern Division ruling, 188

leatherworking, 14. See also horses and
harnesses

Lee County, Tex., 12, 135, 213n36; and
Jeanes teachers, 220n35

Lee, Maggie, 71, 223n51

legislatures/legislation, xx, xxi, xxvii,
xxviii, 5, 11, 15, 18, 21, 53, 69, 93–94,
108, 119, 128, 130, 138, 141, 149, 170,
176, 177, 178, 179–81, 185, 189, 216n48;
Texas state legislature, 3, 42, 119

Leigh 4-H Club, 148

Leon County, Tex., 72

letters, 207n50

Lewis, James, 242n49,

Lewis, W. T. and family, 57

Lewis, Willie Mae, 58

Libassi, F. Peter, 182

Liberty Bonds, 40

Liberty County, 236n5

libraries, traveling library service, 16

life expectancy and mortality, 63, 219n28

Limestone County, Tex., 27, 33, 152,
210n16, 230n37, 232n51, 232n52,
242n49; and Jeanes teachers,
220n35, 221n36; and Sabine Farms,
133, 135

literacy, 7, 19, 20, 105, 207n50

Lindsey, LaVerne Y. and children, 188

Lion's Club, 98

Littig Community, Tex., 42. See also
Manor, Tex.

livestock and shows, xix, xxii, 2, 5, 27,
37, 59, 70–71, 110, 158, 171; breeding/
improved breeds, 109, 152; buffalo,
sheep, goats and rinderpest, 176 ;
canning meat, xxv, 73, 75, 76, 137;
care, 53, 77, 98; demonstrations, 62,
147; as food, 51; improving, 2, 36,
52–53, 155, 169; meat, 111, 131, 148, 158;
purebred, 59; quality of, 51, 52, 59,
62, 98–99, 102, 153, 155 (see also judging contests); shows and exhibitions,
97, 99, 104, 111, 155, 155, 156, 158, 165,
249n35; South Texas Meat Show, 111,
233n59; to supplement income, 50,
58, 59, 62; Third Annual Meat Show,
Tyler, Tex., 158. See also cows, cattle
and beef; hogs, pigs, sows, gilts and
pork; and poultry

Livingston, Ala., 182

Livingston, Polk County, Tex., 202n15

loans. See credit/debt

Lockhart, Tex., 127

Longview, Tex., 69, 233n59

Louisiana, 48, 56, 127, 164, 213n36,
234n65, 261; and automobile ownership, 225n65; and civil rights compliance 182–83; and mattress making,
143; number of extension workers,

162; Opelousas, 183; and roads, 79; Southwest Louisiana branch of the NAACP, 183; Yambilee, 183

Lufkin, Tex., 155

Lusk, John M., 51–52, 59, 62, 71, 103, 122

Lusk, Lea Etta, 59, 64, 69, 71, 91, 102, 103, 122–23, 139, 177–78, 224n58

lynching, 4, 5, 36, 211n23

Macon County, Ala., 184

Madison County, Tex., 24, 72, 82, 236n5, 247n19

Malone, Earline G., 183

Malone, K. H., 122, 123, 132, 137

Manor, Tex., 42. See also Littig Community, Tex.

Marion County, Tex., 82, 92, 101, 117, 185, 245n68; and Jeanes teachers, 220n35, 226n5

markets, xix, 77, 80, 193; curbside markets, 116, 212n33; urban, 69

Marks, Tom, 12

Marsh, Armelia, 61, 231n49

Marshall, Tex., 54, 64, 104, 127, 135, 142, 155, 240n32; Bishop College, 67; Chamber of Commerce, 135; Red Cross, 67

Martin, Oscar Baker, 18, 66, 99, 100, 119, 258–59, 210n17

Maryland, xxiv, 164, 213n36; number of extension workers, 162

Mason, Otis Anthony, 135

Matagorda County, Tex., 223n51, 236n5

materialism, xxi, 35, 108, 110

mattress making and bedding, xxvii, 114, 138–143, 152, 154

Mayberry, B. D., 258–59

Mayes, Thomas A., 82

Mayo, John E., 82–83

McConey, Elijah, 231n49

McGhee, George C., 175–76

McKenzie, Sam, 242n49

McLennan County, Tex., 27, 50, 51, 52, 68, 69–70, 71, 82–83, 84, 89, 93, 104, 108–109, 121, 122, 132, 135, 139, 140,

228n15, 228n25, 237n15; Harrison Switch, 65; and roads, 77

McKinney, Tex., 28

McQuinney, John, 7, 8, 9

Medical and Dental Society, 63, 65

Melton, Willie, 249n40

Memphis, Tenn., 126

merchants, xx, xxi, 96; reducing dependency on, 31, 133

Mercier, W. B., 257–60

Merriwether, Marguerite, 248n27

Merriwether, Sherman M., 230n37

Mexia, Tex., 108, 127

Mexico/Mexican, xxii, 173; Hispanic or Mexican American agents, 173; laborers, xxii

Michigan, 171

middle class. See class

Middle East, 169

migration, xxii, 9, 15, 33, 36, 80, 90, 153; out-migration, xxvii, 63, 115, 123, 124, 145, 159–60, 168, 169, 185, 192, 193

Milam County, Tex., 82, 96, 215n44; and Jeanes teachers, 220n35, 236n5, 240n32

Mineola, Tex., 203n24

Miller, E. A., 129–30

Miller, R. S., 121

ministers, reverends, preachers, pastors and clergy, 2, 48, 64, 65, 76, 96, 120, 159, 193; Methodist Episcopal ministers, 64. See also religion; churches

Mississippi, 11, 13, 48, 56, 164, 183, 205n44, 207n50, 213n36, 216n51, 261, 248n29; and automobile ownership, 225n65; Biloxi, 251n52; and mattress making, 143; Mississippi Cooperative Extension Service (MCES), 188; Mississippi Freedom Democratic Party, 183; Mound Bayou, 11; number of extension workers, 161–62; and roads, 79; U.S. District Court for the Northern District of Mississippi, Eastern Division, 188

Missouri, xxiv, 126; number of extension workers, 162, 239n30

Mitchell, John W., 166–67

modernization, xix, xxiv, 14, 18, 22, 39, 49, 109, 150, 152–53, 155, 180, 261

Mohair, George W. and Leomy S., 242n49

Montgomery Count, Tex., 101, 187, 226n5, 236n5; and Jeanes teachers, 220n35

Moody, Athaniel H., 188

Morgan, David Hitchens, 210n17

Morrill Land-Grant [College] Act: of 1862, xxiv, 5, 200n9; of 1890, xxviii

Morris County, Tex., and Jeanes teachers, 220n35

mortality, 219n28

Morse, Delores, 182

motion pictures and films, 147–48, 151; The Negro Farmer, 148; USDA documentary Helping Negroes to Become Better Farmers and Home-makers, 147; USDA filmstrips, 108

Moton family: Jennie 128, 130, 240n33; Robert R., 40, 128

Mound Bayou, Miss., 11

Mount Enterprise Community, Tex., 127

movable school, 172

mules, 30, 31, 103, 104, 167

Nacogdoches County, Tex., 32, 84, 95, 226n5; Chamber of Commerce, 95; and roads, 77

nation building, 145

National 4-H Club Radio, 147

National Association for the Advance-ment of Colored People (NAACP), 17, 19, 43, 44, 183, 215n44; Southwest Louisiana branch, 183

National Association of Commission-ers, Secretaries and Directors of Agriculture, 251n52

National Association of County Agri-cultural Agents, 160

National Association of Negro Home Demonstration Agents, 160

National Broadcasting Corporation (NBC), 147

National Federation of Colored Farm-ers, 128

National Home Demonstration As-sociation, 160

National Negro County Agents Asso-ciation (NNCAA), 160, 177, 249n39

National Teachers' Association, 96

National Urban League, 149, 246n10

native culture, 171–73

Navarro County, Tex., 82; and Jeanes teachers, 220n35

Neale, Laura F., 222n44

Neches, Tex., 128, 139

Negro County Agricultural Agents' As-sociation, 167

Negro Division, 35, 42–43, 81, 94, 100, 258; and AAA, 114–16, 119–31; annual campaigns, 32; annual meetings, 231n50; black agents serving white farmers, 100; can-ning demonstrations, 66, 68, 69, 72, 143; "community rural develop-ment," 178–79; competition with Tuskegee, 113; constituencies and preferential treatment, xxv, xxvii, xxviii, 18, 19, 114–16, 144, 168, 169, 177, 185, 187–88, 191–92, 224n55, 229n33; county-level organization, 53–55; counties with no agents, 98; and criticisms of, 38, 39, 95, 97–98, 259; defined, 197n2; demonstration work, 25, 27, 56, 62, 68, 87, 93, 141, 147, 149, 153–54, 168; dismantling of, xxv, xxviii, 179–82, 184, 185, 189, 194; district headquarters, 227n15, 228n25; emergency agents/tempo-rary appointments, 68, 91, 177–78, 220n35, 223n51; exhibits 148–50, 154–55, 245n5; firing, 100, 101; first director, 23, 105; and foreign service, xxvii-xxviii, 145, 169–76, 193–94; formation, xix, xxiv, xxv, 18, 19, 22–23, 151; and FSA, 134–36; goals,

25, 87, 101, 169; "good Negroes," 38, 86–87, 99, 113; growing bureaucracy, xxvi, xxvii, xxix, 80–81, 86, 113, 157, 168, 192, 259, 236n5; headquarters, 35–36, 80; history/histories, 150–51, 258; home demonstrations (food, not canning), 64, 140, 143; labor problem, 40; location/extent of activities, 19, 26, 30, 33, 39, 46, 49, 81, 116–18, 121, 157, 161, 163, 236n5; mattress making demonstrations, 138, 141–42; monthly staff conferences, 81; newsletter "Negro Field Activities," 111–12; offices and equipment, 18, 25, 91, 92–93, 96, 101, 109, 143, 148, 151, 168, 179, 194, 209n4; overworked agents, xxiv, xxv, 101, 105, 111, 114, 142–143, 144, 151, 164, 168; professional training/standards, xxv, xxvii, 80–81, 84–85, 93–94, 105, 109, 110–11, 160, 161, 168; program expansion, xxvii, 39, 64, 118, 236n5; program themes (see also Negro Division programming), 52, 55; public relations, 86, 98–99, 104–106, 110–13, 116, 130, 140–41, 145, 146; qualifying counties, 80, 88–89, 90–91, 92, 100, 101, 117–18, 123, 149, 151, 163, 229n34; race protocol, xxvi, 37–38, 85, 88, 97, 99, 100, 108, 113, 118, 125, 146, 163, 193; raising funds, xxvi, 86, 88–89, 92, 94–95, 96–98, 102, 105, 106; relations with white agents, 229n34–36, 238n27; responsibilities, 41, 44, 80, 86, 102, 114, 120, 130, 144, 149; specialists, 157, 161, 185, 247n18; staffing, xxiv, xxvii, 25, 39, 44–47, 48, 66, 81, 89, 90, 94, 94, 100, 114–18, 123, 145, 156, 157, 161, 169, 177, 180, 181, 187, 192, 209nn5–6, 212n31, 228n19, 235n3; state leader/director/acting, 19, 23–25, 34–35, 43, 53, 63, 76, 80, 81, 82, 88, 96, 97–98, 99, 102, 118, 119, 135, 137, 150, 155–56, 159, 163, 164, 173, 181, 226n5; supervisors, xxvi, xxvii,

32, 84, 96, 101, 103, 111, 113, 116, 129, 130, 133, 134, 151, 163, 191; and Texas Centennial Exposition, 149–51; and twentieth anniversary of TAEX and Negro Division, 151; and urban, xxvii, 145, 149, 153, 158, 169, 193; and veterans, 169; visible/measurable evidence of progress, xxvi, xxviii, 18, 42, 86, 89, 99, 102, 103, 104–105, 106, 107, 108, 109, 191; and white landlords, 230n43; and World War I, 39. See also county agricultural agents/ work; district agricultural agents; district home demonstration agents; funding; gender; home demonstration agents/work; professionalism; salaries, expenses and benefits

Negro Division programming, 80, 87, 103–104, 115, 140; "The Balanced Woman," 55; bedroom-improvement campaigns, 138, 140, 143; community/club influence therein, 54–57, 83, 169; community involvement, 63; counties with no agents, 98; counties with only male agents 59, 67, 142; different from TAEX 167; along gender lines, 57–59; "Get a Cow" movement, 52; home improvement program, 141; "Live at Home," 55, 65, 132, 167; New Deal, 118, 120; "Own Your Home," 55, 62; "Steps in Canning," 70; "war on rats flies, and mosquitoes," 64. See also Negro Division

Negro Health Week, 63–64, 65
Negro Industrial League, 117
Negro Medical Association of Texas, 96
New Deal, xxvii, 47, 92, 102, 103–104, 112, 114–15, 117–18, 120, 123, 125, 135, 136, 137, 138, 144, 145, 192, 193. See also Negro Division
newspapers and magazines, 7, 14, 16, 30, 111, 112, 120, 121, 147, 165–67, 185, 188–89, 192, 193; African American newspapers, 36–37, 111, 112; Associ-

ated Negro Press (ANP), 112, 128, 165–66; Associated Press, 188–89; Chicago Defender, 36–37; Daily Oklahoman, 146; Dallas Daily News, 223n51; Dallas Morning News, 126; Dallas News, 111; [Houston] Defender, 111, 112, 233n60; Houston Informer, 111, 233n60; magazines, 112, 177; Opportunity, 113; political cartoons, 185–86; Prairie View Standard, 14, 20, 26, 30, 111–12; San Antonio Daily Express, 14; Terrell Times-Star, 7; Washington Afro-American, 185, 186

Newton County, Tex., 155, 226n5

Nicols, Vera, 242n49

Nicholas, Gabrial, 173

North Carolina, 7, 11, 38, 110, 134, 164, 166–67, 207n50, 213n36, 248n29; black poultry inspector, 251n55; Homemaker's Clubs, 66; and Jeanes teachers, 220n35; North Carolina State Farmers' Union, 212n29; number of extension workers, 161–62

nutrition, health and sanitation, xxiv, xix, xxi, 31–32, 36, 52, 55, 58, 65, 67, 118,136, 154, 169, 170, 172, 173, 191; agents' health, 101, 130, 230n39; and canning, 70, 73, 109; clean up campaigns, 63–64; improving nutrition and health, 51, 58, 63–64, 67, 70, 86, 143, 172; improving sanitation, 58, 63–64, 66; infant care, 17, 64, 219n30; mosquitoes and flies, 63, 64; outhouses, 58, 63, 102; sanitation/health campaigns, xxvi, 63, 116; wells, 63–64; window screening, 58, 63–64, 67, 102. See also diseases

Oakland, Tex., 1, 2. See also Freedmantown

Odd Fellows, 96

Office of the General Counsel, 183

Office of the Inspector General, 182, 183, 184

Oil, 118

Oklahoma, xxiv, 38, 48, 56, 127, 164, 173, 213n36; and automobile ownership, 225n65; Daily Oklahoman 146; number of extension workers, 162; and roads, 79; State Relation Service, 38

Opelousas, La., 183

orchards, fruit and berries, 41, 42, 50, 75, 119; canning fruit/berries, 69, 70, 71, 75; peach trees, 108; plum trees, 108

Osborne, J. Granville, 211n18

Otis, J. R., 167

Ousley, Clarence (Colonel), 17, 19, 20, 23, 25, 29, 33, 35, 39, 210n17; TAEX director, 22, 102, 151

out-migration. See migration

Pace, Elbert E., 135

Palestine, Tex., 75

Pakistan, 173, 176

Panola County, Tex., 101, 133, 236n6

Parish family (Beatrice and Cleo): 71, 223n51

pasture, converting fields to, 50

paternalism, 20, 23, 33, 100, 149

Patterson, Frederick D., 246n10

Patterson, Lafayette, 128

Peasant, George, 147

Pelham, Robert A., 198n7

Pervey, R. P., 128

pests, xxi, 115; eradication, xxiii. See also boll weevil

Petersburg, Virginia, 129, 208n1

Phelps, Ruby O., 93, 109, 139, 140

Phelps-Stokes Fund, 172

Phillips, W. H., 82

Philpot, Isaac, 99

photography, xxvii, 66, 104–13, 149, 151, 154; cameras, 105, 110; and George W. Ackerman, FES photographer, 108–10; TAEX photographers, 108, 111; Teal Studio, 106–108; visual instructor C.H. Hensen, 111

Pierce, John B., 10, 213n36, 216n48, 240n33

pigs. See hogs, pigs, sows, gilts and pork

Pinder, Frank, 175

Piney Grove, 231n49

Piney Woods, 117–18

plantation system/culture, xxii, 27, 67, 76, 80, 103, 123, 172–73

Poe, Clarence, 38, 212n29

Point Four Program, xxvii, 175–76

political influence, African American, xx, xxi, 2–5, 76, 81, 91, 110, 128, 130, 131, 240n33. See also taxes

Polk County, Tex., 71, 92, 105, 215n44, 223n51

Polk, John H., 38

Poole, Preston E., 184, 187

poultry, 2, 9, 75, 95, 98, 130, 155, 231n49, 249n35; black specialists, 251n55; boys and girls raising, 58, 59, 96, 106; clubs, 59; eggs and improving health/diet, 64; purebred, 155; purebred Barred Rock chicks, 155; raising, 14, 31, 50, 52, 55, 62, 77, 103, 108, 148, 223n48; Rhode Island Red pullets and cockerels, 59; selling eggs, 62, 77; turkeys, 52–53

population, African American, xxii, xxiv-xxv, xxvii, 7–9, 11, 12, 16, 17, 19, 115–17, 122, 123–24, 134, 141, 146, 157, 159, 161, 163, 169, 185, 188, 189, 192, 193, 198n9, 216n49, 216n1; demographic shift in, xxiv-xxv, 169; growth of rural African American population, 44, 48; in Texas, 226n2

populism, xxiv, xxv, 1, 3

Porter, Walter C., xxiii, 7, 8

poverty, xix, xxviii, 1, 5, 20, 31, 45, 48, 69, 76, 92, 103, 110, 118, 123, 124, 126, 131, 135–36, 138–41, 144, 151, 155, 161, 169, 175, 191, 193; and health, 63, 70; services for, xxviii, 178–80, 185, 187

Powell, Jack and family, 135, 242n49, 242n50

Prairie View Normal & Industrial Institute (Prairie View A&M), xxviii, 13–14, 19, 20, 22, 24, 27, 33, 35, 41, 47, 65, 73, 82–83, 84, 85, 87, 95–96, 111, 113, 126, 127, 131, 134, 135, 141, 157, 157, 164, 171, 175, 185, 187, 213n36; the "A&M Way," 30, 31; cooperation and tension with Negro Division, 80–81; Cooperative Extension Program, 187, 194; extension agents' annual meeting, 108; farmers' institutes and congresses, 13, 20; first president, 156; graduates not farming, 63; headquarters of the Negro Division and "associate" agents, 19, 36, 80, 105, 109, 175, 181, 182, 227n16, 228n25; principal/president, 13, 22, 24, 25, 33, 63, 80, 97, 111, 150, 150, 151, 156, 173; scholarships and financial assistance, 59, 80–81; short courses, 14, 30, 62, 80, 107, 112, 113, 138, 139, 149, 151, 152, 231n50; training and education for Negro agents, 80–81, 94, 109, 139, 149, 161; underfunding, 81; and War Emergency Conference for Negro Local Leaders, 157; and watermelon blossom-end blight studies, 16

Prairie View Standard, 14, 20, 26, 30, 111–12

prejudice, xix, 97

Prewit, James D., 97, 167–68

Professional Agricultural Workers Conference, 249n40

professionalism, xx, xxv, xxvi, xxix, 2, 44–47, 63, 80–81, 84–87, 90, 105, 109, 113, 114, 141, 144–46, 149–51, 168, 177, 184, 191–93; agents as instructors at summer institutes, 95; contact with black professionals, 64, 96; farming as profession, 63, 67, 193; professional organizations, xxvii, 145, 160, 194; professional gatherings, 146; professional standards, xxv, xxvii, 93–94, 102, 134, 145, 160

Progressive Farmer, 212n29

Progressive reform/ers: xix, xxvi, 14, 21–23, 31, 33, 37, 39, 42, 45, 66, 91, 96, 105, 109, 115, 139, 191

property: accumulation of, xxi, xxii,
2, 3, 15, 32–33, 50, 62, 68, 76, 77, 87,
102, 103, 109, 123, 169, 170, 221n40;
as investment, 43, 125; improving,
3, 32, 32–33, 55–58, 87, 108, 109, 139,
140, 150, 152
Puerto Rice, 173
Purdue University, 167
Pyrtle Community, Tex., 73, 74
Pyrtle School, 73

Quicksall, J. L., 9, 12

race-based (biased) decision making,
xix, xxv, xxix, 18, 21, 36, 44, 88, 114,
124, 146, 160, 163, 170, 177
race relations, xxii, xxiv, xxvi, 18, 20–21,
33, 35–8, 42–44, 95, 97, 99–101, 103,
106, 110, 114, 118, 120, 124, 130, 133,
141, 149–51, 157, 163, 170, 183, 187, 193;
defiance, 78, 96, 97; role reversal,
100; interracial relations/coopera-
tion, xxvi, 14, 15, 21, 88, 90 91, 95, 96,
100–101, 104, 111, 113, 151, 156, 177,
191; Texas Interracial Commission,
96
racial violence, 4, 21, 36, 43–44, 50, 124,
171, 192; Texas Committee on Interracial Violence, 215n45
racial separatism, 38
racism, xxi, xxiv, 9, 12, 13, 20–21, 22, 36,
41, 48, 49, 68, 84, 87, 95, 100, 108,
110, 118, 124, 141, 170, 178, 182–84,
189, 191, 192, 194, 255n26; "race problem," 37–38, 171; white control, xxiii,
1, 2, 20, 85, 172, 192; of white TAEX
officials, 23, 33, 97, 110, 179–80, 182,
191
radio/radio stations and television,
xxvii, 99, 146–47, 157–58, 193; "Food
for Freedom" program, 158; National
4-H Club Radio, 147; National
Broadcasting Corporation (NBC)
radio stations, 147; radio ownership,
146–47, 157–58; Station WTAW in

College Station, 158; television,
193
railroads, companies, and trains, 10, 11,
15–16, 28, 42, 69, 80, 98, 101, 215n43;
Extension Education, 205n39; first
lecture with USDA agents, 202n20;
International & Great Northern
Railroad line, 68; Katy—A&M Col-
lege Agriculture Train, 16, ; Katy—
A&M College Good Roads Special,
16; Rock Island and Frisco Railroad
lines, 12; Texas A&M's educational
trains, 15–16; Texas Midland Railway
Company, 7
Raines County, Tex., 203n24
Rambo, Pinkie, 25, 31, 84, 209n4
Randolph, Emmett A., 157
Rayburn, Sam, 236n10
Reconstruction, xxiv, 5, 21; a second
reconstruction, 177
Reconstruction Finance Corporation
(RFC), 115, 137, 241n40
Red Cross, 40, 67
Red River County, Tex., 27, 226n5,
245n68
Regenbrecht, E. M., 156
Reich, Steven, 43
religion, 64; and agents, 64; Bishop
College, 67; and discrimination,
170, 179, 187; prayer, 43, 49, 64;
shared goals with Negro Division,
65; tension over belief, 37. See also
churches; ministers, reverends,
preachers, pastors and clergy
Republicans, xxi, xxv, 1, 3, 4–5; Texas
Republican Leader, 3; (Texas) Republican State Convention, 4
resettlement projects, 114, 133–36
resistance/skepticism, xix, xxiii, 259;
African American to Negro Division
work, 14–15, 29, 31, 32, 53, 68, 123, 191
Rhombo [Rambo], Mildren Isaacs,
209n4
Rice, C. W., 42
Richardson, C. F., 233n60

Reiff, Lynne, 261
Resnick, Joseph, 183
Rigsby, Hulen T., 249n40
roads, 28, 29, 52, 54, 77, 79, 103; good-roads movement, 77; means of resistance, 78; road improvement, 77–78; Texas Good Roads Association, 77
Roberts, E. D. and family, 77
Robertson County, Tex., 27, 92, 137, 215n44, 223n51, 244n59, 245n68
Robinson, F. J., 75, 128
Robinson, Fred, 184
Rockefeller, John D., 10, 11
Rockwell County, Tex., 142
Roosevelt, Franklin Delano, 108, 113, 119, 129–30, 131
Rosborough, J. F., 108
Rotary Club, 98
Rowan, Iola W., 32, 72, 84, 109, 111, 112, 129, 141–42, 150, 159, 160, 173, 245n5
rubber, 171
Rudder, James Earl, 210n17
Rural Life Committee, 222n44
Rusk, Tex., 82
Rusk County, Tex., 57, 58, 73, 74, 96, 127, 155, 232n51, 226n5

Sabine Farms, 134–36, 241n46, 242n50, 243n53
salaries, expenses and benefits, xxiv, xxvii, 14, 15, 18, 25, 35, 45, 47, 78, 86, 88, 89–90, 92–94, 95, 96–97, 98, 118, 129, 130, 146, 151, 163–64, 165, 168, 181, 182, 187–88, 192, 194, 216n48, 236n7; and photography, 105; TDA, 42
San Antonio, Tex., 43
San Augustine County, Tex., 226n5, 245n68
Sanders, Irene, 32, 56
Sanders, Lue D. and Betsy, 242n49
Sanders, Ruben A., 83
sanitation. See nutrition, health and sanitation
Sandy Point, 215n43

Saturday Service Leagues, 39
Sayles, G. G., 52
Schlup, Lester A., 233n55
schools, xxvi, 2, 3–4, 14, 20, 25, 65–66, 78, 168; African American authority, 3–4; all male, 16–17; acquiring musical instruments, 68; Baptist school, 67; building schools, 67, 87, 220n35; condition of buildings, 65; county training schools, 95; farms, 14; and gardens, 67; and Jeanes teachers, 66; movable school, 172; private, 27; Pyrtle school, 73; and sanitation, 64, 67, 68; state schools, 94
Schor, Joel, 260
scientific agriculture, xxii, 7, 9, 11, 12, 16, 18, 37, 41, 44, 48, 62, 84, 86, 109, 167–69, 171, 172
Scott, Emmett, 215n47
Scott, Milton and Opal, 242n49
Scott, Roy V., 257, 206n47
Seabron, William, 184
Sears, Roebuck and Company, 155; Cow-Sow-Hen Program, 155, 156, 246n16; Sears-Roebuck Foundation, 155
Seastrunk, Dempsey H., xxviii, 157, 185, 254n20
Senate Bill 1800, 130
seeds, 7, 19–20; loans (WWI), 241n40; quality of, 12, 59, 123, 152; seed loans, 131–32; selection, 20, 210n11; spacing, 19; testing, 19, 29
segregation, xix, xx, xxv, xxvi, 3, 4, 12, 18, 20, 33, 35, 38, 81, 85, 86, 104, 108, 112, 149–51, 160, 187, 192; challenges/responses to, 149–51, 160, 165, 177, 182, 194; continued segregation after the Civil Rights Act 179, 181–85, 187, 189; of extension services, xxiv, xxviii, 17–21, 22, 86, 97, 98, 100, 114, 118, 149, 156, 163, 167; and higher education, 161, 171; national and international opposition to, 146; of schools, 3–4; self-segregation, xxviii,

2, 3, 35, 171, 180, 189, 194; separate but equal, xxiv, 47, 167, 177; of Texas Centennial Exposition, 149–50. See also integration/desegregation; lawsuits, court decisions and consent decrees

Seguin, Tex., 51

self-governance/determination, 14

self-help, 3, 35, 170, 173, 180, 193, 194, 261

sewing, 55, 58, 59, 107, 140, 142; rehabilitate clothing, xxvi, 98; sewing clubs, 67; sewing machines, 107, 153

sharecroppers, xxvii, 2, 15, 31, 102, 103, 115, 123, 126, 131, 133, 159, 192, 247n21; displacement, 115, 124; white, 124

Sharp, Annie B., 59

Sharpe, John, 51–52

Shelton, Jack, 112

Shelby County, Tex., 226n5

Shelton, Jessie L., 138, 142–43

Shefield, Charles A., 129

Sheppard, Dr., 65

Shinn, Erwin H., 124–25, 157, 258

Sibley, James L., 175

Simpson, T. G., 222n44

Singleton, John H., 174

Slater, John F. (fund), 95, 228n22

slaves/slavery, 27, 42, 80, 150; emancipation, 1, 2, 150

Smith, A. Maceo, 150

Smith, Belle Isaacs, 2. See also Isaacs, Francis Isabella "Belle"

Smith County, Tex., 92, 96, 153, 155, 222n44, 222n46, 224n52; and Jeanes teachers, 220n35

Smith, Hoke, 19, 206n47

Smith, John Vinson, 52–53, 68, 83, 93, 109, 122, 135

Smith, L. A., 52–53

Smith, Robert Lloyd, 1–4, 12, 13, 15, 22–29, 36, 39, 42, 45, 68, 87, 105, 131, 209n4, 210n10, 216n48, 219n28, 220n35, 223n51, 228n22; one of the Negro Division's first employees 22, 151; president, Texas State Negro Business League, 204n36; and race relations, 43; and roads, 78, 80; State leader (first director) of Negro Division, 23–25, 35, 150; and Texas Interracial Commission, 96. See also FIS

Smith, W. T., 128

Smith-Lever Agricultural Extension Act, xxiv, 12, 18, 19, 41, 151, 178–79, 205n42 207n50

Smoot, Mrs., 50

Snow, A. D., 147

soil, 19–20, 110, 130; conservation/erosion, 43, 108, 122, 126–27, 128, 131, 138, 152; cultivation, 7, 11, 20, 30–31, 36, 42, 50, 99, 123; drainage and subirrigation, 231n50; fertilizer, xix, 19, 122, 123, 152; preparation, 29–30, 77, 99, 210n11; quality, xxi, 27, 110, 117, 123, 126, 135; returning nitrogen to soil, 122. See also terracing

Soil Conservation and Domestic Allotment Act, 120, 126, 128, 130, 239n31

Soil Conservation Service, 260

South, the, xix, xx, xxi, xxii, xxiii, xxv, xxviii, 3, 5, 6, 13, 37, 40, 86, 109, 110, 124, 126, 129–31, 141, 142, 147, 157, 175, 176, 187, 188; and African American farm population, 17, 44, 115, 163, 189; and Civil Rights Act, 179–89; and cotton reduction, 120, 125; and economy, xx, 14, 114, 118; and extension work/workers, xxiv, 18, 38, 40, 47, 49, 86, 87, 98, 125, 159, 162, 163, 165, 171, 176, 178, 180; and first Negro agents, 10–11, 17; and FSA, 133–34; and Jeanes teachers, 66, 220n35; Jim Crow, 18, 49, 161; and land-grant institutions, xxviii, 94, 171, 175; modern/modernizing, xxvi, 39, 86; new south, 193; and migration, xxii, 159, 168, 169, 193; old south, 48; race relations, 20–21, 37, 150, 167, 180; and radio ownership, 146–47; Southern Educational Board, 11; Southern States Office of

Cooperative Extension Work, 99; trans-Mississippi region, 40–41, 48; and travel, 129

South Carolina, 11, 22, 134, 164, 261, 205n44, 207n50, 213n36; Aiken County, 205n42; number of extension workers, 162

South-Wide Extension Conference on Work with Negroes, 159

"Southern 'Fireside Chats,'" 159

Southern States Office of Cooperative Extension Work, 99

Spencer, Lillian, 59

Spencer, W. M. and family, 62

stability, xx

State Teachers' Association, 83, 96

Stein, Ernest, 127

Stockett, Thomas, 186

Stone, Stark, Sr. and wife, 103

Strain, Willie L., 188

Stump Toe, Tex., 69, 222n46

suffrage, 3–5, 21, 164, 183

sugar, 27

Sunny Side, Tex., 107

Surplus Commodity Corporation/ bill, 141

surveying, 106, 120

Tabor College, 213n36

Taeusch Discussion Conference, 129, 131

Tayloe, James, 242n50

Taylor, Hobart, 164–65

Taylor, James, 135, 242n49

Tatum, Tex., 57, 58

Taubenhaus, J. J., 16

taxes, 3, 5, 15, 16, 45, 77, 109, 123, 164, 192

Teal Studio, 106–108, 231n50, 233n59

Teal, Elnora, 106–107, 111

Teal, Arthur Chester, 107, 111

technological innovations, xix, xx, 153, 159, 167–69; truck farming, 14

tenancy/tenants/renters, xxvii, 2, 4, 7, 9, 15, 31, 32, 40, 43, 50–51, 59, 60, 70, 76, 98, 102, 104, 109, 117, 122, 123, 124, 125, 127, 128, 134, 135, 159, 189, 191, 192, 247n21; Bankhead-Jones Farm Tenant Act, 115, 133, 136; becoming landowners, 51–52, 62, 103; bias against, 32, 102, 115, 124, 131, 133, 136; black advantage over white, 202n14; as demonstrators, xxiii, 7, 8, 103; displacement, 115, 124–25; escaping tenancy, 65; Farm Tenancy Conference, 124; Landlord and Tenant Act of 1874, 4; relations with Negro Division, 230n44; Texas Farm Tenant Security Project, 134, 241n46

Tennessee, 126, 163, 164, 213n36, 239n30; and Extension Service programs, 110; and Jeanes teachers 220n35; Memphis, 126; number of extension workers, 162

terraces/terracing and drainage, 100, 126–27, 128

Terrell, A. W. (Judge), 5

Terrell, I. M., 211n18

Terrell, Tex., xxiii, 6–7, 8, 141; Terrell Chamber of Commerce, 91; Terrell Times-Star, 7

Terrell Election Law of 1903, 5

Texas: Blackland Prairie, xxiii, 7, 9, 27, 117, 121, 124; bottomlands, 123; Central, 27, 181, 215n44; East, xxiii, 26, 27, 35, 42, 48, 49, 96, 105, 115, 117, 124, 147, 155, 173, 181; Gulf Coast, 216n49; Gulf Coastal Plain, 27; North, 27; Northeast, 27, 68, 203n24; number of extension workers, 162; Piney Woods, 117–18; Post Oak area, 117; proportion of black to white farmers, 248n29; and roads, 79; South, 27; South Central, 12; Southeast, 185; West, 12. See also African American population

Texas A&M University (Texas A&M). See Agricultural and Mechanical College of Texas

Texas Agricultural Experiment Station, xix, 5, 16, 110

Texas Agricultural Extension Service (TAEX), xix, xxiii, xxiv, xxviii, 1, 5, 33, 39, 86, 94, 97, 124, 126, 128, 136, 151, 167, 249n40, 258; administrators/officials, 15, 20, 23, 29, 97, 164, 181; African American involvement, 46, 97; "associate" agents, 181; booklets, 70; budget, 25; and the Civil Rights Act, 179–85, 187–89, 194; "community rural development" and CRD agents, 178–79; creation of, xxiv, 16; creation of Negro Division, 22; criticism, 117; female appointments, xxvi, 23, 90; friction with Texas Department of Agriculture, 41–42; first black assistant director, 185; and foreign dignitaries, 173; funding and support of Negro Division, 35, 45, 100, 108, 115, 157, 161, 163, 168, 192; goals, 29, 44; headquarters, xxviii, 19, 22, 80, 81, 141, 181, 185, 187; interracial cooperation, 100, 107–108, 112; largest extension Service in U.S., 115; organizational structure, xxv, 18, 21, 34, 137, 181; prohibition of political activities, 249n33; and race relations, 18, 88, 97, 99, 110, 120, 137, 179; specialists, 34, 108, 111, 112–13, 157, 254n20; TAEX director, 17, 19, 20, 22, 66, 88, 90, 97, 99, 100–102, 112, 119, 127, 151, 165, 181–82; twenty-fifth anniversary of TAEX, 145, 151. See also TAEX bulletins; home demonstration agents, county agricultural agents; discrimination; segregation; Negro Division; Negro Division programming

Texas Agricultural Extension Service (TAEX) bulletins: Community Canning Plants, 72; "First Year Sewing," 67

Texas Association of Colored Women's Clubs, 17

Texas Centennial Exposition, 149–51

Texas commissioner of agriculture, 13

Texas Democratic Progressive Voters League, 164

Texas Department of Agriculture (TDA), xxiv, 1, 13, 17; Department of Agriculture, Insurance, Statistics, and History, 5; and farmers' institutes, 13, 42–43, 44, 214n39; first African American volunteers, 42–43; friction with TAEX, xxiv, 41–42

Texas Farm Tenant Security Project, 134–35, 241n46

Texas Farmers' Congress, 12

Texas Governor, 135

Texas Home Canners Association, 68

Texas Negro Farmers' Council of Agriculture, 99, 164

Texas Rehabilitation and Relief, 244n57

Texas Relief Commission (TRC), 137

(Texas) State Bureau of Agriculture, 5

Texas State Farmers' Institute, 42, 43, 222n44

Texas State Negro Business League, 204n36

Texas State Legislature/legislators, 3, 42, 119

third world and developing regions, 145, 169, 175. See also Africa

Thomas, Alvin I., 211n18

Thomas, Ethel W., 58

Thomas, Jesse O., 149, 150–51

Thornton, M. K., Jr., 112–13

tick fever/Texas fever, 53

Tillery, North Carolina, 255n26

timber industry, 117

Toney, Seth T., 51, 97

tradition, 261

trains. See railroads, companies, and trains

Travis County, Tex., 82, 138; and Jeanes teachers, 220n35, 221n36, 228n22

Trent, D. P., 135

Trigg, Edna W., 16

Trinity County, Tex., 226n5, 228n22, 226n5

Trotter, Ide P., 97, 210n17

Trout, Charles E., 174
True, Alfred Charles, 40, 257, 206n47
Truman, Harry S., 175
Tuskegee Institute, 10, 13, 14, 21, 39, 67, 87, 113, 125, 128, 129, 131, 134, 149, 167, 172, 183–84, 188, 206n47, 213n36, 220n35, 258, 240n33, 246n10, 249n40; cooperation with TAEX Negro Division, 234n65; and farmers' institutes, 13; and international reform, 170; principal of, 40, 128; short courses, 14, 249n40
Tyler, Tex., 69, 127, 158

United Brothers of Fellowship (UBF), 96
United Nations, 170; Food and Agriculture Organization (FAO), xxvii, 176; U.N. Declaration of Human Rights, xxviii, 170, 176
United States of America, 114, 118, 171, 175, 192, 193; criticisms of, xxviii, 146, 170
University of Illinois, 171
University of Texas, xxiv, 11, 16, 17, 41, 44; "better baby" clinics, 17; extension education through University of Texas, 41; traveling library service, 16; urban Texans, 17, 41
University of Wisconsin-Madison, 185, 254n20
Upshur County, Tex., ch56
U.S. Congress, xxiv, xxviii, 19, 39, 108, 116, 119, 126, 128–130, 141, 149, 161, 164, 178–181, 183. See also government, federal; and legislators/legislation
U.S. Department of Agriculture (USDA), xix, xxiii, xxiv, xxv, 1, 5, 7, 13, 16, 18, 38, 40, 53, 66, 108, 110, 118, 124, 128, 129, 166–67, 173, 175, 179, 187; assistant to secretary, 33, 184; "associate" agents, 181–82; award for superior service, 177–78; bulletins, 20; and the Civil Rights Act, 179–89; Committee for African Students in North America, 173; crop correspondents' wives, 17; Crop Production Offices, 131; documentary film Helping Negroes to Become Better Farmers and Homemakers, 147; filmstrips, 108; and GEB funding of Negro agents, 10–11, 17; Negro special assistant and special field agents, 118, 128–31, 166, 213n36; Office of Foreign Agricultural Relations (OFAR), xxvii, 169, 173, 175; and race relations, 167; and radio, 146; "School Lessons in Cotton" bulletin, 20; Secretary of Agriculture, 10, 11, 17, 37, 112, 117, 119, 124, 133, 146, 166, 183, 186; special agents and Farmers' Cooperative Demonstration Work, xxiii, 6, 7, 9–12, 13; State Relations Services, 213n36. See also FES; FES circulars
U.S. Department of Commerce, Community Relations Office, 183
U.S. Department of Labor, 40
U.S. Department of State, xxvii, 175; assistant secretary for Near Eastern South Asian-African Affairs, 175–76; minister to Liberia, 171; Near Eastern South Asian-African Affairs Desk, 176; Point Four Program, xxvii, 175–76; Secretary of State, 175
U.S. Department of War, 40
U.S. Food Administration, 40
U.S. presidents, 108; Franklin Delano Roosevelt, 108, 113, 119, 129–30, 131; Harry S. Truman, 175; Lyndon Baines Johnson, 179; Woodrow Wilson, 19, 39
U.S. Supreme Court, 4, 126, 167, 177; Brown v. Board of Education, 167, 177, 178; Plessy v. Ferguson (1896), xxiv, 4, 18, 167

Van Zandt County, Tex., 142, 248n31
vegetables. See garden/ing

veterinarians, 173, 176, 203n31

Victoria County, Tex., and Jeanes teachers, 220n35

Village Improvement Society, 3. See also FIS

Virginia, 13, 134, 164, 175, 213n36, 216n51; Arlington, 146; Boydton 182; and civil rights compliance, 182; Hampton Institute, 10, 87, 167, 213n36, 220n35; and Jeanes teachers, 220n35; Lawrenceville, 182; number of extension workers, 162; Petersburg, 129; Virginia State College, 208n1

Volanto, Keith, 124

Waco, Tex., 15, 35, 52, 82, 84, 90, 104, 109, 227n15, 228n25; Waco Chamber of Agriculture, 91

Wade, Charlie F., 188

Walker County, Tex., 11, 92, 96, 121, 122, 132, 137, 141, 204n38, 228n22, 237n16; County Committee on Agricultural Seed Loans, 132; County Relief and Improvement Committee, 137; Relief Committee of Walker County, 132

Walker, Melissa A., 261

Wallace, Henry A., 112, 113, 117, 119, 124, 133

Waller, Calvin Hoffman, 14, 16, 24, 53, 64, 76, 80, 88–89, 95, 98, 100–101, 102–105, 111, 112, 113, 119, 128, 129, 132, 137, 138, 151, 154, 205n40, 230n37, 234n64, 239n30, 242n48, 246n7; and AAA, 125–26, 128, 130, 131; and FSA, 134, 135, 226n5; and membership in civic/service organizations, 96; and race relations, 100, 103, 118; and Texas Negro Farmers' Council of Agriculture, 99

Waller County, Tex., 27, 71, 123, 135, 141, 223n51; and Jeanes teachers, 221n36

Walton, Cedar A., 124, 165, 237n13

Walton, Thomas O., 33, 35, 90, 210n17, 234n64

war mobilization: World War I, 39, 40, 41, 44; war savings stamps, 40; war securities, 40

Ward, Florence E., 257

Warburton, C. W., 112, 113, 119

Washington, Booker T., 5, 10, 13, 15, 20, 21, 35, 37, 105, 149, 150, 170–71, 207n50, 220n35, 228n22, 234n65

Washington County, Tex., 50, 59, 60, 69, 71, 91, 100, 103, 122, 139, 177–78, 226n12, 227n15, 228n25, 237n16; and Jeanes teachers, 220n35, 221n36; Washington County State Bank, 52

Washington, D.C., 97, 105, 112–13, 119, 125, 128, 129, 141, 159, 167, 173, 182

Weiman, Otto E., 52

Weimar, Tex., 91

Westfield, Tex., 231n50

Wellingham Community, Tex., 222n44

West Columbia, Tex., 147

West Virginia, xxiv, 213n36; Department of Agriculture, 38; number of extension workers, 162

Wharton, Tex., 82, 92, 127, 227n15

Wharton County, Tex., 27, 147, 205n39, 208n1, 222n44, 223n51, 227n15, 226n5

Whayne, Jeannie, 260

Whitaker, John, 242n49, 242n50

Whitaker, Mr., 135

White, George, 174

White, F. S., 12

White, Ralph W., 38

white supremacy, xxiv, 5, 21, 43, 47, 163, 170

Wiley College, 95; Rural Pastor's School, 64, 65

Wilkerson, Doxey A., 258

Wilkins, Alvin, 147

William, Jennifer, 198n7

Williams, E. T., 16

Williams, J. Sheb, 35

Williams, John H., 82, 111, 112, 113, 129, 150, 157, 234n64, 234n65, 247n18
Williams, J. W., 11
Williams, Ned, 67
Williams, Ted, 68
Williamson County, Tex., and Jeanes teachers, 220n35
Williamson, Howard H., 12–13, 19, 20, 97, 99, 101, 112, 113, 119, 127, 129, 151, 210n17
Wilson, James, 10
Wilson, Jesse, 71, 123
Wilson, Mr. and son, 31
Wilson, Woodrow, 19, 39
Wisconsin, University of Wisconsin-Madison, 185, 254n20
women, xxvi, 16–17, 22–23, 33, 34, 45–47, 59, 81, 109, 113, 128, 138–41, 173, 182, 221n40, 258, 243n54; "better baby" clinics, 17; child care, 159; clubs, 67, 75, 136; contributing to farm/household economy, 2, 31, 33, 58, 67, 136; farm women and girls, 17, 18, 50, 55–58, 64, 69–70, 75, 130; Federation of Women's Clubs, 96, 222n44; first employee of TAEX Negro Division, 22; first white female agent in Texas, 16; gender bias in TAEX, 17, 23, 33, 89–90; General Federation of Women's Clubs, 17; and sanitation campaigns, 63; Texas Association of Colored Women's Clubs, 17; Texas Federation of Women's Clubs, 96, 222n44; wives of USDA crop correspondents, 17; women's involvement in Counties with only male farm agents, 59; women's organizations, 41, 83. See also clubs; gender; home demonstra-

tion agents/work; Negro Division, Negro Division programming
Woodland [also known as Bethlehem], Tex., 232n52
Wood, A. J., 82, 228n25
Wood County, Tex., 11, 208n24, 226n5
Woods, Eugenia A., 157
Woodward, C. Vann, 20–21
Works Progress Administration (WPA), 141, 149
World War I, xxv, 36, 41, 44, 69, 71, 115, 167, 177, 220n35; challenge to southern system, 43; and development of Negro Division, 39; "Great Food and Feed Campaigns," 31, 223n48; liberty bonds, 40; post-war, 43–44, 45, 48, 210n17, 215n44; war savings stamps, 40
World War II, xxv, xxvii, 77, 99, 130, 136, 145, 157, 161, 163, 164, 192, 193, 258, 260, 249n35; domestic mobilization, 145, 157, 158, 159; "Food for Freedom," 158; War Emergency Conference for Negro Local Leaders, 157
Wortham, Tex., 224n56

Yates, W. A., 91
youth, African American, 12–13, 14, 18, 19, 20, 22, 55, 59, 62, 67, 68, 87, 98, 106, 147, 153, 155, 160, 167, 177, 187, 188, 192; and education, 27, 59, 62; influence on parents, 65; leaving the farm, 62–63, 80, 192; as next generation agents, educators and reformers, 62–63, 95–96, 160, 161; staying on the farm, 147; undernourished, underweight children, 64; white, 12. See also clubs; schools